The period from 1945 to the present day may not constitute an American century, but it can be seen as the American Moment: the time when, for good or ill, the United States became the predominant political, military, economic, and cultural power in the world. This revised and updated new edition introduces the historic and tumultuous developments in American politics, foreign policy, society and culture during this period. It includes coverage of key recent events, such as the:

- 2008 election of Barack Obama
- global recession
- war in Iraq and Afghanistan
- rise of the internet
- transformation of American Society and Culture
- challenges of the new immigration and multiculturalism
- changing global status of the US in the new millennium

Examining the American Moment in a global context, the authors emphasize the interaction between politics, society, and culture. *America since 1945* encourages an awareness of how central currents in art, literature film, theatre, intellectual history, and media have developed alongside an understanding of political, economic, and social change.

PAUL LEVINE is Emeritus Professor of American Literature at Copenhagen University.

HARRY PAPASOTIRIOU is Professor of International Relations at Panteion University.

D0219235

'A very appealing and useful text for introductory courses in all the American fields: literature, history, art and social science. The co-ordination of chapters offers an effective way of introducing students to the benefits of viewing a historical era from the perspectives of several related disciplines.' – Alan Trachtenberg, Yale University

'A most interesting, even extraordinary book. Juxtaposing historical and political chapters with chapters detailing cultural events it attempts nothing less than that old goal of American Studies: to see American culture whole. As a teaching aid the essays are a valuable tool.' – Jules Chametzky, University of Massachusetts Amherst

'This is a wonderful, searching discussion of the post-WWII period in the United States. It provides a strong narrative without losing sight of the enormous complexity of the period, and the global perspective makes it stand out from many of the textbooks I've read.' – Katherine Ellinghaus, University of Melbourne

A Concise History of Christianity in Canada

EDITOR

TERRENCE MURPHY

ASSOCIATE EDITOR

ROBERTO PERIN

Toronto   Oxford   New York
OXFORD UNIVERSITY PRESS
1996

Oxford University Press
70 Wynford Drive, Don Mills, Ontario M3C 1J9

Oxford   New York
Athens   Auckland   Bangkok   Bombay
Calcutta   Cape Town   Dar es Salaam   Delhi
Florence   Hong Kong   Istanbul   Karachi
Kuala Lumpur   Madras   Madrid   Melbourne
Mexico City   Nairobi   Paris   Singapore
Taipei   Tokyo   Toronto

and associated companies in
Berlin   Ibadan

Oxford is a trademark of Oxford University Press

Canadian Cataloguing in Publication Data

Main entry under title:
  A concise history of Christianity in Canada

Includes bibliographical references and index.
ISBN 0–19–540758–X

1. Canada – Church history.   2. Christianity – Canada.
I. Murphy, Terrence.   II. Perin, Roberto.

BR570.C65   1996   277.1   C95–933329–0

Every effort has been made to determine and contact copyright owners. In the case
of any omissions, the publisher will be pleased to make suitable acknowledgement
in future editions.

Design by Heather Delfino

1 2 3 4 – 99 98 97 96

This book is printed on permanent (acid-free) paper ∞

Printed in Canada

America since 1945

The American Moment

Second Edition

Paul Levine
&
Harry Papasotiriou

palgrave
macmillan

First edition published 2005
Second edition published 2011 by
PALGRAVE MACMILLAN

Palgrave Macmillan in the UK is an imprint of Macmillan Publishers Limited, registered in England, company number 785998, of Houndmills, Basingstoke, Hampshire RG21 6XS.

Palgrave Macmillan in the US is a division of St Martin's Press LLC, 175 Fifth Avenue, New York, NY 10010.

Palgrave Macmillan is the global academic imprint of the above companies and has companies and representatives throughout the world.

Palgrave® and Macmillan® are registered trademarks in the United States, the United Kingdom, Europe and other countries.

ISBN: 978-0-230-25144-1 hardback
ISBN: 978-0-230-25145-8 paperback

This book is printed on paper suitable for recycling and made from fully managed and sustained forest sources. Logging, pulping and manufacturing processes are expected to conform to the environmental regulations of the country of origin.

A catalogue record for this book is available from the British Library.

A catalog record for this book is available from the Library of Congress.

10 9 8 7 6 5 4 3 2 1
20 19 18 17 16 15 14 13 12 11

Printed and bound in Great Britain by
CPI Antony Rowe, Chippenham and Eastbourne

To Lily

To Dora, Kassy and Sotiris

Contents

List of Illustrations

List of Timelines

Acknowledgments

The authors and publishers wish to thank the following for permission to use copyright material:

Associated Press, for the photographs of 'Civil Rights in the Fifties' and of Times Square on VJ Day, on pp. 51 and x.

John F. Kennedy Library, for the photograph of the inauguration of John F. Kennedy on p. 97. Photo no.: SC578830, January 20, 1961, in the John F. Kennedy Library, Army Signals Corps.

Smithsonian Photographic Services, for the photograph of the Vietnam Veterans' Memorial (photo no.: 84-18136-270) on p. 143.

Paul Levine for the photograph of an American restaurant on a busy Shanghai street on p. 191.

Athens News Agency, for the photograph of 9/11 on p. 241.

Every effort has been made to trace the copyright holders but, if any have been inadvertently overlooked, the authors and publishers will be pleased to make the necessary arrangement at the first opportunity.

'Times Square on VJ Day'

Introduction

Paul Levine

In February 1941, Henry Luce, the publisher of *Life* Magazine, wrote an editorial with the prophetic title 'The American Century'. Luce was one of those innovative entrepreneurs who shaped American life in the twentieth century. Like John D. Rockefeller, he combined the Protestant ethic and the spirit of Capitalism in his business magazine *Fortune*. Like William Randolph Hearst, he shaped modern journalism by inventing the weekly news magazine *Time*. And like Walt Disney he altered the way we see the world with *Life*, the famous magazine of photojournalism. Today, 40 years after Luce's death, his magazine empire is a global 'infotainment' colossus that includes *Time* magazine, Warner Brothers movies, and CNN television.[1]

Like his legendary contemporaries, Henry Luce was an American patriot. But he was more of an internationalist than they were. Born in 1898 in China, Luce grew up with a strong sense of America's global mission. His parents were Protestant missionaries and he became the journalistic apostle of the American century. 'To him America was not just a country, it was an idea and an ideal,' wrote David Halberstam in *The Powers That Be* (1979). 'His magazines would celebrate this.' Beginning in the 1920s, Luce sought to promote American values in his increasingly influential magazines. By midcentury, he had become the major media spokesman for the American Dream. 'He sought to make America what it should be and thus, of course, in the pages of *Time*, America *became* what it should be. The dream realized.'

In his 1941 editorial, 'The American Century', Luce urged his fellow countrymen to break with their traditional isolationism and lead the global fight against fascism. In World War I, the United States became a reluctant combatant after German submarines sank three American vessels. In 1919 a triumphant President Woodrow Wilson attended the Versailles Peace Conference with a sweeping plan to create a new world order; but he was thwarted by his French and British allies. After Wilson's failure, the US Congress rejected the peace treaty and refused to join the newly formed League of Nations that Wilson had proposed. After the outbreak of World War II in 1939, skeptical Americans were once again asked to come to the aid of their European allies. With France defeated and Britain beleaguered, the United States had become the last bulwark of Western democracy against Nazi Germany. Now, as citizens of the world's most powerful nation, Luce argued, Americans had an obligation to promote democratic principles throughout the world. Nine months later, the Japanese attacked Pearl Harbor and the United States embarked on a course of action that ultimately transformed modern times into what he called 'the American century'.

Luce's editorial proved to be prophetic; but with some important reservations, as we shall see. Though the United States entered the conflict reluctantly only after the Japanese attack, Americans pursued the war enthusiastically. 'World War II was the most popular in American history,' notes the historian John Patrick Diggins in *The Proud Decade* (1988). 'It was truly a people's war.' While Europe exhausted itself in a brutal conflict, the United States set out to create the most awesomely productive economic and military machine the world had ever seen. Moreover, American losses, though considerable, were slight in comparison to the devastation in Europe and Asia. The Americans suffered 400,000 deaths in battle whereas 35,000,000 Europeans – soldiers and civilians alike – died in just five years. 'In the years since Pearl Harbor the United States had overcome the greatest crisis facing the country since the Civil War,' says Diggins. 'A war that most Americans originally did not want to fight turned into one of the proudest triumphs in the history of the Republic.'

Thus at the end of World War II, the United States emerged as an economic, political and military superpower, a position it has held for more than half a century. As we entered a new millennium, Luce's idea of 'the American Century' took on a new currency. With the collapse of the Soviet Union, economic turmoil in Asia and political disunity in Europe, the United States remained by default the only global superpower. In the realm of culture, too, we have all experienced the long arm of American hyperpower. The world sees American films, hears American music, reads American books, copies American television programs and grumbles about the dangers of American cultural hegemony. The cultivation of efficient techniques of global distribution has created mass culture and spread American values all over the world. Today critics speak anxiously of Globalization and Americanization as if they were the same thing.

We all recognize forms of 'American cultural imperialism', but what is American culture? For many skeptics, it is only McDonald's, Levi's and Hollywood. But a culture is more than a hamburger. When the Nobel Prize-winning novelist Saul Bellow was growing up in Chicago in the 1920s, the city was famous for its stockyards, steel mills, railroads and gangsters. 'What Chicago gave to the world was goods – a standard of living sufficient for millions. Bread, bacon, overalls, gas ranges, radio sets, telephone directories, false teeth, light bulbs, tractors, steel rails, gasoline,' Bellow wrote. 'If you looked here for the sort of natural beauty described by Shakespeare, Milton, Wordsworth, Yeats, you would never find it.'

Yet, as the son of Russian Jewish immigrants, Bellow found something else in Chicago. As he recalled 60 years later in *It All Adds Up* (1994):

The children of Chicago bakers, tailors, peddlers, insurance agents, pressers, cutters, grocers, the sons of families on relief, were reading buckram-bound books from the public library and were in a state of enthusiasm, having found themselves on the shore of a novelistic land to which they really belonged, discovering their birthright, hearing incredible news from the great world of culture, talking to one another about the mind, society, art, religion, epistemology, and doing this in Chicago, of all places.

But critics of American material culture are partly right. In *Land of Desire* (1993) William Leach describes how Americans created the modern world by combining corporate capitalism and consumer culture. 'In the decades following the Civil War, American capitalism began to produce a distinct culture, unconnected to traditional family or community values, to religion in any conventional sense, or to political democracy,' he says. 'The cardinal features of this culture were acquisition and consumption as a means of achieving happiness; the cult of the new; the democratization of desire; and money value as the predominant measure of all value in society.'

Leach traces the evolution of the consumer society from its humble beginnings in retailing through its institutionalization in the consumer and service sectors, to its total acceptance as the American Way of Life. The flamboyant entrepreneurs of the late nineteenth century were transformed into anonymous corporations in the early twentieth century, comprising a network of department stores, investment bankers, advertising agencies, hotels, restaurants, movie theaters, model agencies, fashion groups and public relations firms. In creating a new culture of consumption, the modern captains of industry found unlikely partners in new institutions of higher learning like the Harvard Business School (founded in 1908) and high culture like the Metropolitan Museum of Art (its division of industrial design began in 1914). 'A new society has come to life in America,' noted a French observer in 1928. 'From a *moral point of view*, it is obvious that Americans have come to consider their standard of living as a somewhat sacred acquisition, which they will defend at any price.'

In redefining modern democracy as a mass consumer society, Americans followed a different path from the Europeans. In *Why the American Century?* (1993) Olivier Zunz writes, 'As its size increased and its standard of living improved, the middle class became the hallmark of the "American century." In the "America-as-model" paradigm, the middle class, not the working class, is the revolutionary ideal. Promoting its values became the American alternative to Marxism.' Instead of the Marxist ideology of class conflict, Americans pointed to an expanding middle-class society as the material expression of 'the American dream'. In the postwar years, this celebration of affluence became the hallmark of 'the American Way of Life' and the cornerstone of the ideology of 'the American Century'. Zunz concludes, 'In contrast to the situation in Europe, consumption, not welfare, was the American means of social cohesion.'

Of course, these achievements have had their costs, especially among those groups who were excluded from the American mainstream. But, despite its failures, the United States continues to pursue the prophesy of Henry Luce's 'American Century'. We know how American ideas about the organization of knowledge, the consumer society and multiculturalism have become part of the global cultural landscape as well. After the collapse of the Soviet empire in 1989, the French historian Francois Furet argued that while the Soviet Union had been a superpower, it had never been a civilization. The proof was that it could vanish without leaving any substantial legacy behind. But the opposite is true of the United States. The idea of 'the American Century' became the basis for the establishment of the 'Pax Americana'. Unlike the Soviet Union, says Zunz, 'The United States became a superpower precisely because of its civilization.'

This book is an exploration of American civilization in the period between World War II and the present. If this does not constitute an American Century, it can be seen as the American Moment: the time when, for good or ill, the United States became the predominant political, military, economic and cultural power in the world. In this book, we wish to examine the American Moment in a global context. Our approach is both interdisciplinary and dialogic. By using elements of political science and international relations, media and cultural studies, and social, intellectual and literary history, we try to present a multidimensional picture of the United States in its relation to the larger world. The odd-numbered chapters are written by a political scientist, Harry Papasotiriou; they move chronologically through major events in international relations and American domestic politics. The even-numbered chapters are written by a literary historian, Paul Levine; they explore thematically the central developments in American culture and society. By structuring our book in alternating chapters emphasizing political and cultural developments respectively, we hope to establish a dialogue between the authors and with the reader.

The two authors come from different cultural backgrounds but share similar intellectual interests. Harry Papasotiriou is Greek. He was born in Frankfurt, Germany, in 1961 and grew up in Athens, Greece. He was educated in England and the United States, earning a BA in Philosophy, Politics and Economics from the University of Oxford (1983) and an MA and PhD from Stanford University (1992). In 1992 he joined the faculty of the Institute for International Relations at Panteion University; since 1998 he has taught in Panteion's Department of International Relations, where he now holds the rank of Professor.

Paul Levine is American. Born in Brooklyn, New York, in 1936, he studied English Literature and Art History at Wesleyan University (BA, 1958), American Literature and Intellectual History at Princeton University, and received his PhD in the History of American Civilization from Harvard University (1973). Afterwards he taught at Wesleyan and the University of Rochester and in Canada at York University. In 1975 he became the first Professor of American Literature at Copenhagen University, a post he held until his retirement in 2006. He has also been a visiting professor in American Studies in Hungary and China.

In 1994 Levine became the director of the Athens American Studies Seminar. Over the past decade he and Papasotiriou collaborated on this annual interdisciplinary symposium where American, Greek and other European academics, students and professionals meet to explore a variety of complex issues ranging from the legacy of the Cold War to the crisis of Globalization. As we studied problems ranging from the rule of international law to the role of global media, we became aware of the need for a new kind of textbook to introduce students and general readers to the issues facing the United States and the world. Over the past eight years we have worked together in formulating a new approach, drawing on recently released archives in international relations and the latest research in social science and the humanities. This book, first published in 2005, is the fruit of this collaboration.

But much has happened in the last five years which requires a new edition. Increased instability in the Middle East, the expansion of the European Union eastward, the increasing threat of global warming, the economic rise of developing nations in Asia and Latin America, and the worst global economic recession since the Great Depression have all transformed the international landscape. In the United States, there have been great changes as well, culminating in the stunning election of Barack Obama in 2008. In *A Long Time Coming* (2009) Evan Thomas writes, 'A nation whose Constitution enshrined slavery has elected an African-American president within living memory of days when blacks were denied fundamental human rights – including the right to vote.' In the process, perennial issues of race, class and gender have been transformed.

Meanwhile a generation of cultural icons have died: civil rights activist Rosa Parks, conservative movement godfather William Buckley, diplomat George F. Kennan, economist John Kenneth Galbraith, feminist Betty Friedan, journalist David Halberstam, political scientist Samuel P. Huntington, President Gerald R. Ford, pop idol Michael Jackson, urban critic Jane Jacobs, and three veterans of the Vietnam conflict: General William Westmoreland, antiwar candidate Senator Eugene McCarthy and former Secretary of Defense Robert McNamara. The world of letters lost dramatists Arthur Miller and August Wilson, and novelists Saul Bellow, Norman Mailer, J. D. Salinger, John Updike and Kurt Vonnegut, Jr. Finally, in 2009 a modern political dynasty ended with the deaths of President John Kennedy's sister, Eunice Shriver, and his youngest brother, Senator Edward Kennedy.

As we enter the second decade of the twenty-first century the world looks different. With the economic rise of Brazil, Russia, India and China, some analysts predict the decline of the United States in the next decades. 'Look around,' says Fareed Zakaria. 'The tallest building in the world is in Taipei, and it will soon be overtaken by one being built in Dubai. The world's richest man is Mexican, and its largest publicly traded corporation is Chinese.' Even traditional American icons have been supplanted: the largest Ferris Wheel is in Singapore, the largest gambling casino is in Macao, the largest shopping center is in Beijing. Globalization has transformed the postmodern world in surprising ways.

These are some of the issues we try to address in this new edition.

NOTE

1. In January 2000 the Time-Warner-CNN conglomerate combined with the giant Internet provider AOL in a multi-billion dollar merger that aimed at exploiting the 'synergy' between old and new media. The merger was not successful and in December 2009 they separated.

RECOMMENDED READING

Saul Bellow, *It All Adds Up,* New York: Viking, 1994.
John Patrick Diggins, *The Proud Decades,* New York: Norton, 1988.
David Halberstam, *The Powers That Be,* New York: Knopf, 1979.
Godfrey Hodgson, *America in Our Time,* New York: Doubleday, 1976.
William Leach, *Land of Desire,* New York: Pantheon, 1993.
Evan Thomas, *'A Long Time Coming',* New York: Public Affairs, 2009.
Fareed Zakaria, *The Post-American World,* New York: Norton, 2009.
Olivier Zunz, *Why the American Century?* Chicago, IL: University of Chicago Press, 1993.

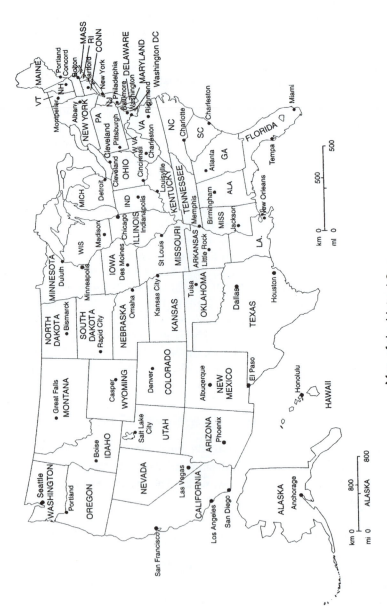

Map of the United States

PART I
The World War and American Power

The Big Three: Stalin, Roosevelt and Churchill at Tehran, November 1943

Year	Politics	Culture
1945	• Yalta Conference • Roosevelt dies in office and is succeeded by Truman • Germany capitulates • Potsdam Conference • Atom bombs are dropped on Hiroshima and Nagasaki • Japan capitulates • The FBI begins to uncover Soviet spying in the United States • The United Nations is created	• Leonard Bernstein, *On the Town* • Tennessee Williams, *The Glass Menagerie* • Richard Wright, *Black Boy* • Rodgers and Hammerstein, *Carousel* • Billy Wilder, *The Lost Weekend*
1946	• End of futile American mediation in China • Republicans gain control of both chambers of Congress in midterm elections • First meetings of the UN General Assembly and the Security Council in London	• Robert Penn Warren, *All the King's Men* • Robert Lowell, *Lord Weary's Castle* • William Wyler, *The Best Years of Our Lives* • Bogart and Bacall in *The Big Sleep* (film) • Eugene O'Neill, *The Iceman Cometh*
1947	• Truman Doctrine • Truman administration loyalty program institutionalizes *Red Scare* • George Kennan articulates containment policy • Marshall Plan is initiated • Taft-Hartley Act restricts labor union activities • HUAC fuels Red Scare • Partition of the former British Indian Empire into India and Pakistan	• Robert Frost, *Masque of Mercy* • Tennessee Williams, *A Streetcar Named Desire* • Arthur Miller, *All My Sons* • Richard Wilbur, *The Beautiful Changes*
1948	• HUAC investigates Hollywood, Alger Hiss • Democratic National Convention endorses civil rights plank; Dixiecrats defect • Berlin blockade begins • Truman is unexpectedly elected president • Democrats recapture both chambers of Congress • UN General Assembly adopts Universal Declaration of Human Rights. • Israel is established. First Arab-Israeli War • Assassination of Mahatma Gandhi by a Hindu nationalist	• T. S. Eliot receives Nobel Prize for Literature • Saul Bellow, *The Victim* • Norman Mailer, *The Naked and the Dead* • Truman Capote, *Other Voices, Other Rooms* • Ezra Pound, *The Pisan Cantos* • Justice Department wins antitrust suit against Paramount Pictures
1949	• NATO is created; Stalin ends Berlin blockade • Soviet Union acquires atom bomb • Mao wins Chinese civil war; PRC is created • Cornerstone laid for present UN Headquarters in New York City • Mao wins Chinese civil war; PRC is established	• Arthur Miller, *Death of a Salesman* • Paul Bowles, *The Sheltering Sky* • Robert Rossen, *All the King's Men* (film)

CHAPTER I

American Politics from Roosevelt to Truman

In 1835 Alexis de Tocqueville gazed into the future of the United States and Russia and declared that each 'seems marked by the will of Heaven to sway the destinies of half the globe'. His famous prediction came true a little over one century later. Yet the rise of these two world powers could scarcely have contrasted more. Russia rose after centuries of intense and often bloody competition in the merciless arena of European Great Power politics. The United States was insulated from Europe's intense political competition by the world's largest oceans; instead it massively expanded its territory from the original 13 states to a continental-sized federation against the weak opposition of the Mexicans and the Native Americans. More Americans were killed in the Civil War of 1861–5 than in any other war in American history. The origin of America's ascendancy in world politics is its phenomenal industrialization in the later nineteenth century, which transformed a nation of farmers, craftsmen and traders into the world's most formidable industrial power. By the end of the nineteenth century the American economy was the largest in the world, has remained so ever since, and is likely to remain so well into the twenty-first century.

Yet the rise of the United States to the top of world politics came just after the Great Depression, the worst economic disaster in American history. In the 1930s America was economically prostrate, diplomatically isolated and militarily weak. Then came World War II, during which the United States emerged as the leading power of our times. The experiences of Depression and world war were so profound, and the United States so transformed by them, that in American parlance the 'modern' begins with this period. The first modern president was Franklin Roosevelt, the master politician and statesman who dominated American politics during those momentous years of crisis and transformation. His successor Harry Truman seemed inadequate at first to follow in Roosevelt's footsteps, but he soon proved his worth as one of America's greatest modern leaders, laying the foundations of America's postwar engagement in world politics.

The legacy of Franklin Roosevelt in American politics

American postwar politics were shaped by the massive realignment that took place in the 1930s. Before the Great Depression, the Republicans had dominated for 70 years, in which only two Democrats had been elected to the presidency (Grover Cleveland and Woodrow Wilson). The Republican Party was a very broad coalition that included conservatives and progressives, industrialists and labor unions, blacks and whites, internationalists and isolationists. A party that had dominated for so long, and that had become especially identified with industrialization and business prosperity, was bound to be held responsible for the Great Depression and to lose the support of the voters. The economic decline during Herbert Hoover's presidency in 1929–33 was almost unimaginably steep. Gross domestic product (GDP) in 1933 was half that of 1929. Agricultural income had declined by two-thirds. Unemployment rose to 25 per cent. Under these circumstances, the Democrats were bound to win the election of 1932.

The Democratic standard bearer who led his party to victory in 1932 was Franklin Delano Roosevelt (FDR), a patrician from upstate New York. Roosevelt became one of the greatest presidents in American history, comparable only to Washington and Lincoln. Yet his earlier career gave few clues to his later mastery. His first steps in politics replicated exactly the career of his distant cousin, President Theodore Roosevelt (1901–9), except that FDR seemed like an inferior copy. His character became less frivolous and gained depth after 1921, when he was struck by poliomyelitis that paralyzed his legs. With enormous willpower he persevered in politics, placing himself at the front rank of the Democratic Party by winning the governorship of New York in 1928, a year in which the Democrats did badly otherwise. Justice Oliver Wendell Holmes shrewdly assessed FDR's qualities: 'A second-class intellect. But a first-class temperament!' Roosevelt proved to be a charismatic leader who reassured and inspired Americans in the depths of the Depression and during the mighty challenges of World War II; an open-minded reformer willing to experiment with new remedies for unprecedented problems; a skillful though often devious manager who dominated his government and his party, securing its presidential nomination four times; and in his last years a world leader who in wartime policy and strategy compares well with Old World giants like Winston Churchill and Joseph Stalin.

FDR's New Deal laid the foundations of the American welfare state and created new machinery for federal engagement in the economy and society, while working within and in effect improving the existing capitalist system. Among its greatest and most lasting achievements are Social Security, which provides old-age pensions; the Securities Exchange Commission (SEC) and the Federal Bank Deposit Insurance Corporation (FDIC), which regulate and stabilize financial markets; the Fair Labor Standards Act and the National Labor Relations Board, which regulate the labor market; and a federal willingness to finance infrastructure development in the United States. The New Deal did not substantially change the income distribution in the United States, nor did it engage in nationalization of production – with the exception of the Tennessee Valley Authority (TVA), a federal agency that helped develop a desperately poor region stretching across seven Southern states. As the historian David Kennedy argued in *Freedom from Fear*, the New Deal was about security:

> security for vulnerable individuals,…for capitalists and consumers, for workers and employers, for corporations and farms and homeowners and bankers and builders as well. Job security, life-cycle security, financial security, market

security – however it might be defined, achieving security was the leitmotif of virtually everything the New Deal attempted.[1]

What was the New Deal coalition?

Franklin Roosevelt shaped postwar American politics because he succeeded in transforming what might have been only a temporary Democratic victory in 1932 into a lasting party realignment. His New Deal coalition dominated American politics until 1968. Its central elements become visible by an examination of the main cleavages in American society in the middle of the twentieth century.

- *North versus South.* This cleavage anteceded America's independence and led to the Civil War of 1861–5, which broke out when the antislavery Republicans won the national elections for the first time in 1860, resulting in the secession of the South. For one century after the Civil War, the South was solidly Democratic. The borderline state of Tennessee, which was split during the Civil War, remained split almost exactly along the same lines until the 1960s, with almost all counties that had sent their men to the Union army voting Republican and those that had fought with the Confederacy voting Democratic. The Solid South was thus one of the most important elements of the New Deal coalition.

- *Creditors versus debtors.* This cleavage pitted farmers and small-scale business-men, especially in the South, the West and the agricultural Midwest, against the great but much despised financial centers of New York and Chicago. The Democrats had aligned themselves with the debtors against the bankers since the nineteenth century. The Midwesterner Harry Truman (Missouri) was a typical representative of this tradition in the mid-twentieth century. On his way to France during World War I, he passed through New York and expressed only contempt for this glittering metropolis (by contrast, he loved Paris). In the early 1920s, he and one of his fellow war veterans opened a haberdashery that went bankrupt because the start-up loans could not be repaid. In politics, he was most effective as a tribune of the common people against the 'Wall Street Republicans'. In this tradition, the New Deal did much to support defaulting homeowners and farmers who faced foreclosures.

- *Employers versus labor.* One of the most significant and lasting changes brought about by the New Deal was the conversion of the labor unions from Republicans to Democrats. The New Deal's Wagner Act, which protected the right of collective bargaining, constituted the most important pro-labor legis-lation in American history, and transformed the unions virtually into compo-nents of the Democratic Party.

- *Rural versus urban.* Before the Great Depression the Democrats were largely a party of the rural South and West, and the Republicans were mostly the party of the industrial Northeast and Midwest. The New Deal altered this alignment and made the Democrats dominant in the cities. In his 1936 reelec-tion, Roosevelt won 102 out of the 104 cities in the United States with a population over 100,000. The subsequent Democratic domination in urban

America brought great power and influence to the urban party bosses who ran the largely corrupt patronage machines.

It should be noted that FDR entered politics as an anti-machine reformer, following in the footsteps of his illustrious predecessor, Theodore Roosevelt. But as president he needed the cooperation of the urban machine bosses to win elections. His successor Harry Truman was a product of the Kansas City machine run by Tom Pendergast, who was one of the most powerful political bosses in the country until his downfall and imprisonment for corruption in 1939. (There was no taint of corruption regarding Truman.)

■ *WASPs versus newer immigrants and blacks.* In 1940, of 140 million Americans, 11.5 million had been born abroad, 23 million had parents born abroad, and 22 million spoke English as a second language. These new immigrant groups were concentrated mainly in the cities of the Northeast and the industrial Midwest. They lived largely in ethnic neighborhoods, in which they preserved some of the traditions of their old countries. Being underdogs in American society, they overwhelmingly supported the New Deal and became a key factor in Democratic electoral politics for decades thereafter. The homogenizing pressures of total warfare facilitated the decline of the ethnic neighborhoods after World War II, but the postwar allegiance of ethnic Americans to the Democratic Party was lasting. At the same time, the New Deal also produced a change in the allegiance of African Americans from the Republicans to the Democrats. After they abandoned the party of Abraham Lincoln, the blacks in time became the most solidly Democratic group in the United States. This fact, though, could not easily be reconciled with the presence of the racist Solid South in the Democratic Party.

Roosevelt led this great New Deal coalition in the direction of federal activism for the cure of the ills in American society, which has become the defining attitude of American liberalism ever since. Yet the New Deal coalition was a very broad church that spanned the mainstream American ideological spectrum, much like the ruling Republican coalition that preceded it. The Solid South, in particular, was essentially conservative and from 1938 onwards acted as a brake to further liberal initiatives by the federal government.

The ability of Southern Democrats to impede liberal activism by the federal government derived from their disproportionate power in Congress, in which the powerful committee chairs were apportioned strictly by seniority within the majority party. Before the 1930s the Democrats were very much the minority party; thus a large portion of the new Democratic congressional majorities in the 1930s and 1940s consisted of representatives and senators with little seniority. Not so those from the Solid South, which had hardly ever elected a Republican to Congress (except during Reconstruction). As a result, the small oligarchies of about two dozen committee chairmen that dominated the House and the Senate were disproportionately from the South.

If postwar liberal activism faced constraints from the conservative elements of the New Deal coalition, it was assisted by a major and lasting expansion in

Table I Income tax in the United States, 1940–60[2]

Year	Lowest bracket income tax, percentage	Lowest bracket income, in $	Highest-bracket income tax, percentage	Highest-bracket income, in $	Millions paying income tax
1940	4.4	4,000	81.1	5,000,000	14.7
1941	10.0	2,000	81.0	5,000,000	25.9
1942	19.0	2,000	88.0	200,000	36.6
1943	19.0	2,000	88.0	200,000	43.7
1944	23.0	2,000	94.0	200,000	47.1
1945	23.0	2,000	94.0	200,000	49.9
1946	19.0	2,000	86.5	200,000	52.8
1950	17.4	2,000	84.4	200,000	53.1
1960	20.0	2,000	91.0	200,000	61.0

the size of the federal revenue base during World War II. The size of the federal government during the Roosevelt presidency increased less during the New Deal reforms than under the pressures of the war. The expanding federal government was paid for by higher income taxes. At the highest brackets the New Deal had raised the income tax to 81.1 per cent, but this applied only to the small number of the truly rich with incomes over $5 million. In 1942 the highest-bracket income tax was raised to 88 per cent. Much more significant, though, was the lowering of the definition of the highest bracket to incomes over $200,000, vastly expanding the number of people who fell into this bracket.

Similarly, at the lowest end the income tax was raised from 4.4 per cent in 1940 to 23 per cent in 1944. At least as important, though, was the lowering of the definition of the lowest bracket from incomes of $4000 in 1940 to $2000 in 1941, which meant that several million Americans were taxed for the first time. The economic boom that began in the 1940s continually added more people to the income groups subject to income tax. The resultant rapid rise in the number of people that paid income taxes is shown in the last column of Table 1.

The rise in income taxes during the war was by and large not reversed after 1945, providing the postwar federal government with a large stream of revenue that made possible not only new domestic programs but also international initiatives like the Truman Doctrine and the Marshall Plan. During World War II, the federal government acquired the revenue base that enabled the United States to move from the periphery to the center of world politics.

American society in the 1940s

In the mid-1940s the United States produced half the industrial product of the world. American per capita income was about double that of the group of next richest countries: Canada, Great Britain, New Zealand, Switzerland and Sweden. Nonetheless, many Americans still lived in surprisingly primitive conditions. In 1947 one-third of American households had no running water, two-fifths had no flush toilets and three-fifths had no central heating. Moreover, in spite of massive industrialization and the attendant urbanization, a majority of Americans still lived in towns with fewer than 10,000 inhabitants. About 17.5 per cent of the population still depended on agriculture for a living. Over 30 per cent of the population was under the official poverty line, in spite of the wartime economic recovery that ended the Great Depression, with black and Mexican-American agricultural laborers at the bottom of the wage ladder.

The American economy in the 1940s displayed far greater regional variations in income levels than today. The South in particular was much less developed than the rest of the United States, constituting a kind of 'third world' within the world's richest economy. Southern economic backwardness was somewhat alleviated by the New Deal's ambitious infrastructure projects such as the TVA that provided electricity and paved roads in much of the region. Still, the South did not catch up with the rest of the United States until the last quarter of the twentieth century.

Internal migrations reveal some of the dynamics in American society in the early postwar period. Throughout American history one major internal migration stream has been from East to West, with people moving from the densely populated Eastern seaboard to the vast expanses of the heartland and the West. This population movement gradually changed the political and electoral balances in the United States. In 1940 New York's population towered above that of any other state. Next in population were Pennsylvania, Illinois, Ohio and California. By 1950 California had jumped into second place, narrowly overtaking Pennsylvania though still far behind New York. Today California has about twice the population of the next state, which is Texas, while New York has fallen to third place. Richard Nixon's meteoric rise – he was elected vice-president in 1952 just before his fortieth birthday – reflected California's growing importance in American politics.

A second migration stream moved from the underdeveloped South to the industrial centers of the North and the West. This interregional population movement largely amounted to a labor movement from the agricultural to the industrial sector of the American economy. With the end of the Great Depression, the American economy entered a long period of high growth that lasted, with but brief interruptions, from the 1940s through to the 1960s. This prolonged economic boom marginalized the agricultural sector, pulling many people from the still largely agricultural South to more developed areas of the country.

A part of the postwar emigration from the South consisted of African Americans, who had more than economic reasons to migrate. At the end of the nineteenth century and the beginning of the twentieth, Southern states instituted a system of racial segregation that separated blacks and whites in schools, churches, parks, restaurants, hotels, public transport and other public facilities. Southern authorities resorted to unconstitutional devices to disenfranchise virtually all blacks in the South, as well as to exclude them from juries in violation of common law rights that went back to the medieval England of Henry II. In addition to these forms of official racial discrimination, blacks often suffered from the violent racism of many Southern whites – 138 were lynched in the period 1930–45 – while the exclusively white judges and juries in Southern courts were hardly unbiased in trials concerning blacks.

The black exodus from the South had begun before 1945, but it accelerated in the early postwar period. Whereas at the beginning of the twentieth century almost all African Americans lived in the South, by 1970 only 53 per cent did. The acceleration of black emigration was related to the fact that one million African Americans served in the armed forces during World War II. Having risked life and limb for their nation fighting against Hitler's racism, many were unwilling thereafter to tolerate racism at home. As one black corporal put it, 'I spent four years in the Army to free a bunch of Dutchmen and Frenchmen, and I'll be hanged if I am going to let the Alabama version of the Germans kick me around when I get home.'[3] The economic boom of the 1940s facilitated the black exodus from the South. For example, a Southern black maid who worked for $3.50 a week moved to California during the war and found work in an armaments plant for $48 a week.

The black migration to the North and the West did not result in greater racial integration, producing the greatest tragedy of postwar American society. As blacks poured into the poorer neighborhoods of the Northern and Western cities, whites started moving out. Without sanction or design by the authorities, substantial racial segregation resulted from the behavior of individuals, as if water and oil had been mixed and then separated. This metaphor is not exact, since racially mixed areas have existed in the Northern and Western cities throughout the postwar era. Yet segregated neighborhoods did emerge at the lower and the higher ends of the socioeconomic scale.

At the bottom, the result was the creation of black urban ghettos, mostly a postwar phenomenon, which in time had explosive consequences for American society and politics. The decline of America's inner cities resulted from a vicious circle in which the flight of whites after the arrival of blacks led to shrinking local employment opportunities, resulting in disproportionately high unemployment rates in the black ghettos. Over time, a significant portion of the ghettos' unskilled blacks found themselves isolated from the surrounding job markets.

At the top, the result was all-white suburbs that expanded rapidly after the war and absorbed an ever-growing portion of America's middle class. The rapid growth of the suburbs resulted from the economic boom in conjunction with two federal programs. Highway construction enabled the daily commute from home in the suburbs to work in the city that has become a prominent neo-nomadic feature of life in the modern world. The GI Bill of Rights of 1944 provided generous housing benefits to the veterans of World War II, about 13 per cent of the population, many of whom were thus able to buy new houses in the suburbs.

In some suburbs African Americans were excluded not only by lack of income. Suburban developers often devised contracts that prohibited the sale or renting of housing units to blacks, in order to protect the value of their investments, since the entry of blacks into a suburban neighborhood could lead to a collapse in real estate values. Such private contracts tended to be honored in practice even after the US Supreme Court declared them unconstitutional and unenforceable in the courts.

The emerging black ghettos were like a wound in the American polity that festered slowly. In the 1940s the wound was still minor. For the vast majority of Americans this decade brought unparalleled prosperity and upward mobility. The awful ruins of the Great Depression receded in the background and faded from the view of a society that optimistically sped forward toward unprecedented material progress and wealth.

American policy in Europe in the 1940s

Before the 1940s, American involvement in the affairs of the eastern hemisphere was limited and fitful, with great swings from isolationism to internationalism. The most ambitious engagement had been Woodrow Wilson's bid to remake world politics according to liberal principles. This was followed by isolationism that peaked in the 1930s, when Congress passed a series of ever more stringent neutrality acts that aimed at precluding any possibility of an American slide into some future European war. At one moment America seemed determined to save the rest of the world, the next moment to have nothing to do with it.

The roots of these American oscillations were in the notions of American *exceptionalism*, according to which the United States was a 'new Jerusalem', a 'shining city upon a hill' with a 'manifest destiny' and a 'special providence' to be a 'beacon' guiding the rest of the world by its principles and its great example. Such notions could lead to either of two perspectives on the Old World. In the Wilsonian version, the United States should become deeply engaged in order actively to save the world according to liberal principles. In the isolationist version, the United States should strive to separate itself from the sordid power politics of the Old World in order to remain pristine and uncontaminated, as if engagement might sully it and dim the beacon's light. What seemed to be precluded was ordinary Great Power behavior predominant in the European tradition, founded upon the operation of the balance of power and guided by the national interest defined in terms of power relations.

It is true that traditional Realist thought was not altogether absent in the American tradition. Alexander Hamilton, one of America's Founding Fathers, and Theodore Roosevelt certainly viewed the world in terms of *Realpolitik*. The Northeastern Republican elites in the 70-year era of Republican domination (1860–1930) had pursued an economic internationalism that was very much guided by a pragmatic understanding of American national interests, in Hamilton's mercantilistic tradition. But these were decidedly elite views; the great mass of Americans were, and on the whole still are, swayed by notions of American exceptionalism.

What few Americans realized was that the exceptional American rise to greatness in isolation from European Great Power antagonisms was made possible by certain cold facts of power politics. The United States was able to grow to a continental-sized federation, to survive the Civil War intact without European intervention that might have enabled the South to secede, and to impose its hegemony on the western hemisphere, because British naval supremacy prevented any other European state from seriously projecting power there. Britain was unable, largely because of Canada's vulnerability to an American attack, to threaten the United States herself. Britain was strong enough to shield the United States from the designs of other European Great Powers, but not so strong after 1814 to menace the United States herself.

This fortunate arrangement in turn depended on the preservation of the balance of power in Europe. Should one Continental nation conquer all others, it would accumulate enough power to subjugate Britain in turn. With the united resources of the Old World it would then overshadow the United States and be able to project power in the western hemisphere. As George Kennan declared in 1950,[4] throughout much of American history

> it was essential to us, as it was to Britain, that no single Continental land power should come to dominate the entire Eurasian land mass. Our interest has lain rather in the maintenance of some sort of stable balance among the powers of the interior, in order that none of them should effect the subjugation of the others, conquer the seafaring fringes of the land mass, become a great sea power as well as a land power, shatter the position of England, and enter – as in these circumstances it certainly would – on an overseas expansion hostile to ourselves and supported by the immense resources of the interior of Europe and Asia.

The arrangement worked well in the nineteenth century; it broke down in the twentieth. The rise first of German and then of Soviet power threatened to overthrow the balance of power despite British resistance. Inevitably, the United States stepped in and saved the machinery upon which was built its own security, growth and greatness. At the hour of maximum danger when survival is at stake, Great Powers move almost instinctively to secure their preservation, cutting through the fog of ideology and quaint national tradition.

Yet ideology and national tradition have a way of asserting themselves in unpredictable ways, as Woodrow Wilson discovered in 1920. Wilson's tragic failure after World War I to lead the United States into the League of Nations and the resultant ascendancy of isolationism haunted Roosevelt during World War II. American policy both during and immediately after the war was guided above all by the overriding determination of the Roosevelt and Truman administrations to prevent a renewed slide into isolationism. After all, American isolationism in the interwar years had fatally weakened the League of Nations and had removed from European politics the one power factor that might have deterred Hitler from launching his war of conquest and Continental domination. Roosevelt and Truman were determined to prevent a similar outcome after World War II; thus they had to shape their policies according to American ideology and national tradition in order to keep the American people on board.

As a result, American responses to pressing geopolitical realities were framed in the terms of American exceptionalism, reflecting various manifestations of American ideology and national tradition in order to mobilize American society. The process was hardly smooth, for it resulted in foreign policy excesses (global anticommunist crusade) and domestic phobias (McCarthyism). But it did secure the main geopolitical objective (containment of the Soviet Union). It also promoted an international order that was immensely beneficial to Western Europe, Japan and, over the long run, much of the rest of the world.

The postwar world began to take shape well before the end of World War II. In examining the policies of the three main allied leaders, one is struck by the clarity of the geopolitical objectives of Churchill and Stalin, and by the comparative vagueness in Roosevelt's geopolitical views. Yet Roosevelt's policy was very focused indeed, once it is understood that his primary objective was to prevent a renewed postwar regression into isolationism, such as had destroyed Wilson's internationalist program in 1920.

Stalin's central geopolitical objective was to expand Soviet territory and domination westwards in Eastern and Central Europe in order to create a buffer zone that would protect the Soviet Union from future invasions. As the leader of a revolutionary Marxist regime, he believed in the ultimate worldwide revolution of the proletariat. Yet this was a very distant goal that could only be promoted by securing the revolution in its only home, the Soviet Union, under the slogan 'Socialism in one country'. Hence Stalin's emphasis on creating a Soviet sphere of influence.

Churchill's central geopolitical objective was to limit the Soviet sphere in Eastern and Central Europe as much as possible, in order to prevent the Soviet Union from emerging after the war as a new menace to the European balance of power in the place of Nazi Germany.

Roosevelt feared that geopolitical antagonisms, spheres of influence and other manifestations of the 'sordid power politics' of the Old World would turn Americans again toward isolationism. Therefore, in order to attain his main geopolitical objective of continued American engagement in Europe, he needed to present the postwar order in the idealistic terms of international cooperation based on liberal principles. Leading the most powerful nation in the alliance against Hitler, Roosevelt was able to a considerable extent to impose his views on his reluctant allies.

His first step was the Atlantic Charter in 1941, a declaration of liberal principles that Roosevelt and Churchill agreed upon, even though the reference to the right of all people to choose their form of government was incompatible with the British Empire. Next Roosevelt put forth the concept of the 'four policemen', that is, the United States, Britain, the Soviet Union and China, as the guardians of postwar peace and security. Neither Stalin nor Churchill thought that China merited such an exalted position, yet in the end they bowed to Roosevelt's wishes. In 1943 Roosevelt put forth his plan for the United Nations with a security council that would include the 'four policemen' as permanent members. Again Stalin and Churchill were unenthusiastic – Stalin proposed regional security organizations instead – yet eventually they went along. But Churchill insisted on including France in the group of veto-wielding permanent Security Council members in order to build her up as a counterweight to Soviet power in Europe. The United Nations Organization was created in 1945 and it was appropriately located in New York, America's greatest city. It originated in an American vision of world cooperation that was strongly supported by the American people.

On matters more directly related to their geopolitical objectives, Roosevelt's two main allies pursued their own agendas. In 1944–5 the Red Army poured into Central and Southeastern Europe, creating new facts that would shape the postwar world. The Soviet Union annexed large territories at the expense of

Germany and other Eastern European states. Poland was shifted westwards, losing her eastern territories to the Soviet Union but gaining new western territories from Germany. Stalin imposed a communist dictatorship on the Poles, beginning the process of Soviet domination in Eastern Europe. Churchill countered by intervening militarily in the Greek civil war, in order to keep the Soviets away from the Mediterranean. Britain was thus already containing the Soviet Union by late 1944, years before the containment strategy was adopted by the United States.

At the Yalta conference in February 1945, Roosevelt and Churchill could do little but accept Soviet domination of Eastern Europe, since the removal of the Red Army from there would necessitate a third world war that neither of them was willing to contemplate. The division of Europe into two spheres was already taking shape. As the allies poured into the vacuum left by the collapse of German power, they had little choice but to respect each other's zones of control, unless they wanted to risk a new war. But the implicit acceptance of the Soviet sphere by Roosevelt and Churchill did not mean that they acquiesced in the imposition of Stalinist dictatorships in Eastern Europe. At Yalta they pressed Stalin to hold free elections in Poland, in effect suggesting an arrangement such as applied during the Cold War in Finland, namely that the Soviet Union would control Poland's foreign and security policy but grant domestic self-rule. During the conference Stalin appeared to give in to their demand, deliberately deceiving his allies.

After his return from Yalta, Roosevelt addressed Congress and declared that the Yalta conference 'ought to spell the end of the system of unilateral action, the exclusive alliances, the spheres of influence, the balances of power, and all the other expedients that have been tried for centuries – and have always failed'. The exact opposite assessment of Yalta would have been closer to the truth. By hiding from the American people the true nature of developments in Europe, Roosevelt facilitated the disillusionment that was to feed the Red Scare a few years later. On the other hand, however devious his methods, Roosevelt did achieve his main objective, which was to secure a permanent American engagement in the eastern hemisphere. There was no isolationist backlash after World War II.

Was the intense Cold War confrontation inevitable?

After the end of the war, the victorious allies moved apart and slid into a confrontation that at times appeared to bring mankind to the brink of a third world war. Yet the division of Europe was complete by the end of the war, and did not change until 1989. Both American and Soviet archives have demonstrated that neither side contemplated a change in this *status quo* by military means, though each side feared that the other might launch an aggressive war. Was the intense Cold War confrontation inevitable, or could the two superpowers have reached a stable *modus vivendi*, such as did emerge in the 1970s?

In order to understand the origins of the Cold War, one must keep in mind the impact of Hitler and the deadliest war in history. Hitler poisoned international politics for years after his death. Neville Chamberlain had striven in good faith to accommodate German demands in order to avoid the irrationality of another great war, but he had been betrayed ruthlessly. Stalin in 1939–41 had appeased Hitler even more than Chamberlain, and had been betrayed even more ruthlessly. The United States had been deeply shocked by Pearl Harbor. Having gone through these traumatic experiences, and through the life-and-death struggle that ensued, the superpowers in the postwar period were highly suspicious of one another. The fear that they might fall victim again to Hitlerite ruthlessness lasted a long time.

In the causal chain that resulted in the Cold War, Stalin bears the main responsibility in the initial phases. Soviet archives have demonstrated Stalin's unshakable belief that a conflict between the capitalist and the communist camps was inevitable, and that he therefore never placed faith in the United Nations and other forms of international cooperation as mechanisms of international security. But this does not mean that he intended to initiate a war. On the contrary, his policy was to postpone the supposedly inevitable war until Soviet power had been built up. It is worth recalling that the American atomic monopoly lasted until 1949 and American superiority in strategic delivery systems until the 1960s. Stalin certainly intended to expand his sphere in Europe in the short run. But his methods were going to be political; he hoped to bring communist parties to power in Western Europe, exploiting the devastation of Western European economies and societies during the war. The most destabilizing aspect of Stalin's policy was the imposition of communist dictatorships in Eastern Europe. The West had in effect accepted his sphere of influence in the geopolitical sense. It was the imposition of totalitarian regimes in Eastern Europe that convinced most people in the West that Stalin was following an expansionist program that aimed at worldwide communist rule.

Unlike Stalin, the Truman administration came to perceive the postwar world in conflictual terms only gradually. It is true that Truman was outraged in 1945 by the Soviet refusal to hold free elections in Poland, in violation of the Yalta agreements. Moreover, the Potsdam conference in July 1945 failed to settle the permanent status of Germany, indefinitely prolonging the occupation arrangements of the four allied powers. Yet despite these tribulations, the Truman administration rapidly demobilized the American armed forces from 12.1 million men in 1945 to 3 million in 1946, 1.6 million in 1947 and 1.4 million in 1948. The nuclear armaments program was also slow – in March 1947 the United States had only 14 unassembled atomic bombs. This was hardly the military posture of a power preparing for conflict.

A ship in calm waters in the open sea may drift for quite some time without danger. But if it approaches a reef, captain and crew must jump to their stations and get the ship moving. The reef that mobilized the United States was the message by the British government in February 1947 that by April it would withdraw its troops from Greece and Turkey and leave the Greek government to deal with the Greek communist rebellion by its own devices, unless the United States moved into Britain's place. With this message, Britain abdicated from its Great Power status and passed the torch to the United States.

With great danger approaching, geopolitical clarity prevailed at once: the Truman administration adopted the policy of resisting the expansion of the Soviet sphere in Europe. Nonetheless, the new geopolitical orientation had to be presented in terms suitable to American exceptionalism in order to bring

American society along. In his address to the Congress on March 12, 1947, Truman announced that the United States would support free peoples resisting subjugation by armed minorities or outside pressure: this became known as the Truman Doctrine. Cloaking geopolitical objectives in an anticommunist mantle was fine in terms of swaying American public opinion, so long as the geopolitical focus remained sharp. But it risked escalating the new engagement in Europe to a global anticommunist crusade without limits, as the future was to show.

In terms of the immediate need to move American society towards an unprecedented American peacetime commitment in Europe, Truman's approach was a historic success. The Greek and Turkish aid bill passed the Senate by 67 to 23 and the House of Representatives by 267 to 107, demonstrating the waning of isolationism. The importance of this vote becomes evident when it is contrasted with the Senate's rejection of the League of Nations in 1920. Truman told his aides: 'it means the United States is going into European politics'.

The Truman administration concentrated next on the task of forming an anti-Soviet coalition in Western Europe. European conditions at the time were appalling. The war had badly damaged European infrastructure, thereby impeding the supply of food, power, water and heating material for large parts of Europe's populations. Tens of thousands froze to death during the unusually cold first and second postwar winters. Conditions were particularly harsh in Germany, where to the destruction of housing and infrastructure was added the burden of 15 million destitute refugees from Stalin's and Czechoslovakia's forcible expulsion policies (possibly the most massive 'ethnic cleansing' operations ever). One million Germans died from cold or hunger after the war, tragically raising the toll that Germany paid for having earlier embraced Hitler. Stalin hoped to exploit Western Europe's misery by promoting the rise of local communist parties to power.

The American response to the challenge in Europe was formulated by the American diplomat George Kennan in an article published anonymously in *Foreign Affairs* in mid-1947, which acquired the aura of a major policy statement once the official capacity of the author was revealed. In the 'X' article Kennan assessed the Soviet objective of world revolution as very long-term, concluding that the Soviet Union would not risk its recent gains in a Hitler-style war of aggression.

> Its political action is a fluid stream which moves constantly, wherever it is permitted to move, toward a given goal. Its main concern is to make sure that it has filled every nook and cranny available to it in the basin of world power. But if it finds unassailable barriers to its path, it accepts these philosophically and accommodates itself to them.

Having resorted to the fluid metaphor to describe the nature of Soviet expansionism, Kennan then proposed 'a long-term, patient but firm and vigilant containment of Russian expansive tendencies'. He also foresaw the end of the story, arguing that if 'anything were ever to occur to disrupt the unity and efficacy of the Party as a political instrument, Soviet Russia might be changed overnight from one of the strongest to one of the weakest and most pitiable of national societies'.

In Kennan's conception, the containment policy was to be implemented mainly by political and economic rather than military means, since the nature of the Soviet threat at that time was not military. His approach is exemplified by the Marshall Plan, which aimed at restoring Western European economic health so that Western European societies would resist the false lure of communism; and at promoting the regional integration of Western Europe, so that it would constitute a united bloc opposing Soviet power.

Secretary of State George C. Marshall's original proposal was an aid package for the whole of Europe, Eastern as well as Western, since the Truman administration wanted to avoid being held responsible for the formal division of Europe. The American leadership presumed that Stalin would reject participation by the Soviet sphere. Actually, Stalin did consider participating at first. But there was little chance of Soviet participation under the American conditions for the aid program, which included the reintegration of Germany into the European economy and, more generally, a multilateral approach to European economic recovery.

Stalin inadvertently furthered the success of the Marshall Plan by first permitting Czechoslovakia to participate, then ordering her to withdraw, and finally overthrowing her government in February 1948 and substituting a Stalinist dictatorship. Czechoslovakia's humiliation and subjugation enhanced the image of the Soviet menace and enabled the Truman administration to emphasize anti-communist arguments in assisting the Marshall Plan's progress in Congress. This display of Soviet domination frightened Western Europeans and helped Truman overcome French and British resistance to the plan's multilateral approach. As a result, the Marshall Plan constituted the first step in European economic integration, leading to the European Coal and Steel Community in 1950, which was designed to place Germany's industrial revival under multilateral control.

The Marshall Plan also resulted in the economic union of the three Western occupation zones in mid-1948 under a single new West German currency. American insistence on including West Germany in Western Europe's economic revival was wise and farsighted. The rapidly growing West German economy in the 1950s acted as the locomotive that pulled the other Western European economies along the track of recovery, prosperity, political stability and European integration, whereby communist influence receded. Western European recovery was also facilitated directly by the Marshall Plan itself, which over the period 1948–52 transferred to Europe $13.2 billion, approximately 1.5 per cent of American GDP.

Stalin's next blunder was the blockade of West Berlin in 1948–9, which disrupted its land transport links with West Germany. A massive American airlift secured the city's food and coal supplies for the duration of the blockade. The main political consequence of Stalin's move was that the leaders of Western Europe demanded from the United States a defensive alliance to guarantee them from Soviet military aggression. It is perhaps ironic in retrospect that European integration originated in American policy and the Atlantic Alliance in Western European fears of Soviet aggression.

The formation of the North Atlantic Treaty Organisation (NATO) in 1949 completed the process by which the Truman administration secured the lasting engagement of the United States in Europe. It was an unprecedented peacetime military commitment by the United States that demonstrated conclusively the waning of isolationism as a significant force in American politics. The contrast with 1920 could hardly have been greater. The American engagement in Europe was dictated by geopolitical necessity: the need to prevent Soviet domination of all Europe. It was also guided by enlightened economic self-interest, since American support for a European economic recovery provided insurance against a return to the Great Depression. Americans had learned the lesson that narrow economic nationalism in the interwar years had contributed to the destabilization of the international economy that resulted in the Great Depression. Yet, undoubtedly, it also derived from some of the most appealing idealistic attributes of America, such as her generosity, her optimism and her self-confidence in the mission of upholding the great liberal tradition in world politics.

The New Deal coalition under Truman's stewardship

Liberals in 1945 looked forward to a new surge in liberal reforms to continue the tradition of the New Deal. Since Congress tended to be under the control of the 'unholy' alliance of the Republican minority and the conservative Southern Democrats, the liberals looked to the presidency as the institution that would lead to new reforms. They wanted a strong liberal president on the model of FDR to arouse public opinion in favor of reform in order to sweep along the more conservative elements of the Democratic Party in Congress.

Harry Truman seemed unlikely to fulfill such high expectations. While anyone succeeding FDR was bound to be dwarfed at the outset by the great man, Truman seemed particularly inadequate. He succeeded FDR upon his death in April 1945, after serving as his fourth-term vice-president for only three months. When he learned of Roosevelt's death he said, 'I felt like the moon, the stars, and all the planets had fallen on me.' He told reporters, 'Boys, if you ever pray, pray for me now.'

A modest man, Truman thought that there must be a million men better qualified for the presidency, though he expected Roosevelt's allies to accept his leadership as FDR's successor. But most liberals doubted his reformist orientation, given his background in Missouri machine politics and his unimpressive congressional career in the 1930s. Truman had only risen to national prominence during the war as head of a Senate committee investigating government waste in the war mobilization, an achievement that did not necessarily imply a zeal for federal activism.

The most significant federal mechanism for social improvement in the early postwar years was the GI Bill of Rights of 1944, Roosevelt's last major legislative achievement, which generously assisted veterans in making the transition to the job market, starting businesses, acquiring housing and gaining access to university education. Federal assistance for university education under the act, for example, benefited 7.8 million veterans between 1945 and 1956, significantly raising the number of Americans who went to college: 497,000 degrees were conferred in 1950, compared with 216,000 in 1940. This facilitated the emergence of a new middle class and the rapid growth of American universities in the postwar years.

Truman was unable to pass legislation of comparable importance. This was not because he was averse to liberal reforms, the suspicions of the liberals not-withstanding. The postwar climate had turned against new reforming endeavors; after the upheavals of depression and world war, Americans wished to enjoy the fruits of the new prosperity. Truman did submit reform bills to Congress. Some, such as his proposal for a national health system, were rejected outright as too 'socialist'. Others, such as his employment bill, were passed only after being weakened beyond recognition by Congress. In addition, Truman found himself clashing with the unions over a series of unpopular postwar strikes that threat-ened to disrupt the new prosperity.

After an inauspicious start, Truman's presidency took a sharp turn for the worse in the congressional midterm elections of November 1946, in which the Republicans regained control of Congress for the first time since 1929–30. The shock of the 1946 elections enhanced the widespread impression that Truman was unable to manage FDR's political legacy and that the Democrats were stuck with a loser. The Republicans were convinced that they would regain the presidency in 1948. The future of the New Deal coalition seemed bleak. But Truman's presidential stature grew considerably in 1947 in the wake of his historic foreign policy initiatives in Europe that were supported in Congress by bipartisan majorities. Nonetheless, domestic developments remained unfavorable for him.

On the left, Truman faced the defection of Henry Wallace, FDR's third-term vice-president (1941–4), who formed the new Progressive Citizens of America Party that supported ambitious progressive reforms at home and reconciliation with the Soviet Union abroad. Wallace's Soviet policy went against the trends of the time and could only appeal to the extreme left wing of the New Deal coali-tion. He never came close to becoming a major electoral force, yet he threatened to bring about Truman's defeat if the 1948 election was close.

On the right, Truman's policies were threatened by Republican majorities in Congress. The most significant legislative initiative of the Republican Congress was the replacement of the New Deal's pro-labor Wagner Act by the Taft-Hartley Act of 1947. Taft-Hartley reshaped labor relations in the United States, confining the right to strike to direct collective bargaining within an industry and prohib-iting solidarity strikes by unions in other industries. Thus the labor movement could no longer strike in the context of generalized class conflict. Truman's veto of the bill was overridden by large majorities in both chambers of Congress, with about half the Democrats in the House and the Senate joining his Republican adversaries.

Truman's strategy for the 1948 election sought to appeal to the New Deal coalition. It was based on the risky, and in the event false, assumption that the Solid South could be taken for granted, so that Truman should aim at securing the black vote in the North by putting forth a civil rights plank. It emphasized his anti-Soviet foreign policy, in order to secure the Democratic advantage among recent immigrant groups who were particularly alarmed by the subjugation of the Catholic peoples of Eastern Europe. It also emphasized recognition of the new state of Israel in order to secure the Jewish vote, which, while not large overall (about 3.5 per cent), was concentrated in a few crucial states with special weight in the Electoral College, the body that actually elects the president.

Truman's foreign policy team opposed recognition of Israel on the grounds that it would amount to 'a declaration of war against the Arab world', as Kennan put it. Truman himself leaned in favor of recognition, in part on account of electoral considerations – he told foreign policy officials that there weren't many Arabs among his voters. Undoubtedly, he was also genuinely moved by the plight of the Jews after the Holocaust, which produced a large pro-recognition trend across American society, well beyond the few states in which Jewish Americans were concentrated.

The aspect of Truman's election strategy that concerned African Americans resulted in greater tribulation. In order to secure their lasting allegiance, Truman took significantly more advanced pro-civil rights positions than FDR, thereby enraging the Southern Democrats. The confrontation culminated at the Democratic National Convention of 1948, which adopted a civil rights plank supported by the liberal wing of the party. Many Southern Democrats reacted by storming out of the convention, waving Confederate banners. They then created the Democratic States' Rights Party, better known as the Dixiecrats, which fielded Governor Strom Thurmond of South Carolina as candidate for the presidency.

As a result, Truman entered the general election race in the fall of 1948 having lost two parts of the New Deal coalition: on the left the supporters of Henry Wallace, and in the South the Dixiecrats. The Republicans nominated Governor Thomas Dewey of New York, who belonged to the moderate and internationalist wing of the party and was thus well positioned to draw centrist voters from the New Deal coalition. Prior to the election, all the opinion polls predicted a Dewey victory. Yet Truman turned the tide through a relentless populist campaign that reminded voters of the Great Depression and the achievements of Democratic rule since 1933. He also did not hesitate to use the anticommunist card against Wallace, declaring that he neither sought nor would accept the political support of 'Wallace and his communists'. Wallace proved tone-deaf to the rising Red Scare in American society, countering that if the communists wanted to support him, he would not stop them. Dewey was so certain of his victory that he declined to campaign energetically. The result was the least predicted election result in recent American history.

The election of 1948 demonstrated the resilience of the New Deal coalition, in spite of its losses and the perceived weakness of Truman's candidacy. Truman received 24.2 million votes (49.6 per cent) against Dewey's 22 million (45.1 per cent), while Thurmond got 1.18 million and Wallace 1.16 million. The Democrats regained control of both chambers of Congress, restoring the New Deal coalition's control over both elective branches of the federal government.

Thurmond's majorities in four states of the Deep South constituted a temporary Southern defection from the Democratic Party that weakened the strong links between the South and the Democrats; though it must be stressed that at the congressional level there was no Dixiecrat defection. On the other hand, the black vote seems to have secured for Truman narrow victories in the closely contested large states of California, Illinois and Ohio, which in the Electoral College far outweighed Thurmond's four states, vindicating Truman's civil rights strategy.

The 1948 election was particularly disheartening for the Republicans, who experienced their fifth presidential election defeat in a row and seemed permanently consigned to a minority status. Their hopes had been raised by their 1946 midterm victory, only to be cruelly dashed in 1948. Their subsequent desperation in the pursuit of power contributed to the increasing acrimony that characterized American politics in the following years. Some Republicans had attempted as early as 1948 to weaken the Truman administration through the growing Red Scare in American society, which Truman used against Wallace. The acting chairman of the House Committee on Un-American Activities Karl Mundt said in September 1948 that the committee's investigations were 'proving very interesting. If the White House refused to cooperate in turning over personnel files, we will crucify the administration. If they do, we are going to be able to dig out more stuff to plague them in the fall campaign'.[5] But some major foreign policy debacle had to occur before the Red Scare could be turned against the Truman administration with real effectiveness. That debacle took place in East Asia.

American policy in East Asia in the 1940s

The American engagement in East Asia in the 1940s was influenced by the intense Sinophilia that had grown in the United States since the beginning of the twentieth century. Few Americans had any real knowledge of China, and those that did tended, like Henry Luce, to arrive at it via Christian missionaries who viewed China through highly idealistic lenses. In spite of the paucity of real knowledge and understanding, an image took hold in the American imagination of China as a 'sister republic', a 'pure' country surrounded by imperialist vultures. But China also represented a vast unexploited market that could bring untold riches to American commerce, so long as America resisted the imperialist spheres of influence in China and insisted on an 'Open Door'.

Pro-Chinese sentiments in the United States grew during World War II, which in Asia began with the Japanese invasion of Manchuria in 1931 and China proper in 1937. In 1942 the *New York Times* wrote: 'It is comforting to believe that the Chinese are inherently a democratic and individualistic people.' The same paper maintained, that 'if the average American loves liberty as much as the average Chinese, and will fight, risk, work and sacrifice as much for it, we need not fear for the future'. Such Sinophile views were also expressed in official circles. A survey by OSS (forerunner of the CIA) in 1942 described China as 'one of the world's staunchest strongholds of democracy'. American policy makers expected China to bear the main burden of land warfare against the Japanese army, much like the Soviet Union against the German army. Roosevelt's high estimation of China was demonstrated when he included her in his 'four policemen', intending to strengthen her as a bulwark against both Soviet and European imperialist ambitions in East Asia.

China's reality was unrelated to the American Sinophile fantasies. Chiang Kaishek's regime was authoritarian and endemically corrupt. It exercised very limited control over the provinces nominally under its authority. Of 300 nominal divisions in the Chinese army, only 40 were directly controlled by the government; the rest were controlled by the semi-autonomous regional warlords that held real power in most Chinese provinces.

The incompetence of the Chiang regime had been demonstrated since the Japanese invasion of China in 1937. Moreover, the Japanese invasion had enabled Mao Tse-tung, the leader of a communist insurgency that defied the government's authority since the late 1920s, to expand the territories under his control. Whereas in 1937 Mao controlled territories with 1.5 million inhabitants out of a total Chinese population of 400 million, by 1943 he controlled 55 million. In the meantime, the American idealization of all matters Chinese extended to Mao's communist movement as well. Even though Mao was a thorough Stalinist, some American officials managed to view him as 'an agrarian reformer' and the Chinese communists as 'so democratic as we are', views for which they paid dearly later.

The Chinese reality was revealed to the Roosevelt administration during the major Japanese offensives in East China in 1944 that easily routed the Chinese armies in their way. The defeat and disorderly retreat of Chiang's forces inflicted a devastating blow to his domestic legitimacy, further weakening a regime with rotten foundations. They also destroyed his standing in the eyes of Roosevelt. Yet FDR was by then committed to the inclusion of China as a permanent member in the Security Council and one of the main pillars of the postwar order. Being now aware of Chiang's weakness, as well as of the growing strength of Mao, Roosevelt attempted to mediate between the two Chinese factions in order to prevent a civil war after the end of World War II.

At Yalta in February 1945, Roosevelt's main concern, in regard to East Asia, was the need to find some ally to do most of the land fighting against Japan, now that China had revealed herself as unable to perform the task. He turned to Stalin, offering him Chinese territory that tsarist Russia had lost in the Russo-Japanese War of 1904–5 as an inducement for an early Soviet entry in the war against Japan after the end of the war in Europe. Chiang was informed of this transaction made at China's expense only afterwards, showing how far he had declined in Roosevelt's estimation.

The lengths to which Roosevelt went to secure the Soviet Union's entry in the war against Japan derived from his perception that the subjugation of Japan would entail massive allied casualties. Japanese resistance to vastly superior American forces in Iwo Jima and Okinawa in the first half of 1945 was futile, yet almost unimaginably fierce. In this light, one must accept the prevailing view among historians that Truman's momentous decision to use the new atom bomb against Japan was motivated by a desire to avoid massive American casualties in an invasion of the Japanese home islands.

The atom bomb made Soviet participation in the war against Japan unnecessary. But Stalin hastily declared war on Japan between the bombing of Hiroshima and Nagasaki, sending several hundred thousand troops into the Chinese and Korean territories under Japanese control in order to maximize his postwar influence. To limit Soviet territorial control, the United States airlifted half a million Chinese government troops into Manchuria. Stalin withdrew his forces speedily – keeping only what was given to him at Yalta plus northern Korea – in order to avoid a confrontation with the West in East Asia, which in his eyes was of relatively low priority. But Mao's forces moved into the territories evacuated by the Soviets, vastly enlarging his territorial base.

In the meantime, Washington was still endeavoring to mediate between the two Chinese factions. But its efforts were doomed to failure, since both sides were determined to fight it out sooner or later. A military intelligence report in July 1945 presciently predicted that the likeliest development after the war was the outbreak of a civil war and that the likely winner was Mao. The diplomats John Service and John Davies reached similar conclusions. The American efforts to mediate between Chiang and Mao ended in July 1946, by which time the Truman administration saw through the duplicitous tactical maneuvers of both sides in the build-up towards their impending military confrontation. Truman's aides now supported an American disengagement from Chiang's corrupt, ineffective and rotten regime, since it was likely to be defeated in the coming civil war.

Unfortunately, American public opinion was unprepared to accept an abandonment of China after decades of Sinophile idealization. Furthermore, the influential China lobby became more powerful after the Republican victory in the midterm elections of November 1946. The Republicans in Congress insisted on a continued American commitment to the Chiang regime as a precondition for passing the Marshall Plan for Europe. After all, wasn't Europe the center of the sordid power politics of the Old World, and China the sister republic that had been threatened by the scheming European imperialists?

The result was a strange dichotomy between the Truman administration's perceptions and its actions. The US archives demonstrate beyond doubt that the Truman administration had written off Chiang's regime well before its fall. At the same time, Truman and his foreign policy team continued publicly to support Chiang and to provide him with aid, in order to secure from Congress the aid packages for Europe. The inability of the Truman administration to explain to the American public the true situation in China was bound to create disillusionment.

Mao's victory in October 1949 shocked the American public and produced deep anxiety. The most populous nation on earth, supposedly a great democracy, had come under communist control, vastly expanding the communist sphere. The question 'who lost China?' dominated politics in the winter of 1949–50, and most Republicans blamed the incompetence of the Truman administration.

In February 1950 Senator Joseph McCarthy moved along a different track with his claim that he had a list of 205 State Department officials who were known to the Truman administration to be communists. Not incompetence but treason was his explanation for the 'loss' of China. This conspiracy theory did not originate with McCarthy, but he gave it a devastating political effectiveness. An anxious and dismayed public that had been fed Sinophile fantasies for decades grasped at his ludicrous treason theory as a way out of its acute cognitive dissonance, giving him enormous power for several dark years.

Prominent among McCarthy's victims were officials and advisors who had the misfortune of being associated with American policy in China during the 1940s, including Professor Owen Lattimore and the career diplomats John Service and John Davies, who were hounded publicly before red-baiting congressional committees, leaving their reputations and careers in ruins. On the Senate floor, McCarthy went so far as to accuse George Marshall of treason. As for relations between the United States and China, before the end of 1950 they would sink into a bloody military confrontation in Korea, which for a whole generation of Americans transformed the 'sister republic' into an enemy more implacable than even the Soviet Union. Thus in the 1940s American society had gone from Depression and isolation to World War II, prosperity and then the Cold War. These historic experiences exerted a profound influence on American culture.

NOTES

1. David M. Kennedy, *Freedom from Fear: The American People in Depression and War, 1929–1945*, Oxford: Oxford University Press, 1999, p. 365.
2. Robert Higgs, *Crisis and Leviathan: Critical Episodes in the Growth of American Government*, Oxford: Oxford University Press, 1987, p. 231.
3. James A. Patterson, *Grand Expectations: The United States, 1945–1974*, Oxford: Oxford University Press, 1996, p. 23.
4. George F. Kennan, *American Diplomacy*, expanded edn, Chicago, IL: University of Chicago Press, 1985, pp. 4–5.
5. Irwin F. Gellman, *The Contender: Richard Nixon, the Congress Years, 1946–1952*, New York: Free Press (Simon & Schuster), 1999, p. 199.

RECOMMENDED READING

Frank Freidel, *Roosevelt: A Rendezvous with Destiny*, Boston, MA: Little, Brown and Company, 1990.

John Lewis Gaddis, *We Now Know: Rethinking Cold War History*, Oxford: Clarendon, 1997.

George F. Kennan, *American Diplomacy*, expanded edn, Chicago, IL: University of Chicago Press, 1985.

David M. Kennedy, *Freedom from Fear: The American People in Depression and War, 1929–1945*, Oxford: Oxford University Press, 1999.

David McCullough, *Truman*, New York: Simon & Schuster, 1992.

James A. Patterson, *Grand Expectations: The United States, 1945–1974*, Oxford: Oxford University Press, 1996.

James L. Sundquist, *Dynamics of the Party System: Alignment and Realignment of Political Parties in the United States*, rev. edn, Washington, DC: Brookings Institution, 1983.

CHAPTER 2

1940s: The Cultural Legacy of World War II

In 1941 Henry Luce announced 'the American Century' on the eve of America's entry into World War II. It may seem surprising that Luce proposed the nation's predominant role during the most serious economic crisis in modern American history. But the creation of a distinctly American culture became the project of many artists in the 1930s. The historian Warren Susman suggests that one of the most significant characteristics of the 1930s was the popular discovery of the anthropological concept of culture, reflected in the remarkable popular success of Ruth Benedict's *Patterns of Culture* (1934). In the 1920s expatriate Modernists like T. S. Eliot and Ezra Pound embraced Matthew Arnold's narrow definition of culture as high culture; now artists adopted the anthropological view that everything a society produced was culture. Susman notes, 'It is not too extreme to propose that it was during the Thirties that the idea of culture was domesticated, with important consequences. Americans then began thinking in terms of patterns of behavior and belief, values and lifestyles, symbols and meaning.' He points out that it was during the 1930s that the phrases 'American Way of Life' and 'The American Dream' became commonplace. 'It is in fact possible to define as a key structural element in a historical reconstruction of the 1930s the effort to find, characterize, and adapt to an American Way of Life as distinguished from the material achievements (and the failures) of an American industrial civilization.'

This effort was reflected in many works that documented the variety of American life. Certainly the most ambitious were the many projects covering every aspect of the nation's cultural life initiated by the New Deal under the auspices of the Works Progress Administration (WPA). But the urge to document American life was not left solely to the federal government. There was also the establishment of the American Institute for Public Opinion and the Gallup Poll (1935), the founding by Luce of the picture magazine *Life* (1936) and the countless artistic efforts to record American reality in words, sounds and images. This effort was evident in all the arts: in John Dos Passos's monumental trilogy, *U.S.A.* (1938) and John Steinbeck's Dust Bowl chronicle, *The Grapes of Wrath* (1939); in Frank Capra's populist films, *Mr. Deeds Goes to Town* (1937) and *Mr. Smith Goes to Washington* (1940); in Aaron Copland's use of American folk songs in the ballet music for *Billy the Kid* (1938); and in three celebrated paintings of 1930: Charles Sheeler's *American Landscape,* Grant Wood's *American Gothic* and Thomas Hart Benton's mural, *America Today.*

Thus by the early 1940s a new sense of American culture had been forged. Nowhere was this sense more apparent than in postwar literature.

The legacy of Modernism

During the past seven decades American literature has been characterized by its splendid multiplicity, its continuing stylistic refinement, and its permanent obsession with the dialectic between the word and the world. As American writers have shed the provincial habits of their literary forebears and claimed their place in the new international literary order, their work has been marked by images of *breakdown* and *breakthrough*: the *breakdown* of distinctions between literary genres or cultural hierarchies, on the one hand, and the *breakthrough* to new imaginative forms and verbal strategies, on the other. Ironically, all this has been accomplished in a period when the writer has felt increasingly threatened with extinction and the critic has continually announced the death of literature.

But this was not apparent half a century ago. The first literary decade after World War II was still dominated by the great figures of the early Modernist movement: in poetry, T. S. Eliot, Ezra Pound and Wallace Stevens; in fiction, Ernest Hemingway and William Faulkner; in drama, Eugene O'Neill. Though most of them had published their best work in the period between the two world wars, they continued to exert a strong influence on the emerging generation of younger writers. Eliot's claim for the 'impersonality' of the poet and Stevens' claim for the 'autonomy' of the imagination shaped the aesthetics of the New Criticism and the practice of the new postwar poetry. Early works like Robert Lowell's *Lord Weary's Castle* (1946), Richard Wilbur's *The Beautiful Changes* (1947) and Theodore Roethke's *The Lost Son* (1948) all reveal an overarching allegiance to poetic tradition and literary decorum. As Richard Wilbur put it,

> Most American poets of my generation were taught to admire the English metaphysical poets of the seventeenth century and such contemporary masters of irony as John Crowe Ransom. We were led by our teachers and by the critics whom we read to feel that the most adequate and convincing poetry is that which accommodates mixed feelings, clashing ideas, and incongruous images.

Similarly, early postwar novels like Vance Bourjaily's *The End of My Life* (1947), Norman Mailer's *The Naked and the Dead* (1948) and William Styron's *Lie Down in Darkness* (1951) were all written in the shadow of the stylistic achievements of Hemingway, Dos Passos and Faulkner.

It might be useful to compare this younger generation with their famous predecessors. The great Modernists, including Hemingway and Faulkner, Pound and Eliot, were all born in the last years of the nineteenth century and grew up in the relative insularity of prewar America only to be educated in the Great War and its aftermath. The literature they produced expressed a profound disillusionment with modern life and mass society, described most eloquently in Eliot's image of 'the waste land'. The younger generation, which included Saul Bellow, Ralph Ellison, Robert Lowell and Arthur Miller, were all born in the years around World War I and grew up in the turmoil of the Great Depression, only to be educated in the Second World War and its aftermath. These writers inherited a dual legacy of disillusionment: one they learned from their experience of the Depression and the War, and the other they were taught by their reading of the Modernists. Their work reveals an anxiety about the human condition, symbolized, for instance, in the titles of Saul Bellow's first novels, *Dangling Man* (1944) and *The Victim* (1948). As Bellow wrote in *Dangling Man*:

> Six hundred years ago, a man was what he was born to be. Satan and the Church, representing God, did battle over him. He, by reason of his choice, partially decided the outcome. But whether, after life, he went to hell or to heaven, his place among other men was given. It could not be contested. But, since, the stage has been reset and human beings only walk on it, and under this revision, we have, instead, history to answer to. We were important enough then for our souls to be fought over. Now, each of us is responsible for his own salvation, which is his greatness. And that, that greatness, is the rock our hearts are abraded on.

Bellow's anxiety was in part a response to the global destruction during World War II. Its most terrible manifestation was the Holocaust in which six million European Jews were systematically murdered. Only months after the revelations of the death camps, when the Japanese authorities refused to surrender unconditionally, American planes dropped the first atom bombs on Hiroshima and Nagasaki, causing mass destruction and creating a second wave of public shock. Some historians have argued that this was the first act of the Cold War. 'The war was over,' wrote the literary critic Alfred Kazin. 'The war would never end.'

A double-edged sense of relief and anxiety permeated postwar society. Morris Dickstein notes, 'Even more than World War I, in which American participation had been brief and casualties relatively light, the Second World War was a watershed, a turning point, in the social history of the nation.' Not only did five times as many Americans die in the second conflict as in the first, but the nation experienced a total mobilization for the war effort. Thus by 1945, American society had been radically transformed. Millions of returning soldiers as well as civilians on the home front were adjusting to a new reality. Movie critics have pointed to the postwar popularity of *film noir,* the dark melodramas and mysteries like *Mildred Pierce* (1945), *The Big Sleep* (1946) and *Out of the Past* (1947). But the problems of adjustment are depicted more directly in movies about returning veterans. In *Pride of the Marines* (1945), John Garfield plays a blinded Marine. In *The Men* (1950), Marlon Brando plays a paraplegic veteran. In *The Best Years of Our Lives* (1946), Harold Russell plays himself, a returning serviceman who has lost both hands in the war.

William Wyler's *The Best Years of Our Lives* is perhaps the best depiction of the early postwar years that we have. Made before the onset of the Cold War, the film exhibits an unusual optimism about the future while still revealing an underlying anxiety about the direction of American society. At the beginning of the film, three returning veterans meet on a plane taking them home to a typical Middle American town called Boone City. The film shows how their separate lives become intertwined as we follow their attempts to readjust to civilian life. Al (Frederic March) is an ex-infantryman who finds it difficult to return to his bourgeois life as a banker and family man. 'Last year, it was "Kill Japs",' he remarks bitterly, 'and this year it's "Make Money".' Fred (Dana Andrews) is a bombardier who suffers nightmares, cannot find a decent job and watches his marriage unravel. Disabled Homer (Harold Russell) cannot cope with the pity and horror expressed by his well-meaning family. In the end, they are all reintegrated into their society, but no one will ever be the same.

In *You Ain't Heard Nothin' Yet* (1999), Andrew Sarris rightly noted the contradictions in the film. 'One of the movie's major problems,' he says, 'is its uneasy mixture of realism and contrivance. The notion of three veterans returning home to three separate layers of society introduces a choice between class conflict and national reconciliation.' The film chooses a facile reconciliation but not without exposing the shadows haunting postwar society. There are no war heroes in this film; instead, in key scenes, each of these psychically or physically wounded men is put to bed like an ailing child by a woman, presaging the profound changes in gender relationships that will occur in the postwar years. Joseph C. Goulden noted in *The Best Years, 1945–50* (1976), 'of course, all the snarls are resolved, and toward the end of the movie someone concludes that they are really enjoying "the best years of our lives"'. In fact, the title is meant ironically and the line is given to Fred's two-timing wife who complains that she has given the best years of *her* life to the war effort and now she deserves some fun. This ambiguity is reflected in the ambivalence of the public response. On the one hand, the film won nine Academy Awards in 1946; on the other hand, the House Committee on Un-American Activities announced that it would call the film's scenarist, Robert Sherwood, as a witness in its first hearings in Hollywood in 1947.

The age of anxiety

Something had changed profoundly with the conclusion of World War II. The United States had entered the war a wounded economic giant and emerged from it as the dominant superpower in the world. By the end of the war, America and Europe had exchanged places. In *Anti-Intellectualism in American Life* (1963), the historian Richard Hofstadter noted, 'In the 1930s Europe lost its political and moral authority.' The rise of fascism, the collapse of the Western liberal democracies and the cynicism of Russian foreign policy undercut the claims to superiority of all European thought and institutions. 'It was no longer possible to look to any foreign political system for moral or ideological illumination. Even the gravest American failures of decency paled when, at the end of the war, the full horror of the death camps was disclosed.' In 1947, after a tour of war-torn Europe, Edmund Wilson, the most cosmopolitan cultural critic of the period, concluded that 'the United States at the present time is politically more advanced than any other part of the world', and that modern American culture represented 'a revival of the democratic creativeness which presided at the birth of the Republic and flourished up to the Civil War'.

But this optimism about America was tempered by a growing pessimism about humanity. The massive destruction of World War II called into question traditional definitions of man and human progress that had flourished since the Enlightenment. In *Europe Without Baedeker* (1947), Edmund Wilson reported a dinner conversation he had with two enlightened English socialists in 1944:

> It was the moment, near the end of April, when the American and the English had nearly completed their hideous work of ploughing Germany under, and the conversation was becoming quietly ghoulish. The official archly remarked that, when the Germans went home after the war, they would find their country 'rather changed.' The radical, in reminding us that Warsaw had been 'completely wiped out,' gave a kind of involuntary grin – but presently caught himself up: 'Who would have imagined,' he said, 'six years ago, that we should soon be talking in this frivolous way about the destruction of whole populations?' I had often thought of this myself. Through the whole of the previous war some humanitarian feeling survived and continued to assert itself: it was assumed that the misery and slaughter were abnormal and undesirable. ... But today it is perfectly plain that human life is no longer an issue. No one pretends to give a damn any more – unless they are someone's close friends or relatives – whether people are killed or not.

Thus World War II undermined the assumptions of humanism that man was the measure of all things. The horrific images of Auschwitz and Hiroshima confirmed that a total war whose primary aim was the subjection, intimidation and destruction of civilian populations had undermined the traditional humanist view by turning human beings into mere numbers. In his iconic novel, *1984*, published in 1948, George Orwell offered an unforgettable vision of the postwar *zeitgeist*. His hero, Winston Smith, is told: 'If you want a picture of the future, imagine a boot stamping on a human face – forever.' The result was a darkening of the intellectual outlook, a rejection of ideas of progress, reason and social activism. 'The key terms which dominate discourse today', noted the sociologist Daniel Bell in *The End of Ideology* (1960), were 'irony, paradox, ambiguity, and complexity', and the key concepts were 'pessimism, evil, tragedy, and despair'.

Literature in the late 1940s

The sense of anxiety and ambiguity among the new generation of writers is evident in three seminal novels published in 1948, the year that Harry Truman won a stunning upset victory in the presidential election. They are Saul Bellow's *The Victim*, Norman Mailer's *The Naked and the Dead* and Truman Capote's *Other Voices, Other Rooms*. Perhaps *The Victim* best captures the *zeitgeist*. Asa Leventhal, the novel's protagonist, lives between the fringes of failure and the edges of success. He has finally succeeded to a level of middle-class respectability when he suddenly finds himself harassed by a multitude of crises. While his wife is away on a trip, Asa must face alone the responsibility of his absent brother's sick child and the burden of another man's failure. His *alter ego* is his anti-Semitic antagonist, Allbee, the victim of the exact failures that Asa himself had escaped by using Allbee. Now Allbee blames Leventhal for the loss of his job and his subsequent decline. Asa totally rejects the accusation but comes to realize that this is at least partly true. Thus Allbee, the anti-Semite, is as much a victim and victimizer as Asa is. But Asa, who wishes to be free from all responsibility, must make the final commitment: he is not only his brother's keeper but Allbee's too. Each man is responsible for his actions because he is accountable for their consequences. 'After all, you married and had children and there was a chain of consequences,' he reflects. 'It was impossible to tell, in starting out, what was going to happen. And it was unfair, perhaps, to have to account at forty for what was done at twenty. But unless one was more than human or less than human … the payments had to be met.'

On each of its levels, *The Victim* is asking what it means to be not less than or more than human. In a crucial conversation, a wise old theater critic named Schlossberg explains to Asa the principle of 'right acting'. 'So here is the whole thing, then,' he says. 'Good acting is exactly human. And if you say I am a tough critic, you mean I have a high opinion of what is human.' To be more than human is to insist on a divine exemption from the contingencies of human life; to be less than human is to refuse the accountability of human action. To be precisely human, Asa learns, is to accept the imperfections of human agency: 'he liked to think "human" meant accountable in spite of many weaknesses – at the last moment, tough enough to hold'. Although *The Victim* begins with the personal problems of Asa Leventhal and the social problem of anti-Semitism, its area of concern widens to include universal questions of human responsibility in a posthumanist world.

Another strand of the new writing focused on the experiences of the world war. Though many war novels were published in the 1940s, perhaps the most powerful was Norman Mailer's *The Naked and the Dead,* which traced the combat experiences of a company of US Marines in the Pacific campaign. Mailer's Marine company is a microcosm of American society in its ethnic and class composition. Thus Mailer follows consciously in the tradition of Modernist fiction in his concern for individual responsibility in a mass society. From Hemingway, Mailer took an obsession with the possibilities of individual heroism and from John Dos Passos he borrowed his analysis of mass society. 'It seems to me,' Dos Passos wrote in *Three Soldiers* (1921), 'that human society has always been that, and perhaps will be always that: organizations growing and stifling individuals, and individuals revolting hopelessly against them, and at last forming new societies to crush the old societies and becoming slaves again in their turn.' Thus for Dos Passos, as for Mailer, 'Whichever won, tyranny from above, or spontaneous organization from below, there could be no individuals.'

In *The Naked and the Dead*, Mailer's hero, Lieutenant Hearn, is a liberal intellectual who, like the author, has gone to Harvard. In the novel, he leads a squad of Marines on an ill-fated mission to liberate a Japanese-held island somewhere in the Pacific. Confronted with an apocalyptic global war and the promise of a reactionary world order to follow, Hearn discovers that the liberal imagination is too weak to understand the new uses of power unleashed by the world war and too ambivalent to offer any heroic alternative to the reactionary irrationalism which he opposes. Thus Hearn's rejection of his liberal past closes the circle of alienation around him and brings him to the point of indecision which leads finally to his own death. Shortly before he dies, Hearn rehearses the options left open to him and discovers there is no way out. 'There were no answers you could find,' he thinks, 'but perhaps there were epochs in history which had no answers.'

After the success of *The Naked and the Dead,* Mailer was famous, but he soon felt the pressure experienced by young writers blessed – and cursed – with early celebrity. In his next two novels, *Barbary Shore* (1951) and *The Deer Park* (1955), Mailer attempted, unsuccessfully, to combine his sense of radical politics with the traditional form of the novel. At the same time he abandoned Marxism for more individualistic forms of existential and sexual politics. As his fiction became more diffuse, Mailer turned to journalism in the 1960s, writing about the Vietnam War, the Space Program and the presidential elections. The high point was his superb account of the 1967 March on the Pentagon when half a million Americans descended on Washington to protest the Vietnam War. In *The Armies of the Night* (1968) Mailer plays the dual role of demonstrator and witness and becomes the author's most memorable character, a combination, he later said, consisting of one-quarter hero and three-quarters clown. Significantly, Mailer described the 'civil war' between young antiwar radicals and their middle-aged parents from a new political perspective. 'Mailer was a Left Conservative,' he wrote. 'So he had his own point of view. To himself he would suggest that he tried to think in the style of Marx in order to attain certain values suggested by Edmund Burke.'

The third novel published in 1948 pointed in another direction that American literature would also take in the future: the exploration of the underworld of sexual experimentation and homosexuality. *Other Voices, Other Rooms* was a poetic first novel by a precocious 24-year-old writer named Truman Capote. An adolescent coming-of-age story in the guise of a fairy tale, it traces young Joel Knox's search for his father from the realistic daylight of New Orleans to the fantastic twilight of Skully's Landing. But when Joel discovers the terrible truth that his father is a helpless invalid, he must look elsewhere for guidance in his search for identity. Thus Joel stands poised between retreating into the private world with his witty homosexual cousin, Randolph, and advancing into the social world with the adolescent tomboy, Idabel.

The novel's theme of sexual initiation was repeated variously in Gore Vidal's *The City and the Pillar* (1948), Paul Bowles's *The Sheltering Sky* (1949) and James Baldwin's *Giovanni's Room* (1956). Though Capote became famous later for his nonfictional account of a gratuitous murder, *In Cold Blood* (1965), his first novel opened new territory in contemporary writing. '*Other Voices, Other Rooms* today seems like a passing phase for its author and a minor moment in American fiction, yet it epitomized many of the qualities of the New Fiction that would develop in the decades after the war,' observes Morris Dickstein. 'Its emphasis on inwardness and style foreshadowed much of the psychological fiction of the 1950s, just as its focus on a boy's coming of age anticipated the direction of the new youth culture that would lead through the Beats to the counterculture of the 1960s.'

If Bellow revised the discourse of humanism in the postwar world and Mailer described the future from a global perspective, then Arthur Miller transformed the conventions of tragedy in modern society. In a celebrated essay entitled 'Tragedy and the Common Man' (1949), Miller explored the possibilities of

tragic art in a democratic epoch. 'I believe that the common man is as apt a subject for tragedy in its highest sense as kings were,' he argued. 'The commonest
of men may take on that stature to the extent of his willingness to throw all he
has into the contest, the battle to secure his rightful place in the world.' Thus,
for Miller, what constituted the tragic condition was the sense of being displaced
from one's world. 'As a general rule,' he said, 'I think the tragic feeling is evoked
in us when we are in the presence of a character who is ready to lay down his life,
if need be, to secure one thing – his sense of personal dignity.'

This quest for personal dignity in a world of impersonal forces lies at the heart
of Miller's two best early plays, *All My Sons* (1947) and *Death of a Salesman*
(1949). Though he has often been called a social dramatist, the conflicts in his
work are more generational than class-determined. Both plays turn on similar
dramatic conflicts between father and son. In *All My Sons,* Chris condemns
his father Joe Keller because he has put material values before human values.
In *Death of a Salesman,* Biff challenges his father Willy Loman because he has
mistaken material values for human values. In each play, the father has betrayed
a trust with respect to his sons; in each, he can restore that trust by sacrificing
himself as much for his son's sake as for his sense of his own personal dignity.
Though both fathers are judged harshly by their sons for their lack of integrity,
the sons are also judged harshly by their creator for their lack of sympathy. At the
end of *Death of a Salesman,* Mrs Loman rebukes her sons for having scorned
their father. 'Willy Loman never made a lot of money. His name was never in the
papers. He's not the finest character that ever lived,' she says. 'But he's a human
being, and a terrible thing is happening to him. So attention must be paid. He's
not to be allowed to fall into his grave like a dog. Attention, attention must be
finally paid to such a person.' In the end, Willy Loman's decline and fall achieves
the status of a modern tragedy.

Other works of the 1940s also failed to find their answers in the realm of politics. Both Robert Penn Warren's study of a populist demagogue, *All the King's
Men,* and Lionel Trilling's portrait of a left-wing ideologue, *The Middle of the
Journey* (1947), turn from reflections on politics to meditations on the nature of
Original Sin or the vagaries of human character. As we shall see, this shift was
reflected in other areas of intellectual activity as well. In 1957, Hans Meyerhoff
looked back at the past decade and concluded: 'Almost all the problems that once
were called "political," now belong to a different context, psychological, socio-
logical, and cultural.' This tendency culminated at the end of the 1950s in Daniel
Bell's influential study of postwar society entitled *The End of Ideology.*

Bellow, Mailer, Capote and Miller exemplified another significant difference
between writers of the younger generation and their predecessors. The early
Modernists were, almost without exception, members of the dominant white,
Anglo-Saxon, Protestant (WASP) culture who shared many of the attitudes
and prejudices of the established society against which they seemed to be rebelling. Eliot, Pound, Hemingway and their contemporaries wrote from inside the
culture they were opposing and felt alienated from the changing world they
were describing. What they rejected in the modern world – the raw vitality,
sexual ambiguity and subtle complexity of urban, immigrant, ethnic and racial
experience – became the subject of the new generation who were more at home

in this world. These writers – including also James Baldwin, Ralph Ellison and Bernard Malamud – were to make a major contribution to American letters. In expanding the realm of American experience depicted in their work and opening up new possibilities of writing in an American idiom, they created the first truly urban American literature.

Los Angeles Noir

The new urban literature, which reflected the transformation of American society in the twentieth century, was identified with two cities: the multiethnic metropolises of Chicago and New York. But in the 1940s, a third city, Los Angeles, became the setting of a very different kind of literature. Whereas Chicago and New York produced major novelists like James Baldwin, Saul Bellow, Bernard Malamud and Richard Wright, Los Angeles attracted a different kind of writer who wrote pulp fiction and screenplays. Dashiell Hammett, Raymond Chandler and, later, James Ellroy and Walter Mosley wrote about the dark side of Los Angeles, producing a new genre of crime fiction called LA *Noir*. It became one of the most popular fictional forms in the postwar period.

This pulp fiction was different in part because Los Angeles was different. California had a long history before it became American. First it was a Spanish colony, then it became part of Mexico. It was invaded by Americans in 1846, annexed in 1848, and became a state in 1850. From the start, California's future was tied to the famous Gold Rush of 1849. In his magisterial multivolume history of California, Kevin Starr says: 'From the beginning, California promised much. While yet barely a name on the map, it entered American awareness as a symbol of renewal. It was a final frontier: of geography and of expectation.'

Los Angeles was founded in 1781 as a Spanish agricultural supply center but it remained a backwater even after American annexation. According to Starr, 'The first American census of Los Angeles County, taken in 1850, presented a picture of nondevelopment. The county had 8,329 inhabitants, half of whom were Indian and most of whom were illiterate. There were no schools or libraries – and no newspapers.' Moreover, Los Angeles was very much a frontier town. 'Cowboys, gamblers, bandits, and desperados of every description brought to the Los Angeles of the 1850s a tone of border-town mayhem. Rough statistics indicate that in 1850 a murder occurred for every day of the year.' Over the next 30 years Los Angeles grew into a modest American city, the capital of a new industrial empire, but it was still a culturally backward place compared not only to New York and Chicago but to San Francisco. In 1910, when the population of New York City exceeded three million and the population of Chicago was over two million, there were only 300,000 inhabitants in Los Angeles.

But after World War I, Los Angeles experienced an economic boom. Whereas New York was the nation's capital of banking and finance, and Chicago was the industrial and transportational hub of the Midwest, Los Angeles owed its growth to a variety of factors: agriculture, tourism, oil, shipping, the fledgling aviation industry, real estate development and, of course, the rise of Hollywood. During the 1920s, two million Americans migrated to California. Three-quarters moved to Southern California and more than one-quarter settled in Los Angeles.

By 1930, the city's population had risen to 1,470,516, which made it the fifth largest city in the United States.

But there is another significant difference. The growth of both New York and Chicago was primarily due to the new immigration from Southern and Eastern Europe at the end of the nineteenth century and the domestic migration of Southern blacks in the early twentieth century. In contrast, Los Angeles's growth was the result of the migration of white Americans from the Midwest. The 1926 census revealed that of a total population of 1.3 million only 105,000 were black, Hispanic or Asian. In other words, the City of the Angels was the most WASP metropolis in the United States.

By the time the boom was over, a major American city had been created. Starr notes that its boosters called Los Angeles 'a City of Dreams', signifying its evolution from a sleepy Mexican village to a bustling metropolis in less than a century. He says:

> Dreams have a way of struggling towards materialization. Los Angeles did not just happen to arise out of existing circumstances, a harbor, a river, a railroad terminus. Los Angeles envisioned itself, then materialized that vision through sheer force of will. Los Angeles sprang from a Platonic conception of itself, the Great Gatsby of American cities.

Like Gatsby but unlike New York and Chicago, LA was a city without a past. It was a boomtown where fortunes were made overnight under mysterious circumstances. But if Los Angeles resembled a Hollywood dreamland, it also had elements of a nightmare city dominated by a reactionary business oligarchy, governed by a corrupt political elite, and patrolled by a repressive and racist police force. At the beginning of World War II, the city experienced another boom as it became the center of a new military-industrial complex. The influx of Mexican and black workers changed the homogeneous character of the city and created the basis of the present multicultural metropolis. It also shaped new racial and ethnic tensions that resulted in the anti-Mexican riots of 1943, the Watts riot in 1965 and the Rodney King riots in 1993.

Out of this witches' cauldron emerged a new popular art form and a new culture hero: the crime novel and the private detective. The private investigator or 'private eye' finds his origin in the tales of detection of Edgar Allen Poe and Arthur Conan Doyle. In many English tales of detection, the crime scene was a bucolic country home and the detective an upper-class amateur. In the 1930s and 1940s American writers like Dashiell Hammett and Raymond Chandler changed all that. In their work, the scene of the crime is the city and the detective is a hard-boiled professional. 'I'm not Sherlock Holmes or Philo Vance,' Chandler's hero, Philip Marlowe, explains to a client in *The Big Sleep* (1939). 'If you think there's anybody in the detective business making a living doing that sort of thing, you don't know much about cops.'

Hammett and Chandler transformed the tale of genteel detection into a story of violent crime, thereby creating a new urban genre. Yet the two men were very different. Hammett was born in 1894, quit school at the age of 14, and worked at a number of jobs, including as an operative for the famous Pinkerton's

National Detective Service. His experience as a detective provided him with the background for his fiction. In 1921, after contracting tuberculosis, he quit his Pinkerton job and began writing crime stories. In 1930 Hammett created a new hero, Sam Spade, in *The Maltese Falcon,* perhaps the best detective novel ever written.

On the other hand, Chandler was born in Chicago in 1888 but grew up in England after his parents divorced. Educated in England, France and Germany, he wrote poetry and read widely in the literary classics, including Ovid and Plato in the original language. In the 1920s he moved to Los Angeles and worked as a business executive until he lost his job in the Depression. He began writing crime stories though, unlike Hammett, he had no direct experience to draw on. Instead he studied the fiction of Flaubert, James and Conrad and read books on forensic medicine and toxicology. After six years of apprentice work, he wrote his first novel, *The Big Sleep.* Chandler became a literary celebrity at the age of 51.

Despite their different backgrounds, Chandler and Hammett created a new type of hard-boiled fictional hero. Chandler's Philip Marlowe and Hammett's Sam Spade are incorruptible individualists operating in a corrupt world. They both possess the curious blend of cynicism and romantic idealism found earlier in Ernest Hemingway's fiction. No wonder that their hard-boiled detective fiction, stylistically influenced by Hemingway, was admired by Jean-Paul Sartre and Albert Camus. In 'The Simple Art of Murder' (1944), Chandler gave a classic description of this new hero:

> But down these mean streets a man must go who is not himself mean, who is neither tarnished nor afraid. The detective in this kind of story must be such a man. He is the hero, he is everything. He must be a complete man and a common man and yet an unusual man. He must be, to use a rather weathered phrase, a man of honor, by instinct, by inevitability, without thought of it, and certainly without saying it. He must be the best man in his world and a good enough man for any world.

Chandler described the 'private eye' as a proud, honest loner and concluded, 'If there were enough like him, I think the world would be a very safe place to live in, and yet not too dull to be worth living in.' Both Philip Marlowe and Sam Spade fit this description but in different ways. Chandler conceived of his hero as a knight-errant in a corrupt world. Hammett's hero does not share Marlowe's chivalric code: in *The Maltese Falcon,* he sleeps with his beautiful client, Bridget O'Shaunessy, but has no compunctions about turning her over to the police. But both 'private eyes' represent the individual conscience in a sexually and politically corrupt urban jungle. Yet the success of *The Maltese Falcon* and *The Big Sleep* cannot be separated from the celebrity of their famous movie versions and especially the performances of Humphrey Bogart who became indelibly identified as the existential *film noir* hero of the 1940s. Both the films and the fiction had a special resonance in the anxious postwar world.

Finally, Hammett and Chandler helped create the new genre: LA *Noir.* Indeed, Chandler captured the character of the city as few writers have done. In *Imagining Los Angeles* (2000), David Fine notes, 'This is what makes Chandler's novels so distinctly Californian: in the land dedicated to the fresh start, the detective is there as a reminder that history is inescapable. One carries one's past into the present, and however successful one is in burning that past for a time, it resurfaces.' After Chandler, a new generation of writers drew on the real or imagined history of postwar Los Angeles. 'The reconstruction of the city's dark history has been a conspicuous feature in Los Angeles narrative since the 1970s,' says Fine.

> The novels and films that constitute this act of historic reconstruction cross a number of boundaries: fact and fiction, past and present, documented act and imaginative reenactment. The resurrection served the more serious purpose of cultural history: history that posits past crime not as individual events but as acts implicated in the larger context of power and hegemony in the city's development.

Though it is certainly not the most crime-ridden city in the United States, Los Angeles has become over the years the crime capital of American fiction. While Chandler depicted the white power structure of the 1940s, recent LA private eyes reflect the changing culture and demography of the city. Walter Mosley's famous detective, 'Easy' Rawlins, is black; Roger Simon's hero, Moses Wine, is Jewish; E. V. Cunningham's detective is Japanese American; Bruce Coo's Mexican-American detective is coyly named 'Chico' Cervantes; Dave Brandsetter writes about a gay detective; and Paula Woods writes about a female African-American LAPD detective aptly named Charlotte Justice. Taken together, they have created a new generation of street-smart 'city boys' and girls who provide a complex multicultural guide to 'the City of Angels'. 'From one perspective,' Kevin Starr explains in *Coast of Dreams* (2004), they 'and the other LA-based novelists who were introducing minority shamuses were crossing the detective story with the novel of manners, in that the communities these heroes and heroines represented had been woefully unchronicled in decades past.'

Hollywood and anticommunism

Perhaps the most ominous aspect of American culture at the end of the 1940s was the growing climate of suspicion that later came to be called McCarthyism. In *The Liberal Mind in a Conservative Age* (1985), the historian Richard Pells explains:

> McCarthyism coincided with the most traumatic episodes of the Cold War: the Stalinization of eastern Europe, the Berlin blockade, Russia's explosion of its own atomic bomb, the 'fall' of China to the Communists, and the military stalemate in Korea. These calamities abroad triggered a series of investigations at home to which many people and institutions across the political spectrum contributed.

McCarthyism took many forms: from security checks and loyalty oaths to the sensational spy trials of Alger Hiss and the Rosenbergs. But no aspect of these 'witch-hunts' earned more notoriety than the congressional investigations of communist infiltration into the movie industry in 1947.

In the 1930s, motion pictures, along with radio, became the prime form of entertainment in America: more people went to the movies every week than attended church. As movies rose in popularity, the large film studios flourished. The motion picture industry became increasingly a vertical monopoly, with large studios controlling the production, distribution and exhibition of films. In order to fill the expanding theater chains they owned, the studios transformed the system of film production. The older method of individual film-making was replaced by a new industrial system where movies were manufactured by an army of workers using mass production techniques. Soon the larger studios were producing one picture a week and Hollywood was turning out one picture every day.

With the advent of sound, Hollywood required writers for its new movies. Whereas artists were drawn to Paris in the 1920s, writers first streamed to Hollywood in the 1930s because of the new economic opportunities offered by the burgeoning movie industry. The introduction of sound and the industrialization of production required a new literary proletariat who could create stories and write dialogue. This was a second California Gold Rush. The novelist Ben Hecht telegraphed his friend, Herman J. Mankiewicz, an invitation to write for Paramount Pictures: 'Millions are to be grabbed out here and your only competition is idiots. Don't let it get around.' Mankiewicz came and wrote with Orson Welles what many critics consider the best American film ever made, *Citizen Kane* (1941).

The army of writers attracted to Hollywood in the 1930s and 1940s was legion, including some indisputably great novelists like William Faulkner, Scott Fitzgerald and Nathanael West. But few screenwriters had such lofty ambitions. Like writers elsewhere, they experienced the twin specters of the collapse of capitalism at home and the rise of fascism abroad. In their search for political alternatives, many were attracted to Marxism and the 'revolutionary' example of the Soviet Union. But these young artists, many from immigrant backgrounds, were also searching for a secure place in American society. The American Communist Party, under the guise of the Popular Front of the late 1930s, seemed to offer them the best of both worlds. The party slogan was 'Communism is Twentieth-Century Americanism'.

The growth of communist support in the film industry was part of a general leftward trend in American intellectual life during the Depression. Beginning in the 1930s, about 300 writers, directors, actors and set designers in Hollywood joined the Communist Party. Many more did not join but actively supported radical causes. However, Hollywood never became the communist haven it was later accused of being: the hundreds who were politically active must be placed in the context of the thousands who were not. In *A Journal of the Plague Years* (1973), the movie critic Stefan Kanfer noted, 'Given the absolute rule of the studio chieftains, given the global and local conditions of the thirties, it is astonishing not that so many were Marxists but that so few were political at all.'

But at the end of the 1930s, history took another turn as the United States peacefully weathered the economic crisis while Europe lurched towards a second world war. At home, the popularity of Roosevelt's New Deal offered an

indigenous alternative to Marxism, which had never attracted widespread sup-
port among the American working class. Abroad, the political expulsion of Leon
Trotsky, the staged Moscow Trials and the Nazi-Soviet Peace Pact led many
American radicals to question their allegiance to Russia. Thus, in 1941, Edmund
Wilson wrote an essay entitled 'Marxism at the End of the Thirties'. It began:
'Marxism is in relative eclipse. An era in its history has ended.' Like Wilson, most
Hollywood radicals abandoned communism before the war.

At the end of World War II, the film industry was at its zenith. The film historian Robert Sklar says,

> In 1946, the first full peacetime year, American movies attained the highest
> level of popular appeal in their half-century of existence. Total weekly atten-
> dance climbed to nearly three-fourths of their 'potential audience' – that is,
> the movie industry's estimate of all the people in the country capable of mak-
> ing their way to a box office, leaving out the very young and very old, the ill,
> those confined to institutions, and others without access to movie theaters.

Moreover, the rich European markets, which had accounted for almost 40
percent of Hollywood's earnings before the war, now reopened with sensational results. For instance, Italy imported more than 1200 Hollywood movies
between 1946 and 1948, almost twice as many films as were actually produced
in those years.

But there were clouds on the Hollywood horizon. In October 1945, the
Justice Department reopened its antitrust suit against the large studios for their
monopoly of the production, distribution and exhibition of films. In 1949, the
Justice Department won its case and the studios were dismantled. By 1948,
Britain, France and Italy reimposed quotas on the importation of American films
in order to encourage their own domestic production. Meanwhile, American
attendance began to fall after 1946 as the suburban building boom and the new
baby boom changed American recreational habits. Soon Hollywood began to
feel the heat of a new competitor breathing down its neck: television. Sklar cites
the legendary film producer Sam Goldwyn, who said in 1949, 'It is a certainty
that people will be unwilling to pay to see poor pictures when they can stay
home and see something which is, at least, no worse.' He was right. By 1953,
nearly half of American families owned television sets and movie attendance had
dropped to half of its 1946 level.

There were internal problems as well. Labor unrest increased as unions struck
at several studios in 1945 and 1946. Studio heads like Walt Disney and Jack
Warner were appalled when the strikes became violent and they blamed it on
the communists. Meanwhile, the elite guilds of actors, directors and writers
began to split into vocal factions along political lines. Increasingly, Hollywood
was divided against itself, though studio executives still believed that they could
deal with their problems without outside interference. This policy was tested in
1947 when the House Committee on Un-American Activities (HUAC) decided
to investigate communist infiltration in the movie industry.

In the 1947 hearings, the committee called 40 witnesses. HUAC claimed it
was interested in the presence of communists in Hollywood and the penetration

of communist propaganda in movies. But, in retrospect, it seems clear that the purpose of the investigations was less to uncover subversive activities than to perform a ritual of exorcism. 'The sole occupation,' says David Caute in *The Great Fear* (1983), 'was naming names – names, names, more names. HUAC already knew the names, of course, either from the researches of its investigators or from executive-session testimony; but only through the humiliating ritual of informing on former colleagues could the penitent ex-communist purge and purify himself and so regain the confidence of the inquisition.'

The Hollywood purges contained aspects of black comedy combining the Marx Brothers and Franz Kafka. The novelist Herbert Gold tells the story of a man accused of being a communist who actually claimed to be a staunch anti-communist. He was told that it did not matter what kind of communist he was so long as he admitted to being one. The more Kafkaesque side was recounted by Arthur Miller in a story about a television writer who had been falsely accused of having radical connections. When he protested his innocence, a network executive explained that this was the problem. ' "You have nothing to give them," he was told, meaning that he had no confession to make, and so he was fired from his job and for more than a year could not recover the will to leave his house.'

Beyond the black comedy, however, there were fundamental ethical and existential questions raised by McCarthyism. How far was an individual willing to go to defend a principle or protect his job? Was he willing to debase himself or harm others in order to support his family? Or should witnesses cooperate with the committee, as some suggested, admit their former sins and demonstrate contrition for past mistakes? 'Eventually, most writers had to confront these questions because they were central to the hearings and investigations of the McCarthy era,' Richard Pells explains in *The Liberal Mind in a Conservative Age*:

> they were being asked not to confess to a crime but to repudiate their youthful commitments and reveal the names of their former associates. Hence an observer had to decide not only what he thought about the morality of these enquiries, but how he would act if he himself were called to testify. For many intellectuals...the experience came as a rite of passage, a test of one's character as much as a defense of one's public principles.

The testimony began with 20 so-called 'friendly' witnesses, including actors Gary Cooper, Adolph Menjou and Ronald Reagan, who supported the committee's investigation. They were followed by 19 'unfriendly' witnesses who challenged the committee's right to even hold hearings into the political beliefs of individual citizens. Only ten hostile witnesses actually testified; they were not celebrities but mostly writers and directors who held well-known radical opinions. They became known as the Hollywood Ten.

The Hollywood community was split on the issue of the HUAC hearings. Conservatives welcomed the committee while liberals quickly formed a counter group, the Committee for the First Amendment, to challenge HUAC and support the right to free expression. But in a series of stormy sessions the ten 'unfriendly' witnesses refused to answer questions and challenged the right of HUAC to examine their political beliefs. They were cited for contempt of

Congress. The contempt citations were upheld by an overwhelming vote in Congress. The Hollywood Ten appealed their convictions and finally lost in 1950. They all went to prison and served short prison terms.

There was an 11th 'unfriendly' witness who also testified. He was, in fact, a famous communist but he didn't go to jail. Before World War II, a large international group of artists came to Hollywood, many as refugees from fascism. They included Arnold Schoenberg, Thomas Mann and Bertolt Brecht. Brecht arrived in Hollywood in 1940 with a *ménage* consisting of his wife, two children and his mistress. He failed to make a career in film but continued to write plays. Though few German exiles mastered English, their presence helped to transform Hollywood into an international center of high Modernism. Otto Klemperer conducted the Los Angeles Philharmonic and philosophers Theodor Adorno and Max Horkheimer brought the Frankfurt School of Social Thought to sunny Southern California.

Brecht was the 11th witness to be called and he was more than a match for the committee. Instead of challenging HUAC's right to examine him as other witnesses did, he played the part of a friendly witness who simply did not understand the committee's questions. Brecht was helped by a well-meaning interpreter whose accent was even thicker than his. The result was a comedy of misunderstanding. When he was asked whether he was a party member, Brecht vehemently denied it, which was a lie. When he was done, J. Parnell Thomas, the committee chairman, praised Brecht as a good example to the Hollywood Ten. He left the hearings, packed his bags and left almost immediately for East Germany. He told a friend in Paris: 'When they accused me of wanting to steal the Empire State Building, it was high time for me to leave.'[1]

The conviction of the radical Hollywood Ten had a sobering effect on the entire movie community, especially the liberal wing, which had defended the right of freedom of speech. The Committee for the First Amendment was quietly abandoned. Within a matter of weeks, the studio heads who had promised to support their employees' right to work capitulated; they fired the Hollywood Ten and set in motion the machinery to exclude workers on the basis of their political beliefs. Four years later, a second investigation threw the movie industry, which was losing customers to television, into a panic. The result was the establishment of the infamous blacklist which purged 350 members of the movie industry during the 1950s. These were the 'Plague Years', as the film critic Stefan Kanfer has called them.

The consequences of the HUAC hearings in Hollywood were a blend of tragedy and farce. The Hollywood Ten all went to jail but some later returned to Hollywood. Edward Dmytryk later recanted and returned to directing films while Trumbo worked afterwards as a screenwriter under assumed names. J. Parnell Thomas, the chairman of HUAC, was not so lucky. In 1948 he was indicted for padding his Congressional payroll. He was convicted and sentenced to 18 months at the correctional institution in Danbury, Connecticut, where he encountered another inmate, Ring Lardner, Junior, one of the Hollywood Ten. Meanwhile, the theme of 'naming names' was taken up a few years later in two of the most powerful dramatic works of the postwar period, Arthur Miller's play, *The Crucible* (1953), and Elia Kazan's film, *On the Waterfront* (1954).

'Naming names'

The story of the friendship of Miller and Kazan and of the creation of these two artistic works is dramatic enough and worth retelling. Kazan was born in Turkey of Greek parents and emigrated to the United States as a child. Miller, the son of Jewish immigrants, was born in Harlem. They met in 1945, when Kazan directed *All My Sons* on Broadway, Miller's first successful play. In 1949, they collaborated on the historic Broadway production of *Death of a Salesman*. At this point, Kazan and Miller were the most famous director and dramatist in America. They were also the best of friends.

After the success of *Death of a Salesman*, Miller turned to a new project. In his Brooklyn neighborhood he heard the story of a young longshoreman who had been murdered because he tried to challenge the corrupt leadership of the local union. Miller wrote a screenplay about the incident, entitled *The Hook*, and he and Kazan offered the script to Harry Cohn, the autocratic president of Columbia Pictures. Cohn was not impressed by the commercial potential of a film about union corruption and he suggested that Miller should rewrite the story so that the villains were communists, not racketeers. Miller refused and Cohn rejected the script in a telegram that read: 'Strange how the minute we want to make the script pro-American Miller pulls out.'

The film project was dropped. However, it was later revived by Kazan with some significant differences. First, he asked Budd Schulberg to write the screenplay. Second, the screenplay was based not on Miller's work but on a series of prize-winning newspaper articles about corrupt labor unions. Third, the film was now called *On the Waterfront*. Finally, and most significantly, the plot no longer concentrated on the murdered longshoreman but now focused on an accomplice in his murder who turns against the criminals and 'names names'.

What had happened in the meantime? In 1951, Budd Schulberg had been called to testify in front of HUAC and named 15 names of former communists. The following year, Kazan was called and named 16 names. Both had joined the Communist Party briefly in the 1930s and then quit over the party's ham-fisted suppression of artistic freedom. Now, 15 years later, Schulberg and Kazan claimed that they were glad to have the opportunity to admit their youthful mistakes and expose the Red Menace. But before he testified, Kazan called on his old friend Arthur Miller and told him of his decision. Miller was appalled and tried to talk him out of it. When he failed, Miller went on to write *The Crucible*. After he testified, Kazan went on to film *On the Waterfront*.

Clearly, both Miller and Kazan were responding to the new political climate in their work. In *On the Waterfront*, Kazan defended the principle of informing under extreme conditions by drawing a parallel between communism and criminality. In *The Crucible*, Miller attacked the principle of naming names by drawing a parallel between the Salem witchcraft trials of the 1690s and the McCarthyite witch-hunts of the 1950s. Taken to their logical extremes, they appeared to be saying opposite things. Kazan argued that the present danger was real: all communists were criminals who threatened the health of the American political system. On the other hand, Miller said that the present danger was illusory: communists presented no greater threat to the nation than the so-called witches did to Salem. Yet this explanation does not account for the strong impression these powerful works continue to make 50 years on.

At its core, *On the Waterfront* is the story of the moral redemption of a young tough, Terry Malloy (Marlon Brando), who unwittingly becomes an accomplice to the murder of an idealistic young longshoreman. The film shows Terry's struggle to redeem his sense of himself by betraying his so-called 'friends' who have in reality been exploiting him all along. With the support of a pious girl and a brave Catholic priest, Terry finally informs on his corrupt pals in an act of conscience. 'I been ratting on myself all these years,' he tells the corrupt Johnny Friendly, 'and I didn't know it. I'm glad what I done.'

At *its* core, *The Crucible* tells the story of the moral redemption of a respectable Puritan farmer, John Proctor, who has transgressed against his sense of himself by first sleeping with the servant girl and then refusing to acknowledge his sin. When the girl accuses his wife during the witchcraft hysteria, Proctor redeems himself by first confessing his sin and then denying the crime of witchcraft. Having lost his good name in admitting his adultery, Proctor reclaims it by refusing either to name names or sign a confession of witchcraft. When asked why he refuses to put his name to the confession that would save his life, Proctor responds: 'Because it is my name! Because I cannot have another in my life! ... How may I live without my name? I have given you my soul; leave me my name!'

This emphasis on moral regeneration suggests that both Kazan and Miller were more concerned with the intimate world of personal relations than with the public world of political actions. Though both *On the Waterfront* and *The Crucible* have been interpreted as essentially political statements on opposite sides of the issue of naming names, they actually have more in common with each other and with other works of the postwar period which depict an alienated hero in a corrupt society who chooses values involving personal integrity over those involving political solidarity. As we shall see, Terry Malloy and John Proctor are not out of place in a decade that produced such alienated heroes as J. D. Salinger's Holden Caulfield, Ralph Ellison's 'invisible man' and James Dean's 'rebel without a cause'.

But the story does not end here. In 1955, Miller returned to the theme of naming names in his short play, *A View from the Bridge,* in which his protagonist violates the code of his Italian-American community by informing on two illegal immigrants who are hiding in his neighborhood. Once again the longshoreman hero is driven by ambiguous motives of sexual guilt and desire but clearly Miller was writing a version of *On the Waterfront* in which naming names leads to tragedy. The following year Miller was called upon to testify before HUAC, where he was willing to speak of his own political activities but he refused to name others. In defending his position, Miller used words very close to those he had written for his character John Proctor only a few years before. 'I am not protecting the Communists or the Communist Party,' he said. 'I am trying to ... *protect my sense of myself.* I could not use the name of another person and bring trouble on him.'

So now the two political and artistic odysseys appear to have achieved a neat symmetry. Kazan had begun by naming names to HUAC and ended by justifying his actions in his art. Miller had begun by attacking the principle of naming names in his plays and had ended by imitating his art by refusing to name names before HUAC. Yet the neatness of the symmetry was only apparent, for life is rarely as satisfyingly shaped as art. Though they were reconciled in 1964 when they collaborated on Miller's new play, *After the Fall,* the scars of their personal conflict never healed. In Hollywood, too, the issue of naming names would remain an open wound for many years. When Kazan, at the age of 89, was given an honorary Oscar in 1999 for 'lifetime achievement', many could still not forgive him for naming names.

With the decline of the studio system and the rise of television, the movie industry was irrevocably changed. The trial of the Hollywood Ten, the Hollywood blacklist and the rise of McCarthyism created an intolerant climate that drove out even a genius like Charlie Chaplin. Brecht left Hollywood in 1947 after testifying before HUAC. Two years later, Thomas Mann moved to Switzerland. Others, like director Jules Dassin, actor Peter Lorre and writer Carl Foreman, followed suit. After providing a home for a generation of European refugees, Hollywood created its own generation of blacklisted American exiles. When Norman Mailer came to Hollywood in 1949 to negotiate the film version of *The Naked and the Dead,* he found a movie community in disintegration. In 1951 producer David Selznick told a friend: 'Hollywood's like Egypt. Full of crumbling pyramids. It'll never come back. It'll just keep on crumbling until finally the wind blows the last studio prop across the sands.'[2] Selznick was wrong. Hollywood would be reborn in the 1960s, but with a new cast of characters.

NOTES

1. Cited in Otto Friedrich, *City of Nets,* New York: Harper & Row, 1986.
2. Cited ibid.

RECOMMENDED READING

Morris Dickstein, *Leopards in the Temple,* Cambridge, MA: Harvard University Press, 2002.

David Fine, *Imagining Los Angeles,* Albuquerque, NM: University of New Mexico Press, 2000.

Otto Friedrich, *City of Nets,* New York: Harper & Row, 1986.

Joseph C. Goulden, *The Best Years,* New York: Atheneum, 1976.

Victor S. Navasky, *Naming Names,* New York: Viking, 1980.

Robert Sklar, *Movie-made America,* rev. edn, New York: Vintage, 1994.

Kevin Starr, *Americans and the California Dream, 1850–1915,* New York: Oxford University Press, 1973.

Kevin Starr, *Coast of Dreams: California on the Edge, 1990–2003,* New York: Oxford University Press, 2004.

Kevin Starr, *Embattled Dreams: California in War and Peace, 1940–1950,* New York: Oxford University Press, 2002.

Kevin Starr, *Material Dreams: Southern California Through the 1920s*, New York: Oxford University Press, 2002.

Warren Susman, *Culture As History,* New York: Pantheon, 1984.

Geoffrey C. Ward and Ken Burns, *War: An Intimate History, 1941–1945*, New York: Alfred Knopf, 2007.

PART II

The Cold War and American Culture

Civil Rights in the Fifties: A black pupil is escorted by federal agents to a desegregated school in the South

Year	Politics	Culture
1950	• McCarthy heightens Red Scare and gives it vicious partisan angle • NSC-68 militarizes containment policy • Korean War begins • China enters Korean War	• William Faulkner awarded the Nobel Prize for Literature • T. S. Eliot, *The Cocktail Party* • David Riesman, *The Lonely Crowd* • Lionel Trilling, *The Liberal Imagination* • Frank Loesser, *Guys and Dolls* • Joseph Mankiewicz, *All About Eve* • Billy Wilder, *Sunset Boulevard*
1951	• Truman dismisses McArthur from Korean command • Truman decides not to seek reelection	• J. D. Salinger, *The Catcher in the Rye* • James Jones, *From Here to Eternity* • William Styron, *Lie Down in Darkness* • Hannah Arendt, *The Origins of Totalitarianism*
1952	• Eisenhower defeats Stevenson in presidential election • Republicans win narrow majorities in both chambers of Congress	• Ralph Ellison, *Invisible Man* • Ernest Hemingway, *The Old Man and the Sea* • Fred Zinnemann, *High Noon* • Reinhold Niebuhr, *The Irony of American History*
1953	• Korean War ends • CIA overthrows nationalist Mossadeq regime in Iran • Julius and Ethel Rosenberg are executed for passing atomic secrets to the Soviet Union	• Saul Bellow, *The Adventures of Augie March* • James Baldwin, *Go Tell It on the Mountain* • Arthur Miller, *The Crucible* • Theodore Roethke, *The Waking*
1954	• US Supreme Court Brown decision begins school desegregation in South • CIA overthrows leftist Arbens government in Guatemala • End of McCarthyism • Democrats regain control of both chambers of Congress in midterm elections • McCarthy is censured by Senate • Worker's uprising against regime in East Berlin	• Ernest Hemingway awarded the Nobel Prize for Literature • Elia Kazan, *On the Waterfront* • Wallace Stevens, *Collected Poems* • William Faulkner, *A Fable* • Eudora Welty, *The Ponder Heart*
1955	• US Supreme Court Brown II decision outlaws segregation in schools • 'Massive resistance' to Brown decisions in the South • Rosa Parks defies bus segregation in Montgomery, Alabama	• James Baldwin, *Notes of a Native Son* • William Gaddis, *The Recognitions* • Norman Mailer, *The Deer Park* • Flannery O'Connor, *A Good Man Is Hard to Find* • Arthur Miller, *A View from the Bridge*
1956	• Martin Luther King organizes black bus boycott in Montgomery, Alabama • Eisenhower is reelected • Democrats increase their majorities in Congress • Popular uprising against regime in Hungary is suppressed by Soviet tanks	• John Berryman, *Homage to Mistress Bradstreet* • Allen Ginsberg, *Howl* • Eugene O'Neill, *Long Day's Journey into Night* • C. Wright Mills, *The Power Elite* • Leonard Bernstein, *Candide*
1957	• Eisenhower enforces school desegregation in Little Rock, Arkansas	• Jack Kerouac, *On the Road* • Bernard Malamud, *The Assistant* • Richard Wilbur, *Poems* • Northrop Frye, *Anatomy of Criticism* • Leonard Bernstein, *West Side Story*
1958	• Khrushchev issues Berlin ultimatum	• John Barth, *The End of the Road* • Vladimir Nabokov, *Lolita* • Edward Albee, *The Zoo Story* • Tennessee Williams, *Suddenly Last Summer*
1959	• Castro gains power in Cuba	• Saul Bellow, *Henderson the Rain King* • William Burroughs, *Naked Lunch* • Robert Lowell, *Life Studies* • Philip Roth, *Goodbye, Columbus* • Harold Rosenberg, *The Tradition of the New*

CHAPTER 3

American Politics from Truman to Eisenhower

In the 1950s the United States launched a worldwide anticommunist crusade, occasionally with painful long-term consequences. In East Asia the Cold War turned hot with the Korean War and the anticolonial struggle in Indochina. In parallel, McCarthyism reached its climax in the early 1950s but came to an end in 1954, closing a dark chapter in American history.

In spite of the heightening of Cold War tensions, for American society the 1950s were a time of growing affluence and stability. Political passions fell and consensus politics prevailed during the period 1955–60 when the Republican President Dwight D. Eisenhower ruled in cooperation with a Congress that had Democratic majorities. Yet under the relatively tranquil surface of post-McCarthy American politics, new forces began to take shape that were later to cause profound political upheavals, particularly concerning the vexed matter of segregation in the South.

The Korean War and the global anticommunist crusade

In the period 1947–9 the Truman administration set the foundations for the West's victory in the Cold War four decades later. Western Europe was transformed into a stable and prosperous pillar of an international order that encompassed the advanced world's democracies. The democratization of West Germany and Japan was a major element in this international order. Another element was the promotion by the United States of an open international economic system that secured unparalleled prosperity for all countries that participated.

In confronting the Soviet threat, Truman's 1947–9 policies were focused on the world's main industrial centers. George Kennan argued at the time that the Soviet Union could be contained so long as four of the five main industrial centers in the world – the United States, Great Britain, Western Europe and Japan – remained grouped against the fifth, the Soviet Union. Regarding the rest of the world, Kennan insisted on strict geopolitical priorities. The West needed to control the North Atlantic, the Mediterranean, the Middle East and the Philippines, in order to secure vital resources and sea lines of communication. Other parts of the world were less important. 'We are not necessarily always against the expansion of communism,' Kennan declared in December 1947, 'and certainly not always against it to the same degree in every area.'

The Truman administration's refusal to get drawn into the Chinese civil war in the later 1940s exemplified these geopolitical priorities. The international enemy was the Soviet Union, not communism as such. Tito's split from Moscow in 1948 encouraged the American leadership to perceive Mao in similar terms. Kennan predicted that Mao's China might become a worse security problem for the Soviet Union than for the United States. His prediction was correct in the long run, but not in the early years of Mao's rule.

In 1950 the Truman administration abandoned geopolitical priorities and moved toward an unrestricted global anticommunist crusade. Henceforth, any advance of communism anywhere in the world was seen as a threat to the credibility of America's anti-Soviet commitments. Moreover, the new concept of containment, put forth by Paul Nitze in the famous NSC-68 policy paper, placed greater reliance on military instruments, unlike Kennan's earlier emphasis on political and economic means of strengthening the anti-Soviet coalition. NSC-68 proposed a major increase in defense spending, economically justified in Keynesian demand stimulus terms, in order to create the military capabilities that would allow the United States to defend its existing commitments and intervene militarily against further communist expansion anywhere in the world. This militant and universalistic version of containment crystallized with the Korean War.

Korea

The North Korean invasion of South Korea on June 25, 1950 took the United States completely by surprise. Coming shortly after the composition of NSC-68, it seemed to confirm the new concept of containment that focused on military threats and therefore the need for military counter-measures. The Truman administration was convinced that the attack was a step in a global program of aggression planned by Moscow, and that if America remained passive and appeased the communists, it would make a third world war more likely. The United States decided to make a stand in Korea in order to demonstrate its resolve and deter further communist aggression elsewhere in the world.

In the first two and a half months of the war, the North Korean forces advanced rapidly down the Korean peninsula and soon confined the South Korean forces and their American allies to the southeastern corner of the peninsula. In September 1950, the UN commander, General Douglas MacArthur, one of America's greatest military leaders, reversed the situation through his daring and brilliant landing at Inchon, near the borders between North and South Korea, which threatened to cut off the North Korean forces further south from their home bases. The North Korean army's retreat was so hasty and disorderly, and its losses so heavy, that it was unable to resist an allied counter-invasion of North Korea.

At this point, Truman decided to expand the political objective of the war from the liberation of South Korea to the conquest of the North and the reunion of Korea under the South's regime. This decision carried the risk of Soviet or Chinese intervention. Stalin refused to enter the war, even though an American conquest of North Korea would bring the American armies to the borders of the

Soviet Union. But Mao was unwilling to risk an American military presence at his borders, since he was mistakenly convinced that the United States intended to invade China next.

China's massive military intervention in the war in November 1950 brought about a new spectacular reversal, causing a largely disorderly retreat of the allied forces to positions well south of South Korea's border. A few months later the front stabilized near the border, and thereafter did not change significantly for years, resulting in a miserable and frustrating stalemate in which no breakthrough seemed possible.

Now two rival strategies were advocated in the United States. The first, proposed by MacArthur, was a widening of the war by including China in the scope of military operations. MacArthur sought a decisive victory in the American tradition through the application of overwhelming force, including atom bombs if necessary, until the Chinese were forced to withdraw from Korea. The second strategy, adopted by Truman, sought to limit the war to Korea and to return to the original political objective of liberating only the South, which had been attained already. Truman thought that Stalin deliberately sought to draw the United States into a major war with China so that he could launch an invasion of Western Europe while American forces were stretched thin. This assumption has since been proved wrong; Stalin certainly had no plans to start a war in Europe. Still, from a faulty premise the Truman administration reached the enlightened conclusion that peripheral wars between members of the two Cold War camps should remain limited, that military moves should be avoided if they risked escalation to a third world war, and that nuclear weapons should not be used in a peripheral conflict. By not contemplating the use of nuclear weapons in Korea, Truman contributed to the notion that they were too blunt and destructive an instrument for any purpose other than deterring their use by the other side.

MacArthur's persistent public disagreement with Truman's policy forced the President to fire him in April 1951. His return to the United States was attended by an astonishing mass delirium. When the popular war hero arrived at San Francisco airport after midnight, he was met by an enthusiastic crowd of half a million people. A similar spectacle occurred upon his arrival in Washington, where he was granted the unprecedented privilege of addressing a joint session of Congress. His speech so satisfied the high emotions of the moment that a Republican congressman, Dewey Short, declared: 'We heard God speak here today, God in the flesh, the voice of God.' From Washington, MacArthur proceeded to New York, where he was met by 7.5 million people in a parade that *Time* described as 'the greatest and most exuberant that the city has ever seen'. Across the country, flags waved at mid-mast, while the White House was swamped by telegrams supporting MacArthur. Nonetheless, MacArthur proved unable or unwilling – he was 71 years old – to capitalize on the mass delirium in order to launch a serious bid for the presidency in 1952. But Truman's popularity never recovered from the depths into which it sank during this period.

The Korean War dragged on until 1953 without any spectacular developments in the field. It ended after China agreed to a return to the *status quo ante* (with some territorial adjustments) and stopped insisting on the forced repatriation of Chinese prisoners-of-war (POWs). Though overshadowed by Vietnam in the popular imagination, Korea was far bloodier. Some 36,000 Americans were killed, together with 14,000 allied troops. China lost half a million. The two Korean sides together lost three million, about 15 percent of the Korean population. Some 70 percent of the dead were civilians, largely because the United States resorted to World War II-type bombardments that destroyed North Korea's cities, much as Germany's and Japan's had been destroyed earlier.

On the larger world stage, NSC-68 and the Korean War resulted in a global anticommunist crusade that created new problems for the American approach to Europe's tottering colonial empires. Until 1950 the United States distanced itself from colonialism and, indeed, under Roosevelt had been actively undermining the colonial empires in the Pacific. This was not unnatural, given that it had been the first new nation to emerge from an anticolonial national liberation struggle. Thus before 1950 France received no American assistance in its struggle to restore its colonial rule in Indochina (which during World War II had been occupied by the Japanese).

Indochina exemplified the new dilemmas. The national liberation movement led by Ho Chi Minh was Marxist and inspired by Mao's revolutionary example. Until 1950, Ho did not appear threatening; but the pressures of the Cold War and the new concepts of NSC-68 produced a change in American policy in May, when the United States began to supply the French with arms in their struggle against the insurgents. China's entry into the Korean War stiffened American resistance to any further spread of communism in Asia and made American support of the French appear even more urgent. European considerations contributed to the change in American policy as well. A quick collapse of the European colonial empires entailed the risk of weakening America's NATO allies at a moment when Soviet aggression in Europe appeared likely.

In the Middle East the United States sided with the colonialists from 1950 onwards, for yet another reason: fear of an imminent Soviet assault on the region. There was no evidence that the Soviets had any such intention; it is now known that Stalin had no interest in meddling in a region that was culturally particularly hostile to communism. Yet in order to stave off an imagined Soviet military threat, the United States ended up relying on Britain's regional network of military and naval bases. For Arab nationalists, who did not feel threatened by the Soviet Union and resented the presence of the colonialists, the new American policy combined with the earlier American recognition of Israel to fuel anti-Americanism.

By the end of the Truman presidency the United States had increasingly become identified with the colonialists in regions of Asia and North Africa, resulting in a nascent anti-Americanism that was to cast a long shadow. Truman's legacy was impressive in Europe and Japan, creating the foundations for the greatest successes in postwar American foreign policy. In other regions of world politics his legacy was mixed, setting the stage for some of the greatest failures in postwar American foreign policy.

Soviet espionage, the Red Scare and McCarthyism

In the 1990s information emerged from Russia that has demonstrated beyond doubt the extent of Soviet spying in the United States in the 1940s. According to the historian of intelligence services, Christopher Andrew, 'during the Second World War Soviet agents had penetrated every major branch of the Roosevelt administration'. Much of this Soviet penetration became known to the Federal Bureau of Investigation (FBI) in the mid-1940s and justifies some of the security measures undertaken by the Truman administration. It does not justify the larger Red Scare and the witch-hunts of McCarthyism that ruined the lives of many innocent and loyal Americans.

The roots of Soviet intelligence's penetration in the United States were in the Great Depression, which seemed to many on the left to demonstrate the bankruptcy of capitalism. To such people the Soviet system appeared more successful in mobilizing the forces of production; the tragic human cost of Stalin's policies was not yet known. The Soviet Union also seemed to be more willing than the Western democracies to stand up to the fascists during the Spanish Civil War (1936–9). During the Comintern's 'popular front' line from 1934 to 1939, communists worldwide were ordered by Moscow to cooperate with socialists and other democratic political forces against the fascist menace. The cooperation of the communists with more mainstream forces made them and the Soviet Union appear less 'untouchable' than before. Under these circumstances, several hundred idealistic leftists became agents of Soviet intelligence agencies.

In April 1941 the NKVD, the People's Commissariat for Internal Affairs, precursor of the KGB, had 221 agents in the United States, excluding the formidable separate spy network of Soviet military intelligence. In the period 1941–5, Soviet intelligence agencies had spies in the White House, the OSS (forerunner of the CIA), the State Department, the Treasury Department, the Justice Department and the Board of Economic Warfare. Their agent network also included an unsuccessful candidate for Congress, a Hollywood producer and a secretary working for the famous journalist Walter Lippmann.

Undoubtedly the greatest success of Soviet intelligence was the multiple penetration of the Manhattan project that permitted the Soviet Union to develop its own nuclear arsenal quickly. The Manhattan project was penetrated on its British side through the recruitment of Klaus Fuchs and Melita Norwood, and on its American side through the network of Julius and Ethel Rosenberg that included Theodore Hall and David Greenglass. According to a KGB official, 'in the USA we obtained information on how the bomb was made and in Britain of what it was made, so that together [it] covered the whole problem'.[1] Truman learned about the Manhattan project only ten days after he became president, whereas Stalin had been informed years earlier through his spies.

What caused the Red Scare?

The heyday of Soviet spying in the United States came to an end in 1945. In September a Soviet intelligence official defected in Canada and provided information regarding Soviet penetration in the United States. In November Soviet intelligence lost Elizabeth Bentley, an American spy who turned against her Soviet masters and provided testimony to the FBI that corroborated earlier information by the former Soviet agent Whittaker Chambers. Matters became even worse for Soviet intelligence in the next few years, when some of its coded wartime messages were decoded by American agencies on the basis of a half-burned Soviet codebook found in Finland (project VENONA), confirming much of the evidence provided by the defectors. As a result, Soviet intelligence was forced to deactivate its agents in the United States in order to save them from arrests and convictions. The FBI could not secure convictions, since it did not catch Soviet agents in the act of passing classified information; the defectors' testimony alone was insufficient in court, while VENONA was kept one of the most closely guarded secrets of Western intelligence for decades (the FBI did not even inform the Central Intelligence Agency (CIA) about it until 1952). Nonetheless, Soviet intelligence in the United States had suffered blows from which it never recovered.

Thus the Red Scare of the later 1940s and early 1950s occurred *after* the neutralization of the wartime Soviet intelligence networks. Undoubtedly, the revelations about Soviet spying in public testimonies by Bentley and Chambers, as well as information leaked by the FBI through a circle of anticommunist supporters, contributed to the paranoid climate of the Red Scare. Yet the lamentable wave of mass hysteria that swept America had deeper roots that were unrelated to actual Soviet spying. A Red Scare had gripped America after World War I as well, when there was no evidence of Soviet spying.

The Red Scare was a prime manifestation of the tyranny of the majority that Tocqueville had warned about in 1835, when he declared that 'in America the majority raises formidable barriers around liberty of opinion'. In *The Liberal Tradition in America* (1955), Louis Hartz analyzed American political culture from this Tocquevillian perspective; he argued that the absence of a feudal past in America resulted in the absence not only of a reactionary, antiliberal conservatism on the right, but also of a countervailing socialist and Marxist tradition on the left. Hence Lockean liberalism has come to dominate American ideology without challenge, becoming a national creed that breeds intolerance of other ideologies. This argument certainly explains the naming of committees of 'un-American activities', as if being a communist was un-American. According to Hartz, the dominant liberal Americanism became particularly insecure regarding 'un-American' creeds in periods when American society came out of its traditional isolation and engaged in greater contact with the Old World and its suspect traditions. This accounts for the Red Scares that followed both world wars.

The argument that the causes of the Red Scare were essentially domestic is confirmed by data from opinion polls in June 1946, which show that large majorities were hostile to domestic communists, while at the same time Americans still desired cooperative relations with the Soviet Union; Churchill's Iron Curtain speech in May 1946 was overwhelmingly denounced in the United States. Congress also raised the issue of loyalty in the federal government in mid-1946, well before it supported an antagonistic stance towards the Soviet Union. The rising tensions in the relations between the two superpowers in the later

1940s and the 1950s certainly fueled and prolonged the Red Scare, but they seem not to have caused it in the first place.

Also noteworthy is the fact that anticommunist activities were often first initiated in center-left circles that had marched with the communists in the Popular Front demonstrations of the 1930s and had become disillusioned with Stalinism. The American Civil Liberties Union (ACLU) purged its national board of communists as early as 1940. The Congress of Industrial Organizations (CIO), the largest labor confederation, began to purge them in 1946, though the struggle continued for several years. The National Association for the Advancement of Colored People (NAACP) followed suit by the end of the 1940s. In 1947 anticommunist liberals founded Americans for Democratic Action (ADA) in order to differentiate themselves from Henry Wallace's communist-infiltrated political movement. When dozens of university professors and hundreds of primary and secondary education teachers were fired in the later 1940s on suspicion of being communists, the leader of the small Socialist party, Norman Thomas, argued that 'the right of the Communist to teach should be denied because he has given away his freedom in the quest for truth'.[2]

The Truman administration contributed to the Red Scare through its federal loyalty program in 1947 that rationalized and streamlined the wartime loyalty programs of the Roosevelt administration. Within four years some 1200 federal employees were fired and a further 6000 resigned because of the loyalty program's questionable procedures. The Truman administration also expanded the Attorney General's list of subversive organizations from 47 during the war to over 150, of which 110 were classified as communist (others were pro-Japanese or fascist organizations from the war). Membership in one of these organizations did not constitute definitive proof of disloyalty; nevertheless the Attorney General's list was used by federal loyalty boards, as well as by various investigating committees in Congress and state legislatures, to harass members of listed organizations.

In 1948 the Truman administration prosecuted 11 leaders of the Communist Party of the United States of America (CPUSA) under the Smith Act of 1940, which outlawed not only subversive acts but even the advocating of the 'duty, necessity, desirability or propriety of overthrowing or destroying any government in the United States by force or violence'. The 11 were convicted and sentenced to five-year jail terms and received fines of $10,000, losing appeals all the way to the Supreme Court, where the vote was seven to two against them. In retrospect, it is known that the leaders of the CPUSA were guilty of aiding and abetting Soviet spying in the United States, but this can hardly justify their persecution on the grounds merely of their beliefs. The Supreme Court declared the Smith Act unconstitutional in 1956, after the Red Scare had waned.

Congress also contributed to the Red Scare through its highly publicized investigating committees, beginning with the House Committee on Un-American Activities (HUAC) during the Republican-controlled Eightieth Congress (1947–8). In 1947 HUAC focused on alleged communist infiltration in Hollywood, illustrating Hartz's point about the insecurities of the dominant Americanism regarding alien dogmas (no security issues were at stake). HUAC was on firmer ground when it investigated allegations by Whittaker Chambers that Alger Hiss, President of the Carnegie Foundation for International Peace, and a former State Department official, had been a communist. The Hiss case divided America deeply, since Hiss was a typical New Dealer, educated in elite universities (Johns Hopkins and Harvard), who served close to the leadership team of Franklin Roosevelt and participated in the Yalta conference. For Republicans such as Richard Nixon, the newest, youngest and ablest member of HUAC, going after Hiss meant striking blows at the entire liberal New Deal establishment.

In the HUAC hearings, Hiss confronted Chambers and challenged him to repeat his allegation outside the chamber, so that he could sue him for libel. Chambers responded by making the much more damaging allegation that Hiss had not merely been a communist, but a Soviet spy. Hiss's decision to sue Chambers was risky. Investigations by the FBI and Nixon, as well as testimony by Elizabeth Bentley, confirmed Chambers' allegations. In 1950 Hiss was convicted of perjury and jailed for several years, though he continued to deny Chambers' allegations to the end of his life.

It is now known from Russian archives that Hiss was indeed a very active Soviet spy, who was decorated by the Soviet Union for his services rendered in the context of Yalta in 1945. This does not mean, as conservatives claimed at the time, that half of Europe was sold out to the Soviets because of Hiss. His contribution to Stalin's diplomacy at Yalta was mainly to inform the Soviet side about the American positions on Poland. On this basis Stalin deceived the Western leaders for a few months by supposedly acquiescing in the Anglo-American demands for free elections in Poland.

The Red Scare culminated in the period 1949–53, when the Cold War caused heightened insecurity in American society. In September 1949 Truman announced that the Soviet Union had tested its first atom bomb, raising for the first time the specter of mass destruction raining upon American cities. In October 1949 Mao gained control over continental China, launching the misleading but domestically potent debate about 'who lost China'. In June 1950 the Cold War turned hot with the war in Korea. During the height of the Red Scare in the early 1950s, Congress undertook 85 separate red-baiting investigations, and in 1950 it passed the severe McCarran Internal Security Act, overriding Truman's veto by 286 against 48 in the House and 57 against 10 in the Senate. These votes and the prominent role of Democratic Senator Pat McCarran demonstrate that the Red Scare was a bipartisan affair. Yet with McCarthy's engagement, it acquired a vicious partisan aspect.

Senator Joseph McCarthy entered the red-baiting game in February 1950, when he began making claims about a list of 205, or 57, or 81 communists in the State Department (the number kept changing). His claims were unsubstantiated, or at best relied on information revealed years earlier. Yet they captured the public mood so well as to turn him into one of the most prominent politicians in America. His unsubstantiated allegations therefore became very potent politically, raising new fears in the public about disloyalty after three years of Truman's loyalty program and five years of the FBI's spy hunts. The Truman administration had no choice but to strike back at him, even though it thereby helped raise him to national prominence. Once the battle was joined between

McCarthy and the Truman administration, it divided Congress mainly along partisan lines, with the Republican leadership in effect using him to strike at the five-term Democratic rule.

McCarthy's demagogic effectiveness derived from his right-wing populism that targeted the liberal New Deal elite. McCarthy appealed to the less educated and poorer strata in American society that were more apt to endorse simplistic conspiracy theories and to resent the upper strata – in this case not the rich (who were targets of left-wing populism) but the well-educated liberal elite that had been in government for two decades. His populism was already evident in his February 9, 1950 speech in Wheeling, West Virginia, that launched his witch-hunting career, in which he declared:

> It is not the less fortunate, or members of minority groups who have been selling this nation out, but rather those who have had all the benefits that the wealthiest nation on earth has to offer – the finest homes, the finest college educations, and the finest jobs in the government that we can give.[3]

This right-wing populism also had an Anglophobic aspect that appealed to many old isolationists in the heartland and especially to Irish Americans. Thus McCarthy described Dean Acheson as a 'pompous diplomat with his striped pants and phony British accent', while his ally Senator Hugh Butler said of Acheson: 'I watch his smart aleck manner and his British clothes and that New Dealism, everlasting New Dealism in everything he says and does, and I want to shout, Get Out!' It is noteworthy that the region least swayed by McCarthyism was the South, which was Anglophile, internationalist and firmly within the New Deal coalition.

McCarthy rarely focused much on actual communist threats, such as the Soviet Union and China, and he never uncovered even a single spy. Instead he railed against imaginary, hidden enemies: 'a conspiracy on a scale so immense as to dwarf any previous such venture in the history of man.' The Republican leadership was at first averse to McCarthy and his methods. But when they witnessed his astounding populist appeal, Republicans saw an opportunity to make electoral gains among working-class voters who had been major constituents of the New Deal coalition. Consequently, they tolerated and sometimes encouraged McCarthy, while keeping a distance from his more hideous practices. When the Republicans won the elections of 1952, their leaders' disposition was to thank the Senator and ask him to end the show, its purpose having been attained. McCarthy had other ideas.

The politics of Eisenhower's presidency

The Republicans entered the electoral year 1952 desperate to return to power after two decades of Democratic rule, yet insecure about their prospects after the nasty surprise of Truman's election in 1948. They appeared to hold good cards at the outset, mainly because of the vulnerabilities of their opponents. Truman's presidency had been weakened by the stalemate in Korea, the assaults of McCarthyism and a bout of corruption scandals in the administration (there were nine prison sentences). But these chinks in the Democrats' armor, summarized in the formula KC2 (Korea, communism, corruption), were somewhat neutralized as electoral issues by Truman's wise decision not to seek reelection; his popularity had remained at low levels since early 1951. Might not the Democrats pull off another 1948 coup by nominating as their candidate a fresh face in American politics who could reenergize the formidable forces of the great New Deal coalition?

This is exactly what the Democrats tried to do, by giving the nomination to Governor Adlai Stevenson of Illinois, a new politician who had not sought elective office before successfully running for governor in 1948. Stevenson artfully presented himself as a reluctant candidate, though in fact he adroitly maneuvered to become the choice of the party bosses. He was genuinely popular, as well as skillful in keeping together the main segments of the New Deal coalition; for example, unlike Truman he was loved by Northern liberals and accepted by Southern conservatives. He might well have attained the presidency, had he not been opposed on the Republican side by another seemingly reluctant candidate who happened to be America's most popular war hero.

General Eisenhower was a conservative who had kept his political views so close to his vest that influential Democrats attempted to draft him as their party's presidential nominee both in 1948 and 1952. He began to reveal his political preferences by allowing Eisenhower-for-president committees to enter his name in Republican primaries in the first half of 1952, while he was still serving as NATO's military commander in Paris. Concealed by this seeming detachment from the crude arts of politicking was Eisenhower's determination to deny the Republican nomination to Senator Robert Taft, known as 'Mr Republican', who represented the conservative and isolationist wing of the Republican Party. While Eisenhower actually shared Taft's anti-New Deal conservatism, he correctly viewed it as unelectable and felt that on this ground a Taft nomination would hand the Democrats a sixth presidential term in a row. But he was at least as alarmed by the prospect that, in the unlikely event that Taft did reach the presidency, he might revive isolationism and unravel Truman's foreign policy in Europe.

The Republican fight for the nomination revealed the main dividing lines within the party. Eisenhower led the Dewey wing that was stronger in the Northeast; he accepted the New Deal reforms and was internationalist in the 'Europe first' tradition. Every Republican presidential candidate since 1940 had come from this wing. Taft led the more isolationist and 'Asia first' wing that was stronger in the heartland; he opposed aid to Europe, embraced McCarthyism and remained anti-New Deal. The fight at the convention was quite close in spite of a string of Eisenhower victories at the primaries. Once Eisenhower secured the nomination, he balanced the ticket by selecting as his running mate Richard Nixon, who came from the West and represented the more respectable face of the Red hunt. Eisenhower deeply detested McCarthy and his closest allies, but did not risk a full break with them at this point.

In the general election Eisenhower won with 55.4 percent of the vote and 442 Electoral College votes against Stevenson's 89. He managed even to carry four states in the outer South. Control of Congress also changed hands, though the

Republican majorities were slim in both chambers. For the first time since 1930, the Republicans controlled both the presidency and Congress.

Nonetheless, this election constituted only an ephemeral weakening of the New Deal coalition. The Democrats regained control of both chambers of Congress in the midterm elections of 1954. In 1956 Eisenhower was reelected with 57 percent of the vote (again facing the unfortunate Stevenson), yet the American people reelected Democratic majorities in Congress. The resilience of the New Deal coalition was demonstrated especially in the midterm elections of 1958, after which the Democratic congressional majorities were 283 against 154 in the House and 65 against 35 in the Senate. The Democrats also occupied 34 out of 50 governorships and had a similar superiority in the state legislatures. They also had a steady advantage in party identification, with almost 50 percent in opinion polls identifying themselves as Democrats, about 30 percent as Republicans and slightly over 20 percent as Independents. The other side of the coin was that the Democrats, being a large coalition, lacked internal cohesion, affirming the comedian Will Rogers's old quip: 'I am not a member of any organized political party. I am a Democrat.' In particular, the liberals and the Southerners were bitterly opposed on many domestic issues.

Eisenhower developed good relations with the congressional Democrats even during the first two years of his presidency when the Republicans controlled Congress, since he needed Democratic votes to overcome the resistance of isolationist Republicans to his foreign policy. In the realm of international relations, Eisenhower actually worked better with Congress after the Democrats regained control in 1955. In return for cooperating with Eisenhower on foreign policy, the Democratic leaders in Congress demanded that the President accept the legacy of the New Deal. Eisenhower's moderate domestic positions, which he affirmed under the slogan of the 'New Republicanism', constituted the domestic side of the consensus politics that marked the Eisenhower presidency.

Eisenhower and the congressional Democrats had one other common ground, their opposition to McCarthy who continued his witch-hunt after Eisenhower's rise to the presidency. The Democratic leaders in Congress had no intention of confronting the ruthless demagogue on their own. Lyndon Johnson, the Democrats' leader in the Senate, shrewdly warned liberal Senator Hubert Humphrey that he 'just eats fellows like you. ... The only way we'll ever get Joe McCarthy is when he starts attacking some conservatives around here, and then we'll put an end to it.'[4] McCarthy moved in this direction in early 1954, when he started to search for communists in the army, a conservative institution that was particularly dear to Eisenhower.

McCarthy's popularity had begun to decline in the first months of 1954, and it declined further during the televised Army-McCarthy hearings from April to June that exposed his shameless methods to the public, at a time when TV ownership was rising very rapidly. His downfall came in one of his confrontations with Joseph Welch, the army's attorney at the hearing and a Republican, whom he accused of having employed a young lawyer who had once briefly belonged to the National Lawyers Guild, 'the legal bulwark of the Communist Party', according to McCarthy. Welch's response was to stand up to McCarthy and denounce his pitiless smearing methods: 'Let us not assassinate this lad further,

Senator. You have done enough. Have you no sense of decency, sir, at long last? Have you left no sense of decency?' The outburst was the catalyst that punctured McCarthy's bubble. McCarthy had for four years been riding so high on baseless smearing and intimidation, that he sensed neither the change in the national mood against him nor the danger in taking on Eisenhower.

His downfall was as swift as his rise. The Senate censured him, though the senators prudently delayed the vote until after the November 1954 midterm elections (his reputation for smearing was still intimidating). The vote was 67 to 22 in favor of the censure. Not a single Democrat voted against, though John Kennedy abstained presumably because he was in hospital. (But Kennedy had more compelling reasons not to vote: his father was an avid McCarthy supporter and McCarthy was particularly popular in heavily Catholic Massachusetts, Kennedy's home state.) After the censure McCarthy became *persona non grata* for the political establishment. Eisenhower removed him from the list of guests for official White House receptions. In the 1956 election campaign, when McCarthy once sat next to Vice-President Nixon, he was asked by a Nixon aide to leave and did so without demur; a reporter then spotted him weeping nearby. A little later one of Lyndon Johnson's assistants bumped into him on the streets of Washington and scarcely recognized him: 'unshaven, needing a bath, bloated from too much booze, almost inarticulate'. He died from alcoholism in 1957 at the age of 48, having impoverished the lives of countless victims and enriched the world's vocabularies with a new word for witch-hunt.

After McCarthy's fall, a new climate of moderation emerged in American politics, facilitating a bipartisan consensus between Eisenhower and congressional Democrats. Liberals such as Arthur Schlesinger, Jr, complained that this was an era of stagnation, yet the bipartisan consensus did produce at least one major federal initiative, the Interstate Highways Act of 1956 that aimed at extending the existing highway network across all regions of the United States. In time, this act contributed to the long-term decline in the economic disparities between regions by stimulating interregional trade and creating more integrated national labor and capital markets. It also contributed over the long run to the growing homogeneity of the United States in terms of political culture. Such developments in turn made the South's system of racial segregation less tenable.

The civil rights struggle in the 1950s

Racial segregation in the South flagrantly contradicted the liberal principles that were so eloquently stated in the American Declaration of Independence. This contradiction became less tolerable in the postwar era, when the development of communications (highways, railways, telecommunications) and the mass media (radio, television) resulted in homogenizing pressures in American society. The South was no longer a remote and isolated region within the vast United States. Furthermore, at the height of the Cold War in the 1950s, when America was conducting a global anticommunist crusade to defend the 'free world', segregation became an American disgrace with international ramifications. Fidel Castro, for example, distributed leaflets in America in 1959 urging blacks to rebel. Consequently, a growing number of Americans came to support desegregation.

The liberals were the strongest opponents of segregation. Yet they coexisted in the Democratic Party with Southern racists. The dominant New Deal coalition covered the entire spectrum of opinion on this matter, from the fiercest opponents to the strongest defenders of segregation. Between the two ends of the spectrum were pragmatic Democratic politicians who cared above all for power. For them what mattered most was the Democratic control of Congress and if possible the presidency in order to secure benefits for their states, cities and party machines. The pragmatists were more willing than the liberal ideologues to tolerate the South's peculiarity in order to keep it in the party fold, though the growing number of black voters in the North and West began to change their calculations.

The Republicans were in the middle of the spectrum. On the whole they were against segregation, and as the party of Lincoln they might have led the struggle for civil rights. Yet most Republicans disliked federal activism in the states on principle. In Congress they had often cooperated with Southern Democrats in blocking liberal initiatives by the Roosevelt and Truman administrations. As a result, they were unwilling to lead the fight for the abolition of segregation, though most of them did vote for civil rights bills in Congress.

The South's main line of defense against federally imposed desegregation was in the Senate and rested on two of the chamber's venerable rules: seniority and the filibuster. Since the South in effect had a one-party system, Southern Democrats tended to have more seniority than Democrats from other regions, securing a disproportionate number of the powerful committee chairmanships. If Southern chairmen could not block a civil rights bill in committee, Southerners resorted to the filibuster, the rule that allowed unlimited debate. By giving endless speeches against an offending bill and indefinitely holding up all of the Senate's other business, the Southerners could blackmail the Senate into shelving the bill. Overcoming Southern resistance in the Senate would thus require an especially determined, and skillfully led, desegregationist bipartisan majority; but this was not forthcoming in the 1950s, when neither Eisenhower nor Stevenson was willing to take a strong stand on civil rights.

The inertia of the Democrats and the Republicans meant inertia by the two elective branches of the federal government. Under these circumstances the initiative against segregation passed to the third branch, the US Supreme Court, the most powerful high court of any modern democracy. Under the leadership of Chief Justice Earl Warren (1953–69), a former Republican governor of California and Dewey's running mate in 1948, the Supreme Court moved very much in a liberal direction. In part this reflected the fact that the Court is, in a very broad sense, part of the dominant coalition, since its members are appointed by the president and confirmed by the Senate. Roosevelt and Truman had changed the Court's composition in a liberal direction, as did Eisenhower by appointing Warren, a decision he later regretted.

For the Warren Court to be able to strike at segregation, someone had to litigate against it and bring the litigation up the appeals process all the way to the US Supreme Court. This task was undertaken by the NAACP which, under the guidance of its chief lawyer Thurgood Marshall, pursued an ambitious legal strategy against segregation. Marshall's decision to begin by attacking segregation in the schools was probably not optimal. People were particularly sensitive to their children's schooling and therefore highly resistant to controversial changes. Given Southern racism, which went back to pre-independence days, there was bound to be strong popular resistance to school desegregation. In retrospect, it seems clear that racist politics in the South began to wane once African Americans were able to vote, forcing politicians to take into account the substantial black electorate in the South. Perhaps if Marshall had opted for black voting rights as his first objective, and if the Warren Court had acted decisively in their favor, the process of abolishing segregation might have been speedier.

Public schools in the South had been segregated since the nineteenth century, and in 1896 the Supreme Court had accepted this as constitutional on the principle 'separate but equal'. In practice, black and white schools were anything but equal, and in the 1930s and 1940s the NAACP had won cases in the Supreme Court that forced Southern authorities to improve black schools. In 1950 the NAACP changed its objective and, instead of striving to improve black education within the segregated system, sought school desegregation. Five cases were brought to the Supreme Court, resulting in the famous *Brown versus Board of Education* decision of 1954. Chief Justice Warren demonstrated impressive judicial leadership by convincing his colleagues to make this a unanimous 9–0 decision, hoping thereby to minimize Southern resistance. With *Brown,* the Court overturned its 1896 precedent on the ground that separate could never be equal, since the very separation derived from the notion of the superiority of one race over another.

Even though Eisenhower's own Attorney General had supported the NAACP's case in the Supreme Court, the President's reaction to the *Brown* decision was unenthusiastic. Publicly, Eisenhower committed himself unequivocally to enforcing the Constitution as interpreted by the Supreme Court, but in private he predicted retrogressive consequences in the South. He had desegregated federal facilities by executive order. But he believed that desegregation at the level of the states had to be brought about by changes in attitudes within the South, rather than by federal intervention. His caution probably helped undermine any chance that Southern resistance to school desegregation might have been overcome quickly.

While more energetic, the Supreme Court was also not decisive enough in imposing school desegregation across the South. With its so-called *Brown II* decision of 1955, it ordered the South's 2200 school boards to comply with the original decision with 'all deliberate speed'. While in some instances there were genuine objective obstacles to quick desegregation, this formulation opened the door for large-scale procrastination that was not justifiable in good faith. It was only in 1969, when the Supreme Court replaced 'all deliberate speed' with 'at once', that formal school segregation came quickly to an end. It is arguable that if Eisenhower and the Supreme Court had firmly insisted on speedy compliance, it might have occurred earlier, since it took the Southern political leaders some time to mobilize their resistance. In this instance, the post-McCarthy consensus between Eisenhower and congressional Democrats had detrimental consequences, given that the civil rights issue was threatening to destroy that consensus.

The political leaders of the South reacted to the *Brown* decisions by launching a 'massive resistance'. Senator James Eastland (Mississippi) claimed that it was the communists who had stirred the blacks into challenging segregation, a belated post-McCarthy resort to the methods of McCarthyism. Governor James Byrnes of South Carolina claimed that school desegregation would not happen in his state for many years. Southern resistance gathered momentum in March 1956, when 19 out of 22 Southern Senators and 82 out of 106 Southern US Representatives signed the 'Southern Manifesto', in which they declared their determination to exhaust all legal means for reversing the *Brown* decisions and preventing the federal use of force in imposing them on the South.

The issue of the use of force came dramatically to the fore in September 1957 in Little Rock, Arkansas, where the local authorities complied with federal court orders to desegregate public schools by devising a token desegregation scheme. Governor Orval Faubus reacted by sending guardsmen to surround a white high school in which nine blacks had been enrolled. His pretext was that he wished to uphold public order in the face of white hostility, but in practice the guardsmen prevented the black pupils from entering the school. This was no longer mere procrastination, but an open and direct defiance by a governor of the law of the land. Eisenhower, who had a constitutional duty to enforce the law, pressured Faubus to change his stance, since he desperately wanted to avoid having to use federal force. After three weeks of negotiations, Faubus withdrew the guardsmen. But this proved to be an empty gesture, since he refused to protect the black pupils from the racist mob that surrounded the school and continued to bar their entry.

Having exhausted all alternatives, Eisenhower took what he described as 'the most repugnant' of all his acts as president and deployed 1100 paratroopers of the 101st Airborne Division in Little Rock to secure the safe entry of the nine black pupils in their school. The South had not witnessed such a use of federal military force since Reconstruction (1865–77). Georgia's Richard Russell, the leader of the Southern bloc in the Senate, talked of 'Hitler's storm troopers'. For Orval Faubus the confrontation brought handsome political benefits, since he was reelected three times in a row, a point not lost on other Southern politicians.

Eisenhower's fears that *Brown* would produce a Southern backlash may seem a poor justification for his half-hearted support in implementing it, but they were not unfounded. Southern violence against blacks did increase after the *Brown* decisions. New members flocked to the racist Ku Klux Klan. There were instances of blacks being killed for seeking to enter or remain on the voting lists. In a case that received prominent national attention, Emmett Till, a young black man from Chicago visiting his uncle in Mississippi, was abducted and murdered for saying 'bye, baby' to a white woman. His abductors were identified by his uncle, prosecuted, but acquitted by an all-white jury. More usually, racist murders did not result in prosecution in the first place; in some cases the likely perpetrators were local law enforcement officers. Blacks were also terrorized by arson, which was sometimes targeted at the homes of prominent civil rights activists like Martin Luther King, Jr.

Despite the climate of fear and intimidation, the black Civil Rights movement grew in a number of streams, which in the 1960s converged and swept segregation away. For all the help that the blacks received from the Warren Court, it is when they rose and stood up to their oppressors that they attained decisive results. It was America's fortune that they did so by nonviolent means, in spite of the violence that was directed against them. The initiative in the mobilization of a black civil society gradually passed from the NAACP, which remained focused on its legal strategy and appealed mainly to middle-class blacks, to the black parishes that constituted the most effective institution for the large majority of Southern blacks at the lower end of the socioeconomic scale. The NAACP's Thurgood Marshall may have ended up in the US Supreme Court (appointed by President Johnson in 1967 and its first black member ever), but the most prominent black leaders since the later 1950s have been preachers. The inspirational, emotionally laden preaching style in black parishes contributed to the rise of ministers in the political leadership of the black community, endowing their political rhetoric with unusual moral gravity and inspirational pulse.

Montgomery, Alabama

Martin Luther King, Jr, emerged as a leader of the black community in the South through what began as minor and local developments in 1955–6 in Montgomery, Alabama, a small city with 70,000 white and 50,000 black residents. The city's buses were segregated, but it was not segregation as such that first sparked black defiance; rather, it was an unfair application of segregation. Not content with segregating the seats in the buses, the bus company had its white-only drivers force blacks to yield their seats so that whites could spill into the black part of the bus whenever all seats in the white section were taken. In December 1955 Rosa Parks, a black seamstress, refused to obey the bus driver and yield her seat, whereupon she was arrested and charged with violating city laws. The black community responded by organizing a highly effective boycott of the bus service, the success of which was secured by Reverend King, then only 26 years old, who rallied his congregation to this nonviolent protest. In spite of racist intimidation, including the burning of King's home, the boycott held for one year, resulting in a sharp decline in the bus company's revenues. In parallel, the blacks went to the courts and appealed against bus segregation all the way to the US Supreme Court. One year after Rosa Parks's initial arrest, the Supreme Court ordered Montgomery to end segregation on its buses.

This African-American victory, coming as it did during the period of 'massive resistance' and racist violence, reverberated across the South's black communities. The boycott was in a sense more important than the legal success, since it demonstrated the potency of organized nonviolent resistance. Fear and intimidation remained the order of the day, but a psychological barrier had been breached, and the oppressors appeared less invincible. A black elite had existed since the nineteenth century that strove to free blacks from white oppression, but it had not succeeded in mobilizing the black masses. The maintenance of racial subjugation did not depend solely on brute force; it required its acceptance by the broad masses of the oppressed as inevitable and habitual, the way things are and always have been. Racial subjugation appeared less inevitable after Montgomery; age-old habits of submission could be broken. The consequences were seen in the 1960s.

Eisenhower's foreign policy

The Eisenhower administration developed a foreign policy that was within the broad path of containment charted by the Truman administration. It accepted the view expounded in NSC-68 that communism was monolithic and that the advance of communism anywhere in the world was a threat to the credibility of American commitments. Therefore, Eisenhower and his Secretary of State John Foster Dulles moved in the direction of a global anticommunist crusade and, like their predecessors, they were apt occasionally to see threats where none existed.

Where Eisenhower differed from Truman was in choosing the means by which the communist threat should be confronted. Truman had decided that nuclear deterrence alone was inadequate; the United States needed strong conventional military capabilities to resist communist aggression wherever it occurred. In 1950–2 he had implemented a massive military build-up, in addition to the mobilization for the war in Korea, which raised defense spending to an alarming 14 percent of GDP. Truman did not worry about the economic effects of a rising military budget, since he thought that increased federal deficit spending would boost the economy, as had happened in World War II.

Eisenhower, by contrast, was a conservative who deeply believed that the growth of military spending threatened to undermine the American economy, as well as traditional liberties in America. His rhetoric is noteworthy, especially coming from a former general. 'Every gun that is made, every war ship launched, every rocket fired signifies, in the final sense, a theft from those who hunger and are not fed, those who are cold and are not clothed', he declared in 1953.[5] At the end of his presidency, he famously warned the American people about the dangers of the military-industrial complex.

The appeal of such rhetoric to a later generation of leftists notwithstanding, its roots were conservative. In Eisenhower's mind the success of the United States came from the vitality of American society, which in turn derived from the freedoms that Americans enjoyed. These freedoms were threatened by militarization and regimentation, which would undermine America's vitality. 'Should we have to resort to anything resembling a garrison state, then all that we are striving to defend would be weakened and, if long subjected to this kind of control, could disappear', Eisenhower declared. Deficit spending could not, in his mind, be justified in Keynesian terms and was bound to lead to inflation and higher taxation, undermining America's long-term economic prospects. Consequently, he strove to attain his foreign policy objectives within a tight cost regime. Communism had to be deterred and resisted worldwide, but on a budget. Cost-effective means had to be substituted in place of the profligacy of the Truman administration. The result was a reduction in conventional military spending and a greater reliance on nuclear deterrence and covert operations.

In the field of nuclear deterrence, the Eisenhower administration put forth the concept of massive retaliation, which threatened to punish any communist aggression by an asymmetric nuclear attack. NSC-68 had sought to expand American conventional capabilities, in order to be able to counterattack symmetrically with conventional means against a conventional communist attack. Otherwise, the United States would face the dilemma: retreat or nuclear war. Eisenhower sought to make conventional communist aggression unthinkable in the first place, by threatening in advance to respond with nuclear weapons.

So long as it deterred communist aggression, Eisenhower's approach was certainly more cost-effective. Nuclear weapons are much cheaper than conventional forces. Moreover, they were necessary to deter a Soviet nuclear attack, which meant that they would be constructed anyway, regardless of the doctrine of massive retaliation. What this doctrine proposed was to put them to use for deterring a much wider range of potential attacks, from a Soviet nuclear strike to conventional communist aggression anywhere in the world. The main test of the doctrine was the Berlin crisis of 1958, the most dangerous confrontation of the Cold War in Europe, which seemed to bring the two blocks to the brink of war.

Massive retaliation was credible so long as the United States had a clear advantage in nuclear delivery systems, since it could more credibly threaten to use nuclear weapons if the Soviet Union was unable to strike back at it with significant nuclear weapons. When the Soviet Union launched the first two Sputniks in space in 1957, it appeared to have acquired the missile capability to send an atom bomb to any American city. American missile development lagged behind. The Soviet leader Nikita Khrushchev exploited the apparent missile gap in order to gain political advantages by terrorizing the West with his belligerent rhetoric and hoping to extract concessions. It is now known that he never intended to start or risk a war between the two blocs, just as Eisenhower never intended actually to retaliate against communist aggression with a massive nuclear strike. Both leaders sought to gain political objectives only by threatening to use, not by actually using, nuclear weapons.

The missile gap, which was feared in the United States and Western Europe and which Khrushchev emphasized theatrically in the late 1950s, was in reality a bluff. The Soviet Union was unable before the 1960s to utilize the Sputnik technology for military purposes: in 1961 it had just four intercontinental nuclear missiles. Furthermore, Eisenhower knew it was a bluff. One of his most important contributions to American strategy was the development of American photographic intelligence, first through the U2 aircraft that flew higher than the range of Soviet air defense systems, and then through satellites. By February 1959, U2s had photographed the entire territory of the Soviet Union, revealing to American intelligence that Khrushchev's supposed missile arsenal did not exist. Yet in order to conceal these American intelligence capabilities from the Soviets, Eisenhower never publicly exposed Khrushchev's bluff. His European allies, the American people and most of his cabinet remained fearful of the supposed missile gap, which Kennedy used to attack Nixon in the 1960 elections. Armed with the secret information, Eisenhower rode through the Berlin crisis without heeding cries for higher defense spending, which under his watch fell from 12.8 percent of GDP in 1954 to 9.1 percent in 1961.

The Berlin crisis began when Khrushchev attempted to undo the postwar status of the city by pressing the psychological advantage that the supposed missile gap conferred on the Soviet side. Berlin was divided into four occupation zones and two city governments, but people could still move freely between the zones. As a result, a growing stream of largely skilled East Germans fled their country by going to West Berlin and then to West Germany. This hemorrhage threatened to undermine East Germany's communist regime. In November 1958, Khrushchev issued a six-month ultimatum demanding that the status of West Berlin be altered to that of a free city without occupiers. Western acquiescence in the ultimatum would have resulted in West Berlin's absorption by the surrounding East Germany, which in turn would have undermined West Germany's morale and weakened NATO's credibility. Eisenhower responded by threatening massive retaliation in the case of any violent move against the Western allies' occupation rights in West Berlin. His firmness paid off. Khrushchev let the ultimatum pass quietly, without attempting to change Berlin's status unilaterally. Yet West Berlin continued to drain East Germany of its population, forcing Khrushchev to return to the matter in the future.

Covert operations

On the periphery of world politics, Eisenhower strove to avoid another costly conventional military entanglement such as Korea in part by resorting to covert operations. If a threat to American security could be eliminated by a covert operation, rather than by an infinitely more expensive military intervention, surely this was preferable. Yet under Eisenhower, covert operations were used in highly questionable ways, in places where the communist threat was imaginary or minor, fueling anti-Americanism in the Third World.

Eisenhower's first covert operation was against the nationalist Iranian Mossadeq regime, which had nationalized British oil assets in 1951. The Eisenhower administration was convinced that Mossadeq was pro-Soviet and that he would open the gates of the Middle East to the Soviet Union. Ironically, it is now known that the Soviet leadership saw him as a 'bourgeois nationalist' unworthy of Soviet assistance. In his first televised press conference in 1955, Eisenhower inaccurately referred to the defeat of communism in Iran as one of the most important successes of his administration (there had been no communist threat in Iran). By overthrowing Mossadeq and substituting the Shah's pro-American regime, Eisenhower did secure a strong regional ally, until the Shah's overthrow in 1978. Thereafter, his covert operation came to haunt American foreign policy, since it was exploited by the Islamic Iranian regime to foment anti-Americanism.

Eisenhower's second covert operation was against the left-wing Arbens government in Guatemala, which the Soviet Union refused to support. The Eisenhower administration grossly overreacted to Arbens, viewing him as a Soviet ally. The CIA organized and trained a battalion of exiles in neighboring Honduras, which in June 1954 'invaded' Guatemala with the support of a small air force hired by the CIA. The bombardments of civilian targets caused such panic that Arbens bowed to American pressure and resigned. A grateful Eisenhower told the Director of the CIA Allen Dulles: 'You've averted a Soviet beachhead in our hemisphere.'[6]

The negative consequences of this victory over a mostly imaginary threat came sooner than in the case of Iran. The Argentine doctor Ernesto 'Che' Guevara was in Guatemala during the bombardments and the coup, and decided thereafter to devote his life to anti-American causes in Latin America. In December 1956 he joined Fidel Castro in a revolutionary guerrilla struggle that overthrew Cuba's Batista dictatorship two years later.

Fidel Castro rose to power at the age of 32, inexperienced and without a sharp ideological orientation, though he was against American hegemony in Latin America. Still, at first his relations with the United States were not antagonistic and Washington recognized his regime six months after it was established. Castro visited the United States in April 1959 and met Vice-President Nixon. But since Castro was determined to avoid the fate of Arbens, he established a strong leftist dictatorship and executed hundreds of political opponents. It was only after he moved in the totalitarian direction of Marxism-Leninism that the Soviet Union embraced his regime.

Once Castro turned communist and secured the support of the Soviet Union, the Eisenhower administration moved against him. In the midst of a global anti-communist crusade that reached distant regions of the planet, Eisenhower could scarcely have tolerated a Soviet ally 90 miles off the coast of Florida. The solution to the problem seemed obvious: it was the Guatemala formula. A group of Cuban exiles was organized and trained by the CIA in order to invade Cuba. But the plan could not be executed during Eisenhower's presidency and was bequeathed to his successor John Kennedy.

In Indochina, Eisenhower continued Truman's policy of assisting the French colonialists in their struggle against Ho Chi Minh's Marxist national liberation movement, which was strongly supported by Mao. America's involvement in the French struggle in Indochina was based on faulty reasoning that was to exert a baneful influence in the 1960s. The Truman administration maintained in 1952 that the fall to the communists of even one of the three countries of Indochina (Vietnam, Laos and Cambodia) would lead to the fall of all Southeast Asia and the Middle East except Turkey and Pakistan. Eisenhower in 1954 expressed much the same view with his metaphor of the row of dominoes in which the fall of one would bring down the rest. This alarmist view was never supported by serious analysis. The experienced Winston Churchill maintained that the West should build up Thailand and Malaysia, countries with stronger and firmer domestic institutions than Indochina, as bulwarks against the spread of communism in the event of a French defeat in Vietnam.

The French position in North Vietnam came under serious threat in the spring of 1954, when Ho Chi Minh's forces surrounded the French stronghold Dien Bien Phu. Eisenhower resisted the pleas by members of his administration to intervene militarily on the side of the French and, after the fall of Dien Bien Phu, advised the French to abandon North Vietnam and seek a partition of the country. The Geneva Accords of 1954 did establish two Vietnamese governments, Ho Chi Minh's communist regime in the North and a weak pro-Western government in the South. Common elections were supposed to take place within two years to create a unified government. But when the time came, South Vietnam's new regime under Ngo Dinh Diem postponed them indefinitely, with Eisenhower's concurrence, reasoning that in the more populated North Vietnam the elections would be rigged by the communist regime to produce a fake overall communist majority.

The perpetuation of Vietnam's division led in the late 1950s to the beginning of an anti-regime guerrilla struggle by the Viet Cong in South Vietnam, whom North Vietnam assisted with supplies and personnel. Having 'lost' half of Vietnam, Eisenhower was determined to assist the other half with generous economic and military aid, as well as 900 American advisors. But the communist insurgency in South Vietnam reached serious proportions only at the end of his presidency, with the establishment of the Viet Cong's National Liberation Front in December 1960. Like Cuba, Vietnam was a problem that Eisenhower bequeathed to Kennedy. These foreign policy matters, as well as civil rights, were forces building up towards an eruption beneath the tranquil surface of American politics in the Eisenhower years. Something similar was happening in American culture.

NOTES

1. Christopher Andrew and Vasili Mitrokhin, *The Mitrokhin Archive: The KGB in Europe and the West,* London: Allen Lane (Penguin Press), 1999, p. 168.
2. James A. Patterson, *Grand Expectations: The United States, 1945–1974,* Oxford: Oxford University Press, 1996, p. 186.
3. Seymor Martin Lipset and Earl Raab, *The Politics of Unreason: Right-Wing Extremism in America, 1790–1970,* New York: Harper & Row, 1970, p. 239.
4. Robert Dallek, *Lone Star Rising: Lyndon Johnson and His Times, 1908–1960,* Oxford: Oxford University Press, 1991, p. 453.
5. John Lewis Gaddis, *Strategies of Containment: A Critical Appraisal of Postwar American National Security Policy,* Oxford: Oxford University Press, 1982, p. 133.
6. Christopher Andrew, *For the President's Eyes Only: Secret Intelligence and the American Presidency from Washington to Bush,* New York: HarperCollins, 1995, p. 211.

RECOMMENDED READING

Christopher Andrew and Vasili Mitrokhin, *The Mitrokhin Archive: The KGB in Europe and the West,* London: Allen Lane (Penguin Press), 1999.
Robert Dallek, *Lone Star Rising: Lyndon Johnson and His Times, 1908–1960,* Oxford: Oxford University Press, 1991.
Richard M. Fried, *Nightmare in Red: The McCarthy Era in Perspective,* New York: Oxford University Press, 1990.

John Lewis Gaddis, *Strategies of Containment: A Critical Appraisal of Postwar American Security Policy,* Oxford: Oxford University Press, 1982.

Seymor Martin Lipset and Earl Raab, *The Politics of Unreason: Right-Wing Extremism in America, 1790–1970,* New York: Harper & Row, 1970.

James A. Patterson, *Grand Expectations: The United States, 1945–1974,* Oxford: Oxford University Press, 1996.

Clinton Rossiter, *Parties and Politics in America,* New York: New American Library, 1960.

CHAPTER 4

Alienation and Affluence in the 1950s

The decade of the 1950s is often criticized as an era of social complacency and intellectual darkness. This was, after all, the time of Senator McCarthy and the Hollywood blacklist; President Eisenhower and the Cold War; Jerry Lewis and television; Pat Boone and suburbia; *Life* Magazine and the 'Silent Generation'. In *Leopards in the Temple* (1999), Morris Dickstein notes,

> The postwar period, especially the 1950s, has been simplified into everything the sixties generation rebelled against: a beaming president presiding over a stagnant government, small-town morality, racial segregation, political and sexual repression, Cold War mobilization, nuclear standoff, suburban togetherness, the domestic confinement of women, and the reign of the nuclear family.

Yet, as Dickstein argues, it was also a flourishing period in all the arts. American culture was transformed in the poetry of Robert Lowell, Richard Wilbur and the New Formalists; in the dramas of Miller, Williams and the Symbolic Realists; in the jazz of Charlie Parker, Dizzy Gillespie and Bebop; in the fiction of Bellow, Ellison and the new ethnic writers; and in the paintings of Jackson Pollock, Franz Kline and the Abstract Expressionists. How can we account for this paradox?

Conformity and alienation

Conformity

In 1950, David Riesman, a social scientist at the University of Chicago, and two colleagues published a pathbreaking analysis of the changing nature of national character. *The Lonely Crowd* became the most influential study of American society for the next three decades. Riesman argued that American social character had changed decisively in modern times – 'a whole range of social developments associated with a shift from an age of production to an age of consumption'. He characterized this transformation as the shift from the 'inner-directed' personality of the nineteenth-century *producer* who found his values within himself to the 'other-directed' personality of the twentieth-century *consumer* who takes his moral and social cues from public opinion.

Whereas the 'inner-directed' person found his bearings by means of an inbuilt gyroscope, the 'other-directed' person navigated socially and morally by means of a radar screen. Riesman explained:

> What is common to all the other-directed people is that their contemporaries are the source of direction for the individual – either those known to him or those with whom he is indirectly acquainted, through friends and through the mass media. This source is of course 'internalized' in the sense that dependence on it for guidance in life is implanted early. The goals toward which the other-directed person strives shift with that guidance: it is only the process of striving itself and the process of paying close attention to the signals from others that remain unaltered throughout life.

Riesman's general theory of social types in a changing mass society found confirmation in more empirical studies like C. Wright Mills' *White Collar* (1951) and William Whyte's *The Organization Man* (1956).

No wonder, then, that in 1954, the critic Irving Howe called the postwar era 'This Age of Conformity'. By this he meant that the social consolidation created by Cold War politics and new economic prosperity was mirrored by conformity in culture. The growing concentration of postwar society in large corporations, government bureaucracies and giant institutions of higher education, sent millions of Americans to work and study in increasingly faceless and standardized organizations. A rising mass culture reflected the growing mass society in which the new priorities of standardization, cooperation and conformity were replacing the older American values of self-reliance, competition and rugged individualism.

For artists and intellectuals, the new social and cultural configurations offered new possibilities as well as pitfalls. The change in their situation was celebrated in a famous symposium entitled 'Our Country and Our Culture', sponsored by the *Partisan Review* in 1952. This symposium, held by a celebrated journal of radical dissent, revealed how far the American intelligentsia had travelled in the years since the Great Depression. 'American intellectuals now regard America and its institutions in a new way,' the editors affirmed. 'For better or for worse, most writers no longer accept alienation as the artist's fate in America; on the contrary, they want very much to be a part of American life.'

Most contributors to the *Partisan Review* symposium agreed with this assessment, but not everyone was optimistic about the future of American culture in the hostile Cold War climate. Radicals like Howe and Norman Mailer decried what *Partisan Review* editor Philip Rahv called 'the *embourgeoisement* of the intelligentsia'. Indeed, Mailer found the postwar period with its snug economic prosperity and its smug intellectual conformity a particularly dangerous time for American writers. 'I would propose that the artist feels most alienated when he loses the sharp sense of what he is alienated from,' he wrote. 'In this context, I wonder if there has been a time in the last fifty years when the American artist has felt more alienated.'

Despite the flush of affluence, a mood of anxiety and alienation cast a shadow over the culture, permeating even popular novels like Sloan Wilson's *The Man in the Gray Flannel Suit* (1955). Tom Rath is a young Madison Avenue executive who must choose between pursuing his career and raising his family. Tom has returned from the war to a 'lunatic world' in which he feels estranged from his wife and past. The old order in which he was raised has faded away with the death of his grandmother; now Tom must live in a brave new world where the gray flannel of personal ambition has replaced the army khaki of social responsibility. Tom lives in a 'crazy world' of large, impersonal forces which he cannot change. Unable to act, he can only muse: 'I can't do anything about the state of the world, but I can put my own life in order.' In a popular form, Wilson's bestselling novel presents the central concerns of postwar fiction: the lack of illusions of the new generation, the decline of values in a competitive economy, the loss of self in an impersonal society.

Similar anxieties about the pressures of conformity were reflected in Arthur Miller's play, *The Crucible* (1953) and Don Siegel's cult horror film, *Invasion of the Body Snatchers* (1956). But there was a new emphasis in the cultural discourse. Whereas writers in the 1930s had focused on the plight of the disadvantaged, intellectuals now turned to the problems of the emerging middle class. In the process, the concept of alienation was translated from the realm of work (economics) to the realm of the family (psychology). Richard Pells notes, 'Where the search for community had captured the imagination of the Left in the 1930s, the search for identity inspired the writers and artists of the 1950s.'[1]

In all the arts there was a similar retreat from the public realm into the private. Poetry, with its emphasis on formalism and 'impersonality', became, in Daniel Hoffman's words, 'the most private, least accessible of the arts in a mass society in which universal literacy, for most, offered the gift of tongues to Caliban'. Private experience was celebrated in the exquisitely formal verse of Richard Wilbur's *Ceremony* (1950); everyday life was examined in Elizabeth Bishop's elegant *Poems: North and South – A Cold Spring* (1955); the domestic world was ironized with colloquial plainness in Randall Jarrell's *The Woman at Washington Zoo* (1960). As Robert Lowell wrote retrospectively in *Life Studies* (1960): 'These are the tranquillized *Fifties,/* and I am forty. Ought I to regret my seedtime?'

A similar turning inward was apparent in American drama. Already in the late 1930s, the success of Thornton Wilder's *Our Town* (1938) and William Saroyan's *The Time of Your Life* (1939) announced the theater's retreat from radical dreams to private fantasies. In the late 1940s, the highpoint of postwar American drama, the three most important plays – Eugene O'Neill's *The Iceman Cometh* (1946), Williams' *A Streetcar Named Desire* (1947) and Miller's *Death of a Salesman* – all described the necessity of illusions in a harsh world. By the end of the decade, the withdrawal from the public realm was nearly complete; with the exception of Miller, American dramatists retreated from the world of ideas into the world of feelings. According to Gerald Weales,

The 1950s was a psychological decade, a period in which playwrights solved problems with the assurance and the profundity of syndicated columnists. The dramatists focused on the personal – family difficulties, loneliness, the uncertainties of adolescence – and if they lifted their eyes to the social, the political, the universal, the wider vistas were somehow domesticated, reduced to problems in how to relate.[2]

Typical of the 1950s were domestic plays like William Inge's *Come Back, Little Sheba* (1950) and Robert Anderson's *Tea and Sympathy* (1953). In summary, as dramatist William Gibson concluded, 'the theater in this country, in this decade, was primarily a place not in which to be serious, but in which to be likeable'.[3]

Fiction, too, seemed to turn inward, as if to catch the nuances of the adolescent flight from the cruel realities of the adult world. In Carson McCullers's *The Member of the Wedding* (1946) and J. D. Salinger's *The Catcher in the Rye* (1951), the adolescent hero became the representative figure in American fiction, a symbol of what literary critic Ihab Hassan called 'radical innocence'. Indeed, Salinger's hero, Holden Caulfield, became the spokesman for a generation of college students and the model on which a series of teenage rebels were based. Yet what distinguishes *The Catcher in the Rye* from its many imitators is not only Salinger's remarkable ear for adolescent speech but the total truth of Holden's characterization. For while Holden's sense of indignation strikes a sympathetic chord, the quixotic futility of his outrage is even more striking. He presents no plan for social reform; he offers no guide to revolution. 'It's hopeless, anyway,' he observes. 'If you had a million years to do it in, you couldn't rub out even *half* the [obscenities] in the world.' Holden's story becomes a casebook of postwar alienation because he can only define himself by negation.

The new alienation

Like the adolescent hero of Nicholas Ray's film, *Rebel Without a Cause* (1954), played by screen idol James Dean, Holden epitomizes what the psychiatrist Kenneth Keniston called the 'new alienation', a feeling of estrangement which 'characteristically takes the form of rebellion without a cause, of rejection without a program, of refusal of what is without a vision of what should be'. Thus when his sister Phoebe tells Holden, 'You don't like anything that's happening', and challenges him to refute the charge, Holden suddenly discovers that he 'couldn't concentrate too hot'. And when Phoebe asks him to name something he would like to *be* in this world, he can only respond with a quixotic occupation: 'I'd just like to be the catcher in the rye and all. I know it's crazy but that's the only thing I'd really like to be. I know it's crazy.'

Here Holden dramatizes his sense of total alienation: his isolation from his peer group and the entire adult world as well as his identification with the transitory state of childhood innocence. In relation to his society, Holden defines himself by negation because he cannot identify positively with anyone who might assist him to act in the social world. But his rebellion is pathetic rather than tragic because he is finally ambivalent about his own predicament. He has contempt for all the 'phonies' he encounters but concludes, 'Don't ever tell anybody anything, if you do you start missing everybody.' His one desire is to be 'the catcher in the rye' but he finally discovers that, 'The thing with kids is, if they want to grab for the gold ring, you have to let them do it and not say anything. If they fall off, they fall off, but it's bad if you say anything to them.' When Holden labels his own actions 'crazy' – as he does frequently throughout the novel – he is really revealing his own ambivalence about his actions. 'If you want to know the truth,' he concludes about his own story, 'I don't *know* what I think about it.'

The alienation of Holden Caulfield illustrates a phenomenon of the 1950s. His preference for innocence, spirituality and pacifism suggests that he is a forerunner of the 'flower children' of the 1960s but, unlike them, Holden has nothing to drop *into* when he drops *out of society*. He can find no subculture with which he can identify. Holden's isolation is really total and that is why the only choice left open to him at the end of the novel is to be socially readjusted at a sanitorium. He considers his actions 'crazy' because he has no standard other than society's by which to judge them. In the 1950s, 'craziness' and alienation suggested a deviation from a norm which still had meaning – even for Holden.

Affluence and anxiety

Thus the postwar period brought Americans a dual legacy of unprecedented affluence and unparalleled anxiety. The affluence was visible everywhere: in the new suburbs, on the new superhighways, and on the ubiquitous television set. The figures tell the story: between 1950 and 1960 the number of American homeowners increased by more than nine million to almost 33 million; in the same period, the number of registered automobiles increased by 21 million. To accommodate the new cars, a new 40,000-mile Interstate Highway System was built. As for television: in 1946 there were 7000 television sets in use; by 1960 there were over 50 million. In *The Fifties* (1993) David Halberstam noted, 'In 1952 *TV Guide* magazine was founded. The frozen TV dinner was introduced in 1954, and by 1956 Americans for the first time were spending more hours watching their sets than working for pay.'

The new economic boom was fueled by the twin engines of private consumerism and public military spending. The theologian Reinhold Niebuhr observed that the Cold War placed Americans in 'an historic situation in which the paradise of our domestic security is suspended in a hell of global insecurity'. The new anxiety was fed by the growing sense of vulnerability that found its most rabid expression in the hysteria of McCarthyism. At first, few were willing to admit that the Cold War was the source of both American affluence and anxiety. Later, many came to see the ambiguous character of the new consumer society. Thus the 1950s, often seen as an era of monolithic conservatism, was actually a time of the gradual unveiling of the nation suspended between its public hopes and secret fears. As Philip Rahv noted, ' "Suspended" is the key word, for a good many other satisfactions of American life similarly exist in a state of insecure suspension.'

'Insecure suspension' suggests the contradictions of affluence and apocalypse felt by Americans throughout the 1950s. This sense of unresolvable crisis leading to a paralysis of will was also reflected in the fiction produced at the end of the decade. Novels like John Barth's *The End of the Road* (1958) and Walker Percy's *The Moviegoer* (1960) describe a world of immanent crisis in which their characters feel suspended over an abyss. Jacob Homer, the narrator of Barth's novel, feels trapped in a corner like his namesake in the nursery rhyme. His struggle to impose a meaning on a life which seems random and arbitrary results in death and paralysis which is just as arbitrary. Binx Bolling, the narrator of *The Moviegoer*, also finds it impossible to find answers or to take sides. Living in a secular society which has abolished the eschatological, Binx desires an apocalyptic ending. He says,

> For a long time I have secretly hoped for the end of the world and believed...with many other people that only after the end could the few who survive creep out of their holes and discover themselves to be themselves and live as merrily as children among the viny ruins.

But both Binx and Jacob have reached the end without receiving any sign of revelation. Binx watches people look up at the sky and shake their heads: all *they* see is the weather. Jacob dreams that he has phoned the weather bureau for the forecast and been told: 'There isn't going to be any weather tomorrow.' Both novels describe a kind of death in life in which people live in suspended animation. Thus *The End of the Road* both describes and epitomizes the end of the Fifties.

Southern writing

Yet the major contribution to the literary culture of the 1950s was made by a new generation of regional and ethnic writers. Though regionalism had always been a strong element in American literature, the predominance of Southern writing in the postwar years requires some explanation. Already in the 1930s a new Southern literature had emerged with the express purpose of defending traditional communal values against the encroachment of Northern-style modernization. In *I'll Take My Stand* (1930) 12 poets and critics, including Donald Davidson, Allen Tate and John Crowe Ransom, had opted for a neoconservative version of the Southern Agrarian tradition in response to the breakdown in civic virtues and social values caused by the rise of urbanization, industrialization and the ideology of advanced capitalism. At the end of World War II a new nostalgia for order, stability and tradition associated with an older bygone world emerged. This pastoral ideal became the lens through which a new generation of writers would view the modern South.

Though the South produced a number of remarkable writers before the war, including Katherine Anne Porter, Erskine Caldwell and Thomas Wolfe, one figure overshadowed the rest and shaped the future of Southern writing. William Faulkner was a direct link with the Modernist movement but, unlike his more cosmopolitan contemporaries who exiled themselves in Europe, he chose to remain in provincial Mississippi where he wrote about what he called his 'little postage stamp' of the South. He remained relatively obscure until 1946, when the critic Malcolm Cowley published an anthology of his fiction entitled *The Portable Faulkner*. Then readers discovered that the saga of a place Faulkner called Yoknapatawpha County was the most daring and sweeping American artistic creation of the twentieth century. The impact on a younger generation of Southern writers was profound. 'The presence of Faulkner in our midst makes a great difference in what the writer can and cannot do,' observed Flannery O'Connor. 'Nobody wants his mule and wagon stalled on the same track the Dixie Limited is roaring down.'

Southern history

In creating his fiction, Faulkner drew on common elements that shaped post-war Southern writing: a rhetorical tradition steeped in the Bible and nourished by oral storytelling; a dark view of life shaped by Protestant fundamentalism; a tragic sense of history marked by the 'peculiar institution' of slavery and the loss of the Civil War; and a romantic vision of the past with its nostalgia for a vanished pastoral ideal and its penchant for lost causes. Faulkner was fond of saying that 'the past is never dead. It is not even past'. Similarly, in postwar works like Robert Penn Warren's *All the King's Men*, Eudora Welty's *Delta Wedding* (1946) and William Styron's *Lie Down in Darkness*, the focus is on 'time and memory'. Thus a father tells his son in Styron's novel: 'always remember where you came from, the ground is bloody and full of guilt where you were born and you must tread a long narrow path toward your destiny. If the crazy sideroads start to beguile you, son, take at least a backward glance at Monticello.'

The burden of Southern history is present in later works as well, from Warren's verse drama, *Brothers to Dragons* (1953), to Styron's historical meditation on the moral costs of slavery, *The Confessions of Nat Turner* (1967). Since then, younger writers have tended to focus on a new South uninhabited by a Faulknerian sense of the past. 'Faulkner ceased to be an influence on Southern novelists when the South at last had its own worldliness to satirize', noted Alfred Kazin. In the fiction of Anne Tyler (*Dinner at the Home Sick Restaurant*, 1982) and Padgett Powell (*Edisto*, 1984) the South lost its regional backwardness and distinctiveness and simply became more like the rest of the country. In *Edisto*, for example, Powell describes an old slave market which has been gentrified and converted into a shopping mall with trendy boutiques.

Southern Gothic

If the historical imagination, with its emphasis on the fallen social world, represents one side of Southern culture, then the gothic imagination, with its emphasis on the fallen spiritual world, represents the other. 'Southern culture', wrote Flannery O'Connor, 'has fostered a type of imagination that has been influenced by Christianity of a not too orthodox kind and by a strong devotion to the Bible, which has kept our minds attached to the concrete and living symbol.' In this view, the manifestation of the grotesque represents not the deviation from the norm but the corruption of the perfect. In McCullers's *The Heart is a Lonely Hunter* (1940), the two central characters are deaf mutes whose affliction symbolizes their 'spiritual isolation'. In Capote's *Other Voices, Other Rooms*, a decaying mansion represents not simply the decadent old South but the disintegration of personality as well. In O'Connor's stories in *A Good Man is Hard to Find* (1955), a one-armed man and a one-legged girl embody the truth of Søren Kierkegaard's observation: 'The greatest danger, that of losing one's own self, may pass off quietly as if it were nothing; every other loss, that of an arm, a leg, five dollars, a wife, etc., is sure to be noticed.'[4]

Strangely enough, perhaps the two most important postwar Southern writers, Flannery O'Connor and Walker Percy, were both practicing Catholics in a predominantly Protestant South. In their work, they dramatized the opposition between religious faith and secular reason, or what Percy called the 'shithouse of scientific humanism'. In her magnificent short stories, O'Connor depicted the tragicomic struggle between the bourgeois ethic and proletarian fundamentalism. For instance, in 'Good Country People', an itinerant Bible salesman teaches a crippled, cynical girl that she 'ain't so smart' by stealing her wooden leg when she had set out to seduce *him*. 'Aren't you just good country people?' she gasps as he disappears with her leg. 'Yeah,' he answers, 'but it ain't held me back none. I'm as good as you any day of the week.' In 'A Good Man is Hard to Find', the old grandmother, confronted by an escaped convict called The Misfit, embraces him as one of her children at the moment when he murders her. It is, O'Connor suggested, 'the moment of grace', leading The Misfit to remark, 'She would have been a good woman if it had been somebody there to shoot her every minute of her life.' Similarly, in 'The Displaced Person', a respectable middle-aged Christian lady learns an elementary lesson about the religion she professes from a violent encounter with a Christ-like Polish refugee.

This conflict between spiritual force and social convention is also at the center of O'Connor's two novels, *Wise Blood* (1952) and *The Violent Bear it Away* (1960). Both novels are about young men who struggle against religious faith before they are scourged by Christian redemption. These reluctant spiritual seekers are less like the middle-class protagonists of her stories than like their demonic antagonists who must murder in order to create. In *Wise Blood*, the hero is confronted by a tableau that epitomizes the conflict between faith and skepticism. At a rural gas station Hazel Motes finds a cage bearing a sign: 'Two deadly enemies. Have a look free.' This is what he sees:

> There was a black bear about four feet long and very thin, resting on the floor of the cage; his back was spotted with bird lime that had been shot down on him by a small chicken hawk that was sitting on a perch in the upper part of the same apartment. Most of the hawk's tail was gone; the bear had only one eye.

The meaning of this grotesque metaphor of the modern world is clear: without a scheme of sin and redemption we are reduced to a mock Darwinian struggle for survival. For the 'practical' rather than 'theological' people in O'Connor's stories who, like Mrs McIntyre in 'The Displaced Person', embrace social convention and believe that 'Christ was just another DP', the presence of Grace will always be a grotesque manifestation. 'My own feeling is that writers who see by the light of their Christian faith will have, in these times, the sharpest eye for the grotesque, for the perverse, and for the unacceptable,' she said. 'The novelist with Christian concerns will find in modern life distortions which are repugnant to him, and his problem will be to make these appear as distortions to an audience which is used to seeing them as natural.'

While few contemporary writers adopted O'Connor's religious orthodoxy, many subscribed to her artistic strategy. 'Ordinary life has a grotesque dimension,' remarks one of Saul Bellow's characters, 'and this has become a theme of the times.' What connects gothic writers of the South with ethnic writers of the North is their common concern not simply for the opposition between self and society but for the confrontation between ordinary experience and what Karl Jaspers calls 'extreme situations'. In works as various as Bellow's *The Victim*, O'Connor's 'A Good Man is Hard to Find' and Styron's *Sophie's Choice* (1979), characters confront forms of extreme behavior which are simply beyond their ability to comprehend. After Auschwitz and Hiroshima, it seems that everything is permissible. The extreme becomes ordinary and, as the critic Lionel Trilling remarked, 'It is now life and not art that requires the willing suspension of disbelief.' This emphasis on extreme experience and aberrant behavior in postwar American writing is reminiscent of Thomas Mann's dictum that 'the grotesque is the genuine anti-bourgeois style'. It suggests that all was not well under the smiling surface of postwar American life.

Ethnic writing

Both Southern and ethnic writers were responding to the radical social and economic changes wrought in the affluent 1950s. But if the flourishing of a regional literature represented a continuity with the past, then the emergence of an ethnic literature represented a break with tradition. The triumph of American culture in the 1950s was its opening up to marginal groups in American society. But this was not achieved without a struggle. For whatever black and Jewish experience may have been, they were not considered typically American; and whatever black and Jewish idiom may have been, they were not considered proper English. In *Writers at Work* (1967), Bellow described the problem that writers from the margin of American society experienced in trying to enter the mainstream of American culture:

> My first two books were well made. I wrote the first quickly but took great pains with it. I labored with the second and tried to make it letter perfect. In writing *The Victim* I accepted a Flaubertian standard. Not a bad standard, to be sure, but one which, in the end, I found repressive – repressive because of the circumstances of my life and because of my upbringing in Chicago as the son of immigrants. I could not, with such an instrument as I developed in the first two books, express a variety of things I knew intimately. These books, though useful, did not give me a form in which I felt comfortable. A writer should be able to express himself easily, naturally, copiously in a form which frees his mind, his energies. Why should he hobble himself with formalities? With a borrowed sensibility? With a desire to be 'correct'? Why should I force myself to write like an Englishman or a contributor to the *New Yorker*? I soon saw that it simply was not in me to be a mandarin. I should add that for a young man in my position there were social inhibitions too. I had good reason to fear that I would be put down as a foreigner, an interloper. It was made clear to me when I studied literature at the university that as a Jew and the son of Russian Jews I would probably never have the right *feeling* for Anglo-Saxon traditions, for English words. I realized even in college that the people who told me this were not necessarily disinterested friends. But they had an effect on me, nevertheless. This was something from which I had to free myself. I fought free because I had to.

Bellow's struggle to find his own true voice as a writer was typical of many ethnic artists of his generation. For black and Jewish writers, the shaping of their experience became one with the forging of an idiom. Both were aspects of the same quest for identity which became the central theme of most ethnic writing.

The central events in Jewish-American consciousness are the mass migration of East European Jews to the United States at the end of the nineteenth century and the mass destruction of European Jews in the middle of the twentieth. The central events in African-American consciousness are the forced migration of black Africans to the New World in the seventeenth and eighteenth centuries and the long journey towards freedom and full citizenship in America in the nineteenth and twentieth centuries. Thus the fate of both Jews and blacks has been deeply imbedded in the terrors of history. As Bernard Malamud noted in *The Fixer* (1966): 'We're all in history, that's sure, but some are more than others, Jews more than some. If it snows not everybody is out in it getting wet.'

Jewish-American writing

Some have argued that the chronicle of Jewish immigrant experience is the American success story *par excellence*. The historian Stephan Thernstrom noted that the rate of Jewish upward mobility was twice that of other immigrant groups. In merely two generations, a large number of Jewish immigrants moved from the impoverished *shtetls* of Eastern Europe to the affluent suburbs of the United States. But the price of success was often high in terms of the sacrifice of traditional Jewish ethics to modern American materialism. This opposition between the Jewish vision and the American dream became the dominant theme in Jewish-American writing. In the 1950s, this theme found its richest expression in Bellow's *Seize the Day* (1956), Malamud's *The Assistant* (1957) and Philip Roth's *Goodbye, Columbus* (1959).

In *Goodbye, Columbus,* for instance, the narrator Neil Klugman must decide what he is willing to sacrifice to catch his Jewish-American princess, Brenda Patimkin. The Patimkins are Jews who have 'made it' in America but at a terrific cost to their identity and character. Even Brenda's nose is not her own after she has had it fixed to conform to the American ideal of beauty. The same conflict occurs in *Seize the Day,* where Tommy Wilhelm has changed his name to make it sound less Jewish in his pursuit of the American dream. Similarly, in *The Assistant,* a poor Jewish grocer named Morris Bober must choose between surviving economically and preserving his ethical values. What is interesting is that in all three works the crass terms of the dream of success are rejected. Morris Bober is exemplary because he refuses to compromise his ethics; Neil Klugman is admirable insofar as he chooses another standard than that of the Patimkins; and Tommy Wilhelm is pathetic because in the end he recognizes that in his pursuit of success he has lost more than he has gained. In much classic Jewish-American fiction, the dream of success takes an ironic twist: as Bellow writes in his richest novel *Herzog* (1964): 'the story of my life – how I rose from humble origins to complete disaster'.

Jewish-American writing after the 1950s

Herzog's lament, like Philip Roth's celebrated *Portnoy's Complaint* (1969), suggests how complex the chronicle of Jewish upward mobility became in the 1960s. Whereas the first generation of Jewish fictional protagonists went into business and contended with failure, a second generation enters the professions and struggles with success. From *Herzog* and *Portnoy* to Norman Podhoretz's memoir, *Making It* (1965) and Joseph Heller's comic novel, *Good as Gold* (1979), Jewish protagonists sweat out identity crises on their way to cultural assimilation. In *Good as Gold*, Heller's antiheroic protagonist Bruce Gold decides to write a book about 'the Jewish experience in America' to add to his fame and fortune. But, as in all of Heller's fiction, there is a catch. 'How can I write about the Jewish experience,' he asks himself, 'when I don't know what it is?' In the course of the novel he comes to know it by realizing that he is living it in all its ambiguity. Gold's rediscovery of his ethnic origins is a victory for old Jewish values over crass American norms.

The quest for traditional Jewish values involves the search for an authentic Jewish identity. This search is exacerbated in America by the pressures of assimilation. 'What does *he* know about being Jewish?' asks Bruce Gold's father of his son. 'He wasn't even born in Europe.' In Jewish-American writing, cultural assimilation is described as the process of eliminating the European, the *authentic* Jewish characteristics. To leave Europe, Herbert Gold observed in his novel, *Fathers* (1966), was 'to abandon history'. But the typically American desire to escape history takes on a tragic dimension in the face of the Holocaust, as poets like Karl Shapiro (*Poems of a Jew*, 1958), Irving Feldman (*The Pripet Marshes*, 1965) and Anthony Hecht (*The Hard Hours*, 1967) remind us. Indeed, the success of Jews in America together with their annihilation in Europe created a complex psychological situation for Jewish Americans which Irving Howe defined as 'inherently schizoid'. In *World of Our Fathers* (1976) Howe explains:

> At home: improvements in social and economic conditions, a growing sense of ease, comfort, security. Abroad: the greatest horror in the history of mankind, the destruction of six million Jews for reasons no mind could fathom, no intuition penetrate. How were these two elements of Jewish experience to be reconciled? The only honest answer was that they could not be; it was a division which anyone who retained even the faintest sense of Jewish identity would have to live with as best he could.

This schizoid tendency is often expressed imaginatively in Jewish-American literature in the encounter between the hero and his double. In some cases these doubles are Jew and Gentile. For instance, in Bellow's *The Victim*, the Jewish hero Asa Leventhal is accused by an anti-Semite named Allbee of ruining his life. The novel investigates a world where all human beings are potential victims yet still responsible for their actions. In Malamud's *The Assistant*, the Jewish grocer, Morris Bober, is robbed by a Gentile, Frank Alpine, who ends up atoning for his crime by becoming a Jew. The novel illuminates a world where all individuals are Jews in that they suffer. But more often the doubles in Jewish-American fiction are the American and European Jew. In Malamud's 'The Last Mohican' (1958), Roth's 'Eli the Fanatic' (1959) and Cynthia Ozick's 'Bloodshed' (1976) the encounters are strikingly similar: the European compels the American to confront and embrace the Jewish identity he has attempted to repress. In Ozick's other fiction, from *The Pagan Rabbi* (1972) through *The Messiah of Stockholm* (1987), there is a continuing obsession with preserving the Yiddish language and traditional Jewish culture that are about to pass out of existence. Thus while writers like Bellow, Malamud and Roth have entered the American mainstream culture that they helped to create, Ozick has self-consciously sought her roots in the vanishing European culture depicted by her Polish models, Bruno Schulz and Isaac Bashevis Singer.

Singer is the anomaly in Jewish-American writing, a Polish immigrant who came to the United States as an adult in the 1930s and refused to assimilate. Writing in Yiddish for an aging audience in America that was declining almost daily, Singer provided a living testament for a European culture that was all but defunct. 'It strikes me as a kind of inspired madness,' Irving Howe observed of Singer: 'here is a man living in New York City, a sophisticated and clever writer, who composes stories about places like Frampol, Bilgoray, Kreshev, *as if they were still there.*' But when Singer turned to Jewish experience in America he sometimes wrote as if America was not there for his displaced persons, so obsessed are they by the European past. In *Enemies, A Love Story* (1972) his characters are refugees from the Holocaust who seem like ghosts possessed by the *dybbuk* of history. 'Everything has already happened,' Singer's protagonist thinks. 'The creation, the flood, Sodom, the giving of the Torah, the Hitler holocaust.' In America, Singer's displaced persons have not so much abandoned history as they have been abandoned by it.

At the end of the 1980s, the critic Ted Solotaroff suggested that as American Jews moved from being marginally American to being marginally Jewish, the traditional themes of Jewish-American writing were being used up. Now that the subjects of assimilation to American materialism and nostalgia for a vanished European tradition had been exhausted, writers who wished to continue writing as Jews and not simply assimilated Americans would have to measure their ethnic identity against new themes. Solotaroff pointed to a recent novel by Philip Roth entitled *The Counterlife* (1987) which exploited the potential of a new theme in exciting ways: the Jewish-American encounter with Israel.

Actually, Roth's richly inventive narrative has several strands that are all concerned with the disparity between the life we live and the life we imagine. The last of a series of fictions about the unsentimental education of Nathan Zuckerman, a controversial Jewish-American writer who bears a superficial resemblance to Roth himself, *The Counterlife* explores the variety of dream lives we lead. In one of them, Zuckerman visits Israel, which comes to stand for a version of the pastoral myth of 'the recovery of a sanitized, confusionless life'. Zuckerman rejects the invitation to stay and, in the process, encapsulates the history of Jews in America. For Zuckerman realizes that his 'landscape' is not 'the Negev wilderness' but 'industrial, immigrant America' just as his 'sacred text' is not the Bible but the Modernist novel. Despite its ambiguities, America remains for him a kind of 'promised land'. He says:

> I was the American-born grandson of simple Galician tradesmen who, at the end of the last century, had on their own reached the same prophetic conclusion as Theodor Herzl – that there was no future for them in Christian Europe, that they couldn't go on being themselves there without inciting to violence ominous forces against which they hadn't the slightest means of defense. But instead of struggling to save the Jewish people from destruction by founding a homeland in the remote corner of the Ottoman Empire that had once been biblical Palestine, they simply set out to save their own Jewish skins. Insomuch as Zionism meant taking upon oneself, rather than leaving to others, responsibility for one's survival as a Jew, this was their brand of Zionism. And it worked.

'Though I don't admit this back in New York,' he adds, 'I'm a little idealistic about America'.

African-American writing

If Jewish-American writing is concerned with the acceptance of identity then African-American literature is concerned with the creation of identity. This is understandable given the conditions of black life in white America. In a situation where black people were kept in servitude for so long, it was hard for them to achieve selfhood. Not surprisingly, this is the theme of many classic black stories: how boys become men. We can even see this theme reflected in the titles of Richard Wright's first three books: *Uncle Tom's Children* (1938), *Native Son* (1940) and *Black Boy* (1945). For black male writers who followed Wright, the theme of identity remained central and was reflected in the titles of some of their most significant books: Ralph Ellison's *Invisible Man* (1952), James Baldwin's *Nobody Knows My Name* (1964) and John A. Williams' *The Man Who Cried I Am* (1967).

Both black and Jewish writing grew out of the same postwar impulses. 'The fallout from World War II had created a rough parallel between Jews and blacks', notes Morris Dickstein in *Leopards in the Temple*.

> As prejudice against blacks and Jews came unstuck in the late forties, ethnic writers found a wider audience and an opportunity to influence the nation's changing attitudes. If Malamud and Bellow presented Jews as exemplary sufferers, emblems of both their people's history and of humanity as a whole, Ellison and Baldwin were determined to avoid portraying blacks mainly as society's victims.

Though Ellison and Baldwin began as protégés of Richard Wright, they soon transcended the social realism of their mentor. In his early essays published in *Notes of a Native Son* (1955), Baldwin rejected the 'protest novel' which reduced characters to political symbols and wondered why Wright was incapable of creating a black character as complex as he was. Instead, Baldwin believed that 'the private life, his own and that of others, is the writer's subject – his key and ours to his achievement'. Thus in early essays and fiction like the autobiographical novel, *Go Tell it on the Mountain* (1954), Baldwin created his most complex character, himself, as a Jamesian observer of American life 'on whom nothing was lost'.

Nowhere is Baldwin's power as a witness to the agony of race relations more evident than in the title essay of his first collection. 'Notes of a Native Son' recounts three major incidents in Baldwin's life that occurred virtually simultaneously: the death of his stepfather and the birth of his youngest child and James's own 19th birthday. These events occur in the summer of 1943 against the backdrop of one of Harlem's worst riots. As he surveys the aftermath of the rioting, he regrets the waste of life and property. 'It would have been better to have left the plate glass as it had been and the goods lying in the stores,' he says. 'It would have been better, but it would also have been intolerable, for Harlem had needed something to smash. To smash something is the ghetto's chronic need.'

The self-hatred manifested in the riots is reflected in Baldwin's troubled relations with his forbidding stepfather, an austere minister who rejected his stepson's ambition to become a writer and whose life had taken a downward spiral into madness. The source of his madness was self-hatred. Baldwin finds that both his stepfather's power as a preacher and his bitterness as a man reside in his conflicted racial consciousness. 'It had something to do with his blackness, I think – he was very black – with his blackness and his beauty, and with the fact that he knew that he was black but did not know that he was beautiful.' When Baldwin finds a similar self-destructive rage in himself, he is shocked. When he is refused service in a segregated New Jersey restaurant, he hurls a glass pitcher at the frightened waitress and smashes a mirror behind her. After he escapes, he is conscious to two 'facts': that he could have been murdered and that he had been ready to commit murder. 'I saw nothing very clearly but I did see this: that my life, my *real* life, was in danger, and not from anything other people might do but from the hatred I carried in my heart.'

During the funeral Baldwin is led to reconsider the legacy his stepfather has bequeathed him: 'This was his legacy: nothing is ever escaped.' As he views the results of rage in the Harlem streets, he realizes what is important.

> It was necessary to hold on to the things that mattered. The dead man mattered, the new life mattered; blackness and whiteness did not matter; to believe that they did was to acquiesce in one's own destruction. Hatred, which could destroy so much, never failed to destroy the man who hated and this was an immutable law.

Baldwin's early essays and novels eloquently describe the struggle to create a complex human identity in the face of white racism. But in his later work, he came dangerously close to becoming the 'protest' writer that he had previously rejected. Instead it was Ralph Ellison who constructed the richest parable of black experience in *Invisible Man* (1952). Ellison's peerless novel adumbrates the theme of achieving identity most eloquently where the movement from invisibility to visibility is accomplished through a process of self-acceptance and self-creation. Though sociologists describe blacks as a minority of 'high visibility' within the dominant white culture in America, Ellison correctly sees them as invisible. As his hero remarks on the first page of the novel: 'I am invisible simply because people refuse to see me…When they approach me they see only their surroundings, themselves, or figments of their imagination – indeed, everything and anything except me.' The problem of the recognition of black people resides, of course, in the blindness of white people. But as Ellison describes it, this white blindness has a profound effect on the way blacks see themselves. What his black protagonist must learn is to *see* himself in order to learn to *be* himself. A primary theme of *Invisible Man* is the search for and creation of identity.

In *Invisible Man* the *bildungsroman* takes on a surreal character. Ellison tells the story of a poor but ambitious black youth who energetically tries to rise in the world but is thwarted by the institutions of racism in America. The invisible man is betrayed at every turn: by conservative black administrators who attempt to 'educate' him in the South and by radical white benefactors who try to 'radical-ize' him in the North. Indeed, the whole of his experience can be summed up in a dream he has at the beginning of the novel. The hero dreams that he was taken to the circus by his grandfather where he was given a briefcase as an award for being a 'good Negro'. Inside the briefcase there is an official letter which holds out the promise of future success. But when he opens the envelope he discovers that it contains another envelope and in that another and so on. When, after a wearying effort, he comes to the final envelope it contains this message which reveals his true situation: 'To Whom It May Concern…Keep this Nigger-Boy Running.'

This dream forms the pattern of the hero's life. At every stage of his develop-ment he is given a piece of paper which states his new identity and promises to take him one more step up the ladder of success. For Ellison, this is the seductive delusion of the American dream. For what the dream really says is: 'Keep this Nigger-Boy Running.' Finally, the invisible man must burn all the pieces of white paper which have governed his life in order to create his own black identity. In the end, he must go underground in order to be able to find himself. And this is what he literally does. Pursued by a black-and-white mob, he falls down an open manhole and decides to stay there until he can figure out what to do. In the epilogue, he decides to resurface in order to take his place in a society which still refuses to recognize his existence.

What is most remarkable about *Invisible Man* is Ellison's decision to situate his novel not in the line of protest novels like Wright's *Native Son* but in the main-stream tradition of classic American literature. 'Indeed,' he wrote in accepting the National Book Award, 'if I were asked in all seriousness just what I consid-ered to be the chief significance of *Invisible Man* as a fiction, I would reply: Its experimental attitude, and its attempt to return to the mood of personal moral responsibility for democracy which typified the best of our nineteenth-century fiction.'[5] Beginning with its epigraph from Melville's novella, 'Benito Cereno', his novel echoes the great nineteenth-century tradition of American writing from Poe through Twain.

Published in 1952, just two years before the Supreme Court struck down segregation, *Invisible Man* is a prophetic book. Though blacks were still virtually 'invisible' in American society in the early 1950s, the Civil Rights movement was poised to change all that. In his novel Ellison made the audacious claim that black experience was as authentically American as apple pie. His nameless protagonist is a typical American hero who claims to belong to 'the great American tradition of tinkers...kin to Ford, Edison, and Franklin'. Like the early leaders of the Civil Rights movement, Ellison believed in integration but not assimilation. He was a true cultural pluralist who saw the United States as the sum of its many ethnic parts. In an essay written after the publication of *Invisible Man,* he argued that all of American culture – 'our jokes, our tall tales, even our sports' – was 'inflected' by jazz and influenced by the African-American notion of 'soul'. He wrote, 'An expression of American diversity within unity, of blackness with whiteness, soul announces the presence of a creative struggle against the realities of existence.'

The audacious achievement of Ellison's novel and Baldwin's essays in *Notes of a Native Son* and *The Fire Next Time* (1963) placed black experience at the center of American life. But in the late 1960s, in a time of intoxicating radicalism, their acceptance of the complex duality of African-American experience came under attack from a younger generation of writers and intellectuals who adopted the politics of Black Power and a separatist 'Black Aesthetic'. Though the black protest movement produced the polemical plays of Le Roi Jones (Imamu Amiri Baraka), the poetic broadsides of Don Lee (Haki R. Mahubuti), and the autobiographical writings of Eldridge Cleaver, it was quickly overshadowed by the artistic achievements of more accomplished artists like the poet Robert Hayden (*Words in the Mourning Time*, 1970) and the novelist Ernest Gaines (*The Autobiography of Miss Jane Pittman*, 1971). Soon they were overtaken by a new generation of talented black women including Toni Morrison and Alice Walker who, as we shall see, revitalized and popularized African-American writing in exciting new ways.

The triumph of ethnic writing

Beginning in the 1970s, writers of other ethnic backgrounds began to receive both popular and critical recognition. Native Americans like Scott Momaday (*House Made of Dawn*, 1968) and Leslie Marmon Silko (*Ceremony*, 1977), Hispanics like Richard Vasquez (*Chicano*, 1970) and Oscar Higuelos (*The Mambo Kings Play Songs of Love*, 1989); Asians like Maxine Hong Kingston (*The Woman Warrior*, 1976) and Amy Tan (*The Joy Luck Club*, 1989) all illuminated other aspects of America's multicultural heritage. Yet despite the success of individual writers, these ethnic groups are still overshadowed by the achievements of black and Jewish writers.

With the awarding of Toni Morrison's Nobel Prize in 1993, African-American literature received international recognition, confirming James Baldwin's claim that 'The story of the Negro in America is the story of America – or, more precisely, it is the story of Americans.' Together with the distinction of Nobel Prize winners Saul Bellow and Isaac Bashevis Singer, the international celebrity of filmmakers Woody Allen and Spike Lee and the global acceptance of jazz as America's classical music, it is clear that a once marginal ethnic consciousness now occupies the center of American culture, prompting the novelist Gore Vidal to complain that the last cultural minority left in America is the white Anglo-Saxon Protestant (WASP).

Abstract expressionism

The dominant characteristics of postwar American literature can also be found in the new painting called Abstract Expressionism that emerged in the decade after World War II: the predominance of an older generation of Modernist masters, a new pessimism about social progress and human nature and a turning inward and retreat from the rendering of social reality to the expression of personal experience. Just as the postwar world of letters was dominated by Hemingway, Faulkner and Eliot, so the art world still lived under the shadow of European Modernism. Picasso was the dominant figure in painting while the two major avant-garde movements between the world wars (Surrealism and Dada) were born and bred in Europe. Though many European artists looked to America for inspiration in their love affair with modernity and popular culture, American painting still represented a provincial backwater.

But at the end of the 1930s this backwater became the home of an entire generation of European artists and intellectuals who fled the rise of fascism. The artists who came to America ranged, literally, from A to Z: including Josef Albers, Andre Breton, Marc Chagall, Salvador Dali, Max Ernst, Ferdinand Leger, Piet Mondrian and Ossip Zadkine. 'When Paris fell to the Nazis in 1940, the center of global art was suddenly cut off from the rest of the world,' Irving Sandler concludes in *The Triumph of American Painting* (1970). 'Thus, by an act of war, New York became the international art capital.'

At this moment, Europe experienced the biggest brain drain in its history. At the same time, the rise of new galleries, museums and art schools made modern art accessible to a new generation of American artists and art lovers. And it made, says Sandler, 'the vanguard in New York ... the most knowledgeable in the world'. The critic Clement Greenberg wrote that by 1940, New York 'had caught up with Paris as Paris had not yet caught up with herself, and a group of relatively obscure American artists already possessed the fullest painting culture of their time'. This was unprecedented in the history of American art.

The rise of fascism called into question the progressive ideologies that flourished in the 1930s. Whereas social critics had stressed utopian tendencies in social thought, now the philosopher Hannah Arendt compared the evolution of German fascism and Russian communism in *The Origins of Totalitarianism* (1951). Whereas social scientists had emphasized the role of environmentalism in eliminating social evils, now the Protestant theologian Reinhold Niebuhr stressed the persistence of Evil in human nature in *The Irony of American History* (1952). Whereas Marxists had depicted the social world of economic behavior as the primary field of human activity, now the neo-Freudian psychiatrist Erich Fromm identified the inner world of psychic experience as the primary sphere in *The Art of Loving* (1956). In intellectual thought, there was a retreat from *society* to *psyche*. Richard Pells explains, 'Above all, having rejected the notion that political ideologies and organized social movements would provide some form of salvation for themselves and their society, the postwar intellectuals reemphasized the virtues of privacy and personal fulfillment.'

In this changed environment, painters began to turn from the representation of the public world to the expression of the private realm. 'In response to World War II and the intellectual climate generated by it, the future Abstract Expressionists came to believe that they faced a crisis in subject matter,' observes Sandler. 'Prevailing ideologies – socialist, nationalist, and Utopian – and the styles identified with them – Social Realism, Regionalism, and geometric abstraction – lost credibility in their eyes.' Instead, 'the Abstract Expressionists turned to their own private visions and insights in an anxious search for new values. The urgent need for meanings that felt truer to their experience gave rise to new ways of seeing – to formal innovations.'

This inward turning became a voyage of discovery. Artists turned to psychology and myth rather than to politics or sociology. Instead they attempted to transform painting into an existential act, which was called Action Painting. In *The Tradition of the New* (1959), the critic Harold Rosenberg described the process. 'At a certain moment the canvas began to appear to one American painter after another as an arena in which to act – rather than as a space in which to reproduce, re-design, analyze, or "express" an object, actual or imagined. What was to go on the canvas was not a picture but an event,' he wrote. 'The painter no longer approached his easel with an image in his mind; he went up to it with material in his hand to do something to that other piece of material in front of him. The image would be the result of this encounter.'

In this way, Action Painting became a process and not a product, calling into question the separation of the world of art from the world of life. 'A painting that is an act is inseparable from the biography of the artist,' announced Rosenberg. 'The act-painting is of the same metaphysical substance as the artist's existence. The new painting has broken down every distinction between art and life.'

Jackson Pollock

No painter exemplified Rosenberg's notion of Action Painting as well as Jackson Pollock. A Westerner, Pollock began as a student of Thomas Hart Benton, the Missouri painter whose celebrations of Americana were so much a part of the quest for an authentic American art in the 1930s. But as Pollock developed, he embarked on an artistic journey from realism through symbolism to pure painting. By the time he discovered his true style, the subject of his paintings was painting itself.

> My painting does not come from the easel. I prefer to tack the unstretched canvas to the hard wall or the floor. I need the resistance of a hard surface. On the floor I am more at ease. I feel nearer, more a part of the painting, since this way I can walk around it, work from the four sides and literally be *in* the painting. This is akin to the method of the Indian sand painters of the West.

I continue to get further away from the usual painter's tools such as easel, palette, brushes, etc. I prefer sticks, trowels, knives, and dripping fluid paint or a heavy impasto with sand, broken glass, and other foreign matter added.

When I am *in* my painting, I am not aware of what I am doing. It is only after a sort of 'get acquainted' period that I see what I have been about. I have no fears about making changes, destroying the image, etc., because the painting has a life of its own. I try to let it come through. It is only when I lose contact with the painting that the result is a mess. Otherwise there is pure harmony, an easy give and take, and the painting comes out well.[6]

Pollock's new drip technique and his allover paintings first challenged and then conquered the postwar art world. Sandler notes, 'The "drip" pictures shocked most people who saw them when they were first shown in 1948. Pollock's departure from traditional techniques did violence to conventional notions of what art was supposed to be; typical was one critic's characterization of Pollock as Jack the Dripper.' But by the time of his untimely death in 1956, he was the first American modern master and perhaps the most influential contemporary artist in the world.

Pollock's celebrity was part of a cultural paradigm shift in the postwar period: the emergence of a romantic antihero sometimes called 'the angry young man' or 'the rebel without a cause'. In *New Art City* (2005), Jed Perl notes, 'there was nothing particularly surprising in the images that were circulating in the early 1950s of Jackson Pollock as a contemporary romantic rebel in blue jeans and a T-shirt, whose stance and demeanor somehow came out of the same crucible as the Marlon Brando of *A Streetcar Named Desire*.' But Brando, Pollock and James Dean, another anguished cultural icon who died in a car crash in 1955, defined the alienation of the early Cold War years.

The abstract expressionists

After World War II, American painters focused almost exclusively on private experience and personal vision. In this inward turning, they were strongly influenced by the Surrealists, many of whom were living in New York. But Surrealism served more as an example than as an influence on the Abstract Expressionists. Pollock observed that the Surrealist emphasis on the unconscious as the source of art interested him more than the Surrealist painters did. Finally, what bound the New York painters was, Sandler says, 'a common esthetic evolution: the rejection of existing realist and geometric tendencies, the attraction to Surrealist content and the technique of automatism, and – during the late 1940's and early 1950s – the achievement of new styles that could no longer be subsumed under existing labels.'

The Abstract Expressionists were not a homogeneous school. Abstract Expressionism contained contrasting streams of gesture painting and color-field painting. What characterizes gesture painting is its expressionistic dynamism, which contrasted with the static, iconic quality of color-field painting. The most famous gesture painters were, after Pollock, Willem de Kooning, Franz Kline and Arshile Gorky. Kline identified gesture painting with drawing, a quality that is evident in his linear black-and-white paintings. Similarly, de Kooning spoke of his 'natural aptitude for drawing'. Like Kline, de Kooning pursued the spontaneous and eschewed the theoretical. He did not like the word 'abstract' because, he said, 'it comes from the lighttower of philosophers' and creates a situation where the aesthetic precedes the painting. De Kooning's rejection of what he called 'the comfort of "pure form"' led him to experiment with reconstructing figurative art but in a highly expressionist way, as in his series of portraits of women. These spontaneous celebrations and deformations of the subject have a highly emotional charge.

In other words, gestural painting is not premeditated. It involves discovering the painting in the process of painting it. Another artist, William Baziotes, said: 'I cannot evolve any concrete theory about painting. What happens on the canvas is unpredictable and surprising to me ... As I work, or when the painting is finished, the subject reveals itself.' Similarly, Arshile Gorky's progress from representation to gestural abstraction was a journey of discovery from outer to inner reality. He began with a memory of his childhood in Armenia and progressed through an inward journey into spiritual autobiography in paintings like *Diary of a Seducer* and *The Liver is the Coxcomb*.

The leading color-field painters, Adolph Gottlieb, Mark Rothko and Barnett Newman, all expressed their affinity with gestural painting. 'To us, art is an adventure into an unknown world ... of the imagination [which] is fancy-free and violently opposed to common sense,' they wrote. At the same time, they pointed to the iconic character of their paintings. Newman asked, 'if we are living in a time without a legend or mythos that can be called sublime, if we refuse to admit any exaltations in pure relations, if we refuse to live in the abstract, how can we be creating a sublime art?' For Newman, the new painting found new subjects for the human desire for exaltation. 'Instead of making *cathedrals* out of Christ, man, or "life", we are making it out of ourselves, out of our own feelings.'

One characteristic of color-field paintings was their large size. Rothko observed that he painted large pictures not to imitate the 'grandiose and pompous' paintings of the past but to create something 'very intimate and human'. In other words, his color-field paintings were created out of the same feeling as Pollock's gestural paintings. And they create a similar sense of awe. Sandler suggests that the color-field painters were visionary artists:

> In the past, revelation has been the function of organized religion – including, of course, religious art. In the modern era, religious dogmas, rituals, symbols, and images have all lost their power to grip the imagination of artists. However, the yearning for a transcendental realm of being has not lessened, and some artists continue to seek means of expressing private visions of their infinite yearnings, in the hope of replacing the time-worn visions of organized religions, and this in a universe the existentially minded believed lacking in ultimate meaning.

The advent of Pop Art

The canonization of Pollock and the establishment of the New York School in the 1950s as the dominant movement in postwar American painting led inevitably to a reaction among artists. Already by the time of Pollock's death, younger painters were rebelling against the hegemony of Abstract Expressionism and its symbolism. Jasper Johns began to paint simple objects like targets and flags in 1955. Elsworth Kelly painted cool hard-edge abstractions like *New York, N.Y.* in 1957. Soon Abstract Expressionism was overtaken by history and the advent of Pop Art. We had entered the era of the commercialization of art and the art of commercialization.

The rise and subsequent decline of Pop Art further fragmented the art scene and eroded its power at the end the 1970s. Like the decline of serious Broadway drama, the commodification of the art work weakened New York's role as a capital of culture. This went hand in hand with the economic decline of the city during the 1980s. Nevertheless, the new painting that emerged in the 1940s and flourished in the 1950s changed the nature of modern art and redefined the project of contemporary painting. In this regard, de Kooning and Rothko had the same impact on the art world that Bellow and Miller had on the world of letters. And here is a final similarity between this generation of American writers and artists: their common immigrant background. As Rosenberg observed:

> The new American 'abstract' art, the first to appear here without a foreign return address, constituted, interestingly enough, the first art movement in the United States in which immigrants and sons of immigrants have been leaders in creating and disseminating a style: Gorky, de Kooning, Hofmann, Rothko, Gottlieb, Lassaw, Reinhardt, Newman, Baziotes, Guston...Apparently, the role for newcomers in the aesthetic affirmation of America has been as significant as in the physical exploration and building of it.

NOTES

1. Richard Pells, *The Liberal Mind in a Conservative Age,* New York: Harper & Row, 1985, p. 187.
2. Daniel Hoffman (ed.), *The Harvard Guide to Contemporary American Writing,* Cambridge, MA: Harvard University Press, 1976, p. 408.
3. Quoted ibid., p. 412.
4. Søren Kierkegaard, *The Sickness Unto Death,* Princeton, NJ: Princeton University Press, 1983.
5. Ralph Ellison, *Shadow and Act,* New York: Random House, p. 102.
6. Jackson Pollock, 'My Painting', *Possibilities* I (Winter 1947–8), p. 79.

RECOMMENDED READING

Daniel Bell, *The End of Ideology,* rev. edn, Cambridge, MA: Harvard University Press, 2000.
Ihab Hassan, *Radical Innocence,* Princeton, NJ: Princeton University Press, 1961.
David Halberstam, *The Fifties,* New York: Villard, 1993.
Haynes Johnson, *The Age of Anxiety,* New York: Harcourt, 2005.
Kenneth Keniston, *The Uncommitted,* New York: Harcourt Brace, 1965.

Richard Pells, *The Liberal Mind in a Conservative Age*, New York: Harper & Row, 1985.

Jed Perl, *New Art City*, New York: Alfred Knopf, 2005.

David Riesman, Nathan Glazer and Reuel Denney, *The Lonely Crowd*, revised edition, New Haven, CT: Yale University Press, 2001.

Harold Rosenberg, *The Tradition of the New*, New York: Horizon, 1959.

Irving Sandler, *The Triumph of American Painting*, New York: Praeger, 1970.

Stephen Whitfield, *The Culture of the Cold War*, second edition, Baltimore: Johns Hopkins University Press, 1996.

PART III

War in Vietnam and Revolution in the Streets

The Inauguration of John F. Kennedy: In the foreground from left to right are Dwight Eisenhower, Chief Justice Earl Warren, JFK, Lyndon Johnson and Richard Nixon

Year	Politics	Culture
1960	• Sit-in protests challenge segregation in the South • John F. Kennedy is elected president • Students for a Democratic Society (SDS) is founded • Students Non-violent Coordinating Committee (SNCC) is founded • Young Americans for Freedom (YAF) is founded and issues The Sharon Statement • FDA approves sale of Enovid as a birth control pill	• Edward Albee, *The Zoo Story* • Paul Goodman, *Growing Up Absurd* • Daniel Bell, *The End of Ideology* • John Updike, *Rabbit, Run* • John Cassavetes, *Shadows*
1961	• Bay of Pigs fiasco in Cuba • Freedom Riders challenge segregation in the South • Berlin Wall is created • President's Commission on the Staus of Women is created	• Jane Jacobs, *The Death and Life of Great American Cities* • Joseph Heller, *Catch-22* • Walker Percy, *The Moviegoer* • Allen Ginsberg, *Kaddish*
1962	• Cuban missile crisis • George Wallace is elected governor of Alabama • University of Mississippi is integrated by federal marshals	• Edward Albee, *Who's Afraid of Virginia Woolf?* • Vladimir Nabokov, *Pale Fire* • John Steinbeck awarded the Nobel Prize for Literature • Ken Kesey, *One Flew Over the Cuckoo's Nest* • Michael Harrington, *The Other America* • John Frankenheimer, *Manchurian Candidate* (film) • SDS issues The Port Huron Statement
1963	• Martin Luther King, Jr. gives 'I have a dream' speech at civil rights March on Washington • Medgar Evers is murdered in Mississippi • South Vietnam military coup overthrows Diem • President Kennedy is assassinated and succeeded by Lyndon Johnson	• Betty Friedan, *The Feminine Mystique* • Mary McCarthy, *The Group* • Thomas Pynchon, *V.* • James Baldwin, *The Fire Next Time* • Stanley Kubrick, *Dr, Strangelove*
1964	• Civil Rights Act • Freedom Summer; three civil right workers are murdered in Mississippi • Gulf of Tonkin Resolution • Johnson wins presidential election by largest percentage of popular vote ever • Berkeley Free Speech Movement (FSM) • Martin Luther King, Jr. wins Nobel Peace Prize	• Saul Bellow, *Herzog* • John Berryman, *77 Dream Songs* • Ernest Hemingway, *A Moveable Feast* • Herbert Marcuse, *One-Dimensional Man* • Marshall McLuhan, *Understanding Media* • Arthur Miller, *After the Fall* • First Beatles tour of the United States
1965	• Johnson's Great Society programs are passed by Congress • Voting Rights Act • Johnson begins major American military engagement in Vietnam • Watts riot • First campus teach-ins against the Vietnam War • Malcolm X is assassinated	• Robert Coover, *The Origins of the Brunists* • Alex Haley, *The Autobiography of Malcolm X* • Flannery O'Connor, *Everything That Rises Must Converge* • *The Autobiography of Malcom X* • Edward Albee, *Tiny Alice* • Robert Lowell, *The Old Glory*
1966	• Deepening American military engagement in Vietnam • Mao initiates the Chinese Cultural Revolution • Crime begins long-term rise • Riots spread in inner cities • Black Panther Party founded in Oakland, California • National Organization of Women (NOW) is founded • Ronald Reagan is elected governor of California	• Truman Capote, *In Cold Blood* • John Barth, *Giles Goat-Boy* • Bernard Malamud, *The Fixer* • Thomas Pynchon, *The Crying of Lot 49*
1967	• Six-Day Arab-Israeli War • Inner city riots climax in Newark and Detroit • 'Summer of Love' originates in San Francisco • Antiwar movement gathers force, March on the Pentagon • Defense Secretary Robert McNamara is disillusioned by Vietnam	• Mike Nichols, *The Graduate* (film) • Arthur Penn, *Bonnie and Clyde* (film) • William Styron, *The Confessions of Not Turner* • Bernard Malamud, *The Fixer* • Richard Brautigan, *Trout Fishing in America*
1968	• Tet offensive • My Lai massacre • Antiwar candidate Eugene McCarthy challenges President in New Hampshire • Johnson withdraws from 1968 presidential race • Martin Luther King and Robert Kennedy are assassinated • Inner city riots damage Washington, DC • Columbia University student strike • Riots at the Democratic Party convention in Chicago • George Wallace runs as third-party candidate for president • Nixon is elected president • American astronauts orbit the moon	• Joan Didion, *Slouching Towards Bethlehem* • Norman Mailer, *The Armies of the Night* • John Updike, *Couples* • Arthur Miller, *The Price* • Galt MacDermott, *Hair*

CHAPTER 5

Kennedy, Johnson and the Crisis of American Liberalism

The era of John F. Kennedy (JFK) and Lyndon B. Johnson (LBJ) represented first the triumph and then the crisis of American postwar liberalism. The great promise of the Kennedy and early Johnson years was followed by violent upheavals that traumatized American society and transformed American politics. Except for the new salience of civil rights, American politics in 1964 would still have been familiar to a New Dealer. This would no longer be the case in 1968, when the war in Vietnam, riots in the black ghettos, new movements like feminism and the counterculture, and a conservative backlash against liberalism produced new cleavages that ended the politics of the New Deal.

The politics of Kennedy's presidency

In his inaugural address, the 44-year-old Kennedy declared that 'the torch has passed to a new generation of Americans, born in this century'. This statement did not just constitute a reminder that the youngest elected president in American history was succeeding the oldest up to then. To an unusual degree, the election of 1960 witnessed the rise to power of a new generation. FDR, Truman and Eisenhower, as well as most of their senior aides, had been born in the Victorian age. By contrast, all presidents from Kennedy to the elder Bush were born in the twentieth century, were shaped during their formative years by the experiences of the Depression and World War II, and rose in politics within the 'American century' that Henry Luce proclaimed in 1941.

Liberals viewed Kennedy as a worthy successor to Franklin Roosevelt who would use the power of the presidency to lead American society to new progressive conquests despite congressional resistance. Moreover, JFK expressed the boundless optimism of the postwar generation that had witnessed unparalleled growth and technological progress; he launched the space program that sent men to the moon. His administration believed in the ability of the federal government to solve intractable social problems by the application of reason and science, putting American ingenuity to work for social improvement by brand-new technocratic methods.

JFK's establishment as the new idol of the liberals was not preordained. The Kennedy family had a past that was controversial. Joseph Kennedy, the family's patriarch, had been a lamentable advocate of appeasement while serving as US ambassador in Britain in the later 1930s and early 1940s. Moreover, the Kennedys had supported McCarthy during the Red Scare; JFK's younger brother Robert even served on McCarthy's staff for several months. Finally, as Catholic Irish Americans, the Kennedys could easily have been identified with the patronage politics of city machines, which still tended to be led by Catholic politicians like Mayor Richard Daly of Chicago.

A large part of JFK's success derived from his upper-class status that separated him from the typical Catholic Irish-American politician. His father Joseph had acquired a fabulous fortune in the stock market in the 1920s and withdrawn it just before the Crash of '29, thereafter using his great wealth to gain political influence for himself and his sons. JFK had gone to prep school, Harvard and Oxford. He was also glamorous and charismatic. In short, he had many of the social advantages of the patrician WASP elite of the Northeast that had benefited the Roosevelts before him.

At the same time, Kennedy's Catholicism strongly appealed to the largely Catholic urban masses of the North, who responded enthusiastically to the opportunity of electing one of their own to the nation's highest office. Kennedy's father also maintained links with the urban machines and used his influence in 1960 to help secure the Democratic nomination for him. Yet in his campaign for the nomination Kennedy needed to prove to his fellow Democrats that his Catholicism would not be an obstacle to victory in the general elections, as it had been for the Democratic candidate Al Smith in 1928.

Consequently, Kennedy conducted a campaign that emphasized the primaries over the party bosses, even though they yielded fewer than one-third of the delegates. By assembling a personal staff under his brother Robert that conducted a well-funded primary campaign, Kennedy pointed to the future of American presidential elections. The key primary was West Virginia, a state in which Catholics comprised only three percent of the population. When Kennedy soundly defeated Hubert Humphrey, one of the leading liberal politicians of that time, after a campaign in which Kennedy had made tolerance the issue, the road to the nomination was open. Lyndon Johnson had sat out the primaries, hoping to get the nomination after a deadlock at the convention. But, by that time, Kennedy already had the image of a winner, which carried many party bosses over to his side. In the end, Johnson, arguably the most powerful Senate Majority Leader ever, became running mate to one of his Senate subordinates who had not left much of a mark there. Amusingly, when Eisenhower called Congress back into session in the summer of 1960, Kennedy felt obliged to return to his seat at the back of the chamber, under the leadership of his running mate.

In the general election Kennedy confronted Vice-President Richard Nixon, who had secured the Republican nomination easily. In the five months up to the elections in November, support for the two candidates in opinion polls was evenly divided. One innovation of the 1960 campaign was the televised debates between the two candidates. In the first debate, which attracted an enormous number of viewers on account of its novelty, Kennedy emerged as the winner, apparently because of his image. Opinion polls found that Nixon 'won' by a small margin among those who listened to the debate on the radio, whereas Kennedy 'won' by a large margin among the five-times larger group who saw the debate on television.

Kennedy's victory in the elections was very narrow. He got just 131,000 votes more than Nixon, 49.7 against 49.6 percent. In the Electoral College he had a comfortable lead of 303 votes against Nixon's 219. But had Texas and Illinois, both decided by narrow margins, gone the other way, Nixon would have won. Local instances of pro-Kennedy fraud were alleged in both states; but Nixon decided against contesting the election, either out of statesmanship or because there had been countervailing instances of pro-Nixon fraud in rural Illinois. The tendency of the Democratic Chicago machine to tamper with vote counts was legendary, but rural Republican machine politicians in Illinois were apt to urge loyal voters to 'vote early and often'. In the days before Watergate, small-scale local voting fraud was not unusual in American politics.

Religion was particularly important in the 1960 election. Kennedy got 78 percent of the Catholic vote, compared with Stevenson's 54 percent in 1956. Protestants gave Kennedy 38 percent, compared with Stevenson's 40 percent in 1956; evidently, Northern and Western white Protestants opposed Kennedy, since he did better than Stevenson in the mainly Protestant South and among black Protestants. Moreover, Kennedy got 81 percent of the Jewish vote, so that his support may be summarized as the South, African Americans and the non-Protestant denominations.

Civil rights

Kennedy's dependence on both the South and African Americans explains his initial hesitation in taking sides in the contested issue of civil rights that gradually moved to the center of national politics in the early 1960s. A new grassroots Civil Rights movement emerged in 1960 when a wave of sit-ins by young blacks challenged segregation across the South. Some 3000 protesters were arrested and jailed for trespassing or disturbing the peace. Still, the 1960 sit-ins remained a matter of only regional concern; civil rights were not a significant issue in the 1960 elections.

This began to change in May 1961, when activists boarded interstate buses in 'freedom rides' across the South, challenging segregation in interstate bus terminals; in December 1960 the Supreme Court had declared segregation at the terminals an unconstitutional barrier to interstate commerce. Racist mobs attacked the freedom riders viciously, raising the specter of large-scale racial violence in the South. In Birmingham, Alabama, the police chief, Eugene 'Bull' Connor, gave the Ku Klux Klan 15 minutes to beat up demonstrators before the police intervened, and one protester suffered permanent brain damage.

Kennedy initially reacted to this racist violence by telling a civil rights aide: 'Can't you get your goddamned friends off these buses?' At this point, he seemed worried primarily about the damage that the violence was doing to the international image of the United States. Kennedy was not unmoved by the plight of the blacks; if necessary, he decided that he would protect civil rights. But he sought to delay movement on this contentious issue, hoping, much like Eisenhower, that in time the South would come to accept reform. Although his election and stirring rhetoric about moving the nation forward had boosted the Civil Rights movement, JFK had to be pushed to action by it. Characteristically, he ordered the desegregation of interstate terminals in September 1961 because the freedom riders defied his wishes and continued their protests. In 1962 he deployed federal marshals and troops to get one black student into the University of Mississippi, much like Eisenhower in Little Rock in 1958.

The struggle over civil rights intensified with the election of George Wallace as governor of Alabama in 1962. Wallace's inaugural address in January 1963 contained such powerful rhetoric in defense of segregation that it made him the leader of the South's defiant resistance to change. Wallace whipped up anti-Northern feelings by complaining that after the Civil War there had been 'no government hand-outs, no Marshall Plan aid,' only 'the vulturous carpetbagger and federal troops.' He declared defiantly, 'from this cradle of the Confederacy, from this very heart of the great Anglo-Saxon Southland, we sound the drum of freedom ... I draw the line in the dust and toss the gauntlet before the feet of tyranny, and I say: segregation now, segregation tomorrow, segregation forever.'[1]

Martin Luther King's magnificent response came during the March on Washington in August 1963, when 200,000 civil rights supporters gathered peacefully in front of the Lincoln memorial. King's speech was the greatest restatement of his generation of the liberal values upon which the United States was founded: 'I say to you, today, my friends, so even though we face the difficulties of today and tomorrow, I still have a dream. It is a dream deeply rooted in the American dream. I have a dream that one day this nation will rise up and live out the true meaning of its creed – we hold these truths to be self-evident, that all men are created equal.' He concluded his speech with these celebrated words:

> When we allow freedom to ring, when we let it ring from every village and every hamlet, from every state and every city, we will be able to speed up that day when all of God's children – black men and white men, Jews and Gentiles, Protestants and Catholics – will be able to join hands and sing in the words of the old Negro spiritual, 'Free at last, free at last, thank God Almighty, we are free at last.'

Not all African Americans were swayed by Martin Luther King's grand pluralist vision. To the violence and the white 'Anglo-Saxon' monism of George Wallace, some blacks wished to juxtapose a violent monism of their own. The black nationalist leader Malcolm X sneered at the 'farce in Washington'. His Black Muslim followers wished to separate themselves from the rest of American society, not to integrate. While relatively few followed Black Islam, it was a reminder that the struggle against segregation could take a more violent turn.

Confronted with the mobilization of clashing political forces and the growing racist violence – including the Ku Klux Klan bombing of a black Baptist Church in Birmingham, Alabama, in September 1963 in which four black girls were killed – Kennedy abandoned his earlier procrastination and firmly supported desegregation. By this time, Americans outside the South had been outraged by the violence against blacks, especially when perpetrated by police forces run by bigots like Birmingham's 'Bull' Connor. The nation had been shocked by brutal images of racist violence in the remote South that were brought by television directly into living rooms across the world. Kennedy's civil rights bill, the most comprehensive legislative plan to end segregation, was proceeding fairly well in Congress before Kennedy was assassinated in November 1963. In this as in other matters, his agenda had to be completed by his successor Johnson.

Kennedy's legislative record is relatively poor, in large part because his presidency was tragically cut short. He was unable to pass major reforms in the manner of FDR since he confronted in Congress the same conservative alliance of Southern Democrats and Republicans that had frustrated Truman's legislative endeavors. Rather than waste political capital in futile legislative battles, Kennedy aimed at getting reelected in 1964 by a more impressive margin than what he called the 'tremendous landslide' of 'one-tenth of one percent' that had 'swept' him into office, so that he could pursue an ambitious legislative agenda in his second term. But there was another reason for the paucity of his legislative record: he focused most of his energies on the grave matters of foreign policy that took up almost his entire inaugural address.

Kennedy's foreign policy

Kennedy's inaugural address was the American leadership's greatest call for the mobilization of America in the worldwide struggle against communism: 'In the long history of the world, only a few generations have been granted the role of defending freedom in its hour of maximum danger.' It also expressed a boundless confidence in America's capabilities that would become unthinkable a few years later. Kennedy proclaimed: 'Let every nation know, whether it wishes us well or ill, that we shall pay any price, bear any burden, meet any hardship, support any friend, oppose any foe to assure the survival and the success of liberty.'

One burden that American society was to bear under Kennedy was increased defense spending – up 13 percent from 1961 to 1964. Kennedy had used the alleged 'missile gap' against Nixon in the 1960 elections and felt committed to increasing the American nuclear arsenal even after he was informed that the missile gap was nonexistent. He increased spending on conventional forces, abandoning Eisenhower's reliance on the threat of a nuclear response to deter Soviet aggression. Instead, Kennedy adopted the doctrine of 'flexible response' that sought to create deterrent capabilities at every level of the ladder of conflict escalation. This meant that the United States needed strong conventional forces in order to be able to respond to conventional aggression instead of facing the dilemma: retreat or nuclear war. While Eisenhower had been deeply worried that high military spending would undermine the American economy, Kennedy thought that it could stimulate aggregate demand and thus expand output. Indeed, he was so much influenced by Keynesian ideas that in 1963 he sought to increase the federal deficit by proposing the first major postwar income tax cut, which Congress passed shortly after his death. Since 1980 this combination of higher defense spending, lower income taxes and larger deficits is associated with Ronald Reagan.

The first test of the new flexible response doctrine came with the new Berlin crisis that erupted after Khrushchev issued a second six-month ultimatum in June 1961, demanding the withdrawal of Western forces from West Berlin. Whereas Eisenhower had reacted to Khrushchev's first ultimatum by threatening a nuclear strike, Kennedy reacted more 'flexibly' by activating 120,000 reservists to demonstrate that he had the option of defending West Berlin by conventional means. Khrushchev would not have risked war for Berlin, anyhow, as the Soviet archives have revealed. In August 1961 he found a different solution to the problem of East Germany's population drain via West Berlin by building a wall around it. The Berlin Wall was a striking admission of failure by the Soviet bloc. It must have been the only time in history that a wall was built not to keep the enemy out, but the citizens in. Still, as a practical matter the Wall did end East Germany's population drain and thereby helped stabilize the European postwar *status quo*. There were no comparably dangerous Cold War crises in Europe thereafter.

His dramatic confrontation with Khrushchev over Berlin notwithstanding, Kennedy thought that the main battlefields of the Cold War were shifting from Europe to the Third World. When Khrushchev announced Soviet support for anticolonial national liberation movements, Kennedy concluded that the next threat to the West would be guerrilla movements in Africa, Asia and Latin America backed by the Soviet Union, China or other communist powers such as Cuba.

Kennedy's thinking on the Third World departed from Eisenhower's in major ways. He sought to distance American policy from right-wing dictatorships and traditional oligarchies and to align it with the forces of socioeconomic and political progress in the Third World. He believed that democratization and modernization would shield developing countries from communist influence, much as postwar reconstruction and prosperity had protected Western Europe. Land reforms should be promoted to reduce wealth inequalities and weaken the traditional landed oligarchies' grip on political power. Industrialization should be facilitated to create a middle class that would make democratization possible. Authoritarian dictatorships should be replaced by elected governments.

Kennedy's 'Alliance for Progress' in the western hemisphere was indicative of this approach. While Franklin Roosevelt's 'good neighbor' policy had been confined to the noninterference by the United States in the internal affairs of Latin American countries, the Alliance for Progress sought to induce progressive reforms. When the Alliance was launched in Punta del Estes in 1961, the United States pledged $20 billion in aid to the 20 Latin American states that participated and agreed to implement progressive economic and political reforms. Kennedy's new approach was so appealing that Che Guevara participated as an observer in the Punta del Estes conference, though Cuba did not join the Alliance for Progress.

The problem with Kennedy's approach was that it underestimated the complexity of the modernization challenges in the Third World. He correctly saw the danger of the United States becoming identified with dictatorships and oligarchies that would sooner or later be swept away by modernization. But the old oligarchies were unwilling to give up their wealth and power without a fight. As a result, forces emerged on the left that had more radical views about needed reforms than Kennedy was willing to countenance. Guerrilla wars broke out in Venezuela, Guatemala and Colombia in 1962 and in Peru in 1965, followed by the short guerrilla war in Bolivia in 1967 in which Che Guevara was killed. Given the Cold War context, Kennedy and his successors were unwilling to allow a spread of Marxist regimes. They wanted reform, not revolution. As a result, Kennedy's initial optimism about progressive reforms in Latin America was overshadowed by the CIA's 'dirty wars' against the guerrilla movements. His progressive vision was often squeezed between the reactionary intransigence of the old oligarchies and the anti-American revolutionary fervor of the Marxist movements. It was only in the 1980s that Kennedy's farsighted vision of modernization and democratization came to fruition in large parts of the Third World.

Kennedy contributed to the polarization between reactionary oligarchies and revolutionary movements through his Cuban policy. By launching the CIA's Bay of Pigs invasion in April 1961, which had been planned under Eisenhower, yet denying the invading force of Cuban exiles the American air support that might have given them a chance to secure a beachhead, Kennedy got the worst of all possible worlds. The operation had no realistic chance of success, yet it fueled anti-Americanism in Latin America. Thereafter, President Kennedy and his brother Robert, the Attorney General, became obsessed with Castro. Under Robert Kennedy's supervision the CIA launched Operation Mongoose, which included 33 attempts to assassinate Castro.

Cuban missile crisis

The Soviet leadership responded to American efforts to overthrow Castro by deciding to deploy secretly in Cuba intermediate-range nuclear missiles, which would have placed most American cities within their reach. Had the deployment been completed, it would have altered the strategic balance by making the United States much more vulnerable to a nuclear attack. Yet the Soviet archives show that the primary Soviet objective was to deter an American invasion of Cuba rather than to change the strategic balance.

When American U2 spy planes revealed in October 1962 the still incomplete installation of Soviet nuclear missiles in Cuba, Kennedy decided to confront the Soviets publicly and demand the withdrawal of their missiles. The ensuing Cuban missile crisis was probably the most dangerous in the Cold War, though the archives have shown that both sides were prepared to fall back to more conciliatory positions than they took in public, rather than risk an escalation of the crisis. Perhaps if Kennedy had approached Khrushchev secretly, without publicizing the Soviet missile build-up in Cuba, he might have made it easier for the Soviets to withdraw the missiles without losing face.

In the event, Kennedy decided on a naval blockade of Cuba that would bar Soviet supplies needed for the completion of the missile systems. While this course was less dangerous than the bombardment of the missile sites that some of his advisors advocated, it still entailed the risk of American warships attacking Soviet transports that refused to allow inspections by the blockading forces. On 22 October an anxious population observed the first Soviet transports coming close to the blockaded area. If they were sunk, would the Soviet Union retaliate in West Berlin? Would an escalation acquire an uncontrollable dynamic towards a third world war?

The crisis began to be defused the next day, when the Soviet ships either sub-mitted to American inspections or turned around and left the area. A deal followed by which the Soviets withdrew the missile systems as well as most of their con-ventional forces from Cuba, while the United States guaranteed that it would not invade Cuba and also secretly withdrew its old intermediate nuclear missiles from Turkey that had already been scheduled for withdrawal before the crisis. Publicly, Kennedy was perceived as the clear winner in the crisis. He had stood up to the Soviets unflinchingly and had forced the withdrawal of their nuclear systems from the western hemisphere. Yet in a sense it is Khrushchev who attained his primary objective: the United States has not invaded Cuba – though Operation Mongoose resumed in mid-1963 – and Castro's regime has outlived the Soviet Union itself. At the time, both Castro and the anti-Castro Cuban exiles were outraged by the deal; Castro thought he was being left unprotected, while the exiles wanted Kennedy to overthrow him. But the two superpowers were wisely unwilling to push for maximal objectives that might risk a world war over Cuba.

Vietnam

In Kennedy's worldwide strategy of resisting communist guerrilla movements, his showcase was South Vietnam, a state covered by the South East Asia Treaty Organization (SEATO), the fall of which would supposedly undermine the cred-ibility of all American alliances. When Kennedy became president, both South Vietnam and Laos faced communist insurgencies. Eisenhower advised Kennedy to make a stand in Laos, since militarily a guerrilla war in South Vietnam could not be sustained without supplies and troops from North Vietnam via Laos. Instead, Kennedy withdrew from Laos under a neutrality agreement that only thinly disguised effective communist control of the country. He did not want to get militarily entangled in Laos because it bordered China; the Korean example in which China intervened militarily was still a recent memory. Yet his decision seriously handicapped his counterinsurgency strategy in South Vietnam.

Should Kennedy also have abandoned South Vietnam under the kind of neu-trality agreement that allowed him to slip out of Laos? The fear of undermining the credibility of SEATO and other American alliances was valid but exagger-ated. South Vietnam was in itself strategically and economically unimportant in the global balance of power. But alliances are undermined if their weakest members are thrown to the wolves because they happen to be unimportant. It must be emphasized that Ho Chi Minh's regime in the North was so harsh that hundreds of thousands of refugees were fleeing from it in the later 1950s and early 1960s. Therefore, abandoning the South would be problematic not only for the credibility of American alliances, but also from a liberal idealistic and humanitarian perspective.

On the other hand, South Vietnam turned out to be a truly rotten apple. The authoritarian regime of Ngo Dinh Diem was unable to control domestic develop-ments and unite its people against the communist insurgency, even though the flood of refugees from the North demonstrated what was in store if the com-munists won. The growth of the communist insurgency – in 1960 half a dozen local government officials were assassinated daily – showed the vulnerability of

the Diem regime. Moreover, Ho Chi Minh, the hero of the Vietnamese anticolonial struggle against the French, overshadowed Diem as a leader of Vietnamese
nationalism.

From the perspective of *Realpolitik,* which emphasizes geopolitical priorities and cost-benefit calculations, no American commitment to South Vietnam
should have been made in the first place. George Kennan argued as much in
1957 in the pages of *Foreign Affairs.* The costs of deepening America's engagement loomed large because of the manifest weakness of the Diem regime. The
costs of withdrawing from South Vietnam were not yet large, since the credibility
of America's alliance commitments would not be shaken if an ineffective regime
were undermined by a largely domestic insurgency. Moreover, the American
withdrawal from Laos had hardly undermined the worldwide credibility of
American alliances. The difference between the two was that South Vietnam was
much better known in the United States, making a withdrawal risky in terms of
a possible revival of McCarthyism.

But Kennedy and his foreign policy advisors, the most brilliant men of the
most powerful nation on earth, were far from making any mundane cost-benefit
calculations. In their boundless self-confidence, they assumed that America had
the resources, the expertize and the ingenuity to transform a rotten apple into
a peach and demonstrate to the communists that their new guerrilla strategy
would be defeated. Yet by deepening America's commitment, they also raised the
stakes. With each step towards a greater commitment, the cost of withdrawal in
terms of American credibility became larger.

The deepening commitment to South Vietnam created new problems for the
Kennedy administration. The loss of Laos worsened the military situation, since
the Viet Cong forces were powerfully augmented by materiel and manpower that
moved from North Vietnam via the Ho Chi Minh trail across southern Laos into
South Vietnam. Furthermore, American efforts to reform South Vietnam were
unsuccessful. Progressive reforms by outside *dictat* cannot quickly transform a
society in the best of circumstances; they were particularly difficult to implement
under conditions of growing insecurity. In addition, Diem resisted American
pressures for reform to avoid antagonizing the landholding oligarchy.

As a result, by August 1963 Kennedy was searching for an alternative to Diem.
When he was informed that a military coup was in the making, he effectively
gave his acquiescence; Diem was not warned about the impending coup, nor were
the coup leaders deterred. Diem was overthrown and murdered on November 1,
1963. Kennedy himself was killed 21 days later, bequeathing to his successor a
deep American commitment in South Vietnam. Under Kennedy's watch the number of American advisors in South Vietnam rose from less than 1000 to 16,000.
American indirect complicity in Diem's overthrow meant a greater political commitment to his successors. But most importantly, Kennedy had elevated South
Vietnam to the position of a test case in his global counterinsurgency strategy.

Lyndon Johnson's triumph

The hopes of the liberals for a strong president who would overcome congressional resistance and follow the liberal reform path charted by the New Deal

materialized not under Truman, nor under Kennedy, but under Lyndon Baines Johnson, who entered politics in the late 1930s as an ardent New Dealer. In the first two years of his presidency Johnson passed a series of liberal reforms that rivaled those of FDR himself. His hopes of becoming the greatest liberal reformer in American history seemed not unreasonable at the height of his success.

Johnson set the tempo by pushing Kennedy's civil rights bill through Congress in the spring of 1964, within months of succeeding Kennedy. He made civil rights his first priority for a number of reasons. First, being a Southerner (from Texas) he wished to escape the tag of a regional politician and to run in the elections of 1964 as a national leader. Second, he genuinely believed that government should help the weakest groups in society, including African Americans. Third, he astutely discerned that segregation was keeping the South behind the rest of the United States, marginalized because of its peculiarity.

In promoting the civil rights bill, Johnson clashed with his former Southern colleagues in Congress, the very men who had elevated him to the Senate's leadership in the 1950s. To overcome their resistance, he needed to create a congressional alliance between non-Southern Democrats and moderate Republicans. This alliance easily passed the civil rights bill in the House in February 1964. But the major battleground was in the Senate, where the Southerners were seasoned masters of the filibuster; in the late 1950s Senator Strom Thurmond had once spoken for over 24 hours, dehydrating himself beforehand so that he would not need to go to the bathroom, in order to filibuster an earlier civil rights bill. A vote for cloture to end a filibuster required two-thirds of the Senate, which meant that the South only needed 34 out of 100 Senators to block passage of the civil rights bill. It took all of Johnson's legendary parliamentary skills to secure 71 votes for cloture, four more than he needed. The bill itself passed easily after this decisive procedural victory. The historic Civil Rights Act of 1964 abolished segregation in the South by outlawing any racial, religious or ethnic discrimination in restaurants, hotels, cinemas, stadiums and other public facilities; in the hiring of personnel by any company with more than 25 employees; and in every activity that was subsidized by the federal government.

Having demonstrated his mastery as a liberal reformer, Johnson concentrated on the goal of winning the 1964 elections by a large margin that would allow him to move out of the shadow of Kennedy, pass a comprehensive program of liberal reforms and establish himself as FDR's greatest successor. Republican disarray furthered his plans.

In order to understand the bitter fight that rocked the Republican Party in 1964, one must be aware of strong currents on the right that went against the prevailing liberal stream in American society. There were lunatic fringe elements like the John Birch Society, founded in 1958, whose members believed that President Eisenhower was controlled by the communists. There were also respectable young Republicans like William Buckley who made a serious case for conservative values. Their modernized brand of conservatism revitalized right-wing politics, which had been marginalized after the death of Robert Taft and the decline of McCarthy.

A group of new conservative activists began to plot the nomination of a right-wing candidate for president two-and-a-half years before the Republican National

Convention of 1964. They persuaded Arizona's Senator Barry Goldwater to run for the presidency, even though he had never expressed such an ambition. Goldwater had emerged as the leading conservative politician in the late 1950s, who was also the most outspoken; for example, he supported a voluntary social security system, abolition of the graduated income tax and privatization of the Tennessee Valley Authority, views that in effect meant a repeal of the New Deal.

A bitter struggle for the nomination pitted Goldwater against Governor Nelson Rockefeller of New York, the leading politician of the moderate Northeastern Republican establishment. But the moderate Republicans were unable to stop the conservative assault. Thus for the first time since the 1930s the Republicans nominated a candidate from the conservative wing of the party. Goldwater defiantly refused to conciliate his moderate opponents and remained firm in his uncompromising conservative politics. At the end of his nomination speech he answered critics who had called him an extremist with these memorable words: 'Extremism in the defense of liberty is no vice! Moderation in the pursuit of justice is no virtue!' Nixon visibly refused to join in the applause.

While Goldwater was moving against the postwar consensus on the right, Johnson was pushing that consensus further left. In mid-1964 he passed antipoverty programs through Congress without serious opposition. He then moved to secure the largest possible majority in the elections. The Democratic convention was carefully choreographed so that nothing would upset Johnson's coronation as the party's standard-bearer. Robert Kennedy, who was passed over as vice-presidential candidate, was programmed to speak after the nominations were safely over, so that the pro-Kennedy emotions in the convention would not threaten Johnson's decision to run with another running mate, Hubert Humphrey. The strength of these emotions was shown by the 22-minute standing ovation with which Robert Kennedy was greeted when he rose to the podium, before even uttering a word.

In the 1964 elections Johnson got 61.2 percent, the largest percentage of the vote in American history. His victory helped elect Democratic candidates for Congress as well, producing the largest Democratic congressional majorities since 1937–8: 295 against 140 in the House and 68 against 32 in the Senate. The historian James MacGregor Burns declared: 'By every test we have, this is as surely a liberal epoch as the 19th Century was a conservative one.' The political scientists Nelson Polsby and Aaron Wildavsky thought that if the Republicans nominated another conservative, 'we can expect an end to a competitive two-party system'. Yet the elections were less lopsided than they appeared at first sight. Apart from his own home state Arizona, Goldwater won five states in the Deep South, suggesting that civil rights were loosening the tie between Dixie and the Democratic Party. Moreover, two years later California elected as its governor Ronald Reagan, who campaigned ably for Goldwater in 1964 and soon emerged as the new leader of the conservatives.

Great society

At the moment of his triumph, Johnson knew that he had to translate it into an impressive legislative record quickly, before its effect faded by the usual frictions of politics. His Great Society reforms, which were passed mainly in the first nine months of 1965, are among the most impressive legislative feats in American history and have had a lasting effect on the American welfare state.

In the field of education, Johnson instituted for the first time federal funding of the public schools that are run by state and local authorities, a provision that in time benefited 90 percent of the local boards of education. Funding was also provided for the fees of needy pupils who went to private religious schools; this was especially important for Catholics. Moreover, his Education Act provided for the funding of impoverished college students, a provision that soon benefited one-quarter of all American students.

In the health field, Johnson created Medicare and Medicaid, two major federal programs that provide health care for the elderly and the poor respectively. The resultant infusion of federal funds in the health-care industry was a major factor in its growth from 5 percent of GDP in the 1960s to 14 percent in the 1990s. In yet another field, the Immigration Act of 1965 resulted in the reallocation of underused European immigration quotas to other continents, facilitating in particular a growing influx of immigrants from Asia that has over time helped diversify the American population.

By creating the Department of Housing and Urban Development (HUD), Johnson provided an administrative umbrella for various specialized initiatives dealing with the problems of housing shortages and inner-city decay. Together with his other antipoverty programs, these initiatives indicated a growing concern among liberals that the unprecedented postwar prosperity had not reached all segments of American society; as Michael Harrington revealed in *The Other America* (1961), there were still major pockets of poverty that needed to be eliminated. But Johnson's approach was overoptimistic, demonstrating the kind of boundless faith in America's ability to solve problems that had also characterized American policy in Vietnam under Kennedy.

While Johnson and Congress were busy with this massive reform program, the civil rights issue flared up again in the South. The Civil Rights Act of 1964 had not dealt with the disenfranchisement of most blacks in the South. Martin Luther King launched a peaceful campaign against this unconstitutional discrimination early in 1965, focusing on Selma, Alabama, in which a mere one percent of eligible black voters was registered. Public opinion was outraged once again by the police brutality that greeted the peaceful demonstrators; in one case, a white Protestant minister was killed.

Johnson reacted by introducing a new civil rights bill to abolish the various devices by which blacks had been disenfranchised. In order to mobilize public opinion, he took the unusual step of addressing a joint session of Congress in support of the bill. In what his biographer Robert Dallek has described as his greatest speech, Johnson warned Congress and the American people that 'should we defeat every enemy, should we double our wealth and conquer the stars, and still be unequal to this issue, then we will have failed as a people and as a nation'. The Voting Rights Act of 1965 was decisive in gradually weakening racist politics in the South. Once millions of blacks were registered to vote, politicians began to include them in their electoral calculations. The transformation of Southern politics was not immediate, but it did ensue inexorably from the benevolent consequences of this act.

Johnson's legislative achievements in 1964–5 constituted a rare instance of presidential dominance in Congress. During the twentieth century only Woodrow Wilson in 1913, Franklin Roosevelt in 1933–5 and Ronald Reagan in 1981 were able to pass comparable legislative programs that were major turning points for the federal government. And Johnson was still in the first year of his first term as elected president! He could look forward all the way to 1972 – in 1965 his reelection for a second term seemed assured – to pass the greatest program of reforms in American history, so long as foreign policy problems did not overshadow his domestic agenda. His wife Lady Bird said in the summer of 1965: 'I just hope that foreign policy problems do not keep mounting. They do not represent Lyndon's kind of Presidency.'

Vietnam

In a 1988 opinion poll asking people which president, from Franklin Roosevelt to Ronald Reagan, set the highest moral standards, Lyndon Johnson came at the bottom of the list, chosen by only one percent of the sample (Nixon was chosen by two percent). This finding is indicative of the lasting collapse of Johnson's standing among the American people caused by the disastrous entanglement in Vietnam.

Recently publicized information has shown that Johnson was aware of the trap in Vietnam from very early in his presidency. On June 11, 1964 he privately told his old mentor and confidant Richard Russell, the venerable Chairman of the Senate Armed Services Committee: 'I don't believe the American people ever want me to run. If I lose it [Vietnam], I think that they'll say *I've* lost it. I've pulled in. At the same time, I don't want to commit us to a war. And I'm in a hell of a shape.' Russell warned him presciently that it would 'take a half million men. They'd be bogged down in there for ten years.' He also told Johnson: 'I do not agree with those brain trusters who say that this thing has got tremendous strategic and economic value and that we'll lose everything in Southeast Asia if we lose Vietnam ... But as a practical matter, we're in there and I don't know how the hell you can tell the American people you're coming out.'[2]

The situation in South Vietnam was going from bad to worse after the overthrow of Diem in November 1963. A series of coups and other violent domestic confrontations, apart from the struggle against the Viet Cong, rocked South Vietnam until 1967, when at last a stable government emerged under General Nguyen Van Thieu. The communist insurgency was gaining strength, challenging the government's authority in many provinces to the point where villages often paid 'taxes' to the Viet Cong. Without an American military presence, South Vietnam would probably have collapsed in 1965.

Johnson was aware that he was trapped, yet he dared not withdraw. Feeling out of his depth in foreign policy, he was reluctant to clash with the internationalist consensus that had supported a worldwide anticommunist crusade since 1950. He kept the entire Kennedy foreign policy team and was unwilling to countermand their policies that had led to a deeper American commitment in

South Vietnam in the first place. Moreover, he was afraid that if he withdrew from Vietnam, he would face another wave of McCarthyism. In February 1964 he told his ally John Knight, Chairman of the Board of the *Miami Herald*: 'what they said about us leaving China would just be warming up, compared to what they'd say now. I see Nixon is raising hell about it today. Goldwater too.'

During 1964 Johnson decided to postpone the major decisions on a military engagement until after the elections and to sustain South Vietnam by infusions of aid and the dispatch of more advisors. In August 1964, though, he took the opportunity provided by two North Vietnamese naval assaults on American electronic intelligence vessels in international waters to push through Congress the infamous Gulf of Tonkin Resolution that authorized the use of force to protect American forces in Vietnam. (The vote was nearly unanimous; only two Senators opposed and one Representative abstained.) What Johnson did not disclose was that the first assault had taken place during a separate South Vietnamese naval raid against North Vietnam, which meant the American intelligence vessel might have been mistaken for part of the raiding force and the second assault might never have taken place at all (it was during a storm and the supposed attack was registered only on radar; no enemy unit was actually seen).

Much has been made about the deception that secured the near-unanimous endorsement of Congress. Yet Johnson could easily have secured a congressional endorsement for military action, if he had sought one on some other plausible grounds. The more serious deception took place during the 1964 election campaign. In order to maximize his electoral appeal, Johnson presented himself as the candidate for peace who at the same time was not abandoning South Vietnam; in effect he was telling voters that they could have their cake and eat it too. He portrayed Goldwater as a dangerous warmonger, a task made easy by Goldwater's excessive belligerency. 'I have not thought that we were ready for American boys to do the fighting for Asian boys,' Johnson declared. 'So we are not going north and drop bombs at this stage of the game, and we are not going south and run out and leave it for the communists to take over.' Yet shortly after his election he was bombing the North and a little later American boys did begin to do the fighting for Asian boys.

Johnson's last chance to avoid the trap was immediately after his landslide election, when he was particularly strong domestically. Some neutrality agreement, such as that the French President De Gaulle had proposed in 1964, would have allowed him to slip out without losing too much face. South Vietnam would have collapsed soon afterwards, with perhaps Cambodia following suit (it was already infiltrated by Ho Chi Minh's forces). It is unlikely that other dominoes would have followed. Johnson's fears about a new McCarthyism were probably exaggerated. But there is no evidence that Johnson ever contemplated such a course. Pessimistic though he was about the prospects of an American military engagement, he evidently thought he had no other option.

America's military engagement in Vietnam was handicapped at the outset by Johnson's domestic priorities. Fearing that Congress would not support his costly Great Society programs during a war, Johnson never mobilized the American people for a difficult military endeavor. In February 1965 he launched Operation Rolling Thunder, the continuous bombardment of North Vietnam, *without any policy announcement.* In the next few months Johnson committed ground forces in Vietnam first to protect American bases and then to conduct limited search-and-destroy missions in surrounding areas, but he pretended that there was no major change in policy. In July 1965, when the communists had launched their most ambitious offensive and the South Vietnamese army was on the verge of collapse, Johnson decided to send more ground forces, which soon took over the main burden of the war. He announced this major escalation in America's military commitment using mild language: 'Our manpower needs there are increasing, and will continue to do so.' Later in the same month, when Johnson announced that troop deployments would rise from 75,000 to 125,000, he declared that this did 'not imply any change in policy whatever'. Thus America entered what would become her longest war up to then with her leadership pretending that nothing had changed.

American military strategy in Vietnam had to operate under severe political constraints. Johnson wished at all costs to avoid a wider war. North Vietnam and Laos were off-limits for American ground forces in order not to provoke China's entry into the war. For the same reason, North Vietnam's rail links with China were off-limits for the American air forces. North Vietnam's ports were not blockaded or mined in order not to risk Soviet casualties and perhaps provoke a Soviet entry in the war. Cambodia was off-limits for the American ground forces in order not to widen the war, even though its unpopulated eastern provinces were used by the North Vietnamese as supply routes reaching the central and southern provinces of South Vietnam, below Laos.

These constraints were severe handicaps for the American war effort. The guerrilla war in the South could be sustained over a very long period, so long as new supplies and fighters infiltrated from the North. Blocking this infiltration along South Vietnam's 1000-mile-long western borders with Laos and Cambodia was physically impossible, given the jungle terrain. There were only two plausible ways for drying up this infiltration: either blockade and mine North Vietnam's ports and bomb its rail links with China to limit the influx of war supplies into North Vietnam, or deploy major forces in southern Laos to restrict the movement of supplies and men from the North to the South. Both these options were off-limits.

Operation Rolling Thunder produced no significant strategic results, even though it dropped more tons of explosives in three years than the US Air Force used during the whole of World War II. It may have damaged North Vietnam's infrastructure, but that was rather rudimentary anyway. Most bombs fell on 'unobserved targets' in the jungle and hit few real targets. The Ho Chi Minh trail proved simply too elusive to block by air bombardments. In their net effect, the massive bombardments may well have actually damaged the American effort. First, they rallied the people of North Vietnam around their leadership against the 'imperialists' and fueled anti-Americanism around the world. Second, according to Pentagon calculations made in 1967, during 1966 some 65 percent of bombs fell on unobserved targets, probably causing only 100 enemy casualties; yet, given the expected portion of unexploded bombs, they may have provided the enemy with 27,000 tons of explosives that could be used to create booby traps. In 1966 alone, such booby traps caused about 1000 American casualties.

It should be noted here that the American air strategy during Vietnam avoided the indiscriminate bombing of cities that had characterized allied strategic bombing campaigns in World War II and Korea. The flattening of cities had not broken enemy morale in these earlier conflicts. It was wasteful in both materiel and downed bomber crews, while killing large numbers of enemy civilians produced no decisive strategic effect. The change in strategy accounts in part for the fact that civilian casualties were far lower in Vietnam than in World War II or Korea. But the technology of precision bombing with 'smart' bombs that further reduced civilian casualties was developed only in the final stages of the Vietnam War under Nixon.

On the ground in South Vietnam the American strategy was also unable to produce decisive results. The American forces enjoyed overwhelmingly superior firepower and therefore sought to fight major battles against significant concentrations of enemy forces. But the insurgents preferred guerrilla warfare, which reduced the conflict to countless hit-and-run raids by an elusive enemy that did not defend ground and simply disappeared in the face of superior force. The communist forces had the enormous advantage that they could retreat into the safety of Cambodia and Laos – off-limits for American forces – in order to recuperate and regroup.

In a guerrilla war without fronts, the American commander General William Westmoreland launched continuous offensive search-and-destroy operations in order to cumulatively reduce the communist forces. But since the enemy's attrition came to be measured in body counts, the American troops had an incentive to count civilian casualties as enemy fighters. Since the enemy was often indistinguishable from civilians, mistaken killings of noncombatants actually counted in favor of American units by increasing the reported body count. Where this situation could lead was indicated by an American major's infamous statement: 'we had to destroy the village in order to save it'. By not always discriminating between enemies and civilians, the American forces can only have helped swell the enemy's ranks with new recruits.

Furthermore, the attrition strategy could not work in any reasonable time frame, since communist losses were simply replaced by new forces sent by North Vietnam. Therefore, attrition had to exhaust not only the Viet Cong, but also North Vietnam. In 1967 the North Vietnamese forces in the South amounted to just two percent of North Vietnam's male labor force (the American forces in Vietnam amounted to one percent of the American male labor force). A guerrilla force needs only a fraction of the numerical strength of its opponents in order to challenge security effectively. In 1967 the communist side had only one-sixth of the numerical strength of its opponents.

Since the attrition strategy was not producing visible results during 1965–7, Westmoreland kept asking for more troops. By the end of 1967 there were more than half a million American troops in Vietnam, without decisive results. Nonetheless, with his job approval showing a continuous decline in the polls since early 1966, Johnson needed to end the war before the 1968 elections. Out of desperation, and perhaps in disbelief that a Third World enemy could sustain its struggle against a massive American military commitment, in late 1967 Johnson launched an optimistic public relations campaign in order to convince the American people that there was 'light at the end of the tunnel'. His popularity improved ephemerally in the opinion polls, since a majority of Americans wanted victory and not a withdrawal from Vietnam, the noisy antiwar demonstrators notwithstanding. Yet the actual situation was so discouraging that Secretary of Defense Robert McNamara, the leading architect of America's engagement in Vietnam, asked to be replaced. In March 1968 Johnson substituted Clark Clifford.

The Tet offensive

On January 31, 1968, the Vietnamese Tet holiday, the communist side launched its greatest offensive in the war, striking at five of the six largest cities and most of the larger towns of South Vietnam. In Saigon it attacked the US Embassy, President Thieu's presidential palace, South Vietnam's general staff and other military and public installations. Westmoreland's command estimated that North Vietnam committed almost a third of its army to the offensive.

From a narrow military perspective, the Tet offensive was a failure. Since the communist side attempted to ignite a general revolution across South Vietnam by striking at a very large number of targets, it diluted the communist forces over many local fronts, making them weak everywhere. By coming out into the open, sometimes in significant concentrations, the communist forces were massacred by the superior firepower of the American forces, which had not been put to such effective use since the previous large-scale communist offensive in 1965. Communist casualties in the two months of the offensive came to 60,000, while American casualties were 4000 and South Vietnam's 5000. Moreover, there was no revolution by the people of South Vietnam.

Nonetheless, the Tet offensive was devastatingly effective on the American home front. After three years of massive air bombardments and the commitment of more than half a million troops, the enemy was able to launch its greatest offensive yet. Live broadcasting of the fighting in the US Embassy compound belied the rhetoric about 'light at the end of the tunnel' in a way that no official account of respective casualties could counter. The American people felt so deceived by their leader that it was impossible for Johnson to call for new sacrifices in order to capitalize on the battlefield successes that destroyed the Tet offensive on the ground.

On March 31, 1968 in a televised address to the American people, Johnson announced a unilateral end of American bombing in all but the southernmost corner of North Vietnam, where the North's troops and supplies began their movement southwards. Johnson ended his address with one of the most dramatic statements in recent American history: 'I shall not seek and I will not accept the nomination of my party for another term as your president.' Johnson's withdrawal from the 1968 race transformed the Tet offensive into a brilliant North Vietnamese political success. Having brought about the downfall of the most powerful leader in the world, Ho Chi Minh had every reason to continue the struggle. There was now light at the end of the tunnel from his point of view.

The failure of the American military engagement in Vietnam derived from the asymmetry in what was at stake for the two sides. North Vietnam was fighting for national unification, a cause sanctioned by nationalism, which has proved to be the most powerful ideology in the era of the nation-state. Nationalism legitimized enormous sacrifices – as Europe had found out in the first half of the twentieth century. The United States by contrast was fighting in a geopolitically insignificant country in order to affirm the credibility of its global anticommunist alliances. This political objective increasingly appeared to the American people as not worth the mounting costs of the war. Furthermore, there was an asymmetry in the two sides' strategic effectiveness. North Vietnam had mastered guerrilla strategy during Ho Chi Minh's anticolonial struggle against the French and perfected it during the American war. The American side was unable to devise an effective counterguerrilla strategy, largely because of the political constraints on military operations. The attrition strategy was particularly poor in strategic imagination – not unlike another disastrous attrition strategy in the trench warfare of World War I – and ended up wasting vast amounts of ordnance in ineffective or counterproductive ways. By 1970 the United States had dropped more tons of explosives in Vietnam than had been used in all previous wars in history, without decisive results.

The cost of the Vietnam War for the United States was enormous. In the entire war, including Nixon's first term, about 58,000 Americans were killed. Over 8000 American aircraft were lost. The economic burden of the war contributed to the destabilization of the American economy that led to the stagflation of the 1970s. Vietnam fueled anti-Americanism worldwide. While America was absorbed in this peripheral conflict, the Soviet Union invested so much in developing its nuclear arsenal as to attain strategic parity with the United States. Moreover, Vietnam powerfully contributed to the domestic upheavals that shook America in the second half of the 1960s.

The turbulent years, 1965–8

The period of American economic growth that began in the 1940s peaked in the 1960s, during which per capita GDP rose by an impressive 41 percent. Income inequalities were somewhat reduced, though they still remained higher than in Europe, except France. In spite of the growing prosperity, waves of violence and disorder swept through American society during 1965–8 that had deep political repercussions. The timing of the disorders was particularly damaging to Johnson, coming as it did after his Great Society reforms that were meant to cure many of the ills in American society. This was particularly true of African Americans; no president since Lincoln did as much for them as Johnson, yet it was his misfortune to preside over the worst postwar outbreaks of black unrest.

Several factors account for the black riots. First, there were the informal conditions of racial segregation in the inner cities of the North and the West, because of white flight from the poorer black neighborhoods. Many poor blacks were stuck in the ghettos, in which unemployment was higher than the national average. Second, there was a collapse of the black family, which Assistant Secretary of Labor Daniel Moynihan identified in a report in 1965. Moynihan pointed out that the migration of blacks from the South to the North and West was partly a failure, resulting in disproportionately high levels of broken families and welfare dependency. In 1963 as many as 23 percent of black births were out of wedlock, compared with only two percent of white births.

There was also a general rise in crime in the United States, which was particularly pronounced in black ghettos. National statistics showed a doubling of murders in the United States between 1963 and 1970, but this increase was disproportionately evident in the ghettos, where large numbers of young black men were unemployed and beyond the traditional discipline of the family. Finally, the Civil Rights movement in the South had shown that age-old structures of segregation could be overturned by protests, thereby creating expectations that other forms of injustice and discrimination would also be challenged. Yet the Civil Rights movement had focused only on legal discrimination and had not addressed the plight of blacks in the ghettos outside the South who faced other kinds of discrimination. Frustrated expectations contributed to the restlessness of many African Americans in the North and the West.

The first major black inner-city riot broke out in New York in July 1964, a few weeks after Johnson signed his first Civil Rights Act. It began in Harlem (Manhattan) and spread to Bedford-Stuyvesant (Brooklyn), causing one death and injuring one hundred people. Far worse was the riot that broke out in Watts, Los Angeles, in August 1965, less than a fortnight after Johnson signed his Voting Rights Act. In Watts 34 people were killed and 400 injured, while the material damages reached $35 million. Sporadic riots with less destructive consequences followed in 1966.

Violence culminated in July 1967 when riots broke out in Newark, New Jersey, and Detroit, Michigan. The Newark riot lasted three days, left 23 dead and ended only after the intervention of the state police and National Guard. The Detroit riot was the worst single outbreak of violence in this disorderly period. Looting, arson and street fighting lasted for a week, during which first the city police and then the state police and the National Guard were unable to restore order. The riot ended only when a force of 4500 paratroopers entered the city. In this terrible unrest 43 people were killed, hundreds were injured and the material damages were in the hundreds of millions of dollars. Overall, during the three years from 1965 to 1967, a total of 130 people were killed in the riots and the material damages came to $715 million.

The consequences of the riots in the ghettos were awful. The inner-city black neighbourhoods suffered damage that took decades to undo, since the collapse in property values made repairs uneconomical for property owners. Local businesses were driven away, sinking the ghettos further into the vicious cycle of lack of amenities and local employment opportunities, high crime, and alienation from the surrounding labor markets. At the same time the middle class accelerated its exodus from the inner cities to the safer suburbs.

Meanwhile, counterculture movements seeking an unconventional lifestyle also fueled the sense of disorder that spread in America at this time. The counterculture's hippies, drugs, acid rock and sexual liberation offended conventional sensibilities. Governor Ronald Reagan of California increased his popularity by expressing the prejudices of the conservative majority with the quip that a hippie 'dresses like Tarzan, has hair like Jane and smells like Cheetah'.

Much more disruptive was the New Left – new in the sense that it was not Marxist – and the antiwar movement that grew with the deepening of the American military engagement in Vietnam. The dissenters' attitude towards Vietnam was expressed well in one of Joan Baez's songs: 'Lyndon Johnson said, it's not really war, we're just sending ninety thousand more, to help save Vietnam from the Vietnamese.' By 1967 young demonstrators were stalking Johnson in his public appearances, shouting: 'Hey, hey, hey, LBJ, how many kids did you kill today?' At the stormy antiwar convention in Santa Barbara in 1967 one activist called for 'completely demoralizing and castrating America', while others chanted the slogan: 'Ho, Ho, Ho Chi Minh, the NLF is gonna win' (the NLF was the National Liberation Front that the Viet Cong had created in 1960). Antiwar activists saw themselves as 'the NLF behind Johnson's lines'. The antiwar movement's strongholds were the colleges, especially the elite universities, where student activists protested against the war with a visibility out of proportion to their numbers.

The Vietnam War divided the country along the lines of age, class and family. Opinion polls showed that support for the war was stronger in the middle class than in the working class. However, the opposite was true of young people from 20 to 29 years, who displayed greater support for the war than any other age group but included the bulk of the antiwar movement in the universities. Given that many antiwar students came from middle-class families supportive of the war, the result was a fierce generational confrontation. Even high-ranking members of the Johnson and Nixon administrations had children who opposed the war. The privileged antiwar students, who benefited from draft deferment, were much despised by the patriotic majority of America's young that was drafted and served in Vietnam. While the working class showed less enthusiasm for the war than the middle class, the unions were strong supporters – in 1967 the AFL-CIO (the merged American Federation of Labour and the CIO) passed a resolution supporting the war by a vote of 2000 to 6.

As the war dragged on, support for Johnson and his Vietnam policy declined. This did not mean that people necessarily wanted Johnson to get out of Vietnam. What most people preferred was some strategy that would secure victory soon. But should this prove unattainable, a growing number wanted to get out. The continuation of a policy that brought mounting costs without bringing victory nearer was what most Americans sensibly thought of as the least desirable option.

In spite of the disorders, the war in Vietnam and the decline in his popularity, at the end of 1967 Johnson still seemed certain to get his party's nomination for another term. Robert Kennedy refused to enter the race as a challenger, even though he was an increasingly harsh critic of the President from the left on both Vietnam and domestic problems. Anti-Johnson activists then persuaded Senator Eugene McCarthy to run against Johnson, but this was widely seen as a protest candidacy that had little chance of weakening Johnson's hold over his party.

The Tet offensive changed the dynamics of American electoral politics in early 1968. In the New Hampshire primary on 12 March, McCarthy got an unexpectedly large percentage – 42 percent against Johnson's 49 percent – that suddenly made the President appear vulnerable to a challenge from the left. Opinion polls later revealed that most of McCarthy's voters were actually hawks that wanted a winning strategy in Vietnam, but the McCarthy candidacy had been boosted.

On March 16, 1968 Robert Kennedy entered the race in a brazen bid to hijack McCarthy's momentum. 'We can change these disastrous, divisive policies only by changing the men who are now making them', he declared. Johnson still had the upper hand for the nomination, in part because his critics were divided between Kennedy and McCarthy. But he felt that having to fight a Kennedy for the nomination meant he would enter the general election race seriously weakened. Johnson had become such a polarizing factor that he would not have been able to govern effectively, even if he had been reelected.

Johnson's decision on March 31, 1968 to withdraw from the presidential race did not bring the turbulence in America to an end. Indeed, some of the most traumatic events of this period took place later in 1968. Nonetheless, Johnson's fall was a watershed in American politics. Lyndon Johnson was the last of the New Dealers, who in 1964–5 had led the liberal wing of his party to its greatest postwar triumph. By 1968 he was no longer acceptable to most liberals, who were now swayed by a new kind of politics that was unrelated to the endeavors of the New Deal. The upheavals of the Sixties that swept Johnson away were strongly reflected in American culture.

NOTES

1. Dan T. Carter, *The Politics of Rage: George Wallace, the Origins of the New Conservatism, and the Transformation of American Politics*, New York: Simon & Schuster, 1995, pp. 10–11.
2. Michael R. Beschloss (ed.), *Taking Charge: The Johnson White House Tapes, 1963–1964*, New York: Simon & Schuster, 1997, pp. 401–3.

RECOMMENDED READING

Robert Dallek, *Flawed Giant Lyndon Johnson and his Times, 1961–1973*, Oxford: Oxford University Press, 1998.

Jim E. Heath, *Decade of Disillusionment: The Kennedy-Johnson Years*, Bloomington, IN: Indiana University Press, 1975.

Godfrey Hodgson, *America in Our Time*, Garden City, NY: Doubleday, 1976.

James A. Patterson, *Grand Expectations: The United States, 1945–1974*, Oxford: Oxford University Press, 1996.

Rick Pellman, *Before the Storm: Barry Goldwater and the Unmaking of the American Consensus*, New York: Hill & Wang, 2001.

Richard Polenberg, *One Nation Divisible: Class, Race, and Ethnicity in the United States Since 1938*, New York: Viking, 1980.

Richard Reeves, *President Kennedy: Profile of Power*, New York: Touchstone, 1993.

CHAPTER 6

The Imaginative Crisis of the 1960s

The turbulent 1960s was a decade of false starts and unfulfilled promises. It began in 1960 with the election of John F. Kennedy, but his presidency was brutally terminated with his assassination in 1963. That same year, Martin Luther King, Jr, delivered his famous speech in Washington, DC, but in 1968 he too was brutally murdered. In that year, antiwar protesters disrupted the Democratic Convention in Chicago. The following year a rock festival at Woodstock, New York, attracted half a million young celebrants of the new counterculture. Yet the roots of these astonishing events can be traced back to some time in the 1950s.

The legacy of the 1950s

During the 1950s American society and culture were being quietly but radically transformed. Politically, the change was heralded by the rise of a new Civil Rights movement that was energized by the 1954 Supreme Court decision outlawing racial segregation in schools, heartened by the success of the 1955 Montgomery Bus Boycott led by the young Reverend King, and galvanized by the student sit-ins in Greensboro, North Carolina, in 1960. Intellectually, a series of books challenged the assumptions of the liberal consensus about the affluent society and thus shaped the ideology of a nascent counterculture: among them, Herbert Marcuse's *Eros and Civilization* (1955); C. Wright Mills's *The Power Elite* (1956); William Appleman Williams's *The Tragedy of American Diplomacy* (1959); Norman O. Brown's *Life Against Death* (1959); and Paul Goodman's *Growing Up Absurd* (1960). Artistically, a new aesthetic emerged that challenged both academic orthodoxy and conventional realism in works like William Gaddis's *The Recognitions* (1955); Allen Ginsberg's *Howl* (1956); Jack Kerouac's *On the Road* (1957); Edward Allbee's *The Zoo Story* (1958); and Robert Lowell's *Life Studies*. In another indication of generational change, three important student organizations were founded in 1960: Young Americans for Freedom (YAF) on the right, Students for a Democratic Society on the left, and the biracial Student Non-violent Coordinating Committee (SNCC) in the field of Civil Rights. By the time of Kennedy's election in 1960 a new cultural frontier had already been established.

Significantly, the publication of Goodman's *Growing Up Absurd* coincided with the election of America's youngest president and the rise of a new student movement. *Growing Up Absurd* was an attack on the values of contemporary

American society which, Goodman said, offered the younger generation few good reasons to become part of it. He argued that increasing numbers of privileged young Americans were 'growing up absurd' and becoming alienated by the destructive demands imposed upon them by their society. He wrote:

> Let us exaggerate the conditions that we have been describing. Conceive that the man-made environment is now *out* of human scale. Business, government, and real property have closed up *all* the space there is. There is no behavior unregulated by the firm or the police. Unless the entire economic machine is operating, it is impossible to produce and buy bread. Public speech quite disregards human fact. There is a rigid caste system in which everyone has a slot and the upper class stands for nothing culturally. The university has become merely a training ground for technicians and applied-anthropologists. Sexuality is divorced from manly independence and achievement. The FBI has a file card of all the lies and truths about everybody. And so forth. If we sum up these imagined conditions, there would arise a formidable question: is it possible, being a human being, to exist? Is it possible, having a human nature, to grow up? There would be a kind of metaphysical crisis.

Goodman's critique was repeated by the leaders of the newly formed youth organization, Students for a Democratic Society. In 1962 SDS published *The Port Huron Statement,* a celebrated manifesto that defined the agenda of the young rebels. It begins with words that might describe a slightly older Holden Caulfield: 'We are people of this generation, bred in at least modest comfort, housed now in universities, looking uncomfortably to the world we inherit.' What is striking about this political manifesto, the historian Christopher Lasch noted in *The Agony of the American Left* (1969), is its apparent lack of political analysis. 'Both the strengths and the weaknesses of the New Left derive from the fact that it is largely a student movement based on "alienation". From the beginning, the New Left defined political issues as personal issues.'

This emphasis on 'personal' rather than 'political' issues is not surprising. Todd Gitlin, an early student leader, said that the SDS circle comprised 'a surrogate family, where for long stretches of time horizontal relations of trust replaced vertical relations of authority'. He noted that 'as many as one-third or one-half of the early SDS elite came from visibly broken or unstable families: a disproportionately large number for that generation. But even those who grew up in more stable families shared the fervent desire to find a community of peers to take seriously and be taken seriously by.' Thus a key word in the *Port Huron Statement* is 'values'.

Goodman's criticism was echoed in popular films and rock music that reflected the malaise of the affluent young who were 'growing up absurd' and announced, with the famous singer-songwriter Bob Dylan, that 'the times, they are a-changing'. In Mike Nichols's popular film *The Graduate* (1967), Dustin Hoffman plays a college graduate who feels alienated from his parents' values. Benjamin Braddock is an older, wiser and even more alienated Holden Caulfield. When a family friend suggests a career in 'Plastics', he is repelled. When his father asks what he wants out of life, he responds: 'Something different.' *The Graduate* owes as much to Salinger as it does to Goodman. It suggests that by the end of the 1950s the glacial quality of American life and the uniform character of the Cold War consensus were already breaking up.

Catch-22

No literary work encapsulates this breakup as brilliantly as Joseph Heller's outrageous novel about World War II, *Catch-22* (1961). In Heller's retrospective view, the war was fought not to make the world safe for democracy but to make it safe for a mysterious multinational corporation named M&M Enterprises. His hero, Yossarian, a bombardier who 'has decided to live forever or die in the attempt', discovers that there is a conspiracy against his life between his own superior officers who send him up on bombing missions and the enemy gunners who try to shoot him down. Acting out of a deep moral concern for his own personal safety, Yossarian seeks ways out of combat, only to be thwarted at every turn by a mysterious military law called 'Catch-22'. It turns out that Catch-22 is administered, like the war itself, not by the military but by M&M Enterprises.

Perhaps we can understand the changing sensibility best by comparing *Catch-22* with *The Catcher in the Rye,* which was published exactly a decade earlier. Holden Caulfield's alienation was a phenomenon of postwar conformity and Salinger's attitude towards his adolescent hero's 'craziness' was at least ambiguous. Ten years later, however, the writer's attitude towards social maladjustment is no longer ambivalent. If, as the psychiatrist R. D. Laing observed in *The Politics of Experience* (1968), 'Normal men have killed perhaps 100,000,000 of their fellow normal men in the last fifty years,' then what ought to be questioned is not the definition of 'insanity' but the definition of 'normality'. In *Catch-22,* Heller puts the question of normality in World War II this way:

> Men went mad and were rewarded with medals. All over the world, boys on every side of the bomb line were laying down their lives for what they had been told was their country, and no one seemed to mind, least of all the boys who were laying down their young lives. There was no end in sight.

It seems that *Catch-22* turns the problem of 'craziness' raised in *The Catcher in the Rye* upside down: society may think the hero is crazy but we never do. Thus *Catch-22* begins as a farce about individual survival in an institutional world and ends as a tragicomedy about collective responsibility in the Cold War years. Yossarian sets out as a kind of Sancho Panza, dedicated to the principle of dishonor before death; but when the corpses of his friends begin to pile up around him, he becomes a quixotic rebel against the System, an idealistic defender of childhood innocence. 'Somebody had to do something sometime,' he thinks. 'Every victim was a culprit, every culprit a victim, and somebody had to stand up sometime to try to break the lousy chain of inherited habit that was imperilling them all.' In short, he becomes a radical catcher in the rye.

Yossarian's decision to desert at the end of the novel is an awakening to his real situation in a world where victory in World War II will not culminate in peace but in a Cold War manipulated by M&M Enterprises. Here Heller's novel departs significantly from Salinger's. Whereas Holden was readjusted to his society because he really had no alternative, Yossarian secedes from his society because it offers him no alternative. In other words, the alienation expressed in the fiction at the beginning of the 1950s was transformed into a comprehensive social critique just ten years later. Citizens like Yossarian become radicalized when they realize that the System created by the Cold War no longer works for them. In *Catch-22*, he hears a man shout, 'Police! Help! Police!':

> Yossarian smiled wryly at the futile and ridiculous cry for aid, then saw with a start that the words were ambiguous, realized with alarm that they were not, perhaps, intended as a call for police but as a heroic warning from the grave by a doomed friend to everyone who was *not* a policeman with a club and a gun and a mob of other policemen with clubs and guns to back him up. 'Help! Police!' the man had cried, and he could have been shouting of danger.

Catch-22 is prophetic of the changes that transformed American life and literature during the decade of the Sixties.

The imaginative crisis of the Sixties

With President Kennedy's election in 1960, Americans entered a new era of intensified public awareness and accelerating historical consciousness. Soon the signs of history were everywhere: in the televised slaying of the president and of his assassin, Lee Harvey Oswald, which were repeated endlessly in slow motion; in the film clips of the Vietnam War that Americans watched on the evening news over their suppers; and in the photographs of civic riots and political demonstrations that adorned the front pages of the daily newspapers. As Leo Braudy observed, 'History was no longer a pattern of factually and philosophically analyzable causes; it was a nightmare, an allegory of good and evil, a metaphysical comic book.'

The apparent absurdity of modern life, the distrust of social conventions, the primacy of personal freedom, and the possibility of utopian solutions were manifest not only in novels like *Catch-22*; they were also reflected in the new American cinema exemplified by Robert Rossen's *The Hustler* (1961), John Frankenheimer's *The Manchurian Candidate* (1962) and Stanley Kubrick's *Dr Strangelove* (1963). *The Manchurian Candidate* is a case in point. It was made by three talented people: dramatist George Axelrod, director John Frankenheimer, and actor Frank Sinatra. Based on a novel by Richard Condon, the film was meant to be a combined spy thriller and political satire of the Cold War and the McCarthy era. The story takes place during the Korean War and involves the efforts of the Communists to brainwash some American soldiers and transform one of them into a robot political assassin. Thus the outrageous plot focuses on the political assassination of a presidential candidate at a political rally. But the history of the film itself is even more far-fetched. It was released in 1962 as a kind of black comedy but it was not a box-office success. A year later, President Kennedy was murdered. In 1964 the film was withdrawn from exhibition; it was not re-released until 1989. (In 2004, it was remade by Jonathan Demme as a dark commentary on the Bush era.)

Two years before Kennedy's assassination, Philip Roth wondered aloud how writers could compete with the fantastic nature of contemporary reality. In 'Writing American Fiction' (1961) he described in hilarious detail a grotesque murder case in Chicago that became a bizarre media event when the mother of two dead teenage girls was showered with gifts, including two parakeets and new kitchen appliances. Roth asked, 'And what is the moral of so long a story?' He answered:

> Simply this: that the American writer in the middle of the twentieth century has his hands full in trying to understand, and then describe, and then make *credible* much of the American reality. It stupefies, it sickens, it infuriates, and finally it is even a kind of embarrassment to one's meager imagination. The actuality is continually outdoing our talents, and the culture tosses up figures daily that are the envy of any novelist.

Given this situation, American writers were faced with a series of artistic problems that amounted to a crisis in imagination. In *The Golden Notebook* (1964), the Nobel Prize-winning novelist Doris Lessing identified this imaginative crisis as 'the thinning of language against the density of our experience'. If language was an inadequate tool against history then writers would have to find new modes of speech, discover new forms of expression.

Poetry

Interestingly enough, the etiolation of 'language' was felt first in the most personal medium of poetry. In the late 1940s, two iconic poets of the prewar generation had published works which challenged the predominant New Critical aesthetic with its preference for classical form and metaphysical ambiguity: William Carlos Williams's *Paterson* (1946) and Ezra Pound's *Pisan Cantos* (1948) attacked cherished notions of the poet's 'impersonality' and poetry's ironic understatement. Then in the mid-1950s, poets associated with Black Mountain College began publishing a more open and immediate poetry based on Charles Olson's theory of 'projective verse'. The publication of Olson's *Maximus Poems* (1953) was followed by Denise Levertov's *Here and Now* (1957) and Robert Duncan's *The Opening of the Field* (1960).

Meanwhile, in San Francisco, Beat Generation poets like Kenneth Rexroth, Lawrence Ferlinghetti and Allen Ginsberg were producing an irreverent and unkempt verse culminating in the publication of Ginsberg's electrifying poem *Howl*. Other movements sprang up in such disparate places as Minnesota (Robert Bly and James Wright) and New York (Frank O'Hara and John Ashbery), leading to what Daniel Hoffman called 'the balkanization of contemporary poetry'. Yet all these movements shared a perception of the breakdown of the old poetic order. 'The various rebellions against the aesthetic of the fifties,' noted Hoffman, 'involved rejections of poetic tradition and literary decorum. Along with the casting off of strict meters came abandonment of received structures, a new demotic diction, rejection of narrative and sequential organization and paraphrasable content, and the reintroduction of personal subjects – Oedipal tensions, sexual confessions, suicidal urges, madness – presented without the mediation of masks or historical analogues.'

But the most important new development was Confessional Poetry which rejected indirection and 'impersonality' in favor of a frank expression of the poet's private and public life. Its most influential practitioners were the two greatest poets of the postwar generation, Robert Lowell and John Berryman. Both underwent a similar poetic odyssey from formalism to spontaneity and from song to speech, culminating in their greatest works, Lowell's *Life Studies* and Berryman's *The Dream Songs* (1969), in which they described the poet's attempt to cope with the pressures of his inner and outer life. Berryman wrote, 'I am obliged to perform in great darkness/operations of great delicacy/on my self.' Like Berryman, Lowell recounted his own version of the Dark Night of the Soul. 'My night is not gracious, but secular, puritan, and agnostical,' he wrote. 'An existential night.'

But in its attempt to combine personal memory with public history, *Life Studies* is also concerned with historical continuity. 'Of all poets since the war, Lowell has the finest historical imagination, the most powerful capacity for juxtaposing past and present, public and private, and discovering significance in the juxtapositions,' observed the critic Richard Gray. Thus Lowell's title, *Life Studies,* refers to both the study *of* life and studies *from* life: that is, still life, portrait, autobiography and general history. In its variety, *Life Studies* shows how we may study life in different ways and how they are all poetry. Lowell writes about decline and decay but he stops short of the apocalyptic only in his sustaining belief in the continuity between past, present and future. Perhaps this is what is meant by the redemptive potential of history.

Other poets followed suit, including three of Lowell's former students: Sylvia Plath, Anne Sexton and W. D. Snodgrass. 'The times have changed,' Lowell observed in 1962. 'A drastic experimental art is not expected or demanded. The scene is dense with the dirt and power of industrial society.' Soon no subject was exempt from the poet's scrutiny, no matter how private or public: from self-hatred (Plath, *Ariel*, 1965) and suicide (Sexton, *Live or Die*, 1967) to feminism (Adrienne Rich, *Snapshots of a Daughter-in-Law*, 1963) and ecology (Gary Snyder, *The Back Country*, 1969).

Theater

The American theater also experienced a breakdown of traditional forms in this period as the center of gravity in serious drama moved from Broadway to Off-Broadway, then to Off-Off-Broadway, and finally to the new regional theaters scattered around the country. Beginning at the end of the 1950s, a new generation of playwrights challenged both traditional themes and conventional forms. In plays like Edward Allbee's *The Zoo Story* (1958) and Jack Gelber's *The Connection* (1959), Off-Broadway held out a promise of the rejuvenation of American drama which was never quite redeemed.

On the one hand, controversial subjects like racism and homosexuality were explored in Leroi Jones's *Dutchman* (1964) and Mark Crowley's *The Boys in the Band* (1968). On the other hand, experimental troupes like The Open Theater and the Living Theater created total theatrical events and improvisatory works like *America Hurrah* (1966) and *Paradise Now* (1971). But with the exception of Edward Allbee (*Who's Afraid of Virginia Woolf?*, 1962; *Tiny Alice*, 1964; *A Delicate Balance*, 1966), no one seemed capable of sustaining a career as a playwright. Instead the theater moved from text-centered drama to performance-centered spectacle like the rock musical *Hair* (1968). Thus in the theater, the imaginative crisis was reflected in the rejection of the word in favor of sight, sound and spectacle. Perhaps the ultimate theatrical events of the Sixties took place in the streets: at the 1967 antiwar March on the Pentagon or the 1969 musical happening at Woodstock.

Prose

The imaginative crisis also resulted in the explosion of the traditional forms of writing prose. Under pressure from the density of contemporary experience, some novelists moved to hybrid forms of Realism they called the 'New Journalism' or the 'nonfiction novel': for example, Baldwin's *The Fire Next Time* (1963), Capote's *In Cold Blood* (1966), and Mailer's *The Armies of the Night* (1968). Feeling the thinning of language, other writers turned to black humor, paranoid visions, or a kind of linguistic guerilla warfare where they blew up the English language; for instance, Heller's *Catch-22*, William Burroughs's *Naked Lunch* (1959) and Ken Kesey's *One Flew Over the Cuckoo's Nest* (1962). Aware of the exhaustion of literary forms, still others like John Barth, John Hawkes and Kurt Vonnegut explored the vein of reflexive and antirealistic writing now called 'postmodernist'. But whatever their orientation, perhaps Vonnegut spoke for all the writers of the 1960s when he wrote in *Slaughterhouse-Five* (1969), 'everything there was to know about life was in *The Brothers Karamazov*, by Fyodor Dostoevsky. But that isn't enough any more'.

Slaughterhouse-Five is a representative novel of the 1960s in its attempt to find a new form adequate to its content. In it, Vonnegut tried to recount his experiences as a prisoner-of-war during the dreadful firebombing of Dresden in 1945. But he discovered that mere reportage could not do justice to the horrific events, that it was nearly impossible to frame an imaginative response adequate to the suffering. Furthermore, there was the problem of assigning meaning to the nihilistic destruction he had witnessed. But how does a writer give meaning to senseless carnage or write a parable against violence when he believes that pacifist tracts don't achieve anything?

No wonder, then, that *Slaughterhouse-Five* is missing all the usual ingredients of conventional fiction. It lacks characters and dramatic conflict because these are absent in the real misery of war. 'There are almost no characters in this story and almost no dramatic confrontations,' Vonnegut tells us, 'because most of the people in it are so sick and so much the listless playthings of enormous forces. One of the main effects of war, after all, is that people are discouraged from being characters.' It lacks form and suspense because these are not qualities produced by total destruction. 'It is so short and jumbled and jangled,' he says, 'because there is nothing intelligent to say about a massacre. Everybody is supposed to be dead, to never say anything or want anything ever again. Everything is supposed to be very quiet after a massacre, and it always is, except for the birds.'

Finally, it is not surprising that the author calls his own book 'a failure' because what we read is an antiwar novel by a writer who doesn't believe in writing antiwar novels. In other words, we are confronted by an imaginative work whose meaning is called into question by its own creator, a novel that defies fictive conventions because they are inadequate to the reality being described. *Slaughterhouse-Five* is a novel that can only be told 'in the telegraphic schizophrenic manner of tales of the planet Tralfamadore, where the flying saucers come from' because this reality can only be made comprehensible from that far-out perspective: realism considered as science fiction, the world viewed from the perspective of another planet.

Like *Slaughterhouse-Five,* other imaginative works of the period are filled with apocalyptic images. Consider the titles of some of the decade's representative books: Ginsberg's *Kaddish* (1961); Baldwin's *The Fire Next Time;* and Joan Didion's *Slouching Towards Bethlehem* (1968). This literature is replete with images of social breakdown and scenes of terrifying violence: the brutal murder of the Clutter family in Capote's *In Cold Blood,* the destruction of Dresden in Vonnegut's *Slaughterhouse-Five,* and the Detroit riots in Joyce Carol Oates's *them* (1969). In each book, the author tries to find some meaning in the enveloping destruction and civil breakdown. Similarly, many novels turn on the discovery of an apocalyptic plot, a dangerous conspiracy against the individual on the part of a murderous collectivity. In Heller's *Catch-22,* Kesey's *One Flew Over the Cuckoo's Nest* and Thomas Pynchon's *The Crying of Lot 49* (1966), the protagonists must wake up to the fact that there may be a plot against their lives. The perception of conspiracy becomes a necessary imaginative act for survival. Paranoia becomes a sign of health.

In their inversion of conventional definitions of sanity and insanity and their subversion of accepted social norms like patriotism and capitalism, these novels became part of the prevailing social critique of the time. In *Asylums* (1961), the sociologist Erving Goffman noted the tendency of certain social agencies like asylums, prisons and boarding schools to become 'total institutions' in the sense that they totally administered the life of their inmates. 'Total institutions are not a separate class of social establishments,' observed Samuel E. Wallace, 'but rather specific institutions, which exhibit to an intense degree certain characteristics found in all institutions. The issue is not which institutions are total and which are not. But rather, how much totality does each display?' In *Catch-22,* the army is part of a vast empire called M&M Enterprises, a harbinger of the new multinational corporate world to come. In *One Flew Over the Cuckoo's Nest,* the mental asylum administered by Big Nurse is part of 'the Combine', a metaphor for the entire therapeutic society whose aim is social control and adjustment. In *Naked Lunch,* the underworld of drug addiction is simply the underside of 'Freeland', the ultimate consumer society and junk culture of the future. All three novels are versions of contemporary society as a total institution described by Paul Goodman in *Growing Up Absurd* and Herbert Marcuse in *One-Dimensional Man* (1964).

The artistic legacy of the 1960s

As we shall see, the 1960s ended not with the expected bang but with a whimper: the dissolution of the New Left and the rise and fall of a violent radical faction called the Weathermen; the dissolution of the Civil Rights movement and the rise and fall of an angrier but less coherent Black Power movement; the dissolution of the counterculture after Woodstock and its absorption into the mainstream consumer economy. Only the new Feminist movement appeared to prosper while other political-cultural movements became marginalized or self-destructed. With the election of Richard Nixon in 1968, the country turned away from activism. Though the Vietnam War would grind on for seven more years, the antiwar movement never again cohered as it did in 1967–8. As the country became depoliticized, so did the culture, thus creating an imaginative crisis in the 1970s and 1980s. One name for this crisis is Postmodernism.

Poetry after the 1960s

This enervation could be seen in all the arts. For instance, poetry retreated from the public world to the college campus and settled back into the closed universe of private experience, linguistic manipulation and self-reflection. 'Contemporary poetry flourishes in a vacuum', Joseph Epstein argued in a polemical essay entitled 'Who Killed Poetry?' (1988). He complained, 'just now the entire enterprise of poetic creation seems threatened by having been taken out of the world, chilled in the classroom, and vastly overproduced by men and women who are licensed to write it by [college] degree if not necessarily by talent or spirit'. Not everyone agreed with Epstein's diatribe. In a caustic rejoinder called 'Death to the Death of Poetry' (1989), the poet Donald Hall pointed out that the proliferation of poetry readings, magazines and books had contributed to the creation of a new audience for contemporary verse. 'Our trouble is not with poetry but with the public perception of poetry,' Hall argued. 'Although we have more poetry today, we have less poetry reviewing in national journals...we need a cadre of reviewers to sift through the great volume of material. The weight of numbers discourages readers from trying to keep up. More poetry than ever: how do we discriminate?'

The stream of published poetry became an indiscriminate flood in the Eighties as 246 small poetry-book publishers started up between 1980 and 1987. Yet with the death of Berryman, Bishop, Jarrell and Lowell, few major names emerged to take their place. Instead, poetry was decentralized in distinct, self-defined groups of which new women poets were the most distinguishable. The success of Carolyn Forché (*The Country Between Us*, 1981), Sharon Olds (*The Dead and the Living*, 1983) and Marilyn Hacker (*Assumptions*, 1985) led Alicia Ostriker to claim a feminist renaissance in *Stealing the Language: The Emergence of Women's Poetry in America* (1986). She wrote: 'There is reason to believe that American women poets writing in the last 25 years constitute a literary movement comparable to Romanticism or modernism in our literary past and that their work is destined not only to enter the mainstream but to change the stream's future course.'

But out of the bewildering array of new poetry, only a few voices emerged to claim a wider public, among them John Ashbery, Allen Ginsberg and Adrienne Rich. Despite their successes, however, it was clear that the audience for poetry was limited to college campuses or, as the poet Wendell Berry lamented, restricted to other poets. What Randall Jarrell observed in *Poetry and the Age* (1953) was just as true nearly 40 years later: 'Tomorrow morning some poet may, like Byron, wake up to find himself famous – for having written a novel, for having killed his wife; it will not be for having written a poem.'

But in the 1990s, some poets moved in another direction as the academic dominance was challenged by the rise of a new public. In *Poetry and the Public* (2002) Joseph Harrington chronicles the development of a changing poetic community. 'The new poetry scene largely emerged outside of the traditional institutions of literature, such as universities, literary journals, or academic and commercial presses,' he says. 'Rather, much new work by poets appeared, at least in the first instance, in other social settings: on the sides of buildings, in performance spaces, in poetry films, open readings in coffee-houses, poetry slams [public competitions] in bars or community centers, workshops in homes or in libraries.' The new poetry is more public than private, performative than premeditated, demotic than academic. In fact, according to Dana Gioia, it is more heard than read, as more people attend poetry readings than buy poetry books. In this way, the new poetry scene resembles recent developments in the theater.

The theater after the 1960s

In drama too there was the sense of an ending in the 1960s as the theater closed the book on one of its most turbulent decades. The critic C. W. E. Bigsby describes the situation well:

> By the early 1970s the American theatre seemed in one of its periodic crises. The promise of Off- and Off-Off-Broadway had largely dissipated; its leading companies had closed, and the social and political pressures which had given it a special significance for the best part of a decade had relaxed. It was no longer possible to pretend that the theatre was at the heart of a debate about central moral issues or was conducting a radical revision of artistic form. Meanwhile, the major figures of the American theatre, Arthur Miller, Tennessee Williams and Edward Albee – people who had dominated the 1940s, 1950s and 1960s – seemed to disappear from public view … With rapidly increasing costs, Broadway was less willing than ever to present the work of new American playwrights, preferring musicals, comedies and British imports already tested out in London's West End.

By the mid-1970s, the center – Broadway and its environs – was no longer holding, as a new generation of playwrights began fruitful collaborations with various regional theaters around the country. The best new plays were now being premiered in Dallas, Louisville or Minneapolis *before* they moved to New York. They were often more traditional in form though certainly not conservative in content: Charles Fuller's gripping account of the impact of racism on black consciousness in *A Soldier's Play* (1981); Harvey Fierstein's tough and sentimental melodrama about homosexuality in *Torch Song Trilogy* (1982); and Marsha Norman's harrowing version of a dysfunctional mother-daughter relationship in *'night Mother* (1983). But in these years arguably only three talented dramatists managed to produce a body of consistent work illuminating the dreams and nightmares of American life: Lanford Wilson (*The Hot l Baltimore*, 1973; *The Fifth of July*, 1978;

Talley's Folly, 1979); Sam Shepard (*The Tooth of Crime,* 1973; *Buried Child,* 1978; *Fool for Love,* 1983); and David Mamet (*American Buffalo,* 1975; *Glengarry, Glen Ross,* 1984; *Speed-the-Plow,* 1988). Though radically different from each other, all three shared a sharp ear for the nuances of American speech and a brilliant grasp of the inner theatricality of contemporary American life.

By the end of the 1980s, three new directions in the American theater could be discerned. The first was the growing domination of urban 'regional theaters' like New York's Public Theater, Washington's Arena Stage and Los Angeles's Mark Taper Forum as alternatives to Broadway's commercial theater. These regional theaters resembled similar publicly funded theaters in Europe but, as Hilary DeVries noted, 'American theater, unlike its European counterpart, has been characterized by artists rather than institutions.' These 'artists' might include performers like Meredith Monk, directors like Peter Sellars or producer/ entrepreneurs like the late Joseph Papp. By the time he retired in 1991, Papp had created a formidable theatrical empire in New York, combining elements of experimental, populist and commercial theater in both his year-round Public Theater and the summer productions of Shakespeare in Central Park.

The second was the emergence of a new generation of dramatists whose work reflected the social concerns that emerged in the 1960s. Some dealt with questions of sexuality, gender and religion, like Tina Howe (*Coastal Disturbances,* 1986; *Pride's Crossing,* 1997) and Wendy Wasserstein (*The Heidi Chronicles,* 1987; *The Sisters Rosenzweig,* 1993). Others drew on ethnic and racial experience, for instance August Wilson (*Fences,* 1987, *The Piano Lesson* 1990, *Gem of the Ocean,* 2003) and Henry David Hwang (*M. Butterfly,* 1988; *Golden Child,* 1996, revised 1998). Of all the playwrights of his generation, the late August Wilson was the most ambitious. In a series of plays, each set in a different decade in the twentieth century, Wilson aimed to explore the whole range of black experience. Not surprisingly, several plays were informed by the African-American musical heritage: *Ma Rainey's Black Bottom* (1984), *The Piano Lesson* (1990), *Seven Guitars* (1996) and *Gem of the Ocean* (2004). 'I'm taking each decade and looking back at one of the most important questions that blacks confronted in that decade and writing a play about it,' said Wilson. 'Put them together and you have a history.' The deaths of Wilson and Arthur Miller in 2005 deprived the American stage of two of its greatest social dramatists.

But perhaps the most striking characteristic of the new American theater was its formal eclecticism and technical innovation. In musicals, dramas and comedies there was an attempt to meld traditional theatricality with new technology in order to appeal to an audience weaned on television and movies, rock concerts and music videos. 'Theater has to reinvent itself in the next generation,' observed Peter Sellars. 'Because traditional theater is no longer relevant to a whole generation, and the most exciting developments today are electronic, theater must remake itself from an electronic standpoint.' Part of this transformation involved the popular cannibalizing of high culture classics. For instance, the Pulitzer Prize-winning musical *Rent* (1996) updated Puccini's *La Boheme* by transporting its bohemian artists from Paris's Left Bank to New York's East Village and transforming the nineteenth-century disease of tuberculosis into the twentieth-century plague of AIDS.

This new eclecticism was something the contemporary theater shared with the other arts. It was manifested in the breakdown of boundaries between high and low cultural forms and between various performative genres. Sam Shepard pointed to this common characteristic when he noted, 'I'm interested in exploring the writing of plays through attitudes derived from other forms such as music, painting, sculpture.' He observed that in the other arts the

> single most important idea is the idea of consciousness... For some time now it's become generally accepted that the other art forms are dealing with this idea to one degree or another. That the subject of painting is seeing. That the subject of music is hearing. That the subject of sculpture is space.

This concern with consciousness resulted in an *avant-garde* theater which combined all three 'subjects' synchronically, perhaps best exemplified in the work of Richard Foreman (*Café Amérique*, 1981) and Robert Wilson (*Einstein on the Beach*, 1976). This new theater was truly postmodern in its deconstruction of older classics and traditional genres and its reconstruction of hybrid forms. 'The avant-garde is usually born out of legitimate social confrontation,' observed Robert Brustein. 'That doesn't exist anymore [in today's society]. As a result, the avant-garde is not a political force, but an aesthetic and metaphysical one.'

Despite the successes of individual practitioners, American theater did not flourish in the 1990s. Robert Wilson worked mostly in Europe while Shepard and Mamet spent more time making movies than writing plays. The only new playwright of the 1990s to rival them was Tony Kushner, whose Pulitzer Prize-winning drama, *Angels in America*, was the most celebrated work of the decade. It reached an even wider audience when an award-winning production directed by Mike Nichols was shown on television in 2003 and released on DVD in 2004. In 2009, Kushner returned to similar themes in another epic drama with an ambitious title, *The Intelligent Homosexual's Guide to Capitalism and Socialism With a Key to the Scriptures.*

Angels in America consists of two parts: *Millennium Approaches* (1991) and *Perestroika* (1992). Subtitled *A Gay Fantasia on National Themes,* Kushner's epic drama combines realism and fantasy to explore major themes of politics, sex and religion. Its cast includes fictional characters, celestial angels and historical figures like Ethel Rosenberg and Roy Cohn, Senator Joseph McCarthy's aggressive assistant who pursued communists and homosexuals alike and died of AIDS in 1986. But aside from Kushner's triumph, drama, like poetry, was in transition. 'For all the expansion of regional theatre and the consolidation of Off-Broadway and Off-Off Broadway, forty years later the theatre has in large degree reverted to a minority interest,' concluded Bigsby. 'Its leading writers and directors are for the most part unknown to the public, their experiments seem arcane, their relationship to their culture is problematic.'

Postmodernism

After the 1960s, literary culture changed radically in the United States. The highbrow academicism of contemporary poetry and the lowbrow eclecticism of contemporary theater were both reflected in the state of American publishing in the last quarter of the twentieth century. In *A Few Good Voices in My Head* (1987), Ted Solotaroff wrote a jeremiad about the widening gap between commercial publishing and literary culture. 'Increasingly ruled by corporate values and mass-marketing methods, the publishing business can be said to have moved most of its product and spirit to the shopping mall,' he observed. 'Meanwhile, in response to the loss of its institutional home, the community of letters and ideas has been moving its product and spirit to the campus, where many of its books, magazines, and authors lead their dispersed but sheltered lives.' As popular writers like Stephen King, Judith Krantz and Elmore Leonard occupied the center stage of mainstream culture, others were pushed to the academic wings where they taught in creative writing programs and published with small regional presses. Solotaroff concluded, 'The hospitality and security the academic community offers comes with its relative insularity and remoteness from the common life and its overt and underlying issues that are pressing for expression.' As serious writing became a mandarin activity, it threatened to become more remote from the mainstream of American life and culture.

Academicism, eclecticism and remoteness from ordinary life – qualities that could be discerned as well in fiction – are all aspects of the new aesthetic which came to be called Postmodernist. In recent years there has been a great deal of critical discussion – and critical confusion – about the meaning of Postmodernism, leading Ihab Hassan to lament that the term might fade 'from awkward neologism to derelict cliché without ever attaining the dignity of a concept'. Called variously 'fabulism', 'metafiction', 'post-realism', or 'surfiction', Postmodernist fiction points to the rejection of Realism by a significant group of writers, often teachers of creative writing on college campuses. They reject both the conventions of Realism, with its emphasis on plot, character and mimetic representation, and the ideology of Modernism, with its nostalgia for order, faith in high culture, and often reactionary politics. 'Postwar experimental writing may be seen as a search for ways to deal with the violence, brevity, and rigidity of life,' observed the critic Josephine Hendin.

> It carries to great extremes the themes of combativeness, fragmentariness, coolness, and meaninglessness that are marks of modern fiction. It may originate in the modernist sense of life as problematic, but unlike the great experimental fiction of the 1920s, it does not lament the brokenness of experience as a sign of the decline of Western civilization. Instead it offers an acceptance of dislocation as a major part of life and perhaps a hope that the displacement of traditional ideals might permit new ways of dealing with the human situation.[1]

Already in the 1940s American writers were turning from the naturalistic treatment of the social world to deal with the subjectivity of experience in what the critic Jonathan Baumbach called 'the landscape of nightmare'. In the gothic dream world of Capote's *Other Voices, Other Rooms* and the exotic spiritual landscape of Paul Bowles's *The Sheltering Sky,* fiction found new forms to deal with 'the underside of consciousness'. In the 1950s, other writers turned from the

content of subjective experience to the form of aesthetic experience in such seminal works as William Gaddis's *The Recognitions* and Vladimir Nabokov's *Lolita*
(1958). In *A World More Attractive* (1963), Irving Howe complained that

> those writers who wished to preserve the spirit of rebellion also found it
> extremely hard to realize their sentiments in novels dealing with contem-
> porary life. Most of them were unable, or perhaps too shrewd, to deal with
> postwar experience directly; they preferred tangents of suggestion to frontal
> representation; they could express their passionate, though amorphous criti-
> cism of American life not through realistic portraiture but through fable, pica-
> resque, prophesy and nostalgia.

Postmodernist fiction

In the 1960s a new aesthetic was formulated as, in Malcolm Bradbury's words,
'the tension between massive public history and the dwarfed artistic imagination
pushed writers into examining the potential of the form they possessed'. In a celebrated essay entitled 'The Literature of Exhaustion' (1967), John Barth argued
that conventional fictional forms had been used up. In *The Death of the Novel
and Other Stories* (1969), Ronald Sukenick demanded that writers begin over
again with a new sensibility: 'Reality doesn't exist, time doesn't exist, personality doesn't exist.' In *Surfiction* (1975), Raymond Federman went even further,
proclaiming, 'In the fiction of the future, all distinctions between the real and
the imaginary, between the conscious and the unconscious, between the past
and the present, between truth and untruth will be abolished.' Finally, in 'The
Death of the Author' (1984), William Gass declared that art was less creation
than translation. 'Because we borrow, beg, buy, steal, or copy texts,' wrote Gass,
'we are, in effect, translating texts from one time to another and one context to
another and one language to another.'

Though these pronouncements sound suspiciously programmatic,
Postmodernist writers did not form a school and, indeed, displayed a surprisingly wide variety of approaches to writing. Donald Barthelme's stories in *City
Life* (1970) are minimalist fragments constructed out of the 'dreck' of modern
life. Barth's mammoth novel, *Giles Goat-Boy* (1966) is a maximalist celebration
of the possibilities of imaginative form. Robert Coover explored the debased
manifestations of American popular mythology in fictions that were often amusingly irreverent: religion in *The Origins of the Brunists* (1965), sports in *The
Universal Baseball Association* (1968) and film in *A Night at the Movies* (1988).
Finally, Vonnegut combined popular literary genres with experimental fictional
techniques in homely parables of the terrors of contemporary life like *Breakfast
of Champions* (1973) and *Slapstick* (1976).

What all these different books share is a sense of the changing nature of the
writer's view of his own calling. These are 'texts', Brian McHale explains in
Postmodernist Fiction (1991):

> which are strongly self-conscious, self-reflective, self-critical; which, by laying
> bare their own devices, continually raise the problem of the relation between

the game-like artifices of fiction and the imitation of reality; which actively resist and subvert the reader's efforts to make sense of them in the familiar novelistic ways; the sort of texts which the French would be apt to call texts of the 'practice of writing'.

Several critics have made a useful distinction between 'invisible' and 'visible' writing to describe the polarities of Realism, with its emphasis on writing as a transparent medium between reader and subject, and fabulism or *écriture* which self-consciously calls attention to its own artifice. Such self-referential works as Nabokov's *Pale Fire* (1962) and Barth's *Letters* (1979) created, in William Gass's pregnant phrase, 'the world within the word'.

By critical consensus, the most brilliant of the Postmodernist writers is Thomas Pynchon. His two major early novels, *V.* (1963) and *Gravity's Rainbow* (1973), are massive attempts to contain modern history within the pages of a book in the manner of *Ulysses* and *Moby-Dick*. These are works of such vastness, range and difficulty that, as Tony Tanner said of *Gravity's Rainbow,* they defy summary and at the same time provide an exemplary reading experience. 'The reader does not move comfortably from some ideal "emptiness" of meaning to a satisfying fullness,' noted Tanner in *City of Words* (1971), 'but instead becomes involved in a process in which any perception can precipitate a new confusion, and an apparent clarification turn into a prelude to further difficulties. So far from this being an obstacle to appreciating the book, it is part of its essence. It is the way we live now.'

But Pynchon's strategy is perhaps more perfectly worked out in his classic short novel, *The Crying of Lot 49.* The site of his novel is Southern California in the 1960s, which seems a far cry from Raymond Chandler's Los Angeles in the 1940s. The home of military research, popular entertainment, waste culture and rampant narcissism, Pynchon's California seems less a physical place than a state of mind. The heroine, Oedipa Maas, becomes the executrix of the vast estate of her former lover, an eccentric millionaire named Pierce Inverarity. Like her *alter ego,* Oedipus Rex, she embarks on a quest which involves her in the solution of a mystery. In *At the Edge of History* (1971), William Irwin Thompson notes, 'She searches for an inheritance from a past that is dead, discovers an imagined system of communication in a land where human communication fails, and finds in the rubbish of the state the fertile decay for her own ambiguous regeneration.'

As Oedipa explores the extent of Inverarity's estate she becomes aware of a series of plots and counterplots involving a shadowy group called the Tristero. These conspiracies may be real or they may be projections of Oedipa's increasingly paranoid vision. But as she attempts to pierce the mystery surrounding Inverarity's legacy, which may include all of America, she is tempted by glimpses of transcendent meaning and yet cannot be sure of her own senses. 'Another mode of meaning behind the obvious, or none,' Pynchon writes of his heroine's dilemma.

> Either Oedipa in the orbiting ecstasy of a true paranoia, or a real Tristero. For there either was some Tristero beyond the appearance of the legacy America or there was just America and if there was just America then it seemed the only

way she could continue, and manage to be at all relevant to it, was as an alien, unfurrowed, assumed full circle into some paranoia.

The novel leaves Oedipa – and the reader – waiting for a clearer sign of 'revelation' that will never come. But both are finally united in their imaginative search for meaning, committed to unraveling the plot. In later novels like *Vineland* (1990) and *Inherent Vice* (2009) Pynchon returned to California as a national site, a state of mind and the scene of a crime.

However, by the end of the 1970s some voices were raised against the developing symbiotic relationship between avant-garde writing and advanced literary criticism. In *The Post-Modern Aura* (1985), Charles Newman attacked the 'inflation of discourse' where Postmodernist fiction evolved ever more sophisticated formalist techniques to 'unmask its own fictionality' while post-structuralist criticism developed 'secondary languages which presumably "demystify" reality, but actually tend to further obscure it'. In an age when all authority is questioned, including the authority of the writer and the critic, then both literature and criticism are turned back on themselves. As literature ceases to deal with life so literary criticism ceases to deal with literature. Finally, a literature and a criticism which take themselves as their own subject become distorted mirrors of each other: 'self-reflexive, involuted, solopsistic, cerebral, hermetic, privatized and cut off from the sources of life'.

By the beginning of the 1980s, even celebrated Postmodernist writers were publicly wondering about the usefulness of these critical categories. Barth admitted that his own work appeared to have 'both modernist and postmodernist attributes, even occasional premodernist attributes,' while Coover confessed, 'Maybe I think that all my fiction is realistic and that so far it has simply been misunderstood as otherwise.' In a new article entitled 'The Literature of Replenishment' (1979), Barth cautiously revised his earlier estimate in 'The Literature of Exhaustion'. After the conscious elitism of experimental fiction, he now hoped that the novel would return to its historical roots in 'middle-class popular culture'. 'The ideal postmodernist novel will somehow rise above the quarrel between realism and irrealism, formalism and "contentism", pure and committed literature, coterie fiction and junk fiction,' he wrote. 'Alas for professors of literature, it may not need as much *teaching* as Joyce's or Nabokov's or Pynchon's books, or some of my own.'

Yet the process of transforming the conventions of traditional fiction was not ended. Just as Barth and Coover were redefining their own fictive efforts, so several unreconstructed Modernists were challenging their larger audiences to follow them into more experimental territory. In a trio of long novels, *Bellefleur* (1980), *A Bloodsmoor Romance* (1982) and *Mysteries of Winterthurn* (1984), Joyce Carol Oates sought to revitalize in Postmodern terms the nineteenth-century popular genres of the gothic family saga, romance and mystery. In *Loon Lake* (1980), E. L. Doctorow pursued the possibilities of a seamless multivoiced narrative. His tale of the pursuit of the American Dream by several individualists during the Depression 'is the account in helpless linear translation of the unending love of our simultaneous but disynchronous lives'. And in *The Counterlife* (1986), Philip Roth closed his multivolume series of novels about a celebrated Jewish-American writer tantalizingly like himself with an exploration of the relationship between the creator and his characters. In Roth's view, the 'obsessive reinvention of the real' never stops either in life or in art. 'The treacherous imagination is everybody's maker,' he observes, 'we are all the invention of each other, everybody a conjuration conjuring up everyone else. We are all each other's authors.'

Minimalism and Maximalism

At the same time that the premises of Fabulism were being scrutinized, the techniques of Realism were being refined in the new movement of Minimalism. Minimalist writers like Raymond Carver (*What We Talk About When We Talk About Love*, 1981) and Bobbie Ann Mason (*Shiloh*, 1982) dealt with ordinary life in simple language within the confines of the short story. Carver was the acknowledged master of the genre, describing people on the edge of breakdown with the precision of Hemingway. But, Allan Lloyd Smith noted,

> Carver's people resemble Hemingway's damaged heroes, the walking wounded of stories like 'Big Two-Hearted River'; but Carver's people suffer not from the ravages of war but the atrophy of their culture: they have the brain-damage caused by TV, bowling alleys and trailer parks, the lack of money and the lack of words to cope with their experiences.

If the Minimalism of Carver's short stories represented one revision of conventional Realism, then the Maximalism of Tom Wolfe's fat novels, *The Bonfire of the Vanities* (1987), *A Man in Full* (1997) and *I Am Charlotte Simmons* (2004), represented another. Wolfe began as the spokesman for the New Journalism, which combined the methods of objective reporting with the techniques of subjective fiction. In books like *The Electric Kool-Aid Acid Test* (1968) and *The Right Stuff* (1979), he documented the startling range of American lifestyles from hippies to astronauts. But in his fiction, Wolfe turned his documentary style on the excesses of post-Reagan America. In an essay entitled 'Stalking the Billion-Footed Beast' (1989), he challenged American novelists to confront the new social reality. 'The past three decades have been decades of tremendous and at times convulsive social change, especially in large cities, and the tide of the fourth great wave of immigration has made the picture seem all the more chaotic, random, and discontinuous,' he observed. 'The economy with which realistic fiction can bring the many currents of a city together in a single, fairly simple story was something that I eventually found exhilarating.'

In creating a panorama of urban life stretching from the skyscrapers of Manhattan to the shopping malls of Atlanta, Wolfe portrayed new immigration and commercial greed, the decline of civic virtue and the rise of cynical mass media, the racial and class tensions of American cities. In *The New Journalism* (1973), he argued 'that nonfiction had displaced the novel as American literature's "main event"'. In his novels, he mixes documentary and satire in the manner of Balzac or Sinclair Lewis to create a carnivalesque country. In 'Stalking the Billion-Footed Beast,' Wolfe declared, 'If fiction writers do not start facing the obvious, the literary history of the second half of the twentieth century will record that journalists not only took over the richness of American life as their domain but also seized the high ground of literature itself.' We shall examine Wolfe's challenge in the next chapters.

Art in the streets

In the 1960s, political protesters took to the streets. So did American artists. The streets of the city became a contested space where urban life was being redefined. Nowhere was this more evident than in New York City. Though New York grew rapidly after the Civil War, its distinctive skyline was not created until the 1930s. During the Depression, three major landmarks were constructed that changed the face of the city: the Chrysler Building (1930), the Empire State Building (1931) and Rockefeller Center (1929–39). When the Swiss architect Le Corbusier entered New York harbor for the first time in 1935 he was struck by the magnificent skyline. 'We saw the mystic city of the new world appear far away, rising up from Manhattan,' he said.

> It passed us at close range: a spectacle of brutality and savagery. In contrast to our hopes the skyscrapers were not made of glass, but of tiara-crowned masses of stone. They carry up a thousand feet in the sky, a completely new and pro- digious architectural event; with one stroke Europe is thrust aside.[2]

Le Corbusier was impressed with the Manhattan skyline but he thought he could improve it. He was puzzled that most New Yorkers lived in brownstone row-houses, walk-up apartments and low-rise tenements: 'Between the pres- ent skyscrapers there are masses of large and small buildings. Most of them are small. What are these small houses doing in dramatic Manhattan? I haven't the slightest idea. It is incomprehensible.' So he proposed clearing them away and building instead massive high-rise apartment blocks that could each house 3000 people. In *City Life* (1995), the architectural critic Witold Rybczynski explains, 'Instead of streets and sidewalks, there were elevators and corridors, or "interior streets", as he called them. It was all very rational – "Cartesian" was a favorite Le Corbusier term – cars over there, living over here, work above, play below. Voila! The city of the future.'

Le Corbusier wanted to build high-rise and abolish the street. But American painters and photographers like Edward Hopper, Ben Shahn and Berenice Abbott continued to depict the low-rise life of the street. In Abbott's landmark book of photographs, *Changing New York* (1939), and Hopper's urban paintings, the neighborhoods of New York were immortalized. Indeed, the street atmosphere of Hopper's famous painting, *Nighthawks* (1942) was often reproduced in *film noir* classics like Abraham Polonsky's *Force of Evil* (1948) and John Huston's *The Asphalt Jungle* (1950).

Le Corbusier didn't get to build his city of the future in New York, but after World War II others tried. When the federal government released billions of dollars to build new roads and housing, the city was transformed by a new gen- eration of architects and city planners who had been taught by Le Corbusier to think big. In place of unplanned urban growth, they proposed gigantic urban renewal projects which changed the face of the city. They replaced low-rise build-ings with enormous high-rise complexes and reduced pedestrian sidewalks to create wider streets for automobile traffic. Old neighborhoods were bulldozed to make way for new highways; the old city was destroyed in the name of Urban Modernism.

It was in this context that Jane Jacobs published a groundbreaking book in 1961 entitled *The Death and Life of Great American Cities.* Jacobs created a new paradigm of urban planning and changed the way people saw the city. Jacobs began by turning the conventional wisdom about modern cities on its head. Instead of more modern high-rise complexes, she demonstrated how a mixture of old and new low-rise and high-rise buildings was economically necessary and aesthetically desirable. Instead of building more parks and highways, Jacobs wished to preserve the city streets. She wrote:

> Streets and their sidewalks, the main public places of a city, are its most vital organs. Think of a city and what comes to mind? Its streets. If a city's streets look interesting, the city looks interesting; if they look dull, the city looks dull... To keep the city safe is a fundamental task of a city's streets and its sidewalks.

Instead of viewing the city as simply a larger small town, Jacobs argued that modern cities are intrinsically different. 'They differ from towns and suburbs in basic ways and one of these is that cities are, by definition, full of strangers.' Instead of suburban 'togetherness', urbanites prize personal freedom. Instead of small-town 'friendliness', city-dwellers desire anonymity. 'Cities are full of people with whom, from your point of view, or mine, or any other individual's, a certain degree of contact is useful or enjoyable; but you don't want them in your hair. And they don't want you in theirs either.' Finally, instead of orderly urban plan-ning she proposed unplanned order:

> Under the seeming disorder of the old city, wherever the old city is working successfully, is a marvelous order for maintaining the safety of the streets and the freedom of the city. It is a complex order. Its essence is intricacy of side-walk use, bringing with it a succession of eyes. This order is all composed of movement and change, and although it is life, not art, we may fancifully call it the art form of the city and liken it to dance.

It may seem odd that Jacobs would celebrate street life in a decade when urban crime was a grim reality. Even an ardent admirer like Marshall Berman questioned her idyllic urban vision in *All That Is Solid Melts Into Air* (1988). 'Sometimes her vision seems positively pastoral,' he notes; 'she insists, for instance, that in a vibrant neighborhood with a mixture of shops and residences, with constant activity on the sidewalks, with easy surveillance of the streets from within houses and stores, there will be no crime. As we read this, we wonder what planet Jacobs can possibly have been thinking of.' Similarly, the chaotic character of urban life is portrayed by Saul Bellow in *Mr Sammler's Planet* (1970) as less than pastoral. Where Jacobs described safe neighborhoods, Bellow depicted a derelict city. In two vivid scenes he showed an elegant black pickpocket plying his trade on a crowded city bus and later being beaten to a pulp in front of a crowd of passive bystanders. No wonder that in an apocalyptic moment Bellow's protagonist Mr Sammler concludes: 'New York makes one think about Sodom and Gomorrah, the end of the world.'

Nevertheless, when Jacobs said, 'The ballet of the city sidewalk never repeats itself,' she was pointing in the direction that modern art would take in the Sixties. For in this decade, all the arts took to the streets. Berman notes that 'even as Jacobs assimilated the life of the street to dance, the life of modern dance was striving to assimilate the street'. Beginning in the Sixties, choreographers Merce Cunningham and Twyla Tharp brought randomness, chance and non-dance movements into their performances into which they introduced not music but silence, radio static and random street noises. Berman says, 'sometimes dancers would move directly into New York's streets, and onto its bridges and roofs, interacting spontaneously with whoever and whatever was there'.

Film, poetry, painting

The symbiosis between street life and dance life was reproduced in all the arts. The new American cinema of John Cassavetes and Sidney Lumet used the streets of New York in films like *Shadows* (1961) and *The Pawnbroker* (1965). Soon a younger generation of filmmakers, including Paul Mazursky and Woody Allen, were making the New York cityscape the subject of films like *Next Stop, Greenwich Village* (1976) and *Manhattan* (1979). Indeed, films about New York created indelible urban images in various ways. In *Hannah and Her Sisters* (1986), Woody Allen filmed the interiors in the apartment on Central Park West that belonged to his star and then partner, Mia Farrow. In *Do the Right Thing* (1989), Spike Lee transformed a street in the Bedford-Stuyvesant section of Brooklyn into a movie set that resembled a Hollywood sound stage. In the famous opening scene of *West Side Story* (1961), Jerome Robbins scrambled the city's geography by combining a West Side street and an East Side playground. 'Dancers would jump up on the West Side', said Robbins, 'and come down on the East Side.'

In poetry, too, John Ashbery, Kenneth Koch and Frank O'Hara wrote a new kind of urban verse which became identified as the New York School. It was spontaneous and colloquial, as in O'Hara's celebrated poem on the death of jazz singer Billy Holiday, 'The Day Lady Died' (1959). In *The Last Avant-Garde* (1998), David Lehman described the origins of the New York School in the early 1950s. He depicted O'Hara and his friends as 'the band of outsiders who brought the avant-garde revolution to American poetry'. In *All Poets Welcome* (2003), Daniel Kane chronicled the evolution of a group of disparate artists on New York's Lower East Side who comprised an informal political and aesthetic avant-garde characteristic of the 1960s. It began with impromptu poetry readings in coffeehouses like Le Metro and Les Deux Mégots and culminated in the formation of the Poetry Project at St Mark's Church. The Poetry Project, said Allen Ginsberg, became an 'immediate neighborhood community and family' which attracted poets as different as Ginsburg, O'Hara and Anne Waldman.

O'Hara was also an art critic who wrote a book about Abstract Expressionist painter Jackson Pollock and a poem for pop artist Robert Rauschenberg. Like film, poetry and dance, painting moved into the streets as well. Even before Pollock's death in 1956, a new generation of painters began rebelling against the hegemony of Abstract Expressionism. Robert Rauschenberg produced 'combine paintings' out of discarded objects in 1954; Jasper Johns painted simple objects like targets and flags in 1955. With the triumph of Pop Art we entered the era of art commerce which celebrated both consumer commodities and street art. Ben Heller wrote in 1963, 'art has become a big business, is now a party to modern merchandising. Taking advantage of the burgeoning interest in culture in general and art in particular, and responding to the demands of an almost voraciously grasping public, the art world has rapidly and radically changed'.

Rauschenberg observed that art begins in the streets. 'The everyday world is the most astonishing inspiration conceivable,' said Allan Kaprow. 'A walk down 14th street is more amazing than any masterpiece of art.'[3] Berman notes that a new generation of artists, including Rauschenberg, Jim Dine, Red Grooms, George Segal and Claes Oldenburg, were moving away not only from the dominant forms of abstraction but from the flatness and confinement of painting itself. He says, 'They experimented with a fascinating array of art forms: forms that incorporated and transformed non-art materials, junk, debris, and objects picked up in the street; three-dimensional environments that combined painting, architecture and sculpture.' A prime example is Rauschenberg's celebrated 'combine', *Monogram* (1955–9), which features a stuffed Angora goat that the artist had bought on the street from a failing office-supply store for 35 dollars.

The new street art that emerged in the 1960s followed the aesthetic line established by Ralph Waldo Emerson more than a century earlier. Emerson wrote: 'I embrace the common, I explore and sit at the feet of the familiar, the low.' The essential thing, Oldenburg said, was to 'look for beauty where it was not supposed to be found'. Emerson wrote: 'What would we really know the meaning of? The meal in the firkin; the milk in the pan; the ballad in the street; the news of the boat; the glance of the eye; the form and gait of the body; – show me the ultimate reason of these matters.' Oldenburg said:

> I am for an art that is political-erotical-mystical, that does something other than sit on its ass in a museum. I am for an art that embroils itself with the everyday crap and comes out on top. I am for an art that tells you the time of day, or where such and such a street is. I am for an art that helps old ladies across the street.[4]

The artistic celebration of the street became a dominant mode of culture in the late twentieth century: in colorful graffiti and rap music as well as modern dance and Pop Art. This celebration persists in the new millennium. In E. L. Doctorow's novel, *City of God* (2000), Manhattan is described as the 'capital of literature, the arts, social pretension, subway tunnel condos'. In a memorable passage, Doctorow describes how street life is at the heart of urban experience:

> But I can stop on any corner at the intersection of two busy streets and before me are thousands of lives headed in all four directions, uptown downtown east and west, on foot, on bikes, on in-line skates, in buses, strollers, cars, trucks, with the subway rumble underneath my feet ... and how can I not know I am momentarily part of the most spectacular phenomenon in the unnatural world? There is a specie recognition we will never acknowledge. A primatial over-soul. For all the wariness or indifference with which we negotiate our public spaces, we rely on the masses around us to delineate ourselves. The city may begin from a marketplace, a trading post, the confluence of waters, but it secretly depends on the human need to walk among strangers.

NOTES

1. In Daniel Hoffman (ed.), *The Harvard Guide to Contemporary American Writing*, Cambridge, MA: Harvard University Press, 1979, p. 240.
2. Quoted in Witold Rybczynski, *City Life*, New York: Scribner, 1995, p. 156.
3. Quoted in Marshall Berman, *All That Is Solid Melts Into Air*, Harmondsworth: Penguin, 1988, p. 319.
4. Quoted ibid., p. 320.

RECOMMENDED READING

Marshall Berman, *All That Is Solid Melts Into Air*, New York: Penguin, 1988.

C. W. E. Bigsby, *A Critical Introduction to Twentieth-Century American Drama, Volume Three*, Cambridge: Cambridge University Press, 1985.

Gerard J. DeGroot, *The Sixties Unplugged*, Cambridge, MA: Harvard University Press, 2008.

Anthony Flint, *Wrestling with Moses*, New York: Random House, 2009.

Todd Gitlin, *The Sixties: Years of Hope, Days of Rage*, New York: Bantam, 1987.

Mark Harris, *Pictures at a Revolution*, New York: Penguin, 2008.

Daniel Hoffman (ed.), *Harvard Guide to Contemporary American Writing*, Cambridge: MA: Harvard University Press, 1979.

Jane Jacobs, *The Death and Life of Great American Cities*, New York: Vintage, 1992.

G. Calvin Mackenzie and Robert Weisbrot, *The Liberal Hour*, New York: Penguin, 2008.

Brian McHale, *Postmodernist Fiction*, London: Routledge, 1991.

Tony Tanner, *City of Words*, New York: Harper & Row, 1971.

Leonard Wallock (ed.), *New York: Capital of the World, 1940–1965*, New York: Rizzoli, 1968.

PART IV
The Ambiguous Legacy of the Sixties

Vietnam Veterans' Memorial

Year	Politics	Culture
1969	• Moratorium antiwar demonstrations • Nixon appeals to 'silent majority' • Stonewall Riots in Greenwich Village, NY • Weather Underground's 'Days of Rage' • People's Park in Berkeley, California	• Joyce Carol Oates, *Them* • Philip Roth, *Portnoy's Complaint* • Kurt Vonnegut, *Slaughterhouse-Five; or The Children's Crusade* • Woodstock Festival in upstate New York • Altamont Rock Concert in California
1970	• American land forces invade Cambodia • Kent State demonstrators killed	• Donald Barthelme, *City Life* • Joan Didion, *Play It as It Lays* • Tom Wolfe, *Radical Chic and Mau-Mouing the Flak Catchers*
1971	• Kissinger secretly visits China • Pentagon Papers are leaked • 'Plumbers Unit' is created in the White House	• E. L. Doctorow, *The Book of Daniel* • Ernest Gaines, *The Autobiography of Miss Jane Pittman* • Bernard Malamud, *Tenants*
1972	• Nixon visits China • Easter offensive in Vietnam • Nixon visits the Soviet Union • Watergate burglars are arrested • Nixon is reelected by a landslide	• John Barth, *Chimera* • Francis Ford Coppola, *The Godfather* • Ishmael Reed, *Mumbo-Jumbo*
1973	• Supreme Court *Roe versus Wade* decision • Watergate cover-up is revealed • Vice-President Agnew resigns, is succeeded by Ford • Yom Kippur War • Oil crisis fuels high inflation	• Thomas Pynchon, *Gravity's Rainbow* • Frank O'Hara, *Selected Poems* • Kurt Vonnegut, *Breakfast of Champions* • Stephen Sondheim, *A Little Night Music*
1974	• Nixon resigns, is succeeded by Ford	• Francis Ford Coppola, *The Godfather Part II* (film) • Roman Polanski, *Chinatown* (film) • Tillie Olson, *Yonnondio* • Gary Snyder, *Turtle Island*
1975	• Fall of South Vietnam • Congressional investigations of CIA • Helsinki Accords	• John Ashbery, *Self-Portrait in a Convex Mirror* • Saul Bellow, *Humboldt's Gift* • E. L. Doctorow, *Ragtime* • Lisa Alther, *Kinflicks* • Milos Forman, *One Flew Over the Cuckoo's Nest* (film) • Steven Spielberg, *Jaws* • Michael Bennett, *A Chorus Line*
1976	• Outsider Jimmy Carter defeats Ford in presidential election • Chinese Cultural Revolution ends, the Gang of Four are arrested and Mao Tsetung dies	• Alex Haley, *Roots* • Martin Scorsese, *Taxi Driver* (film) • *Kinflicks*
1977	• Carter's legislative program is stalled in Congress	• Woody Allen, *Annie Hall* • Michael Herr, *Dispatches* • Toni Morrison, *Song of Solomon* • David Mamet, *American Buffalo* • George Lucas, *Star Wars*
1978	• Camp David Peace Accord between Israel and Egypt • Proposition 13 cuts property taxes in California • Deng Xiaoping begins economic reforms in China • Lech Walesa and coworkers begin to organize the first free trade union in Poland	• Michael Cimino, *The Deer Hunter* • John Irving, *The World According to Garp* • Isaac Bashevis Singer awarded the Nobel Prize for Literature • Sam Shepard, *Buried Child* • Lanford Wilson, *The Fifth of July* • Michael Cimino, *The Deer Hunter*
1979	• Fall of Shah's regime in Iran • Hostage crisis begins in Teheran • Soviet invasion of Afghanistan • Jerry Falwell founds Moral Majority	• Francis Ford Coppola, *Apocalypse Now* • Norman Mailer, *The Executioner's Song* • William Styron, *Sophie's Choice*

CHAPTER 7

American Politics from Nixon to Carter

The 1968 election brought about the collapse of the New Deal coalition without establishing a dominant conservative alternative. Nixon reshaped American foreign policy after the debacle of Vietnam. He also exploited new wedge issues involving patriotism, crime prevention, school busing and racial equality in order to secure a triumphant reelection in 1972. Nonetheless, the Democrats remained firmly in control of Congress. After Nixon's resignation over Watergate, American politics temporarily shifted leftwards, indicating the potency of the new post-New Deal liberal politics. But by the end of the 1970s the weak presidencies of Gerald Ford and Jimmy Carter and their foreign policy failures had contributed to a strong political swing to the right.

The 1968 election

By the time of President Johnson's withdrawal from the presidential race at the end of March, the election of 1968 was already marked as unusually turbulent and unpredictable. The Tet offensive and the resultant fall of a strong president, coming as they did on top of violence and unrest in the ghettos and growing antiwar protests during 1965–7, contributed to a widespread sense of crisis in American society. Worse was to follow.

On April 4, 1968 Martin Luther King, Jr, was assassinated. The riots that broke out after this calamity hit 130 cities, causing 46 deaths and material damage in excess of $100 million. The worst violence took place in Washington, DC, the nation's capital, where black rioters set white-owned stores on fire, disregarding the damage to apartments above where blacks lived. Among the neighborhoods destroyed by arson was the shopping area on 14th Street, just two blocks from the White House.

The assassination of King, the great moderate leader, raised fears that racial conflict would escalate out of control. Robert Kennedy made the largest gesture for bridging the widening racial gap when he entered the ghetto of Indianapolis during the riots, climbed on the roof of a car and with an emotional extemporaneous appeal won over the initially hostile crowd that gathered around him. For most liberals who in the spring of 1968 were in despair over the quagmire in Vietnam and the racial conflict at home, Kennedy appeared increasingly as the only hope. Kennedy was doing better in the primaries than Johnson's original challenger, Senator Eugene McCarthy, while

Vice-President Hubert Humphrey, who entered the race after Johnson's withdrawal and ludicrously proclaimed his belief in 'the politics of joy', avoided the primaries altogether.

On June 5, 1968, just after his victory in the California primary, Robert Kennedy was assassinated. Liberals saw their world crumbling around them. Their sons and daughters were protesting in increasingly shrill ways; Columbia University shut down in the spring of 1968 after being taken over by antiwar protesters. Blacks had lost their great civil rights leader, while liberals had lost the only politician who seemed capable of both defusing racial conflict and taking America out of Vietnam.

Kennedy's assassination changed the electoral dynamics yet again. Humphrey's nomination was now secure and the main issue at the Democratic National Convention in late August was the party's program. Since Humphrey, who was personally overshadowed by Johnson, felt unable to deviate publicly from the administration's policy in Vietnam, the antiwar wing of the party went to the convention prepared to fight.

The Democratic National Convention in Chicago was a disaster. Chicago Mayor Richard Daley, the most powerful old-style machine boss in America, was determined to maintain order in his city's streets against the inevitable antiwar demonstrators. Coming from a working-class, Irish-American background, Daily was unenthusiastic about the war in Vietnam, but fiercely patriotic. Highly publicized preparations by the Chicago police for dealing with demonstrators deterred many from going to Chicago; only about 10,000 gathered, hardly an unmanageable amount for Chicago's 11,000 policemen to cope with, supported as they were by the Illinois National Guard. Nonetheless, on the evening of Humphrey's nomination the Chicago police launched a vicious attack on the young protesters that shocked television viewers. A subsequent official inquiry placed the blame squarely on the police; yet opinion polls showed that a majority of Americans sided with the police.

Developments within the convention hall were also disastrous. The antiwar wing was so vocal that Johnson abandoned any thought of appearing in person, even though he had timed the convention to coincide with his sixtieth birthday. The fight between the two wings of the party transcended the bounds of civility. When Connecticut's Senator Abraham Ribicoff denounced from the podium the 'Gestapo tactics on the streets of Chicago', Daley shouted back from the floor: 'Fuck you, you Jew son of a bitch, you lousy motherfucker go home.' The Democrats seemed to be falling apart. The unfortunate Humphrey, a lifelong liberal more progressive than either the two slain Kennedys or Johnson, won the nomination fighting against the most liberal wing of his party and with the solid support of the mostly conservative Southern Democrats that Johnson lined up for him.

The collapse of the New Deal coalition in 1968 resulted from a polarization of its elements: the liberal wing of the party moved leftward while the white working class, including immigrant groups previously loyal to the New Deal, moved to the right. These hardworking blue-collar ethnics lived in the poorer neighborhoods of American cities near the black ghettos where the riots were taking place. They resented special Great Society programs in support of the inner cities and the blacks, which their hard-earned tax dollars paid for. They were hostile to judicial schemes of integrating schools by busing white children to black neighborhoods and vice versa. While racism among Northern blue-collar groups was widespread, there were other reasons, especially an upsurge in crime, behind the white backlash that followed the enactment of the Civil Rights Acts and the Great Society.

The South also defected from the Democrats in the presidential election of 1968. This process had begun with the defection of the Dixiecrats in 1948. Eisenhower had won some states of the Outer South and Goldwater five states of the Deep South. But never before had a Democratic candidate fared as badly in the South as Humphrey, a vocal supporter of civil rights, who lost ten out the 11 Southern states and won only Johnson's Texas.

In a conventional two-way race, the Democratic losses in the South and among blue-collar ethnics in the North would have led to a Republican landslide. But Alabama's former governor George Wallace decided to run as a third-party candidate, and he discovered that his bigotry had an appeal well beyond the South. In the North, Wallace was especially strong in white ethnic districts that neighbored the expanding black districts. Visiting such areas was likened by pollster Samuel Lubell to 'inspecting a stretched-out war front' where every pro-Wallace precinct was like 'another outpost marking the borders to which Negro residential movement had pushed'.[1]

The Republicans in 1968 nominated Richard Nixon, after a three-way race that pitted him against Nelson Rockefeller on his left and Ronald Reagan on his right. Nixon secured the nomination by winning the support of the Southern Republicans. He emphasized his support for the Brown decisions in the 1950s and the Civil Rights Acts of the mid-1960s in order not to be tagged as a racist; but he argued against further federal activism in support of civil rights, especially school busing, thus earning the support of Senator Strom Thurmond, the leader of the Dixiecrats in 1948 who had defected from the Democrats and joined the Republicans in 1964. To general surprise, Nixon chose as his running mate the hitherto obscure Governor of Maryland, Spiro T. Agnew, the son of a Greek immigrant who had taken a tough law-and-order stand during the riots that followed Martin Luther King's assassination and who, in Nixon's calculations, would appeal to blue-collar ethnics.

The election of 1968 was surprisingly close. Nixon got 43.4 percent of the vote against Humphrey's 42.7 percent and Wallace's 13.5 percent. Moreover, the Democrats continued to control Congress, though congressional Southern Democrats were likely to work with Nixon on many issues. But if 1968 did not signify the creation of a new Republican majority, it did mean the end of the New Deal coalition. First, Nixon got more working-class votes than Humphrey, suggesting that the class-based allegiances shaped during the Great Depression were being displaced by new cleavages involving race, school busing, law and order, and Vietnam. Second, Humphrey won only four states south of the Mason-Dixon line and west of the Mississippi (Texas, Minnesota, Washington and Hawaii), losing traditional New Deal strongholds. Third, while over 61 percent had voted for Johnson in 1964, 57 percent voted against the Great Society in 1968. The 1960s gave us the New Left, feminism, sexual liberation, minority rights, new forms of activism and Woodstock. They also gave us the beginning of a long-lasting rightward shift in American politics.

Nixon's foreign policy

When Nixon became president, the edifice of postwar American foreign policy was badly shaken. The global anticommunist crusade that a bipartisan consensus had supported resulted in the Vietnam quagmire, draining American resources and undermining the consensus at home. The Soviet Union had caught up with the United States in nuclear weapons and for the first time attained strategic parity. Furthermore, the American economy no longer towered above all others as it had in the early postwar years, due to the growth of rival economies in Western Europe and East Asia. This combination of factors amounted to a weakening of the United States in the international distribution of power.

At this difficult juncture, the reins of American foreign policy were taken over by unusually able leaders. Nixon and his National Security Advisor Henry Kissinger were able to restructure foreign policy and place it on sounder foundations, guided by a geopolitical *Realpolitik* approach that was similar to Kennan's in the 1940s, but that was otherwise more in the European than in the American tradition. Nixon and Kissinger did not entirely depart from the global anticommunist fixations of their predecessors, as their intervention in Chile against President Allende showed. But in more central aspects of world politics their approach was different.

The Nixon administration inherited the pressing Vietnam problem, which would inevitably absorb much of its energy. Nixon was determined to marginalize the Vietnam War and pursue other major foreign policy objectives. But he was not prepared to exit Vietnam in humiliating defeat, which would have created the image of an American 'paper tiger', thus emboldening America's international adversaries (as actually happened in the later 1970s). His objective was to secure some 'peace with honor' that would not be the equivalent of defeat. Since the leaders of North Vietnam were relentless in their pursuit of Vietnamese unification, Nixon's quest for an 'honorable' exit prolonged the war for four years.

A central element of Nixon's Vietnam policy was 'Vietnamization', the gradual withdrawal of American soldiers and their replacement by South Vietnamese forces. From mid-1969 to November 1972 the American military presence in Vietnam reduced from 550,000 troops to 20,000, resulting in a steep decline in American casualties. The new technology of the 'smart bombs' also reduced American air losses; whereas previously it took one hundred sorties to destroy a bridge in the face of enemy antiaircraft fire, with 'smart bombs' it took only seven. These developments did not placate the antiwar movement, but they kept the patriotic majority on Nixon's side.

Nixon also changed the strategy in Vietnam, placing more emphasis on protecting South Vietnamese population centers than on destroying enemy forces. Moreover, the new strategy aimed at disrupting the movement of supplies and reinforcements from the North to the South via Laos and Cambodia. When the American bombing of North Vietnam resumed in February 1969, it was extended for the first time to the eastern provinces of Cambodia that the Ho Chi Minh trail traversed. In 1970 Nixon ordered the 'invasion' – more like a series of raids – of Cambodia in order to make communist use of her eastern provinces more difficult. These moves did not end the flow of supplies and reinforcements from the North to the South, but they did weaken the communist presence in South Vietnam sufficiently to facilitate Vietnamization.

While the war in Vietnam continued, Nixon worked on attaining *détente* with the Soviet Union. Conditions were ripening for an improvement in superpower relations. Europe's division had stabilized without major crises after Berlin in 1961. The nuclear balance of terror made a third world war unlikely. Yet the situation was still dangerous. Kissinger likened the superpowers to

> two heavily armed blind men feeling their way around a room, each believing himself in mortal peril from the other whom he assumes to have perfect vision…Each tends to ascribe to the other side a consistency, foresight and coherence that its own experience belies. Of course, over time even two blind men can do enormous damage to each other, not to speak of the room.[2]

Nixon and Kissinger were able to transcend the Manichean view of the Soviet Union that had characterized earlier American attitudes. They continued to regard it as an adversary, but not as a demoniacal power bent on world conquest. The policy of *détente* that they pursued was not based on some unrealistic notion that superpower antagonisms would end completely. *Détente* sought to place limits to these antagonisms and make them less dangerous. Nixon and Kissinger wished to integrate the Soviet Union as a normal power in the existing states system, helping it move away from its original revolutionary mission.

Nixon's opening to China

The progress of *détente* in superpower relations was facilitated by Nixon's greatest success, his opening to China. Sino-Soviet tensions had been visible to American policy makers since the early 1960s, but they were thought of as the product of a hostile Chinese ideological rigidity. In reality, they derived from an underlying Sino-Russian geopolitical clash in Northeast Asia that went back to the times when tsarist Russia had expanded to the Pacific. Stalin had confirmed traditional Russian geopolitical ambitions in Northeast Asia when he had grabbed Chinese lands at Yalta as the price for entering the war against Japan. Thus China had historical reasons for fearing Soviet power. The Soviet Union on its side had reason to fear that an overpopulated China would covet its vast and mostly empty territories in the Russian Far East. Sino-Soviet tensions erupted in 1969, when fighting broke out between border forces.

Once Nixon and Kissinger understood the true nature of the Sino-Soviet split, they realized that the United States could maneuver itself to the strongest position in a triangular geopolitical relationship, in which the other two sides would fear each other more than the United States and would each strive to attain American favor. The breakthrough in Sino-American relations came with Kissinger's secret visit to China in 1971, the first by an American official since the communist victory in 1949. Kissinger's mission successfully opened the way for Nixon's official visit to China in February 1972, the first ever by an American president. During secret talks, Nixon asked Mao Tse-tung to contemplate why the Soviet Union had more forces at the Sino-Soviet borders than at its front with Western Europe. Mao did not need to do much contemplating. At one point when the two leaders were discussing the differences between leftists and rightists in the West, Mao declared, 'I like rightists', because they were more anti-Soviet. In the face of the common Soviet threat, Nixon and Mao simply bypassed their vexed bilateral problems, such as Taiwan, and focused on the big picture.

Nixon's China move was a brilliant success. In the assessment of historian John Lewis Gaddis, it 'is difficult to think of anything the Nixon administration could have done that would have produced a more dramatic shift in world power relationships of greater benefit to the United States at less cost'.[3] Whereas his predecessors had entangled America in Vietnam at enormous cost in order to contain global communism, Nixon with one costless move had worsened the Soviet Union's strategic situation drastically and had regained the global initiative. The extent of Nixon's success is seen by the reaction of the Soviet side. Negotiations between the two superpowers to promote *détente* proceeded more quickly after Nixon's visit to China; arrangements were made for Nixon to visit the Soviet Union in May 1972.

Preparations for Nixon's Moscow trip were disrupted by a general communist offensive in South Vietnam that began on March 30, 1972. This 'Easter offensive' was North Vietnam's third bid to overthrow South Vietnam – the previous two were in 1965 and 1968. The timing of the offensive, at approximately the same point in the American electoral cycle as the Tet offensive of 1968, suggests that the communists hoped to produce another major domestic upheaval in the United States. But Nixon reacted very differently from Johnson, escalating the war by mining Haiphong harbor, North Vietnam's main port, even though this inevitably entailed Soviet naval losses. In South Vietnam the communists suffered major losses in the face of the superior firepower of the South Vietnamese and American forces. Like Tet, the Easter offensive was a failure militarily, but without producing a significant political backlash on Nixon's home front.

The Nixon administration feared that its tough Vietnam policy would undermine Nixon's planned trip to Moscow. To its surprise, the Soviet side did not delay the trip by even a single day. After Nixon's opening to China, the Soviet Union could not afford worsening relations with the United States. Thus Nixon became the first American president ever to visit the Kremlin. In Moscow in May 1972 Nixon and Soviet leader Leonid Brezhnev signed the first major strategic arms control agreements (SALT I and ABM) between the two superpowers. With these agreements the United States in effect accepted strategic parity with the Soviet Union, which in turn took a major step towards integration in the existing states system. The danger of an escalation of superpower tensions towards a third world war receded.

Nixon's successes in China and the Soviet Union overshadowed Vietnam both internationally and within the United States. But the war still dragged on. America's extrication came after Nixon's triumphant reelection in November 1972. In December Nixon ordered the most intense bombardment of

North Vietnam in the entire war. North Vietnam exhausted its entire antiaircraft arsenal within the first eight days of the bombardment, and then asked for new negotiations. The failure of its Easter offensive, improved American relations with China and the Soviet Union, and Nixon's reelection must have had a discouraging impact on its leadership.

However, the January 1973 cease-fire did not constitute an American victory, since it permitted North Vietnam's forces in the South to remain there. Had the United States not been exhausted by this long war in a geopolitically insignificant country, it could have pressed for a more advantageous agreement. But Nixon had reason to fear a congressional rebellion that might have forced him to abandon South Vietnam without any agreement. The January 1973 cease-fire avoided a humiliating American exit from Vietnam, but it was not the end of the story. Like Neville Chamberlain before him, Nixon consciously borrowed Benjamin Disraeli's phrase 'peace with honor'. Yet with prescience more applicable to his later imitators than to himself, Disraeli had confided that 'if there is no peace, the people are apt to conclude there is no honor either'.

The Middle East

During the Nixon administration, Americans began to experience unfamiliar constraints of energy scarcity and the consequent energy dependence on the Middle East. In previous years the United States had been practically self-sufficient in energy, since domestic oil sources could easily compensate for any shortfall in imports. In the Arab-Israeli Six Days War of 1967 Johnson had supported Israel, which defeated Egypt, Syria and Jordan and occupied the Sinai Peninsula, the Golan Heights and the West Bank. Most Arab oil-producing states had declared an oil embargo against Israel's Western supporters, but the United States had raised its oil production to cover the shortfall in the world's energy markets; the embargo failed and was abandoned by the end of the summer of 1967. But a combination of increasingly wasteful energy consumption and the depletion of domestic oil wells increased American dependence on oil imports in the 1970s.

Developments were thus very different during the Yom Kippur War that broke out in October 1973 when Egypt and Syria launched a surprise attack against Israel. After the initial successes of the Egyptian and Syrian offensives, Israel was able to launch strong counterattacks. This time the ensuing Arab oil embargo was very successful. Since it came at a time when worldwide oil consumption was rising fast, it soon led to a quadrupling of oil prices. This major shock destabilized the world's economies. Gas shortages appeared in the United States, as the world's most powerful nation discovered to its dismay that its wasteful consumerism could be disrupted by decisions taken in distant Third World states.

The Nixon administration used the Yom Kippur War to strike a blow at Soviet influence in the Middle East. The key was, as Nixon told Kissinger early in the war, that the American stance should not be excessively pro-Israel. After the Arab invasion, a successful Israeli counterattack led Israeli forces to the western side of the Suez Canal, threatening to cut off the Egyptian Third Corps that was still to the east of the canal. Had Israel completed the encirclement of the

Egyptian Third Corps and forced its surrender, the war would have ended, as in 1967, with Egypt's humiliation. The two superpowers agreed upon a cease-fire that saved the Egyptian Third Corps from captivity. Israel reluctantly went along, but then violated the cease-fire and completed the encirclement of the Egyptians. Kissinger was able at this point to deter a direct Soviet involvement on the ground, as well as to secure the supplies of the encircled Egyptians, so that they would not be forced to surrender. This demonstrated to Egypt that the only way she could get concessions from Israel was through the United States. Soviet influence in Egypt waned henceforth and the road opened for the Israeli-Egyptian Peace Treaty of 1978.

Since Egypt was the most populous Arab country, her shift from Soviet to American influence constituted a major change in the relative position of the two superpowers in the Middle East. With his *Realpolitik* Nixon had not only changed the world balance in America's favor, but also the balance within a region that was becoming increasingly important in the new era of energy scarcity. But this last major foreign policy success did not give Nixon much satisfaction, since his presidency was collapsing at home.

Nixon's triumph and fall

In domestic politics the Nixon presidency presents at first sight an enigma. In some respects, Nixon seems to have been one of the most liberal presidents ever. Yet he hated the liberals, and they returned the compliment with an intensity that is impressive even for a nation that has often witnessed great polarizations in its history. How then is one to interpret Nixon? Was he the last of the liberal presidents, the first of the conservatives or something different altogether?

The answer to the riddle is that Nixon mixed liberal policies with a conservative populism. He was not willing to take on the postwar consensus on the economy and the welfare state. Ever since the Great Depression, opinion polls consistently showed that voters trusted the Democrats more than the Republicans on the economy. Nixon therefore pursued economic policies that followed centrist policy trends. He also knew that whenever class became the main polarizing cleavage in American politics, as it had been in the 1930s, the Republicans were at a disadvantage because they were identified as the party that favored the wealthy. Therefore, Nixon supported federal programs that took the sting out of class politics. In these matters, he in no way pointed towards the Reagan Revolution of the 1980s.

In his liberal version, Nixon created the Occupational Safety and Health Administration (OSHA), which had been the AFL-CIO's top priority in 1969. He created the Environmental Protection Agency (EPA), which addressed new concerns about the environment. In an effort to undermine the liberal public housing bureaucracy of the Great Society, he supported housing subsidies for the poor so that they could afford homes in the free market. In order to help African Americans find employment and stop depending on Great Society antipoverty agencies, the Nixon administration also promoted a more advanced version of affirmative action than Johnson, explicitly introducing the notion of hiring quotas in favor of blacks for construction companies doing public works.

Nixon even proposed a national health system, though, as with Truman before him (and Clinton after him), it was voted down in Congress. Federal nondefense spending rose faster under Nixon than at any other comparable period in the postwar era; it doubled between 1968 and 1975, an astounding leap even if one discounts for inflation.

The politics of polarization

The conservative side of Nixon was evident in the new polarizing politics that revolved around issues such as law and order and patriotism. In order to realign American politics and create a new Republican majority, Nixon strove to exploit polarization on these issues that favored the conservatives, while reducing polarization on economics and class issues that favored the liberals. His politics may be summarized as right-wing populism that appealed to Southerners and Northern ethnics on flag and race, and centrist moderation on economic issues that disturbed only the economic conservatives whom he took for granted. His strategy worked very well at the level of presidential elections, but not at the congressional level where the Democrats remained so heterogeneous as to accommodate almost every shade of opinion in American politics.

The Nixon-era polarization derived to a large extent from the continuing war in Vietnam. Antiwar sentiments rose in the fall of 1969 when antiwar activists launched the so-called Moratorium, nationwide demonstrations that began on 15 October and were planned to resume every 30 days. Nixon countered on 3 November with a televised address in which he appealed to 'the great silent majority of my fellow Americans – I ask for your support...North Vietnam cannot defeat or humiliate the United States. Only Americans can do that.' A Gallup poll found that 77 percent of respondents supported Nixon's appeal. His job approval rating went up from 52 percent to 68 percent. The Moratorium demonstrations withered.

Antiwar sentiments rose sharply again at the beginning of May 1970, when Nixon launched ground operations in Cambodia. Antiwar demonstrations broke out all over America against this perceived widening of the war. The situation became even more tense on 4 May, when inexperienced National Guardsmen opened fire on a crowd of peaceful demonstrators at Kent State University and killed four students and bystanders. Yet two weeks later 100,000 people demonstrated in New York in support of the president, led by the strong local construction union (whose members were at the time building the World Trade Center's Twin Towers). In opinion polls 58 percent blamed the demonstrators for Kent State and only 11 percent blamed the National Guard, while 50 percent supported the Cambodia operations and only 39 percent were opposed.

Crime was another polarizing issue that Nixon used against the liberals. The rise in crime created threatening conditions in American cities that had not been seen for generations. Between 1960 and 1980 there was a tripling in murders, armed robberies and rapes. Opinion polls in 1975 showed that most Americans and, particularly, three-quarters of women in large cities were afraid to walk in their neighborhood after dark.

The crime wave had a clear racial dimension. While blacks constituted only 12 percent of the population, they amounted to half the perpetrators of serious crimes. It must be emphasized that the overwhelming majority of African Americans were law-abiding and that a disproportionately large percentage of the victims of serious crime were also black: much of the crime wave consisted of black criminals harming black victims. White victims of the crime wave were concentrated in blue-collar neighborhoods that were closer to the ghettos.

Liberals blamed black crime on the legacy of slavery and the subsequent discrimination against blacks. But from the standpoint of practical politics, the liberals faced the enormous problem that the crime wave surged immediately after Johnson's Great Society reforms that had supported blacks as never before. Liberal analysis in the universities and the suburbs of the underlying causes of crime did not interest blue-collar whites who suffered the consequences in their neighborhoods. Their views were shown in opinion polls by the rise in the support for the death penalty from 38 percent in 1965 to 67 percent in 1976.

The polarization over crime revolved largely around US Supreme Court decisions in the 1960s in favor of the rights of suspects, as well as the tendency of the courts in the 1960s and early 1970s to be lenient in sentencing. There were good reasons for both these developments: *Miranda*-type rights, where the suspect has the right to remain silent and request the presence of an attorney at a police interrogation, protect the innocent who might otherwise be coerced into confessing, while long prison terms can brutalize inmates, making them worse criminals. But these rulings incensed many whites who suffered under the crime wave. Clint Eastwood's popular film *Dirty Harry* (1971), which explicitly attacked the Supreme Court's *Miranda* decision, reflected conservative attitudes in this period.

Particularly strong opposition arose against the US Supreme Court's busing decisions. While people outside the South had supported the abolition of legal segregation in public schooling, most disagreed with what Nixon described as 'forced integration' by busing children to distant neighborhoods. Again, this was an issue that affected blue-collar families that could not afford private schooling. For whites, three-quarters of whom opposed busing, this matter was related to the crime issue, since busing might send their children to schools in crime-infested ghettos. Opinion polls showed that African Americans were evenly divided on the busing issue, since many black parents preferred to keep their children in schools in their own neighborhoods. The crime and busing decisions of the Supreme Court contributed to the decline of its high confidence ratings in the opinion polls from 83.4 percent in 1949 to 32.6 percent in 1973.

Nixon's abuse of power

The Achilles' heel of the Nixon presidency was a pattern of abuse of power that gradually entangled the White House in illegal activities. Nixon wanted the FBI and the CIA to continue Johnson-era practices such as extensive domestic surveillance of antiwar and radical black organizations that Nixon, like Johnson before him, suspected of being infiltrated by communists and Soviet intelligence. But the times had changed. The Director of the FBI, J. Edgar Hoover, who had held that post since the 1920s, sensed correctly that Congress and the press would no longer tolerate the illegal surveillance of American citizens. In 1970 Hoover told an interagency committee on intelligence:

> For years and years and years I have approved opening the mail and other similar operations, but no. It is becoming more and more dangerous and we are apt to get caught. I am not opposed to doing this. I am not opposed to continuing the burglaries and the opening of the mail and other similar activities, provided someone higher than myself approves of it.[4]

In short, Hoover demanded a written authorization by Attorney General John Mitchell, one of Nixon's closest aides, in order to be covered.

Hoover's refusal to continue past practices inflamed Nixon's persistent feeling that the 'Eastern Establishment' treated him unfairly. This Eastern Establishment had not decried illegal domestic surveillance under Kennedy or Johnson, he thought. Why should they deny it to him? Furthermore, Nixon hated and feared the media. He explained to a colleague:

> If you consider the real ideological bent of the *New York Times*, the *Washington Post, Time, Newsweek,* and the three television networks, you will find overwhelmingly that their editorial bias comes down on the side of amnesty, pot, abortion, confiscation of wealth (unless it is theirs), massive increases in welfare, unilateral disarmament, reduction of their defenses and surrender in Vietnam.[5]

His hatred of the influential mainstream media he deemed 'liberal', especially the *New York Times* and the *Washington Post,* prevented him from acknowledging the new climate of distrust in government that Vietnam had produced in American society.

The key step in the direct involvement of the White House in illegal activities, after Hoover's refusal to undertake them himself, came after the leak to the press in June 1971 of the *Pentagon Papers,* a large internal Pentagon survey commissioned by Robert McNamara in 1967, with thousands of classified documents concerning America's entanglement in Vietnam under Nixon's four predecessors. Even though the *Pentagon Papers* did not concern his administration, Nixon feared that their leak was part of a wider liberal plot to undermine his Vietnam policy. As a result, Nixon created the so-called 'Plumbers' Unit' in the White House to stop leaks and do other dirty business. The plumbers broke into the office of the psychiatrist of Daniel Ellsberg, Kissinger's former aide who had leaked the *Pentagon Papers,* hoping to find material with which to discredit him. Moreover, in the summer of 1971 Nixon began to create 'enemies' lists' that included prominent liberal opponents, so that the Internal Revenue Service (IRS) and the Justice Department could harass them.

Given the paranoid atmosphere in the White House, it is unsurprising that Nixon's reelection campaign in 1972 would also resort to illegal methods, especially when the Plumbers' Unit was transferred to it. Yet the plumbers were amateurs compared to the FBI, which had undertaken illegal surveillance for decades.

They were caught in June 1972 in the Democratic National Committee's offices in the Watergate complex trying for a second time to bug phones, since they did not get it right the first time.

The Watergate break-in was not a big story during the election campaign of 1972. To neutralize the danger that the arrested burglars would implicate their superiors in the Nixon campaign who had ordered the break-in, Nixon resorted to a cover-up that involved providing them with secret hush money. By such means he postponed any major scandal until after the election, but at the risk of making the scandal much more damaging, if the cover-up was revealed.

In the 1972 elections Nixon was helped when George Wallace decided to seek the Democratic nomination rather than run again as a third-party candidate. Wallace's candidacy drew voters away from centrist candidates like Hubert Humphrey and Edmund Muskie, thus paradoxically helping the candidate of the most liberal wing of the party, George McGovern, win the nomination narrowly.

The Democratic National Convention in July 1972 constituted a revenge of the liberal wing of the party against the old establishment for the Chicago convention of 1968. Taking advantage of the new rules for delegate selection that required quotas for women, blacks and the young, the convention rejected the 'official' delegates of Illinois, including Chicago's Mayor Richard Daley, and chose instead a group that included the black activist Jesse Jackson; one McGovern aide surmised correctly: 'I think we just lost Illinois.' The climate in the convention harmed the Democrats when inexperienced young delegates from the antiwar movement took the opportunity to attack 'the system': for example, they nominated Mao Tse-tung as McGovern's running mate (presumably they were not aware that Mao now liked rightists). The party program that the convention adopted reflected the advanced liberalism of McGovern: promoting gender equality and gay rights, pro-choice on abortion, in favor of busing and, most emphatically, for an immediate withdrawal from Vietnam and a more general scaling down of America's defense establishment and overseas presence. This last aspect, which McGovern stressed most in his campaign, cost him the endorsement of the AFL-CIO.

By nominating their most liberal candidate, the Democrats in 1972 found themselves in a similar predicament to the Republicans with Goldwater in 1964. Nixon, who before June 1972 seemed quite vulnerable in the opinion polls, thereafter dominated McGovern by almost two to one. In the election he received almost 61 percent of the vote, one of the largest percentages in American history, though slightly below Johnson's 1964 record. In the Electoral College Nixon did better than Johnson, since he lost only one state, Massachusetts. But the Democrats maintained their comfortable lead in both chambers of Congress.

Nixon's second term began with a constitutional confrontation between the Republican President and the Democratic Congress concerning war powers, appropriations (Nixon in early 1973 grossly abused the presidential power of impoundment by not spending funds appropriated by Congress) and campaign irregularities regarding the 1972 elections. Liberals now talked about the 'imperial presidency', sharply reversing their earlier support of a strong FDR-style presidency that would move the nation forward against the opposition of the reactionary Congress.

This constitutional confrontation acquired a new dynamic in April 1973, when the press began to uncover the Watergate cover-up. On 30 April Nixon was forced to dismiss his White House chief of staff Bob Haldeman and other leading aides in a desperate attempt to contain the damage to his presidency. But his situation worsened in June when his former counsel John Dean testified in Congress that he had repeatedly discussed the cover-up with Nixon, implicating the president directly in illegal activities. Since Nixon denied Dean's charges, the matter came down to the president's word against Dean's. Nixon's situation worsened decisively in July 1973, when one of his aides revealed in congressional testimony that Nixon had installed in his office a recording system that taped all his conversations. It was now possible to prove whether Nixon or Dean had been truthful on the cover-up.

For one year Nixon, claiming executive privilege, refused to release the relevant tapes. During this period of Nixon's slow-motion collapse, when the matter of the release of the tapes was moving through the courts, the press was in the grip of an unprecedented frenzy, hunting for – and finding – new scandals in the Nixon administration. The chief victim of this intense media scrutiny was Vice-President Agnew, who was forced to resign after instances of corruption and tax evasion from his years as governor of Maryland were revealed. In October 1973 Nixon replaced him with the Republican House Minority leader Gerald Ford.

The end of the Nixon presidency came on July 24, 1974, when the Supreme Court unanimously ordered the release of the tapes to the courts and Congress. The content of the tapes appalled congressional Republicans who had been defending Nixon throughout this period. By the end of July, the House Judiciary Committee had voted for Nixon's impeachment on a number of charges. Leading congressional Republicans then persuaded Nixon that he had no chance of preventing his impeachment by the full House. Having lost any hope of salvaging his presidency, Nixon resigned on August 9, 1974, 21 months after his electoral triumph. He was succeeded by Vice-President Gerald Ford who, upon assuming office, caused a public outcry by pardoning Nixon for any crimes committed during his presidency.

The Watergate scandal deepened the crisis of confidence in America's public institutions that had begun with Vietnam. The deference that Americans had earlier shown to their leaders was lastingly shaken. This has been particularly evident in the intense way that the media have ever since scrutinized leading public figures, which would have been unthinkable in the days of Roosevelt and Johnson.

In the short term, the Republican Party paid dearly for Watergate. In the midterm elections of November 1974 the Democrats gained 46 seats in the House and four in the Senate. In 1976 the Democratic presidential candidate Jimmy Carter defeated Ford with 51 percent of the vote. Yet these developments in the immediate post-Watergate years obscured only temporarily the underlying conservative trends in American society that had been evident since 1968. No

Democratic presidential candidate since 1976 reached Jimmy Carter's percentage of the vote in that year until Obama's election in 2008.

Trends in American society and politics in the 1970s

From the point of view of political geography, the most important change in American society since the 1970s has been the net migration from the North to the West and the South. While the West had always attracted new domestic immigrants, the South in the early postwar period had been losing population, especially African Americans. This trend was reversed after the 1970s, producing an influx from the North that included both whites and blacks. Whereas in the first three postwar decades five million blacks had left the South, from the mid-1970s to 2000 some 100,000 moved from the North to the South annually.

These migration patterns altered American political geography by ending the political primacy of the North in favor of the South and the West. Of 22 presidents from the Civil War to the mid-1970s, only two were Southern politicians, Andrew Johnson and Lyndon Johnson (Woodrow Wilson came from the South but he entered politics in New Jersey), and another two were from the West, Herbert Hoover and Richard Nixon. By contrast, all presidents since the mid-1970s, except Obama, have resided in the South (Carter, Clinton and Bush father and son) or the West (Reagan).

Several factors account for these demographic trends. First, the South and the West have by and large been booming economically, whereas parts of the North that industrialized earlier have been stuck with older declining industries and have come to be known as the 'rust belt'. The tendency of newer growth industries to invest in the South and the West was facilitated by the lower taxes and antiunion traditions of many states in these regions compared to most in the North. As a result, the South has drastically narrowed the gap between its per capita income levels and those of the rest of the United States, though on average it still remains behind the nation at large.

A second factor that encouraged migration to the West and the South was racial tension in Northern cities, a sad legacy of the riots and crime wave of the 1960s. The end of segregation in the South resulted in a normalization of race relations to the point where, astonishingly, Southern cities seemed more habitable than many Northern cities, accounting for the return of large numbers of blacks to the South since the mid-1970s. Indicatively, the Supreme Court's decision in 1971 to sanction busing for the racial integration of the public schools of Charlotte, North Carolina, was received more positively and with less hostility than busing schemes in Northern cities.

Table 2 Population of United States regions, 1965 and 1987, in thousands[6]

	Northeast	Midwest	South	West
1965	52,354	54,224	54,680	32,204
1987	56,078	59,538	78,084	49,699

A third factor was the invention of air conditioning in the 1960s, which made the 'sunbelt' (from the South to the lower West) more attractive, since people can enjoy its warmer climate while insulating themselves from its negative consequences. The sunbelt climate has proved highly attractive for old-age pensioners, who in growing numbers have been leaving the North and retiring to Florida, Arizona and other sunbelt states.

These trends have resulted in the homogenization of American society. As Johnson had predicted when passing his historic Civil Rights Acts, the South is no longer an underdeveloped anomaly set apart from the rest of the United States. Politically this has resulted in the rise of two-party competition in the previously solidly Democratic South, with Southern Democrats largely adopting liberal positions and Republicans attracting Southern conservatives. This development was evident first in presidential elections with Eisenhower winning parts of the Outer South, Goldwater the Deep South and Nixon both. Gradually the Republicans in the 1970s and 1980s increased their overall strength in the South and became the majority party by 1996, as is shown in Table 3.

In the long run the emergence of two-party competition in the South ended the postwar dominance of the Democrats in Congress, which depended on the unnatural cohabitation of Northern liberals and Southern conservatives in the Democratic Party. The gradual movement of Southern conservatives to the Republican Party and the concomitant movement of both Southern and Northern liberals from the Republican to the Democratic Party eventually resulted in an ideologically clearer division between the two parties.

The continuing growth of the suburbs since the 1970s was another important demographic development in American society. It resulted in large part from the swelling of the middle class and the shrinking of the traditional working class that resulted from the 'postindustrial' transformation of the American economy, characterized by increasing automation of industrial production and the growth of the service sector. It was also related to racial tensions in the cities, which fueled the exodus of whites to the suburbs.

Busing was an important factor in this respect. The Supreme Court's *Milliken versus Bradley* decision in 1974 concerning Detroit confined the use of busing for the racial integration of public schools to the city itself; there was to be no busing across city boundaries. Thus the suburbs were left out of the cities' busing

Table 3 Party strength in the South, 1956–96, at eight-year intervals[7]

Governors	US Senators Dem.	US Representatives Rep.	Dem.	Rep.	Dem.	Rep.
1956	11	0	22	0	99	7
1964	11	0	20	2	90	16
1972*	8	3	14	7	74	34
1980*	6	5	11	10	69	39
1988	6	5	15	7	77	39
1996	3	8	7	15	54	71

Note: * In 1972 and 1980 Virginia Senator Harry Byrd was an independent, so that the Senate totals in the table are one short of the South's 22. The Southern states are: Virginia, North Carolina, South Carolina, Georgia, Florida, Alabama, Mississippi, Louisiana, Texas, Arkansas and Tennessee.

systems of integration. For many white parents that were against busing their children to schools in decaying inner-city neighborhoods but could not afford private schools, moving to the suburbs became a viable alternative. Boston's federal court-mandated busing scheme that began in 1974 bused pupils from the black Roxbury ghetto to predominantly Irish blue-collar South Boston and vice versa. Black pupils that were bused to South Boston had to face the hostility of white racist mobs, while white pupils that were bused to Roxbury sometimes fell victim to the local high crime rate. Both ended up needing police escorts in transit and police protection within the schools. By the time the busing scheme ended in 1988, the pupils in Boston's public school system had fallen from 80,000 to 57,000, of which only 15,000 were white, demonstrating white flight to the suburbs or private schools.

The racial tensions in America's cities undermined the idealistic vision of liberals such as Martin Luther King and Hubert Humphrey, who had sought to integrate blacks into the American mainstream. In the 1970s liberals began to support the new notion of multiculturalism, according to which African Americans and other minorities could retain their distinctive cultural features and coexist with the Anglo-American tradition without being assimilated by it. Since the 1970s it has been conservatives who have supported the traditional assimilation of minorities, fearing that multiculturalism will lead to a 'balkanization' of American society.

The feminist movement reached its high watermark in the early 1970s, but then suffered setbacks. Betty Friedan, author of the highly influential *The Feminine Mystique* and founder of the National Organization for Women (NOW), led the effort in favor of the Equal Rights Amendment (ERA), which would prohibit any legal gender discrimination. The ERA had originally been proposed in 1923, had been endorsed by the Republican and Democratic National Conventions in the 1940s, but had failed in Congress before the 1970s. Then it passed by overwhelming congressional majorities in late 1971 and early 1972, and was endorsed by Nixon. A majority of states ratified it soon afterwards. But a backlash stalled its progress in the second half of the 1970s, leaving it with the endorsement of only 35 states, three short of the three-quarters required to ratify a constitutional amendment. Part of the backlash derived from traditional and religious women led by activist Phyllis Shlafly, who defended traditional gender roles. The ERA also became entangled in the backlash against the Supreme Court's *Roe versus Wade* decision in 1973 that legalized abortion, which leading feminists strongly supported. The backlash was so strong in conservative segments of American society, that the 1980 Republican National Convention removed endorsement of the ERA from its platform for the first time since 1940. Still, feminists could take solace in the fact that the courts promoted legal gender equality by reinterpreting the Constitution.

Another development was the decline of the urban patronage machines and their powerful bosses, which had been a prominent feature of American politics from the 1830s to the 1960s. Three factors account for the waning of the patronage system. First, the 'postindustrial' transformation of the American economy created tens of millions of well-paid white-collar jobs in the private sector, making civil service employment less attractive than before. Second, the welfare state, founded by the New Deal and enlarged by the Great Society, covered some pressing needs of the poor and made them less dependent on the patronage of the party bosses. Third, Vietnam and Watergate resulted in a very widespread demand in American society for honesty in government; in the new climate, people were no longer prepared to tolerate the corrupt machines in which votes were traded for jobs and the beneficiaries of patronage turned a blind eye to the illicit enrichment of their benefactors.

While the decline of the patronage system was undoubtedly a major step in the direction of cleaner politics and more merit in the civil service, it also removed a factor that had provided coherence in American politics. In their hey-day, the urban political machines were able to elect representatives, senators and governors, and even presidents, in return for economic benefits (called pork) to the machine and its electorate. A president like FDR could deal with a few pow-erful bosses and thereby line up a significant part of Congress. When the party machines declined, candidates for elective offices relied on personal campaign organizations to get elected – as Kennedy had done in 1960 – resulting in greater atomization in politics. The rise of television as the main news medium also con-tributed to less coherence in politics, since candidates no longer depended on the mobilization of party organizations, but needed to raise funds on their own to run expensive advertising campaigns. As a result, more politicians were self-made and hence more independent-minded.

A related development in the 1970s was the decline in party affiliation. The traditional voter identified strongly with one of the two parties and voted the party ticket in elections. Party identification in the 1970s was lower than in the 1950s, with the Democrats falling from approximately 50 percent to 40 per-cent and the Republicans being tied with the independents at around 30 percent. Ticket splitting became a common phenomenon; from 1968 to 1990, voters tended to elect Republican presidents and Democratic majorities in the House. Many voters now identified less with parties and more with interest groups on issues like legalized abortion, environmental protection and gun control, which again tended to result in less party coherence in politics.

Coherence was also weakened by the new rules for the presidential nomi-nation that the Democrats adopted after 1968 and which the Republicans also imitated. Before 1972, a large majority of the delegates in the national conventions were controlled by the party leaderships in the states and cities; only a minority of delegates were elected by the people through primaries. Consequently, party leaders in effect chose the presidential candidates who enjoyed their confidence and would more likely be able to work with them if elected. The new rules established the primaries as the main method of delegate selection and democratized the alternative caucus methods that a minority of states use. It is now the people rather than the bosses that choose the delegates. One consequence is that each candidate for the nomination must now set up a personal campaign organization many months before the primaries in order to raise money for the expensive primary campaigns. Ironically, election reform has meant that money has become even more important than before in presi-dential elections. Eisenhower and Stevenson, for example, did not campaign at all before the conventions in the summer of 1952. Under the new rules they would not have been nominated or they would have had to start campaigning well before the beginning of 1952.

On the other hand, the new system of primaries has promoted greater ideological coherence within the two parties and a sharper ideological distinction between them. Under the old system, party leaders often chose moderate presidential candidates in order to appeal to the center and maximize the chances of victory. But since the more ideological voters are more likely to vote in the primaries – voter turnout in the primaries is much lower than in the general elections – the new system often rewards the more ideological candidates. This has been particularly evident in the Republican Party, where the moderate Dewey-Eisenhower-Nixon wing that had dominated from 1948 to 1976 was subsequently eclipsed by the conservative wing. As ideological differences between the two parties have become sharper than in the earlier period of consensus, the old organizational factors of coherence in American politics have been replaced by ideological factors.

American foreign policy under Gerald Ford and Jimmy Carter

Nixon's collapse brought about a temporary weakening of the presidency in favor of Congress, reversing the trend towards a strong presidency that went back to FDR. Whereas in the decades of the Cold War consensus Congress usually deferred to the presidents on major foreign policy issues, Vietnam resulted in the fracturing of this consensus and led to congressional assertiveness and defiance.

The shift in power from the presidency to Congress coincided with an intense questioning within the United States of the foreign policy of Nixon and Kissinger. *Realpolitik* did not fit well with the more idealistic American traditions about foreign policy. Thus it was attacked both from the right and from the left. Critics from the right still saw the world in terms of a struggle between good and evil; they saw *détente* as a policy of appeasement that failed to take into account the inherent expansionism of Soviet totalitarianism. Their ranks included not only conservative Republicans but also Democratic hawks like Senator Henry 'Scoop' Jackson. The CIA's long-serving head of counterintelligence, James Jesus Angleton, thought that the Sino-Soviet split was a gigantic communist scheme of deception aimed at lulling the West into a false sense of security. Angleton went so far as to explore the possibility that Kissinger was a Soviet agent.

Critics from the left also saw the Cold War in terms of a struggle between good and evil, but they opposed unilateral American interventionism and 'imperialism' as evil and supported international agreements and global cooperation as good. Thus they rejected not only the earlier worldwide anticommunist crusade that had led to Vietnam, but also Nixon's *Realpolitik*, which viewed the world in cynical power terms. They supported a speedier improvement in superpower relations and a return to Kennedy's progressive concepts regarding the Third World, though without their anticommunist dimension. In a broad sense, they were heirs of Woodrow Wilson's idealism, hoping to replace power politics by benevolent schemes of world cooperation. Under the influence of the liberal tradition and the Civil Rights movement in America, they supported human rights internationally.

After the Watergate scandal, voters elected an unusually liberal Congress, where Nixon's critics on the left were dominant in the mid-1970s. By the end of the decade, however, international and domestic developments led to a swing of the pendulum all the way to the other extreme, resulting in the ascendancy of Nixon's critics from the right during the 1980s.

The liberal post-Watergate Congress reduced American aid to South Vietnam in 1974. In January 1975 the communist side launched its fourth and largest general offensive against South Vietnam, committing 17 North Vietnamese divisions in the assault. South Vietnam could not resist this offensive without massive American aid. But Congress resisted the Ford administration's emergency aid request, making South Vietnam's collapse inevitable in April 1975. Saigon's fall was so rapid that many high officials of the Thieu regime had no time to flee the country. Many of them gathered with their families in the American Embassy hoping desperately that the Americans would fly them to safety. US engagement in Vietnam ended ignominiously with scenes broadcast worldwide of packed helicopters lifting off the Embassy roof. The fall of South Vietnam undermined the Cambodian government as well, which Congress also refused to assist with aid. One devastating by-product of the communist victory in Vietnam was Pol Pot's murderous dictatorship in Cambodia, which lasted for three grim years, during which two million Cambodians were killed because of the regime's genocidal policies.

In order to prevent any new American entanglements in the Third World, Congress voted towards the end of 1975 against any American involvement in the Angolan civil war, in which Cuban forces were active with Soviet support. Congress forbade not only the use of overt American funds in Angola, but also any covert operations by the CIA. At the same time the CIA itself came under intense congressional scrutiny, with liberals seeking to uncover illegalities committed during the previous quarter-century. The congressional investigations were triggered by leaks about the CIA's covert efforts to undermine Chile's leftist Allende government during 1970–3. The democratically elected Allende was overthrown in 1973 by General Pinochet, who established a brutal right-wing dictatorship that lasted until the later 1980s. Under the post-Vietnam and post-Watergate climate of suspicion regarding secret government operations and abuses of power, the Church Committee in the Senate and the Pike Committee in the House examined, then leaked to the press and officially publicized in their reports a vast amount of classified information that exposed many illegal practices in the CIA's recent past.

Undoubtedly, much of what was publicized ought to have been made public, particularly the CIA's illegal surveillance of American citizens under Johnson and Nixon. But the leaking of sensitive information regarding spying operations went beyond the bounds of propriety, since it put active CIA personnel in danger. The climate within the United States turned against the investigations after the assassination of the CIA's station chief in Athens in December 1975, even though his name had probably not been leaked by either of the two congressional committees that Ford and his allies blamed implicitly.

Given the prevailing liberal orientation in Congress, it is unsurprising that the greatest foreign policy success of the Ford administration was the Helsinki Accords of 1975 that normalized relations between the two blocs in Europe. The Soviet side gained Western recognition of the territorial *status quo* that had emerged after World War II, including East Germany. The West gained a Soviet commitment to respect human rights. While few expected the Warsaw Pact governments to comply strictly with the human rights provisions of Helsinki, these did encourage vigorous dissident movements in the Soviet bloc. Subsequently, Andrei Sakharov in the Soviet Union, Lech Walesa in Poland and Vaclav Havel in Czechoslovakia, along with many other dissidents, contributed to the delegitimization of the monolithic communist regimes.

Jimmy Carter

In American presidential politics, 1976 was the year of the outsider. Ford only narrowly survived a strong challenge in the primaries from the former governor of California, Ronald Reagan, the leader of the Republican Party's conservative wing. In the general elections Ford faced Governor Jimmy Carter of Georgia, who had prevailed in the Democratic primaries against other Democratic candidates with far greater experience in national affairs. Ford was handicapped by the fact that he had pardoned Nixon in September 1974, a move that raised suspicions that a secret deal had been made when he was chosen by Nixon as Agnew's replacement. Moreover, Carter as a Southerner was able to arrest the slide of the South towards the Republicans. At the same time, he was a moderate who showed the new post-segregationist face of Southern politics. Yet in spite of Ford's handicaps and Carter's advantages, the presidential election was close. In Congress on the other hand the Democrats retained the large majorities in both chambers that they had secured in the post-Watergate 1974 midterm elections. But ominously for Carter, few congressional Democrats were helped by his election and thus few felt they owed him their cooperation, accounting for the failures of his legislative program.

Central to Carter's foreign policy was the worldwide support of human rights, by which Carter hoped that the United States would regain the Wilsonian moral high ground that it had lost with the Vietnam War and Nixon's amoral *Realpolitik*. The human rights policy entailed a distancing of America from right-wing dictatorships that had earlier been supported in the name of the anti-communist crusade. It also entailed a cooling of American relations with China and the Soviet Union, who disliked being lectured by the United States on their internal human rights abuses. From a pragmatic point of view, therefore, the human rights policy complicated American foreign policy. Still, it proved to be the most enduring legacy of Carter's presidency.

Carter's greatest foreign policy success was the Camp David agreement of 1978 that produced peace between Egypt and Israel. While Kissinger had opened the way in 1973–4 by facilitating Egypt's detachment from the Soviet Union's embrace, it was Carter who personally mediated between Egyptian President Sadat and Israeli Prime Minister Begin. The historic land-for-peace agreement removed the most populous Arab state from the ranks of Israel's uncompromising enemies, thereby securing Israel from a conventional Arab attack. Camp David was a major step towards the pacification of the Middle East. It was Jimmy Carter's finest moment. Thereafter, fortune smiled on him no more.

One set of foreign problems that undermined Carter's presidency derived from the Soviet Union. While Carter and his aides were hardly naïve idealists, his administration was affected by a prevailing revisionist view that blamed the United States as much as the Soviet Union for the Cold War. Liberals thought that rapid improvements in superpower relations were both desirable and easily attainable, if only the United States would abandon the earlier Cold War fixations and the Nixonian emphasis on power politics. Thus when Carter took office in 1977, he announced that it was time to move beyond the view 'that Soviet expansion was almost inevitable but that it must be contained' and beyond 'that inordinate fear of communism which once led us to embrace any dictator who joined us in that fear'.

In reality, the Soviet Union in the 1970s made the fateful decision to take advantage of the American post-Vietnam retreat in order to maximize worldwide Soviet power and influence. If the Soviet leadership had pursued improving relations with the West by abandoning its worldwide revolutionary mission, and if in parallel it had been willing to implement liberalizing economic reforms in the manner of Deng Xiaoping's communist China in the 1980s, the Soviet Union might not have collapsed. Instead, the sclerotic Brezhnev regime opted for an ambitious foreign policy, which proved so menacing to the rest of the world that it produced within a few years an immense global anti-Soviet mobilization, which eventually doomed the Soviet Union. Three Soviet policies were particularly menacing.

First, the Soviet Union aggressively supported the spread of communist dictatorships in the Third World, especially in Ethiopia and South Yemen. In Central America, leftist regimes emerged in Grenada and Nicaragua with Cuban support. Castro also helped the leftist insurgency in El Salvador, which neighbors Nicaragua. Combined with the earlier fall of South Vietnam and Cambodia, as well as Cuba's military presence in Angola's civil war, a pattern emerged of expanding communist power and influence on three continents. While none of these developments alone was particularly threatening to the West, together they seemed to create an alarming communist trend in world politics.

Second, the Soviet Union steadily increased its nuclear arsenal, aiming at superiority over the United States. During the second half of the 1970s it deployed a large number of intermediate nuclear SS-20 missiles, which threatened Western Europe and China. In time, the SS-20s led to a massive nuclear arms build-up in Britain, France and China, as well as the United States, disastrously worsening the Soviet Union's security situation.

Third, in December 1979 the Soviet Union invaded Afghanistan with large forces in order to prop up the collapsing Afghani communist regime. This was the first expansion of the Soviet sphere by the direct use of Soviet military force since 1945; it led to the collapse of *detente* and the revival of Cold War antagonisms. A few days after the invasion, Carter declared that 'the action of the Soviets has made a more dramatic change in my opinion of what the Soviets' ultimate goals are than anything they've done in the previous time I've been in office'. In retaliation, Carter imposed economic sanctions on the Soviet Union and withdrew the United States from the 1980 Moscow Olympics.

The Carter administration also had to confront a new type of threat in Iran after the collapse of the Shah at the beginning of 1979 and the rise of Ayatollah Khomeini's Islamic fundamentalist regime a few months later. The fall of the Shah meant the loss of one of America's most important allies in the Middle East. This geopolitical loss took a more humiliating form in November 1979, when Islamist students invaded the US Embassy in Tehran and took 52 American diplomats hostage. This violation of diplomatic immunity was indicative of the international image of the United States as a 'paper tiger' following the collapse of South Vietnam and the retreat of American influence in various parts of the world. Khomeini characteristically said of Carter: 'He sometimes threatens us militarily and at other times economically, but he is aware himself that he is beating on an empty drum.' Khomeini's assessment was not entirely accurate, since Carter did launch a military raid in April 1980 to rescue the hostages. But the aborting of the raid after an accidental collision and destruction of American aircraft in the Iranian desert enhanced the image of American weakness.

By the end of the 1970s, the pendulum within the United States swung from the liberal critics of Nixon's *Realpolitik* to the opposite conservative side. In 1980 the American people elected Ronald Reagan as president, who had been attacking the Nixon-Kissinger policies from the right. The rightward movement of American society in the 1980 elections resulted not only in the defeat of Carter, but also in the exit from Congress of prominent liberals, including Senator George McGovern who had been among the most forceful critics of Nixon and Ford from the left. The strong opposing currents that characterized American politics from Nixon to Carter also left their mark on American culture.

NOTES

1. Dan T. Carter, *The Politics of Rage: George Wallace, the Origins of the New Conservatism, and the Transformation of American Politics,* New York, Simon & Schuster, 1995, p. 349.
2. Michael Howard, *The Causes of Wars,* Cambridge, MA: Harvard University Press, 1984, p. 227
3. John Lewis Gaddis, *Strategies of Containment: A Critical Appraisal of Postwar American National Security Policy,* Oxford: Oxford University Press, 1982, p. 297.
4. Christopher Andrew, *For the President's Eyes Only: Secret Intelligence and the American Presidency from Washington to Bush,* New York: HarperCollins, 1995, p. 367.
5. Quoted in Michael Schudson, *Watergate in American Memory,* New York: Basic, 1993.
6. Estimates provided in Michael Barone, *Our Country,* New York: Free Press, 1990, pp. 601–5.

7. Augustus B. Cochran III, *Democracy Heading South: National Politics in the Shadow of Dixie,* Lawrence, KS: University of Kansas Press, 2001, p. 128.

RECOMMENDED READING

Christopher Andrew, *For the President's Eyes Only: Secret Intelligence and the American Presidency from Washington to Bush,* New York: HarperCollins: 1995.

Dan T. Carter, *The Politics of Rage: George Wallace, the Origins of the New Conservatism, and the Transformation of American Politics,* New York: Simon & Schuster, 1995.

Robert Dallek, *Nixon and Kissinger: Partners in Power,* London: Allen Lane, 2007.

David Frum, *How We Got Here: The 70s, The Decade that Brought You Modern Life,* New York: Basic, 2000.

Rick Perlstein, *Nixonland: The Rise of a President and the Fracturing of America,* New York: Scribner, 2008.

Richard Reeves, *President Nixon: Alone in the White House,* New York: Simon & Schuster, 2001.

Bruce J. Schulman, *The Seventies: The Great Shift in American Culture, Society, and Politics,* New York: Free Press, 2001.

CHAPTER 8

The Clash of Two Countercultures

When did the Sixties end? In *America's Uncivil Wars* (2006) Mark Hamilton Lytle describes the 1960s 'as a set of experiences that stretch over 20 years, beginning somewhere in the mid-1950s and drawing to a close in the mid-1970s.' He divides the epoch into three phases: 'the era of consensus, from 1954 until the assassination of John F. Kennedy in November 1963; the years from 1964 to 1968, during which most of the phenomena associated with the sixties emerged; and finally the era of essentialist politics, from 1969 until the fall of Richard Nixon in 1974.'

When did the radical Sixties end? Today we would place the date in November 1968, when Richard Nixon was elected president. But in the two years before the election, The crucial period occurred in the two years before Nixon's election in 1968 when Americans experienced a flood of traumatic events that transformed their world. When the poet Robert Lowell published *Notebook 1967–68* (1968) he listed the important events that figured in his text, including the Arab-Israeli Six Days' War, the Russian invasion of Czechoslovakia, black riots in Newark and Detroit, student rebellions in Paris and New York, the murders of Martin Luther King and Robert Kennedy, and growing opposition to the Vietnam War. Yet Lowell's list did not cover one of the most traumatic events of the epoch: the Chinese Cultural Revolution. In *The Sixties Unplugged* (2008) Gerald De Groot reports that in 1968, 200,000 people died in pitched battles between rival armies in Guangxi Province alone, and 3000 'class enemies' were slaughtered in ritualized acts of cannibalism.

Looking back on those fateful years, Todd Gitlin later wrote: 'one can see the late Sixties as a long unraveling, a fresh start, a tragicomic *Kulturkampf*, the long overdue demolition of a fraudulent consensus, a failed upheaval, an unkept promise, a valiant effort at reforms camouflaged as revolution – and it was all of those.' But for Gitlin they were mainly apocalyptic years filled with 'the rhetoric of showdown and recklessness'. He notes that the key film of 1967 was *Bonnie and Clyde* and the key song was the Doors' 'The End'. 'The end was always near,' Gitlin says. 'The zeitgeist screamed until it was hoarse.'

The fateful years

The 1960s had begun with civil rights demonstrations against the system of racial segregation in the South. But by 1965 the momentum shifted to Vietnam

THE CLASH OF TWO COUNTERCULTURES

as American troop numbers and casualties increased sharply. New Left activists became the cutting edge of the antiwar movement. 'As the war became more militant, so did the antiwar movement – in demands, in spirit, in tactics,' notes Gitlin. Between 1965 and 1967, as American troops in Vietnam doubled and redoubled and redoubled twice more, most antiwar movers and shakers shook off their leftover faith in negotiations and endorsed immediate withdrawal.' Radicalized members of the New Left no longer represented a loyal opposition but actively supported an NLF (National Liberation Front) victory. Viet Cong flags began to appear at antiwar rallies alongside American flags. 'Surely those NLF flags were part of the explanation for one of the stunning political facts of the decade: that as the war steadily lost popularity in the late Sixties, *so did the antiwar movement*.' In the months leading up to the 1968 election, leftist radicals chose to move away from constructive engagement and adopted a strategy of destructive disruption, culminating in the protests in Chicago at the Democratic Party Convention. Lytle calls this increasing cacophony the transformation of the 'civil wars' of the decade into 'uncivil wars'.

After Nixon's election, revolutionary enthusiasm waned as the United States showed few signs of radical political change. The New Left fell as spectacularly as it had risen, the victim of the same factional disputes and internecine warfare that had plagued the Old Left. Having attempted to abolish history, the young radicals became its victims instead. 'When the New Left started it made much of the difference between it and earlier radicals,' observed the historian William O'Neill in *Coming Apart* (1969). 'It was open, undoctrinaire, independent where they had supposedly been conspiratorial, dishonest, and sectarian. But in scarcely more than eight years the New Left recapitulated practically the whole history of American radicalism.'

Thus 1968 was a year of extremes when, as the novelist Joan Didion said, 'the center was not holding'. It was a time of both ends against the middle: the liberal consensus was under attack from a counterculture on its left and a counterrevolutionary movement on its right. For there was *another* cultural revolution in the making in 1968 within the discontented white middle class. Roosevelt's New Deal coalition held together for three decades until the pressures of racial integration, cultural change and Big Government tore it apart. In 1968 Alabama Governor George Wallace launched his third-party movement; though his campaign faltered, it was a watershed in modern American politics. Kevin Phillips, a young political analyst, detected in the Wallace phenomenon a rising cultural populism that was changing the political landscape. He wrote in his influential book, *The Emerging Republican Majority* (1969):

> The great political upheaval of the 1960s is not that of Senator Eugene McCarthy's relatively small group of upper-middle-class intellectual supporters, but a populist revolt of the American masses who have been elevated by prosperity to middle-class status and conservatism. Their revolt is against the caste, policies and taxation of the mandarins of Establishment liberalism.

Phillips understood what others had missed; he provided Richard Nixon with the basis of his 1972 'Southern Strategy' to create a new right-wing populist coalition appealing to 'the Silent Majority'. So began two decades of nearly uninterrupted Republican presidential rule.

The New Realism

A new politics of resentment emerged on both the left and right. The Vietnam War created a crisis in confidence in the whole political system. Take the example of Robert McNamara, the brilliant Secretary of Defense under Presidents Kennedy and Johnson. McNamara was a systems manager whose reliance on statistics as the only accurate gauge of reality was legendary. After he returned from his first inspection tour of Vietnam he declared, 'Every quantitative measure we have shows we're winning this war.' Because he had no independent means to gather data, McNamara was forced to rely on the South Vietnamese to provide him with the facts. One Vietnamese general observed, '*Ah, les statistiques!* Your Secretary of Defense loves statistics. We Vietnamese can give him all he wants. If you want them to go up, they will go up. If you want them to go down, they will go down.'

But McNamara was not merely the victim of invented statistics, he was the perpetrator of fictions as facts as well. In *The Best and the Brightest* (1973), David Halberstam recounted an incident where McNamara silenced critics of his hawkish policy at a National Security Council meeting by offering statistics which, it later turned out, he had simply made up on the spot. Thus the highest decision-makers in the government were reduced to making policy on the basis of pure fantasy. This confusion of fact and fiction reached its apogee during the 1968 Tet offensive when American public opinion turned against the war. During Tet, American credibility suffered a fatal blow while the Viet Cong actually suffered a military defeat. Ironically, it was here that the Johnson administration won the battle but lost the war. From then on, Vietnam policy would not be left to generals and politicians alone to decide. Instead, beginning in the 1970s, journalists and historians, novelists and filmmakers began to record American reality in new ways. But how were artists and historians to represent the fading line between fantasy and reality that covered large areas of American experience?

By the late 1960s it was clear that American literature was being pulled in opposite directions: toward a greater exploration of pure fantasy and a greater exploitation of pure fact. On the one hand, there was the development of a new experimental fiction which refused the mimetic urge. On the other hand, there was a renewed interest in the social world on the part of novelists who took over areas of experience previously reserved for journalists, historians and social scientists. Some literary critics made much of this radical division between Fabulists and Realists but, in truth, the lines were never so clearly drawn. 'What matters is the use to which the writer puts his technique,' observed Keith Opdahl in *Contemporary American Fiction* (1987). 'In postmodern hands, realistic detail can be so intense, so compulsively focused, that it defamiliarizes the world. In realistic hands, on the other hand, fabulistic devices can express a feeling or experience the reader recognizes immediately as his own.'

Whereas Fabulists stressed the reflexive nature of art, New Realists found their material in the social and political issues that dominated the 1960s: women's estate, black consciousness and the Vietnam War. In a sense, the cultural life of the 1960s was shaped more by images than by words, just as print culture was dominated more by social criticism than by imaginative writing. Among the most influential books of the decade were Herbert Marcuse's *One-Dimensional Man*, Betty Friedan's *The Feminine Mystique*, *The Autobiography of Malcolm X* and the now forgotten little red book, *Quotations of Chairman Mao*. As we shall see, the political and cultural *analysis* which shaped the movements of the 1960s paved the way for the imaginative *experiencing* of controversial areas of American reality during the 1970s. Yet the New Realism was not simply a reflection *of* the concerns of an alternative culture but a reflection *on* the illusions and delusions of an apocalyptic decade.

Women's estate

This change was apparent in the outpouring of women's fiction in the early 1970s. The new feminist consciousness in the 1960s was expressed first in programmatic prose and then in the highly personal poetry of Adrienne Rich, Sylvia Plath and Anne Sexton. Though a few novels like Plath's *The Bell Jar,* Mary McCarthy's *The Group* and Joan Didion's *Run, River* appeared in the same year as Friedan's *The Feminine Mystique* (1963), women's fiction did not emerge as a significant force until ten years later. Instead it was Friedan's social analysis which recorded a breakthrough in feminist consciousness.

In *Woman's Proper Place* (1978), Sheila M. Rothman showed how the role of American women had changed in the twentieth century. During World War II, women had gone to work in unprecedented numbers as men were drafted to fight the war. But afterward, they were asked to relinquish their jobs to returning servicemen. As women were relegated to the isolation of the new suburbs, many, especially college graduates, began to chafe at their limited lives as simply house-wives. When Friedan interviewed her 1942 Smith College classmates 15 years on, many were bitter about their new loneliness and feelings of social uselessness. Six years later, in *The Feminine Mystique,* Friedan explored the roots of this bitter-ness. She argued that 'the core of the problem for women today is not sexual but a problem of identity – a stunting or evasion of growth that is perpetuated by the feminine mystique'. As with ethnic writers in the 1950s, the 'problem of identity' became a dominant theme in the new women's writing in the 1970s.

If *The Feminine Mystique* wrote the text, then the protest movements of the 1960s provided the training for the women's movement. The first generation of feminists actually learned their organizational skills in the civil rights and antiwar movements where they were asked to play subordinate roles. Todd Gitlin recalls, 'Men sought [women] out, recruited them, took them seriously, honored their intelligence – then subtly demoted them to girlfriends, wives, note-takers, coffee makers.' In *Personal Politics* (1979) Sara Evans observed that women learned firsthand how 'the personal was political'. Another female activist asked, 'How could those men be so smart and still so sexist?'

So the women's movement was born out of disillusionment with both bour-geois society and the radical left. After 1968, the left was in shambles as the Civil Rights movement adopted the violent rhetoric of Black Power and the

New Left adopted the terrorist tactics of the Weathermen. As male activists turned to fantasies of revolutionary violence, female activists turned to new women's consciousness-raising groups. Women discovered that power relations shaped domestic as well as political life and they took up the slogan, 'The personal is political'. Thus the women's movement was born out of the ashes of the imploding New Left. Gitlin concludes, 'Sisterhood was powerful partly because movement brotherhood was not.'

Soon local consciousness-raising groups were being forged into a decentralized national movement which adopted the slogan, 'Sisterhood is powerful'. The National Organization of Women (NOW), founded by Friedan in 1966, became its mainstream political voice. *Ms* magazine, founded by Gloria Steinem in 1972, became its mainstream cultural voice. During the 1970s, women achieved a series of stunning political and legal successes, including eliminating criminal penalties for abortion, changing prejudicial rape laws, banning job discrimination against pregnant women, sharing property distribution at divorce, and guaranteeing equal treatment for women in education. By the 1990s, American society had been radically transformed. In 1950, women comprised only 20 percent of college undergraduates; by 1990, they comprised 54 percent. In 1960, only 35 percent of women worked outside the home; by 1990, the figure was 58 percent. In the same period, the number of female lawyers and judges rose from 7500 to 108,200 and the number of female doctors from 15,672 to 174,000.

In *The World Split Open* (2000), Ruth Rosen recalls lecturing on the impact of the women's movement to a large class of young female students in the early 1980s. When she asked her students to name the political changes in women's estate that had occurred in the past 20 years, they looked bewildered. When she began to list the changes, they were astounded. 'It wasn't just the enormity of all that women had challenged that still seemed breathtaking,' she explains. 'What stunned me was that the changes in women's lives had been so deep, so wide-ranging, so transformative. I realized the women's movement could not be erased, that it has brought about changes that these young people now took for granted.'

But not all the changes were positive: the flowering of the sexual revolution and the withering of the nuclear family created alarming numbers of unmarried mothers and single-parent families living below the poverty line. Nor has the path to greater equality been smooth. Neoconservative forces opposed to social change mobilized, especially after the election of Ronald Reagan in 1980, to oppose the ERA. Moreover, the women's movement itself began to split into warring factions as mainstream Women's Liberationists clashed with marginalized Radical Lesbians. A new phenomenon called 'trashing' emerged in which women's groups attacked movement leaders because of their 'elitism'. One woman said: 'Sisterhood was not all it was cracked up to be.' Rosen concludes: 'The personal often became *too* political.'

Women's writing

Thus the new women's literature of the 1970s grew directly out of the feminist movement without necessarily reflecting its contested ideology. Elizabeth

Fox-Genovese observed, 'If contemporary female culture cannot be understood independent of the women's movement, it cannot be identified with feminism *per se*.' In some novels – for instance, Judith Rossner's *Looking for Mr Goodbar* (1975) and Diane Johnson's *The Shadow Knows* (1976) – the heroine is cast in the role of the victim of a patriarchal society. But in others, like Alice Walker's *Meridian* (1976) and Marge Piercy's *Vida* (1979), she is a true heroine who succeeds through a courageous political act. *Meridian* combines feminism with the Civil Rights movement and *Vida* combines feminism with New Left politics; both novels demonstrate how, in Sara Evans's phrase, the personal becomes political.

Mainstream women's writing dealt with neither victims nor role models but rather with women who were alienated from the pressures of middle-class life. Not surprisingly, many novels defined the 'problem of identity' in terms of the theme of leaving home; the heroine suddenly confronts new opportunities resulting from a death in the family. But here the death *in* the family stands for the death *of* the family as the heroine reconsiders her traditional roles of daughter, wife and mother. In Gail Godwin's *The Odd Woman* (1974), Lisa Alther's *Kinflicks* (1975) and Mary Gordon's *Final Payments* (1978), the situation is nearly identical: the heroine, approaching the magical age of 30, finds herself at a crossroads where she must choose between an old security and a new freedom. All three heroines are divided women, in transit from old to new values, trying to shake a new consciousness out of an older sense of feminine identity. As one character puts it in *The Odd Woman*, 'I think I was one of those people who have the misfortune to grow up with one foot in one era and the other foot in the next.' These novels, like their bestselling counterparts, Erica Jong's *Fear of Flying* (1973) and Marilyn French's *The Women's Room* (1977), describe the pitfalls and possibilities in women's quest for self-realization.

Lisa Alther's *Kinflicks* is the best representative of the genre, a truly comic *bildungsroman* about a young Southern woman's coming-of-age in the 1960s. In a key scene, the heroine Ginny Babcock fantasizes that she is in a 'huge department store'. At the top of the escalator stands her father, at the bottom stands her mother. With the aid of all her mentors, mainly men, she is trying to get off this treadmill. But each time Ginny comes close she is swept away by another authority figure who forces her to either run up the down escalator or down the up escalator. Finally, she collapses in exhausted frustration.

> As she was being carried under the moving steps, down in the guts of the department store, she reflected that after all that effort, she hadn't made any progress, as Hegel had promised she would. And as she imagined the escalator mechanism chewing her to bits, she sighed with relief.

Ginny's fantasy symbolizes her predicament: she is trapped within the family in a social world confined to a department store, the symbol of the consumer society. For Ginny, social and family pressures are, in fact, the same thing. In her life, she has changed roles as she has exchanged costumes. In fact, her costumes define her roles. But now as she sits with her dying mother and tries to decide whether to return to her estranged husband, she recognizes the identity of social and family pressure. Both mother and daughter must strip away their illusions in order to face death and life respectively. Ginny must be weaned away from her mother's influence; both must learn to let go. This occurs when the dying mother refuses her authoritative role and tells her daughter, 'You must do as you think best.'

> Ginny's eyes snapped open, as though she were Sleeping Beauty just kissed by the prince. She stared at her bruised mother. Mrs. Babcock opened her good eye and stared back. Was it possible that the generational spell had actually been broken? They smiled at each other, their delight mixed with distress.

In *Kinflicks,* as in other women's fiction, personal liberation means liberation from the family: the burden of history is generational. Only by breaking 'the generational spell' can Sleeping Beauty be awakened. But Sleeping Beauty cannot wait for the prince; she must wake herself up.

During the 1980s, female protagonists became older and wiser as women writers continued to explore the feminine world. The titles of later novels by the same writers illustrate the point: Gordon's *The Company of Women* (1980); Godwin's *A Mother and Two Daughters* (1982), and Alther's *Other Women* (1984). In her novel, Godwin quotes approvingly Montaigne's dictum: 'To storm a breach, conduct an embassy, govern a people, these are brilliant actions; to scold, to laugh ... and deal gently and justly with one's family and oneself ... that is something rarer, more difficult, and less noticed in the world.' In any event, mainstream women's fiction, with its roots in the traditional novel of manners, remained aesthetically conservative in its allegiance to the conventions of realism even when it was attacking the conventions of middle-class society.

Joyce Carol Oates

But not all women writers dealt with the conventions of bourgeois realism. In *The Left Hand of Darkness* (1969) and *The Beginning Place* (1980), Ursula Le Guin established a cult following by describing social relations in the utopian form of science fiction. In *Small Changes* (1973) and *Braided Lives* (1982), Marge Piercy cultivated a loyal readership by depicting sexual and class oppression in the didactic manner of social realism. But no author defies conventional categorization as readily as Joyce Carol Oates who publishes fiction, poetry and essays on subjects ranging from feminism to boxing. 'What is the ontological status of the writer *who is also a woman?*' Oates asks in *(Woman) Writer* (1988). 'A woman who writes is a writer by her own definition; but she is a *woman* by others' definition.' In novels as various as *them, Childworld* (1976), *Marilyn* (1999) and *The Gravedigger's Daughter* (2008) she has explored not only the ontological condition of women but the dream life of America.

Perhaps Oates's talents are best revealed in *them,* a violent chronicle of family life over three decades in proletarian Detroit. She describes the struggle of two siblings, Maureen and Jules Wendall, to escape the trap of brutalizing poverty into which they were born. The plot is long and complex, sensational and nearly unbelievable, though Oates insists that the story is based on reality. Maureen becomes a prostitute, is beaten up, suffers a breakdown, recovers and ends up a middle-class housewife in the suburbs. Jules becomes a petty criminal, elopes with a rich but psychotic young woman who subsequently shoots him; he recovers and ends up a street revolutionary during the Detroit riots of 1968. In the last scene of the novel they confront each other for the last time, the sister who has achieved her dream of bourgeois security and the brother who is still pursuing his dream of radical transcendence. In the end, both affirm different versions of the same American dream of spiritual rebirth by an act of individual will.

What Oates conveys brilliantly is the brutal energy of American life: the resilience of spirit amid the rigidity of class, the persistence of dreams amid the urge to violence. She describes the struggle for liberation from the oppression of *them*: those who are defined as 'the other', whether they be the poor, the rich, the blacks, the whites, the family, the working class, the man or the woman. It is finally women like Maureen and her mother who are most memorable: women dreaming, waiting, suffering and loving. 'A woman is like a dream,' Jules's girlfriend tells him. 'Her life is a dream of waiting. I mean she lives in a dream, waiting for a man. There's no way out of this, insulting as it is, no woman can escape it.' 'But how do you fall in love?' Maureen wonders. 'I heard Ma say to a friend of hers that there was nothing in life but men, nothing but love … Why did she open herself up to such pain? Again and again she opened herself up.' 'What does it mean to be a woman?' asks Oates. 'How do these people endure it, how do they keep going? – dragging about in the envelope of their bodies, their skin puffy over their bones, living. They keep on. Sleeping.'

Black women's writing

Alongside the dominant white culture has developed another stream of women's writing which has its roots in neither bourgeois society nor conventional realism. Beginning in the early 1970s, a new generation of talented black women who found their source in an older rural communal life and oral folk cultural tradition began to revitalize African-American writing by portraying their experience in sharply different ways from older male writers. Whereas Wright and Baldwin had focused on the plight of the male adolescent in a disintegrating family environment, younger writers like Morrison and Walker concentrated on the efforts of black women to preserve the family structure without sacrificing their integrity. Whereas Alther and Godwin depicted white women who must choose between traditional gender roles and potentially new identities, Walker and Morrison described black women who chose to seek their roots in the past and to find strength in the continuity of traditional cultural arrangements.

In other words, while black male and white female writing were concerned with the theme of 'leaving home', black women writers dealt with the theme of 'finding home'. This quest for identity is best characterized by Walker in the title of her collection of essays, *In Search of Our Mother's Gardens* (1983). It is also apparent in her luminous short story, 'Everyday Use', in which a mother must choose on which daughter to bestow the gift of an old homemade quilt: the beautiful daughter who has left home and the South in search of liberation in the North or the homely daughter who lacks the ability to leave and achieve but not the character to stay and love. For the beautiful daughter the quilt has become an art object – a relic of a distant past – to be hung on the wall but not used.

But for the homely daughter the quilt is, like the past it represents, something usable, part of a living tradition. The story, like Walker's popular novel, *The Color Purple,* is a parable about the uses of the past and a hymn to the unsung black women who made home, family and community possible under the most difficult circumstances. Here she creates a world of female bonding, extended family relationships and enduring communal values, which is at odds with the concerns of traditional male black writing.

Toni Morrison

The most distinguished example of this new literature in the 1970s is Toni Morrison's *Song of Solomon,* which rewrites the crisis of black male adolescence from a feminist perspective. She tells the story of two sides of the Dead family: the patriarchal side, headed by Macon, which prizes orderliness, respectability, the patient accumulation of wealth and the sanctity of the nuclear family, and the matriarchal side, headed by his sister Pilate, which values spontaneity, love, immediate gratification and the broader ties of the extended family. The novel describes the son's rebellion against his father and his search for his real familial roots. This quest takes the adolescent hero Milkman Dead on a journey to his ancestral home in the South. If the traditional black story describes the quest for freedom as a journey from South to North, then Morrison depicts the search for roots as a journey from North to South.

   The epigraph to *Song of Solomon* is: 'The fathers may soar/And the children may know their names.' In these two images are contained the significant actions of the novel. Naming is a common trope in ethnic literature which takes as its theme the quest for identity. The immigrant who comes to America and changes his name casts off his old identity and claims a new one as an American. In African-American literature this process is complicated by the fact that the new name the African was given upon coming to American shores was that of his slave master. To find one's original (African) name or to forge a new one become acts of self-definition. In *Going to the Territory* (1986) Ralph Ellison explains, 'For it is through our names that we first place ourselves in the world. Our names being the gift of others, must be made our own.' Similarly, Morrison shows how naming is both an assertion of collective identity and a declaration of independence. The quest for identity is not simply a process of self-creation but an act of archeology as well, discovering the roots of one's given name. In naming, we do not simply face the future but also record and preserve the past.

   Here the process of naming becomes entangled with the act of soaring. Milkman's wish to fly, like that of his ancestor Solomon in the song, expresses his desire for transcendence. This motif can be traced back to slave tales and African folklore. As we have seen, it is also a major theme in the work of Wright and Ellison. But in Morrison's novel, Milkman learns that flying is ambiguous because the male desire for flight is often a wish for escape from masculine responsibility. This is what Pilate had learned as a child from the ghost of her dead father:

'You just can't fly off and leave a body,' he tole me. A human life is precious. You shouldn't fly off and leave it. So I knew right away what he meant... He meant that if you take a life, then you own it, you responsible for it. You can't get rid of nobody by killing them. They still there, and they yours now.

When Milkman understands Pilate's reluctance to fly like the male, he comprehends the strength of her feminine rootedness in life which is a kind of love. 'Now he knew why he loved her so,' he understands. 'Without ever leaving the ground, she could fly.'

Pilate is only one of several powerful female figures in Morrison's fiction, who also include the protagonists of *Sula* (1974), *Beloved* (1987) and *Paradise* (1998). Together with the heroines of Toni Cade Bambara's *The Salt Eaters* (1980) and Gloria Naylor's *Mama Day* (1988), they comprise a remarkable portrait gallery of strong black women which radically revises our understanding of African-American experience. What they share is a belief in being rooted in an authentic black tradition as a precondition for achieving identity. The preservation of the past as history and folklore is a central task in this radically conservative fiction. These writers insist on the necessity of cultural continuity against the inroads of mainstream American ideology with its emphasis on inevitable change.

The effort to preserve the past is present in other women's ethnic fiction as well. Popular Hispanic writers focus on the ordeal of immigrant experience from many perspectives, reflecting the rich tapestry of Latino culture. In *The House on Mango Street* (1985) and *Caramelo* (2002) Sondra Cisneros writes of Mexican life in Chicago. In *How the Garcia Girls Lost Their Accent* (1992) and *Yo!* (1996) Julia Alvarez depicts three decades of Dominican-American experience. In *Dreaming in Cuban* (1992) Cristina Garcia writes about three generations of Cuban women. From *When I Was Puerto Rico* (1993) to *The Turkish Lover* (2004) Esmeralda Santiago traces her own journey from rural Puerto Rico through Brooklyn to Harvard University.

It is striking how many of these fictions are multigenerational narratives. The same is true of Chinese-American writers like Maxine Hong Kingston and Amy Tan. In her much-acclaimed novel, *The Joy Luck Club,* Tan depicts the history of two generations of Chinese women: the mothers who are immigrants still connected to the Old World, and their daughters who are children of the New World. In a key scene, one daughter confronts the older generation and experiences their fear of the American future. 'In me, they see their own daughters, just as ignorant, just as unmindful of all the truth and hopes they have brought to America,' she thinks. 'They see daughters who will bear grandchildren born without any connecting hope passed from generation to generation.' She affirms her solidarity with the past, acknowledging the necessity of cultural continuity. 'And gradually, one by one, they smile and pat my hand. They still look troubled, as if something were out of balance. But they also look hopeful that what I say will become true. What more can they ask? What more can I promise?'

Multiculturalism

The breakthrough of ethnic writers gave rise to a new multicultural movement which helped to redefine American society. A new literary generation, defined by race, gender and ethnicity, brought first white, then black, then Native American, Hispanic and Asian-American women into the front ranks of American writers.

But this breakthrough occurred along the entire cultural front. From the television success of Alex Haley's *Roots* to the films of Spike Lee, a once marginal ethnic consciousness entered the cultural mainstream. In *Movie-Made America* (1975, rev. 1994), Robert Sklar describes how avant-garde filmmakers began to distinguish themselves from the Hollywood mainstream in the 1980s. 'The most telling sign', he notes, 'was the labels filmmakers chose for themselves and their work. Instead of adhering to groups by virtue of aesthetic doctrines or common styles, they emphasized affinity with multicultural identities that were taking bold form in the social world.'

But an uncritical emphasis on ethnic authenticity can be counterproductive as well. Even a writer like E. L. Doctorow, who is sympathetic to multiculturalism, recently questioned its relevance to literary quality. In *Reporting the Universe* (2003), he writes:

> I think something peculiar – and politically inert – is going on when I walk into a bookstore and see it sectioned off with shelves devoted to gay and lesbian writers, or African-American writers, as if the expected readers of these books can only be gays and lesbians and African-Americans, as if Edmund White and Toni Morrison are consumer products, or as if the genres are primary, the writers secondary – as in Inspirational, or Cooking, or Self-Help.

Roots

Still, the connection between ethnic experience and literary expression raised new questions about the relationship between art and the identity of the artist. A cultural turning point was the publication of Alex Haley's *Roots* in 1976. Haley was an African-American journalist who had ghostwritten *The Autobiography of Malcolm X* in the 1960s. Later Haley became interested in his own biography. Through research in Gambia, he traced his family genealogy back seven generations to an African named Kunta Kinte who was brought to America as a slave in 1767. Out of this personal history he fashioned an imaginative family chronicle about the enforced African migration to America. *Roots* became a sensational bestseller and was awarded a special Pulitzer Prize. When it was translated into a television mini-series in 1977, millions of Americans stayed home to watch it night after night. It became the most successful program in television history and inspired a wave of ethnic pride that sent Americans, black and white, in search of their ancestral roots.

But, inadvertently, the *Roots* phenomenon raised other questions about ethnic identity that were more difficult to answer. In reviewing *Roots,* the black novelist Ishmael Reed noted that Haley chose to trace his mother's genealogy back to Gambia. But, he said, 'If Alex Haley had traced his father's bloodline, he would have traveled twelve generations back to, not Gambia, but *Ireland.*' Reed, who also claims Irish ancestry, wondered what this said about the American obsession with ethnicity. Haley could have followed his Irish family genealogy but would anyone have taken him seriously? Reed once mentioned his Irish-American heritage to a Professor of Celtic Studies at Dartmouth College who laughed at the notion. Why is this funny?

In *Postethnic America* (1995) David Hollinger notes that Haley's dual ethnic inheritance involved a contradiction between American theory and practice. In *theory*, the United States is a nonethnic nation. The Declaration of Independence states that 'All men are created equal' and the Constitution protects freedom of religion and makes no mention of ethnicity. 'The national ideology', says Hollinger, 'is nonethnic by virtue of the universalist commitment... to provide the benefits of citizenship irrespective of any ascribed or asserted ancestral affiliations.' If the United States truly practiced what it preached then Haley could in fact have chosen to be Irish – or African-American – or both.

But in *practice*, the United States has an ethnic history which contradicts the theory. Historically, race is a fiction which was socially constructed as an ideology. We do not choose our racial identity; the larger society chooses it for us. The history of slavery and racism determined that Alex Haley saw himself – and was seen by others – as a black man. No other choice seemed rational. 'The persistence of the "one-drop rule" [the law of racial purity from the time of slavery] deprives those with any hint of black skin of any choice in their ethno-racial affiliation,' says Hollinger. It even denies the reality that blacks and whites in America share a substantial gene pool. The historian Barbara Fields points out that many Americans still believe in a racial paradigm 'that considers a white woman capable of giving birth to a black child but denies that a black woman can give birth to a white child'.

Identity politics and MISC

Out of this contradiction between theory and practice, a new fashion of 'identity politics' was born. People who found themselves disadvantaged by America's racial history began to identify more with their marginalized group than with the country. They defined themselves not as part of the whole community but as members of a particular subculture with which they chose to affiliate. Catharine R. Stimson explains,

> Identity politics is contemporary shorthand for a group's assertion that it is a meaningful group; that it differs significantly from other groups; that its members share a history of injustice and grievance; and that its psychological and political mission is to explore, act out, act on and act up its group identity.

A group may define itself in terms of race, gender, class, ethnicity or any other characteristic. In defining a group ideal, says Stimson, 'identity politics offers stability in a shifting, swiftly changing world'.[1]

Identity politics has thrived in American universities. Especially on large multiethnic campuses like Berkeley it is possible to mobilize students to demand a multicultural curriculum, separate facilities for special groups or preferential treatment for racial minorities. But there has been a cost as well. Identity politics balkanizes college campuses into hostile groups, alienates the majority of white students, divides the society over the issue of Affirmative Action, and creates a sterile academic debate about 'canon formation' and 'political correctness'.

In recent years a new development has also raised questions about both identity politics and multiculturalism. Supporters of multiculturalism often point out
that the percentage of non-Hispanic whites in the population is falling; by 2050
some estimate that the majority of the population will be nonwhite. But the situation is more complex than that. In the 2000 census nearly half of the people
who called themselves Hispanic also identified themselves as white. Richard
Alba and Victor Nee argue that the American mainstream is in the process
of being redefined in ways that undermine the foundation of identity politics.
'Given demographic trends, the mainstream is likely to evolve in the direction
of including members of ethnic and racial groups that were formerly excluded,'
they predict; 'in the next quarter century, we expect some blurring of the main
ethnic and racial boundaries of American life'. Just as excluded ethnic groups like
Italians and Jews were 'whitened' in the early twentieth century so, one hundred
years later, Cubans and Chinese are also entering the American mainstream. 'For
portions of nonwhite and Hispanic groups, the social and cultural distance from
the mainstream will shrink: these individuals will live and work in ethnically and
racially mixed milieus, much of the time without a sense that their social interactions are greatly affected by their origins.' While this will not mean an end to
racial inequality, still 'it will alter the racial compartmentalization of American
society to an important extent'.

The multicultural debate

The attack on the idea of a hegemonic culture in the name of cultural diversity
has led to a rethinking of aesthetic categories and a revision of accepted can-
ons of cultural taste. But the debate over cultural standards still rages in the
strident controversy over political correctness, an unappealing idea which con-
firms Robert Hughes's observation that, 'If the first law of American corporate
life is that dead wood floats, the corresponding rule of liberation-talk is that
hot air expands.' In *The Twilight of Common Dreams* (1999) Todd Gitlin tells
an instructive story about the excesses of identity politics. About every seven
years the state of California chooses new textbooks to be used in its public
schools. In 1990 a new series of history textbooks came up for review. It was
written under the direction of Professor Gary Nash, a distinguished social historian who writes extensively about minority groups. Nash and his colleagues
departed from the old-style textbooks which celebrated American history as a
pageant of progress shaped by great white men. Instead they emphasized the
multicultural character of American history by including those 'silent' groups
like blacks, immigrants, women and the working class who tended to be left
out of the textbooks. The new textbooks were scheduled to appear in time
for the 500th anniversary of Columbus's discovery of America so that they
could be used in teaching the impact of white European exploration on native
American people.

When these revisionist textbooks came up for review at public hearings there
was an outcry against them, not from the Radical Right but, strangely enough,
from the Multiculturalist Left. Gitlin says, 'To great media fanfare, a number
of group representatives testified passionately that the books were "racist,"

religiously discriminatory, and otherwise demeaning. Muslims, Jews, Chinese Americans, gays, and, most vigorously, African Americans objected.' Some criticisms were legitimate but most were trivial or irrational. Eventually, the textbooks were approved by the state board of education but they were rejected by the local board of Oakland, a city with a multiethnic population. At a time when state expenditures for education were being sharply reduced, left-wing groups chose to protest not budget cuts but multicultural textbooks that were not multicultural enough. 'One consequence was that when Columbus Day rolled around in 1992, Oakland's [elementary school] teachers had no textbooks at all to help them teach about California's Indians or, indeed, about anyone else.'

The Vietnam experience

Men and Vietnam

Just as the feminist movement of the Sixties nurtured the development of a new women's writing in the 1970s so the antiwar movement spawned a new literature about the Vietnam experience after the war was over. First, the field was dominated by historians, social scientists and journalists who produced a polemical debate about American involvement in Southeast Asia. Only later did imaginative works reveal other aspects of America's most controversial war. In *Dispatches* (1977), Michael Herr explained why 'objective' reporting was finally not sufficient to describe the war:

> The press got all the facts (more or less), it got too many of them. But it never found a way to report meaningfully about death, which of course was really what it was all about. The most repulsive, transparent gropes for sanctity in the midst of the killing received serious treatment in the papers and on the air. The jargon of Progress got blown into your head like bullets, and by the time you waded through all the Washington stories and all the Saigon stories, all the Other War stories and the corruption stories and the stories about brisk new gains in ARVN [Army of the Republic of Vietnam] effectiveness, the suffering was somehow unimpressive.

In *Dispatches,* Herr transcended the facts by projecting himself as both witness and participant in a brilliant example of the New Journalism. Others found different ways to describe their experience. In poetry like Michael Casey's *Obscenities* (1972), novels like Tim O'Brien's *Going After Cacciato* (1978) and memoirs like Philip Caputo's *A Rumor of War* (1977), we came to a new understanding of the bitter legacy of Vietnam. These writers taught us to see the war from ground level; from that perspective we could not simply stand aside and judge without becoming implicated in the terrible ambiguities of power, violence and extreme situations. Caputo depicted this ambiguity best when he described his own ambivalence about his war experience. 'Anyone who fought in Vietnam, if he is honest about himself, will have to admit he enjoyed the compelling attractiveness of combat. It was a peculiar enjoyment because it was mixed with a commensurate pain,' he wrote. 'It was something like the elevated state of awareness induced by drugs. And it could be just as addictive, for it made whatever else life offered in the way of delights and torments seem pedestrian.'

Yet Caputo and the others did not glamorize the war. Instead they showed how Vietnam transformed the people who experienced it firsthand. Caputo joined the Marines as an idealistic volunteer and left the military both disillusioned and disgraced, but he still spoke of his irrational desire to return to Vietnam even though he now opposed the war. This strange compulsion arose 'from a recognition of how deeply we had been changed, how different we were from everyone who had not shared with us the miseries of the monsoon, the exhausting patrols, the fear of a combat assault on a hot landing zone.' He explained,

> I was involved in the antiwar movement at the time and struggled, unsuccessfully, to reconcile my opposition to the war with this nostalgia. Later, I realized a reconciliation would be impossible; I would never be able to hate the war with anything like the undiluted passion of my friends in the movement. Because I had fought in it, it was not an abstract issue, but a deeply emotional experience, the most significant thing that had happened to me. It held my thoughts, senses, and feelings in an unbreakable embrace.

Though much Vietnam writing is indebted to the realism of Hemingway and Mailer, many writers stress the irrational nature of the war experience. By the end of *Dispatches* we sympathize with the correspondent who 'said he didn't mind his nightmares so much as his waking impulse to file news reports on them'. This sense of modern history as a nightmare from which its participants are trying to awake is pervasive in modern literature but nowhere more relevant than in Vietnam literature. In *American Fictions: 1940–1980* (1983), Frederick Karl calls attention to this surreal quality in the new war writing. 'Vietnam novels and memoirs...are, in a sense, removed from history, roving outside time and space,' he notes. 'What distinguishes fiction about the Vietnam War from that about World War Two is its disembodied quality; it is unassociated with anything occurring back home or even back at the base.' This quality is most fully represented in Tim O'Brien's *Going After Cacciato,* perhaps the most brilliant novel to come out of the war.

In this new war writing, many drew on their own experiences as soldiers or journalists in Vietnam. As acts of imaginative reconstruction, they described the separation of the war from ordinary life. In the Academy Award-winning film *The Deer Hunter* (1978) director Michael Cimino portrayed his working-class heroes as traumatized victims incapable of adjusting to civilian life. They are soldiers who could not save South Vietnam but who tried to rescue their comrades. In the next decade, the flow of autobiographically-based writing became a flood, to be followed by similarly autobiographically-based films like Oliver Stone's *Platoon* (1986). But many books and films dealt less with the war against the North Vietnamese than the inner conflict experienced by American soldiers. As the narrator in *Platoon* confesses: 'We didn't fight the enemy, we fought ourselves, and the enemy was in us.' So it remained for another group of writers to imaginatively reclaim the war experience from a different perspective and bring it back home.

Women and Vietnam

If Vietnam literature and women's writing were the two dominant modes of the New Realism produced in the 1970s and after, they clearly represent a mainstream divided by gender. Except for John Updike (*Marry Me,* 1976) and John Irving (*The World According to Garp,* 1978), few male authors ventured into the world of domestic relations. Aside from Frances FitzGerald (*Fire in the Lake,* 1972) and Sally Emerson (*Winners and Losers,* 1976), few female writers explored the subject of war. But in the mid-1980s several novels appeared which, in different ways, attempted to reimagine the Vietnam experience from a new (feminine) perspective. Both Jayne Anne Phillips's *Machine Dreams* (1984) and Bobbie Ann Mason's *In Country* (1985) depicted the impact of Vietnam on Middle America by describing how their young heroines coped with the loss of a father or brother. In both novels young women imaginatively reconstruct the Vietnam experience of their male relatives in an effort to connect with history. For instance, in the moving conclusion of *In Country,* the heroine visits the Vietnam Memorial in Washington (designed by Maya Lin, a Chinese-American female architecture student) to see her father's name, to touch it, and thus reclaim her past.

Joan Didion's *Democracy* (1984) is also concerned with a woman's efforts to confront history, though, as its title suggests, it has larger ambitions. Didion named her novel after Henry Adams's nineteenth-century satire on the corruption of American political life in the Gilded Age. Like Adams, she sees Washington as a world of entropy in which the intimate connection between moral style and practical politics has broken down. And like Adams, she is a self-proclaimed conservative who is concerned with the rupture of private and public history. Just as Phillips and Mason describe a Middle America insulated from history, so Didion draws a satirical portrait of Washington where politicians still believe that America is exempt from the exigencies of history. This is the hard lesson that her heroine learns. Here we see two themes coalesce in a new kind of Vietnam literature: the heroine's coming-of-age as a woman and as an American. Didion's heroine becomes a liberated woman when she leaves her politician husband to make her own life; she comes of age as an American when she ceases 'to claim the American exemption' from history and goes to work in a refugee camp in Kuala Lumpur.

An astonishing number of Vietnam war narratives and domestic dramas are resolved in liberating acts of divorce and flight or purgative rituals of remembering and mourning, like the funeral in *The Deer Hunter* and the Vietnam Memorial visit in *In Country.* In *Echoes of Combat* (1996), Fred Turner calls such stories '*therapeutic narratives* whose conventionalized dynamics of character and plot, crisis and resolution offered Americans a highly formalized and emotionally secure environment in which to recall the chaotic, rage-provoking years of conflict.' Vietnam films and novels provide a safe way of recalling horrendous violence, but few works have the political dimension of Didion's *Democracy.* Turner notes, 'to the degree that they have helped us forget the political decisions that sparked the war, as well as the support millions of citizens gave to those decisions, such therapeutic constructions have also made it easier for us to make the same mistakes again.'

The end of victory culture

But Vietnam books and films evoke something more. In *The End of Victory Culture* (1995), Tom Engelhardt argues that Vietnam marked the culmination of the unraveling of the myth of American exceptionalism. For a hundred years, Americans had watched the narrative of Manifest Destiny played out on the silver screen in the struggle between cowboys and Indians. But in Vietnam the traditional roles in Western films were reversed: in My Lai and elsewhere the Americans were now the savage marauders and the Vietnamese were the innocent victims or disciplined victors. 'The war mysteriously robbed Americans of their inheritance,' he says.

> On screen and off, they were transformed from victors into, at best, victims; from heroes into, at worst, killers; their leader [Richard Nixon], a self-proclaimed madman; their soldiers, torturers; their democratic public, a mob of rioters and burners; their army, in a state of near collapse; their legislative bodies, impotent. They had become the world's most extraordinary (because least expected) losers.

Thus Vietnam represented not merely the loss of a war but the loss of a culture. 'It is now practically a cliché that, with the end of the Cold War and the "loss of the enemy," American culture has entered a period of crisis that raises profound questions about the national purpose and identity.'

In the last two decades of the twentieth century, American writers created a new politicized fiction which took as its starting point the changing national character in the post-Vietnam era. In the 1980s, several novelists linked American involvement in Central America with Vietnam. Both Robert Stone's account of failed revolutionary politics, *A Flag for Sunrise* (1981), and Robert Houston's parable of a nineteenth-century American adventurer in Nicaragua, *The Nation Thief* (1984), use the southern hemisphere as a reference point for descriptions of the end of American innocence. In the 1990s, several prize-winning fictional works, including Tim O'Brien's *The Things They Carried* (1990) and Robert Olen Butler's *A Good Scent from a Strange Mountain* (1992), returned to the Vietnam tragedy. This focus continues in *They Marched into Sunlight* (2004), journalist David Maraniss's brilliant recreation of a traumatic week in 1967 when American troops were fatally ambushed in Vietnam at the same moment that American students were protesting the war in Wisconsin.

More than 40 years after the first American 'advisors' arrived and 30 years after the last soldiers departed, Vietnam remains a fixed point in the national memory. After the swift allied victory in the 1991 Gulf War, President Bush exulted, 'By God, we've kicked the Vietnam syndrome once and for all.' But not everyone agreed. Three years later, a Vietnam veteran complained, 'What happened twenty years ago feels like yesterday and what happened yesterday feels like twenty years ago.' In the new millennium Vietnam reappeared like Banquo's ghost casting a long shadow over the 2004 election, George W. Bush's embattled presidency, his catastrophic occupation of Iraq, and Barack Obama's controversial war in Afghanistan. Critics on left and right continued to draw parallels between the failures in Vietnam and these later wars, leading Michael Herr to conclude: 'All the wrong people remember Vietnam. I think all the people who remember it should forget it, and all the people who forgot it should remember it.'

Metahistorical fiction

History and fiction

Vietnam writing illustrates that one of the legacies of the 1960s was its challenge to traditional ways of interpreting history. Already at the beginning of the decade, 'revisionist' historians were beginning to question the conventional view of American history which stressed consensus, assimilation and progress. In the process they opened up exciting new areas in the social history of previously 'silent' groups like blacks, immigrants, women and the working class. But much of this 'new history' was based on quantitative research and microhistorical analysis which tended to fragment our understanding of American history as a whole and to reduce its intelligibility for a larger general audience. Thus while aspects of the American past looked different, complained the social historian Herbert Guttman, '*American history* itself does not look different. And that is the problem.' He concluded, 'A new synthesis is needed, one that incorporates and then transcends the new history.'[2]

At the same time, semiologists and historians began to question the traditional distinctions between the writing of history and fiction. In different ways, Roland Barthes and Hayden White attacked the special status of history as a representation of reality by noting the similarity between the linguistic structures and rhetorical strategies of historical and imaginative writing. There no longer seemed to be a privileged view of the past, no such thing as 'objective' history. Facts did not speak for themselves but were selected and organized according to the particular narrative vision employed by the historian. As E. L. Doctorow noted, both historians and novelists 'lied' in their selective presentation of reality but novelists were 'honest liars' because they called their work fictions and so were to be believed.

The breakdown of the traditional distinction between history and fiction did not go unnoticed among novelists. In the 1960s, writers like Barth, Styron and Thomas Berger imaginatively reinvented mythic aspects of the American past. In the ensuing years, a renewed interest in history was taken up by a wide spectrum of American novelists. In a series of novels, including *Burr* (1973), *1876* (1976), *Lincoln* (1986) and *Hollywood* (1990), a traditional realist, Gore Vidal, reinterpreted 'the history of the United States from beginning to now' in the light of the political present. In *The Book of Daniel, Ragtime* (1975), *Loon Lake* (1980) and *City of God* (2000) a modernist, E. L. Doctorow, gave us an imaginative history of the twentieth century shaped by radical politics, popular culture and the restless pursuit of the chimerical American dream. In *V., Gravity's Rainbow, Mason & Dixon* (1997) and *Against the Day* (2006) a postmodernist, Thomas Pynchon, created a history of the modern world out of fragments of science and technology, politics and popular culture.

E. L. Doctorow

The most interesting of these new metahistorical novels combined fact and fiction, conventional and experimental literary techniques, to challenge the idea of historical objectivity and undermine the assumption that there is a single ascertainable order of history. For instance, in Robert Coover's *The Public Burning* (1977) and Doctorow's *The Book of Daniel,* the trial and execution of Julius and Ethel Rosenberg is shown to be the key symbolic event of the Cold War. But neither novelist is ultimately concerned with questions of guilt or innocence. Instead, the Rosenbergs are treated as pathetic but complicit scapegoats in some anthropological ritual. Whereas Coover invents outrageous situations for historical figures in order to portray Cold War hysteria, Doctorow creates his own characters and immerses them in history to suggest something larger about twentieth-century American radicalism.

The Book of Daniel is a political novel in the form of a Freudian family romance. It is not simply a fictional account of the Rosenberg case but a description of the generation gap between prewar and postwar America. In the final analysis, Doctorow suggests, the book is not about the Rosenbergs at all but about the *idea* of the Rosenbergs. Here it matters little that he has changed some facts: the Rosenbergs are now called the Isaacsons and their two sons have been transformed into a brother and sister, Daniel and Susan. It also matters less whether the accused are innocent or guilty – in the novel Daniel never finds out – than that they have been cast as scapegoats in a ritual drama beyond their comprehension. Instead, the Isaacsons come to symbolize the legacy that one generation leaves to another: the legacy of the Cold War, on the one hand, and of the Old Left, on the other. The subject of the novel is this legacy, Daniel's legacy, and that is why it is Daniel's book: a moving meditation on memory, mourning and what Christopher Lasch called 'the agony of the American Left'.

Similarly, in Doctorow's *Ragtime* the traditional interpretation of American cultural history is subverted and then rewritten 'from the bottom up'. In *Ragtime* the true shapers of modern American culture turn out to be precisely those people who had been written out of the history textbooks: blacks, immigrants, women and the working class. On the private level, he chronicles the lives of three 'families' – WASP, immigrant and black – who lead segregated lives. By the end of the novel, these three families have become one. On the public level, *Ragtime* describes the transformation of American society from small-town Anglo-Saxon homogeneity to big-city ethnic heterogeneity. The immigrants and blacks who were excluded from the American mainstream at the beginning of the novel have by the end become part of the family.

At the center of the novel, as in all of Doctorow's fiction, lies the question of justice. Coalhouse Walker, the black ragtime pianist, gives up his art when he learns that he will never receive justice in a racist society. Tateh, the immigrant filmmaker, surrenders his radicalism when he learns that revolution will never create justice in a capitalist society. Whereas Coalhouse abandons the piano and becomes a terrorist, Tateh escapes working-class poverty by becoming a commercial artist and pointing 'his life along the lines of flow of American energy'. Both represent aspects of the third artist in the novel, the famous magician Harry

Houdini, whose daring escape acts symbolize the universal desire of people to throw off their chains.

The comparison between the fictional Coalhouse and the historical Houdini suggests the remarkable way that Doctorow combines historical and imaginary figures. *Ragtime* is shaped by the conflation of history and fiction where the boundary line between the two seems to disappear. Not only does he invent incidents in the lives of historical personages like Houdini, Freud and Emma Goldman, but his 'real' and 'imagined' characters meet and mingle promiscuously on an equal footing, both victims and agents of their own projections of history. When asked whether some of the events he depicts had actually happened, Doctorow responded: 'They have now.' In his view, 'history is a kind of fiction in which we live and hope to survive, and fiction is a kind of speculative history, perhaps a superhistory, by which the available data for the composition is seen to be greater and more various in its sources than the historian supposes'.

Don DeLillo

Similarly, Don DeLillo uses an historical event to examine the dream life of the nation. In *Libra* (1988), DeLillo explores the assassination of President Kennedy as an expression of the underside of contemporary American history, 'that moment in Dallas, the seven seconds that broke the back of the American century'. For DeLillo, the Kennedy assassination is the key moment in postwar American history. 'I think Americans lost their sense of coherent reality as a result of the assassination,' he observes. 'It was as if we'd suddenly entered the world of randomness and ambiguity – something *outside* traditional American experience. Something which I think we associated with the darker age of Europe; with the literature of Kafka and similar writers.' What attracts DeLillo to the assassination is the indeterminacy of the event. Though we have the physical act on film, on television, in the thousands of pages of the Warren Report, the historical facts are still open to countless interpretations. 'There is a sense,' he says, 'in which fiction can rescue history from its confusions. The fiction writer has the liberty to invent characters and clear up events. A novel working within history is simultaneously outside it, correcting, clearing up, finding patterns and balances and symmetries. The kind of balances that we don't encounter in ordinary life.'

For DeLillo and Doctorow, history is not something we are given but something that we compose. 'The nature of things was to be elusive,' DeLillo writes in *Libra*. 'Things slipped through his perceptions. He could not get a grip on a runaway world.' 'Everything is elusive,' Doctorow writes in *Daniel*. 'God is elusive. Revolutionary morality is elusive. Justice is elusive. Human character.' In both novels, America is invented as history is composed, not to suggest that reality is illusory but to demonstrate that it must be imagined. Perhaps history has become an organizing principle of contemporary American fiction, like Marxism in the 1930s and Existentialism in the 1950s. Certainly, in novels like *Ragtime* and *Libra*, writers provide a new synthesis of American experience that Herbert Guttman found missing in contemporary American historiography. Or as Harry Truman remarked: 'There is nothing new in the world except the history you do not know.'

Postscript on Watergate

Meanwhile history continued to prove the validity of Philip Roth's claim that public events surpassed the inventions of even the most imaginative novelists. In 1972 an apparently trivial burglary in Washington, DC, led to the resignation of the world's most powerful leader, President Richard Nixon, in 1974. The story is quite simple. During the 1972 presidential election campaign, five men broke into the Democratic Party National Headquarters in the Watergate Building in Washington, DC. They were discovered by a black security guard named Frank Mills who phoned the police. The burglars were arrested and their arraignment in a Washington court was attended by a young reporter from the *Washington Post* named Bob Woodward. When he returned to the newspaper to file his report, his editor, Howard Simons, said: 'That's a hell of a story.' Simons decided to team Woodward with another young reporter, Carl Bernstein, who had a passion for rock music. They were an odd couple: Woodward's family was conservative Republican; Bernstein's background was left-wing and countercultural.

It soon became clear that they were dealing with more than a bungled break-in. Several of the arrested men were Cuban exiles living in Miami. One was carrying a large amount of cash. Another man, James McCord, had connections with the CIA; he had an address book with interesting names in it. It turned out that McCord worked for CREEP, an apt acronym for the Republican Committee to Reelect the President. In fact, they all worked for 'the Plumbers', the clandestine White House gang organized in 1971 after Daniel Ellsberg leaked the Pentagon Papers to the *New York Times*. Thus Watergate connected three government fiascos: the failed invasion of Cuba in 1961; the publication of the *Pentagon Papers* in 1971, revealing the secret history of the Vietnam War; and the bungled Watergate burglary a year later exposing government involvement in illegal activity at the highest level.

Yet the Watergate scandal, which ended with the resignation of a president for the first time in American history, almost didn't happen. In *The Powers That Be* David Halberstam noted: 'For such a landmark story in American journalism, *Watergate* was filled with ifs.' He explained:

> If the story had broken on a weekday instead of an a weekend, perhaps the *Post* might have assigned a senior political reporter from the national staff, a reporter already preoccupied with other work, and the story might have died quickly. If the first marriages of both Bob Woodward and Carl Bernstein had not ended, leaving them both bachelors, they might have been pulled away by the normal obligations of home and might not have been willing to spend the endless hours that the story required ... If Howard Simons, the managing editor, had not in some way been titillated by the story, and had not decided on his own to assign two reporters full-time ... If, if, if.

'Watergate overwhelms modern journalism,' says the sociologist Michael Schudson. 'No other story in American history features the press in so prominent and heroic a role.' Indeed, the story of how two unknown journalists uncovered the greatest political scandal of the postwar years helped to transform journalism into a celebrity vocation. When *All the President's Men* was published in May 1975, less than a year after Nixon's resignation, it became the fastest-selling non-fiction book in the history of American publishing. Robert Redford purchased the movie rights before the book was published and the film was released in 1976 to great acclaim. According to Schudson, the continuing celebrity of Watergate is mainly due to the film.

All the President's Men celebrated the role of journalism as the guardian of the public interest. But there was a downside to the medal of celebrity. As the number of applicants to journalism schools rose after the Watergate scandal, many aspired simply to become famous without learning the ethics of their craft. In 1981, Janet Cook, an ambitious junior reporter for the *Washington Post*, wrote an affecting story about an eight-year-old drug addict, 'Jimmy's World', which won a Pulitzer Prize. But it turned out that there was no Jimmy; the story was invented and the prize was returned. The *Post* was embarrassed and so was Cook's editor, Bob Woodward. She was only the first of many ambitious young journalists who were determined to achieve celebrity at any price, including falsifying their reportage.

Another negative consequence of the new fashion of investigative reporting was the increasing invasion of the privacy of public figures. The separation between the private and public spheres was eroded with the publication of a second book by Woodward and Bernstein about Nixon's last weeks in office. *The Final Days* (1976) was an inside account of Nixon's decline and fall, complete with humiliating descriptions of his excessive drinking, racist rantings and bizarre behavior. The extensive use of direct quotation without citing sources raised eyebrows in the journalistic community. CBS news commentator Eric Severeid worried about the invasion of privacy and noted that in the past journalists waited until presidents like Roosevelt and Kennedy were dead before they exposed their personal shortcomings. 'Not even the cannibals feasted on living flesh,' said Severeid.[3] The erasure of the boundary between public and private life reached its nadir in 1998 in the sensational press coverage of the scandal surrounding President Clinton's affair with a White House intern named Monica Lewinsky. The media circus and impeachment proceedings tarnished the reputation of both the press and the Congress, not to mention the predatory president.

Meanwhile many leading figures in the Watergate fiasco survived their disgrace. Some went to prison but most ended up exploiting their scandalous celebrity. Charles Colson, Nixon's special counsel, became a born-again Christian. After serving a short prison sentence, he teamed up with former Black Panther Eldridge Cleaver to form an unlikely interracial evangelical team. Others found a different path to redemption. John Ehrlichman, Nixon's advisor on domestic affairs, and John Dean, his legal counsel, became successful writers. Dean published a bestselling book entitled *Worse than Watergate: The Secret Presidency of George W. Bush* (2004). It seems the only Watergate figure who did not cash in on the scandal was Frank Mills, the black security guard who had discovered the break-in. Instead he was arrested twice for shoplifting and sentenced in 1983 to a year in jail for trying to steal a pair of tennis shoes. His fate provides a stark contrast to the white Watergate felons who fashioned successful new careers out of their crimes.

And what of the master criminal Richard Nixon? According to Michael Schudson, the disgraced president 'self-consciously sought to rebuild his reputation from the day he resigned'. From 1974 until his death in 1994, Nixon campaigned to restore his tarnished reputation through a series of public gestures. In 1976 he visited China, the scene of his greatest foreign policy triumph. In 1977 he made a series of television interviews with David Frost and in 1978 he published his *Memoirs*.[4] In 1990 he opened the Richard M. Nixon Library in his birthplace, Yorba Linda, California.

But despite these efforts, his reputation remained tarnished. 'Richard Nixon was a serial collector of resentments,' notes Rick Perlstein in *Nixonland* (2008). Memories of his early divisive political campaigns when he earned the name 'Tricky Dick' remained. He once told his friend, Leonard Garment, 'You'll never make it in politics, Len. You just don't know how to lie.' When he was interviewed by *Time* magazine in 1990, he was asked: 'How do you expect the Watergate affair to be judged in the future?' Nixon answered by telling a story. After his last trip to China, his friend Claire Booth Luce told him that every historical figure could be summed up in one sentence and his would be, 'He went to China.' Nixon disagreed. He said that historians were more likely to write: 'He resigned his office.'

NOTES

1. Catharine R. Stimson, *The Nation* (December 18, 1995), p. 791.
2. Herbert G. Guttman, 'Whatever Happened to History?' *The Nation* (November 21, 1981), p. 554.
3. Quoted in Michael Schudson, *Watergate in American Memory*, New York: Basic Books, 1992.
4. The interviews were dramatized in Ron Howard's 2008 film version of Peter Morgan's play, *Frost/Nixon*.

RECOMMENDED READING

Loren Baritz, *Backfire,* New York: William Morrow, 1985.
Tom Engelhardt, *The End of Victory Culture,* New York: Basic, 1995.
Todd Gitlin, *The Twilight of Common Dreams,* New York: Henry Holt, 1995.
David Halberstam, *The Best and the Brightest,* New York: Random House, 1972.
David Hollinger, *Postethnic America,* New York: Perseus, 1995.
Mark Hamilton Lytle, *America's Uncivil Wars,* New York: Oxford University Press, 2006.
Rick Perlstein, *Nixonland,* New York: Scribner, 2008.
Ruth Rosen, *The World Split Open,* New York, Viking, 2000.
Michael Schudson, *Watergate in American Memory,* New York: Basic, 1992.
Fred Turner, *Echoes of Combat,* New York: Anchor, 1996.
Tom Wells, *The War Within,* Berkeley, CA: University of California Press, 1996.

PART V
From the Cold War to Globalization

An American restaurant on a busy Shanghai street

Year	Politics	Culture
1980	• Ronald Reagan is elected president • Republicans gain control of Senate after decades of Democratic rule • Democrats retain control of House	• E. L. Doctorow, *Loon Lake* • Galway Kinnell, *Mortal Acts, Mortal Words* • Joyce Carol Oates, *Bellefleur* • Lanford Wilson, *Talley's Folly*
1981	• Reagan tax cuts • Reagan defense build-up begins • Congress resists steep domestic spending cuts	• David Bradley, *The Chaneysville Incident* • Sylvia Plath, *Collected Poems* • John Updike, *Rabbit is Rich*
1982	• Deep recession ends era of high inflation	• Saul Bellow, *The Dean's December* • Don DeLillo, *The Names* • Bobbie Ann Mason, *Shiloh and Other Stories* • Steven Spielberg, *E.T., The Extra-Terrestrial*
1983	• Reagan launches SDI • Suicide bombers hit Marine barracks in Lebanon • Invasion of Grenada	• Richard Rodriquez, *The Hunger of Memory* • Sam Shepard, *Fool for Love* • Alice Walker, *The Color Purple*
1984	• Reagan withdraws troops from Lebanon • Reagan is reelected by a landslide	• Joan Didion, *Democracy* • Louise Erdrich, *Love Medicine* • David Mamet, *Glengarry Glen Ross*
1985	• Reagan's first meeting with Gorbachev	• Don DeLillo, *White Noise* • Carolyn Kizer, *Yin* • Sharon Olds, *The Dead and the Living* • Philip Roth, *Zuckerman Bound*
1986	• Iran-Contra scandal • Democrats regain control of Senate	• Gore Vidal, *Lincoln* • Larry McMurtry, *Lonesome Dove* • Anne Tyler, *The Accidental Tourist*
1987	• Reagan fires top aides over Iran-Contra	• Rita Dove, *Thomas and Beulah* • August Wilson, *Fences* • Tom Wolfe, *Bonfire of the Vanities* • Oliver Stone, *Wall Street*
1988	• De-escalation of arms race between superpowers • Vice-President Bush defeats Governor Dukakis in presidential election	• Don DeLillo, *Libra* • Toni Morrison, *Beloved* • Alfred Uhry, *Driving Miss Daisy*
1989	• Communist regimes in Eastern Europe collapse • Fall of the Berlin Wall • Tiananmen Square Massacre of students and workers in Beijing	• Oscar Hijuelos, *The Mambo Kings Play Songs of Love* • Amy Tan, *The Joy Luck Club* • Wendy Wasserstein, *The Heidi Chronicles*
1990	• Iraq conquers Kuwait • German reunification	• E. L. Doctorow, *Billy Bothgate* • Tim O'Brien, *The Things They Carried* • John Updike, *Rabbit at Rest* • August Wilson, *The Piano Lesson*
1991	• US-led coalition liberates Kuwait • Violent breakup of Yugoslavia results in Croatian War • Dissolution of the Soviet Union	• Russell Banks, *The Sweet Hereafter* • Tony Kushner, *Angels in America* • Leslie Marmon Silko, *Almanac of the Dead*
1992	• Outbreak of Bosnian War • Clinton defeats Bush in presidential election	• Don DeLillo, *MAO II* • Francis Fukuyama, *The End of History and the Last Man* • David Mamet, *Oleanna*
1993	• Clinton withdraws American troops from Somalia after 18 casualties	• Robert Olen Butler, *A Good Scent from a Strange Mountain* • Richard Powers, *Operation Wandering Soul* • Toni Morrison awarded the Nobel Prize for Literature
1994	• Clinton's bill for a national health system is defeated in Congress • Republicans gain control over both chambers of Congress	• Edward Albee, *Three Tall Women* • Paul Auster, *Mr. Vertigo* • William Gaddis, *A Frolic of His Own*
1995	• NATO intervention helps end Bosnian War • Budget deadlock between Clinton and Republican Congress	• Benjamin Barber, *Jihad vs. McWorld* • T. C. Boyle, *The Tortilla Curtain* • Jane Smiley, *Moo* • Barack Obama, *Dreams from My Father*

1996	• Congress backs down in budget crisis • Congress passes Clinton's welfare reform • Clinton defeats Dole in presidential election	• Allegra Goodman, *The Family Moscowitz* • Mary Gordon, *The Shadow Man* • David Foster Wallace, *Infinite Jest*
1997	• Crime declines and the American economy booms	• Don DeLillo, *Underworld* • Thomas Pynchon, *Mason & Dixon* • Philip Roth, *American Pastoral*
1998	• Monica Lewinski scandal • House votes in favor of impeaching Clinton • Republican majorities in Congress are reduced in midterm elections	• Richard Powers, *Gain* • Philip Roth, *I Married a Communist* • Tom Wolfe, *A Man in Full*
1999	• Senate acquits Clinton • NATO intervenes in Kosovo War	• Ralph Ellison, *Juneteenth* • Susan Sontag, *In America: A Novel* • Colson Whitehead, *The Intuitionist*

CHAPTER 9

American Politics from Reagan to Clinton

The Reagan Revolution moved American politics out of the malaise of the 1970s, completing the party realignment that had begun under Nixon. Reagan's presidency, the first to survive two full terms since Eisenhower's and the most successful since FDR's, restored the confidence of most Americans in their nation. His politics were much in evidence in the 1990s, with Clinton accepting the main thrust of the Reagan Revolution in economics and welfare but clashing with the conservative coalition on cultural issues. In foreign policy, the 1980s witnessed both the decline of the Soviet Union and the rise of post-Cold War problems, especially in the Middle East. The pivotal years 1989–91 brought both the end of the Cold War and the first Gulf War, the peaceful dissolution of the Soviet Union and the beginning of Yugoslavia's ethnic conflicts. In the 1990s, the world was increasingly divided into zones of peace, democracy and economic interdependence on the one hand, and of religious and ethnic conflict, failed states and humanitarian disasters on the other. But foreign policy in the 1990s was not salient for the American public, which basked in the misleading sense of security of the 'unipolar moment' and enjoyed the fruits of the two longest economic booms in American history during the Reagan and Clinton years.

The Reagan Revolution

Three major currents in American society converged in 1980 and produced Reagan's conservative revolution. The first was a revival of American national-ism, which the American political elite, still traumatized by its failure in Vietnam, failed at first to discern. This nationalistic surge began in the mid-1970s, when the Ford administration initiated and the Carter administration completed the transfer of the Panama Canal to the Republic of Panama. The canal had been under American sovereignty since its construction early in the twentieth cen-tury. For Latin Americans it was a resented symbol of American hemispheric hegemony. Giving up sovereign rights over the canal did not threaten American strategic interests, since the United States could easily prevent its takeover by a hostile power. Yet this peripheral issue upset many Americans, as Ronald Reagan discovered in the 1976 primaries when crowds responded enthusiastically to his line: 'we built it, we paid for it, it's ours, and we're going to keep it'. The Panama Canal Treaty barely passed the Senate in 1978 by the two-thirds majority needed in order to ratify treaties. But 20 senators who had supported the handover were subsequently defeated in the 1978 and 1980 elections, while only one opponent did not get reelected.

American nationalism was further inflamed by the Iranian hostage crisis that began in November 1979 and dragged on until the end of the Carter presidency. It was also fueled in the later 1970s by a revival of anti-Soviet fears, brought about by communist advances in the Third World, the Soviet Union's ambitious armaments programs and, above all, the Soviet invasion of Afghanistan. Truman's former aide Paul Nitze, the architect of NSC-68 in 1950, revived the bipartisan Committee on the Present Danger, which in 1980 produced alarmist television spots warning of the dangers of Soviet nuclear superiority. The Republican National Convention in 1980 received Henry Kissinger, the architect of *détente,* with a notable lack of enthusiasm.

The second aspect of the Reagan Revolution was related to the economy. Since 1974 the American economy had experienced the combination of high inflation, high unemployment and low growth that became known as 'stagflation'. The double-digit inflation of the later 1970s that rose to 16 percent in 1980 became the ordinary citizen's primary economic problem, displacing fears of recession and unemployment that had been the main American economic worry since the Great Depression. Earlier habits of frugality that went back to the Depression were undermined; savings were drastically devalued by inflation while real debt shrank for those who were living on credit. A new economic culture of living on credit emerged; the substitution of the credit card for cash was its most ubiquitous legacy. But by 1980 high inflation produced interest rates of 21 percent, at which point many Americans willingly accepted the cost of a recession to force inflation out of the system.

Moreover, inflation drastically raised the tax burden of the average American. As workers' incomes rose due to inflation, they came under higher tax brackets and were taxed more heavily. Since tax brackets remained fixed in nominal terms, high inflation produced the equivalent of a continuous rise in the real income tax. Furthermore, as property values were greatly inflated, some households could no longer afford the resulting higher property tax and had to sell their homes. Overall, between 1971 and 1977 the price index rose by 47 percent while the total tax receipts at all three levels of government – federal, state and local – rose by 60 percent. The political establishment was happy to spend the growing tax influx, but most Americans turned against the increased government spending that their rising taxes financed.

The result was a grassroots tax revolt that took the political establishment by surprise. California opened the way with the tax-cutting Proposition 13, which was placed on the ballot after antitax activists gathered a phenomenal 1.25 million signatures in their petition. Two-thirds of the voters supported Proposition 13 in the elections of June 1978. Twenty states from Alaska to Maine followed California's example and cut taxes by referendum. Thirty-seven states cut property and state income taxes by regular legislation.

The tax revolt reached the federal government with the introduction in Congress of the Kemp-Roth bill that proposed a 30 percent cut in federal income tax over three years. Reagan endorsed Kemp-Roth in March 1980, which led George H. W. Bush, his chief rival in the 1980 Republican primaries, to accuse him of 'voodoo economics'. But Reagan's tax-cutting stance helped him win the nomination in 1980.

The third aspect of the Reagan Revolution was the political activation of evangelical and fundamentalist Protestants on the Republican side. Traditionally, the evangelical Protestants of the South and the heartland had been Democrats. It was William Jennings Bryan, the Democratic presidential candidate in 1896, 1900 and 1908, who in the famous Scopes trial of 1925 led the anti-Darwinian side and upheld the fundamentalist version of the world's creation. But after World War II, evangelical Protestants withdrew from active politics. The popular preacher Jerry Falwell declared in 1965: 'I would find it impossible to stop preaching the pure saving Gospel of Jesus Christ and begin doing anything else, including fighting communism or participating in civil rights reforms ... Preachers are not called upon to be politicians but to be soul winners.'[1]

Developments in the 1960s and 1970s resulted in a new cultural cleavage in American society that led to the political emergence of the Christian Right in 1980. Feminism, sexual liberation and gay rights challenged traditional morality. The Supreme Court protected pornography and forbade prayer in public schools under the First Amendment. In 1973, in its landmark *Roe versus Wade* decision, it maintained that a woman's right to abortion was adumbrated in the Constitution and that therefore neither Congress nor any state could pass a law making abortion illegal. The McGovern Democrats in 1972 had placed the Democratic Party firmly on the liberal side of this new cultural divide.

These developments coincided with the phenomenal growth in the 1970s of the evangelical churches at the expense of the more established Protestant congregations. The new churches flourished not only in numbers, but also in their finances. Financial prosperity permitted evangelicals and fundamentalists to operate their own TV stations, schools, colleges and publishing houses, through which they maintained their subculture. Their entry into the political arena was finally induced by the abolition of their tax exemptions by the IRS in 1978, ironically under Carter, who was a born-again evangelical Protestant. To the evangelicals this seemed like a move to force them to send their children to public schools that offered no prayers and taught Darwinism. 'We are not trying to jam our moral philosophy down the throats of others,' Falwell declared in 1980. 'We're simply trying to keep others from jamming their amoral philosophies down our throats.' In contrast to his 1965 position against evangelical participation in politics, Falwell now declared that 'the day of the silent church is passed ... Preachers, you need as never before to preach on the issues, no matter what they say or what they write about you. Get involved, registered, informed, and voting.' In 1979 he founded Moral Majority, which in the 1980 elections attacked prominent liberal senators in TV advertisements.

Ronald Reagan

In 1980 the Republicans nominated Ronald Reagan; it was only the second time in the postwar era that the nomination went to the candidate from the conservative wing of the party. But while Goldwater had been crushed by Johnson in 1964, now Reagan easily defeated Carter. That he went on to become the most successful American president since Roosevelt is an indication of the rightward shift in American society that had taken place since 1968.

Among conservative forces Reagan's victory resembled a revolution: the conquest of the Bastille of Big Government. The Republicans gained not only the presidency but also, for the first time since 1953–4, the Senate. Still, the conservative victory was incomplete. The House remained under Democratic control, though the Republicans narrowed the margin enough to be able to pass their bills in cooperation with Southern Democrats. Reagan's own victory was not particularly impressive in terms of the popular vote. He got 51 percent while Carter was repudiated decisively by getting only 41 percent; another 8 percent went to the liberal Republican congressman John Anderson, who ran as an Independent. Nonetheless, it was the most conservative election result since the 1920s.

In his inaugural address Reagan declared: 'Government is not the solution to our problem; government is the problem.' Thus he demonstrated his intention to curb the size of the federal government, which had grown alarmingly in the 1970s, in order to restore America's vigor and greatness. He also proclaimed, that 'we are too great a nation to limit ourselves to small dreams. We're not, as some would have us believe, doomed to an inevitable decline...It is time to reawaken this industrial giant, to get government back within its means and to lighten our punitive tax burden.' In his infectious optimism, Reagan was much like Roosevelt, for whom he had voted every time and of whom, paradoxically, he still spoke with glowing enthusiasm in the 1980s.

Reagan's strategy in the spring of 1981 was first to pass a major income tax cut, a popular measure that Congress was unlikely to resist, and to cut federal spending afterwards, when the tax cut would presumably impose congressional spending restraint. His strategy was complicated by the fact that at the same time he sought a major rise in military spending, which was added to the already sizable increase in the defense budget that Carter had implemented after the Soviet invasion of Afghanistan. The income tax cut was passed in the spring of 1981 as Congress voted to cut tax rates by 25 percent over three years, while reducing the top rate from 70 percent to 37.5 percent. Moreover, tax brackets became inflation-indexed.

However, Reagan was unable to induce the domestic spending cuts needed to counterbalance both the tax cuts and the rise in defense spending. He effectively exempted the main pillars of the federal welfare state, such as social security, Medicare and Medicaid. Consequently, the main burden of the spending cuts was to be borne by discretionary federal programs. Yet members of Congress were unwilling to cut specialized programs that benefited their own constituents. The result was that instead of real cuts in domestic spending, there were mere reductions in the rate of growth of domestic programs; domestic spending kept rising in absolute dollar terms, though it declined somewhat as a portion of GDP.

The combination of income tax cuts, defense spending increases and an only modest arrest in the growth of domestic spending inevitably resulted in large federal deficits. In nominal terms, the federal government accumulated more debt under Reagan than in the entire previous history of the United States. The result was a paradoxical reversal in the position of the two parties on deficits.

Traditionally, it was the Republicans who insisted on fiscal discipline and the Democrats who were willing to condone deficits on Keynesian demand-stimulus grounds. Eisenhower had sought to restrain defense spending in order to avoid deficits, whereas Kennedy had increased defense spending and cut income taxes in order to stimulate the economy. In this respect, Reagan was closer to Kennedy; the Democrats who attacked him for his deficit spending were closer to Eisenhower.

Nonetheless, Reagan differed from Kennedy fundamentally, since he did not regard deficit spending as positive in itself. Reagan supported fiscal discipline, provided it was attained at low taxation levels. Confronted with the unwillingness of Congress to cut domestic spending significantly, Reagan learned to live with large deficits as the price for enforcing Congressional restraint on the growth of domestic spending, which had exploded in the 1970s. Politically his strategy was effective, in that the Democrats who attacked him for the large deficits were unable simultaneously to propose major increases in domestic spending.

The Reagan Revolution also focused on deregulation, freeing major sectors of the economy from tight federal control. This process had begun under Carter, who had deregulated telecommunications, trucking and air travel, with favorable results in terms of fewer anticompetitive practices and lower prices for consumers. Reagan deregulated energy and the capital markets. The abolition of price controls for oil and a change in federal priorities in favor of domestic oil exploration contributed to the halving of the price of oil in the 1980s.

Deregulation of the capital markets resulted in the growth of new and more flexible forms of finance such as venture capital and so-called 'junk bonds', which in combination with the tax cuts made the American capitalist system more dynamic and fluid. In the first three postwar decades a small number of giant corporations dominated the American economy. In 1969 the 25 largest corporations employed seven percent of the American labor force. By 1998 that number had declined to 4.5 percent. Since the 1980s new companies have risen more frequently than before, financed by more flexible capital markets. The explosive growth of information technology in the 1980s and 1990s, which was largely produced by penniless Stanford or MIT graduate students with bright ideas, exemplifies the new dynamism of the American economy that has left many old established corporations weakened and in decline.

The greater dynamism of the American economy and the relative decline of established corporations contributed to the decline of the labor unions, which had flourished under the more stable corporate framework of the 1940s. The part of the nonagricultural labor force that was unionized fell gradually in the first three postwar decades, from 35.5 percent in 1945 to 27.4 percent in 1970. Thereafter the decline accelerated, from 23.6 percent in 1980 to 15 percent in 1995.

The most difficult moment for the Reagan Revolution came in 1982, when the tight monetary policy of the Federal Reserve Board, which aimed at forcing inflation out of the system, caused America's deepest postwar recession. The Republicans suffered serious losses in the midterm congressional elections of 1982, though they kept control of the Senate. Reagan's popularity fell to a mere 35 percent in January 1983. To many Democrats it seemed quite possible that the

1980 election might turn out to be a temporary aberration rather than a major realignment. Nonetheless, Reagan continued to support the tough anti-inflation policy and maintained his faith in a recovery based on tax cuts, deregulation and the eradication of inflation. In the event, the 1982 recession did eliminate high inflation and was followed by the longest American postwar boom up to then. With the end of stagflation, Reagan's popularity revived.

In 1984 Reagan's campaign adopted the slogan: 'It's morning again in America'. This message resonated with American voters who, since President Kennedy's assassination, had witnessed Vietnam, riots in the ghettos, the murders of Martin Luther King and Robert Kennedy, the resignation of President Nixon, energy crises, stagflation and the failed presidencies of Ford and Carter. With Reagan, Americans seemed at last to have a successful presidency that was pulling the nation out of the years of crisis and malaise.

The 1984 election confirmed the Reagan Revolution. Reagan got 59 percent of the popular vote and won every state except Minnesota, the home state of his opponent Walter Mondale, Carter's former vice-president. The Republicans made gains in the House and retained control of the Senate. Yet the rightward realignment under Reagan remained incomplete, since the House was still under Democratic control. Moreover, in opinion polls more Americans identified themselves as Democrats than as Republicans, though for the first time since the Great Depression more Americans trusted the Republicans than the Democrats on the economy. But the continuing resilience of the Democratic Party was demonstrated in the 1986 congressional midterm elections, in which the Democrats regained control of the Senate after a six-year interval of Republican rule.

Even if Reagan did not secure the Republican domination of Congress, he did preside over a rightward shift in the ideological orientation of America. The term 'liberal' acquired such a negative connotation for most Americans that fewer Democratic politicians identified with it. The long dominant New Deal faith in federal activism as the instrument for curing society's ills was replaced by a traditional American distrust of big government and a renewed faith in free enterprise. The historian Bruce Schulman has concluded, that the 'domestic agenda of Richard Nixon, even the "Modern Republicanism" of Dwight D. Eisenhower, would have made those men too liberal for the Democrats by the late 1980s'.[2]

The 1988 elections confirmed the rightward shift in American society. Neither party had hitherto won three presidential elections in a row after the 1940s. In 1988 the Democrats nominated the liberal Governor Michael Dukakis of Massachusetts. Dukakis tried to distance himself from liberalism by declaring in his acceptance speech that the issue was 'competence, not ideology'; yet in the end he was unable to evade the liberal tag. The Republicans nominated Reagan's vice-president, George H.W. Bush, a centrist candidate who presented himself as a 'milder, gentler' version of Reagan's conservatism. Bush's victory with 54 percent of the popular vote resembled FDR's reelection for a third term in 1940 with 55 percent, thus confirming the conservative realignment in American politics.

The consequences of the Reagan Revolution for American society were multifaceted. Inequalities in income distribution increased somewhat. The portion of the population under the official poverty level rose from 11.4 percent in 1979 to 12.8 percent in 1989. On the other hand, the number of households with annual incomes over $50,000 in constant 1990 dollars rose during the 1980s from 30.9 percent to 35.9 percent, demonstrating the growing affluence of the middle class. The number of individuals declaring annual incomes over $1 million rose from 5000 to 35,000, while the number of millionaires in assets trebled from half a million to a million and a half, demonstrating in part the flourishing of entrepreneurship.

The economic boom of the middle class and the expansion of the ranks of the rich took place during the boom of the 1980s, which continued, aside from the brief recession of 1991–2, throughout the 1990s. The poorest segments of American society did not benefit from this boom; the average income of the poorest tenth of the population rose under Reagan only from $6494 to $6994. Nonetheless, the American economy as a whole no longer declined in relation to its main international competitors, as had happened during the 1970s; instead the United States recaptured an impressive worldwide lead that constituted one of the firmest foundations of its global leadership at the start of the twenty-first century.

Reagan's foreign policy

The central thrust of Reagan's foreign policy was a deliberate bid to undermine the Soviet Union and its communist sphere. Reagan's conviction that the Soviet Union was both a dangerous military power and a collapsing economic system was not derived from any deep knowledge of international relations. Yet he proved to be the proverbial right man in the right place at the tight time. By whatever means he arrived at his views, he drew from them policy directions that were devastatingly effective in undermining the rotten Soviet edifice. Because of the high oil prices of the 1970s, the Soviet leaders avoided serious economic reforms, such as those that saved China under Deng Xiaoping. Instead, they relied on oil revenues as a means of keeping their decrepit economy going. By the early 1980s the Soviet Union was becoming a hollow shell, with an unreformed and increasingly backward industrial base. Thus it was highly vulnerable to the pressures that the Reagan administration was planning.

From the outset, Reagan moved against *détente* and beyond containment, encouraging instead 'long-term political and military changes within the Soviet empire that will facilitate a more secure and peaceful world order', according to an early 1981 Pentagon defense guide. Harvard's Richard Pipes, who joined the National Security Council, advocated a new aggressive policy by which 'the United States takes the long-term strategic offensive. This approach therefore contrasts with the essentially reactive and defensive strategy of containment.' Pipes' report was endorsed in 1982 and formulated the policy objective of promoting 'the process of change in the Soviet Union towards a more pluralistic political and economic system'.[3]

A central instrument for putting pressure on the Soviet Union was Reagan's massive defense build-up, which raised defense spending from $134 billion in 1980 to $253 billion in 1989. This raised American defense spending to seven percent of GDP. But in its efforts to keep up with the Americans, the Soviet

Union was compelled in the first half of the 1980s to raise the share of its defense spending from 22 to 27 percent of GDP, while it froze the production of civilian goods at 1980 levels.

Reagan's most controversial defense initiative was the Strategic Defense Initiative (SDI), the visionary project to create an antimissile defense system that would remove the nuclear sword of Damocles from America's homeland. Though critics compared it to *Star Wars,* George Lucas's popular sci-fi Hollywood epic, experts still disagree about the long-term feasibility of missile defense. But the SDI's main effect was to demonstrate America's technological superiority over the Soviet Union and her ability to expand the arms race into space. This helped convince the Soviet leadership under Gorbachev to bid for a de-escalation of the arms race.

Particularly effective, though with unintended long-term side effects, was Reagan's support for the *mujahideen* (holy warriors) that were fighting against the Soviet forces in Afghanistan. Reagan was determined to transform Afghanistan into the Soviet Vietnam. Therefore, in 1986 he decided to provide the *mujahideen* with portable surface-to-air Stinger missiles, which proved devastatingly effective in increasing Soviet air losses (particularly helicopters). The war in Afghanistan cost the United States about $1 billion per annum in aid to the *mujahideen;* it cost the Soviet Union eight times as much, helping bankrupt its economy.

Apart from his defense policies, Reagan also weakened the Soviet Union through economic moves. His supporters' claims that he brought about the fall of the Soviet Union are somewhat weakened by the fact that he ended Carter's grain embargo, which had produced alarming food shortages in the Soviet Union. On the other hand, Reagan was able to reduce the flow of Western technology to the Soviet Union, as well as to limit Soviet natural gas exports to Western Europe. One of the most effective ways in which his economic policies weakened the Soviet Union was by helping bring about a drastic fall in the price of oil, thereby denying the Soviet Union a large influx of hard currency.

Reagan and the Third World

In the Third World, Reagan was determined to overcome the Vietnam syndrome and to revive both covert operations by the CIA and the overt use of armed force. He revived the pre-Vietnam global anticommunist crusade. He also pursued a more forceful policy than Carter against America's newer enemies in the Muslim world, though his record in this respect is mixed. His assertive and forceful policy faced significant resistance in Congress. There was also resistance to the use of armed force in the Pentagon, which was afraid of being entangled in another unpopular war in distant lands.

Strong domestic resistance emerged against Reagan's efforts to overthrow the leftist Sandinista regime in Nicaragua, forcing the Reagan administration to abandon any thought of a military intervention. Instead, Reagan resorted to covert operations by the CIA, which mined Nicaraguan harbors (in violation of international law) and supported the guerrilla campaigns of the anti-Sandinista 'Contras'. But in the mid-1980s Congress passed a law that forbade any commitment of federal funds in support of the Contras. The Reagan administration responded with appeals for private and foreign funding of the Contras; for example, it persuaded the Sultan of Brunei to contribute $10 million.

Reagan was more successful in overcoming the Vietnam syndrome with the invasion of Grenada in 1983, which he launched on the slim pretext that a coup within the Grenadian leftist regime had put American students on the tiny island in danger. Carter mockingly referred to 'the conquest of Grenada', and indeed it was hardly a mighty military feat. Yet Eastern European archives have revealed that it was a nasty jolt for both Castro and his Soviet patrons.

Reagan's bid to end Lebanon's civil war had a less fortunate conclusion. In October 1983 suicide bombers struck a Marine barracks in Lebanon and killed 241 American troops while a second suicide bombing at a French barracks killed 58 people, raising fears that the Western peace-keeping mission in Lebanon – in the wake of the Israeli 1982 invasion – might turn into a grim morass. Reagan decided a few months later to withdraw the Western forces, thus escaping from a nasty vipers' nest relatively unscathed. However, this early success of a terrorist strategy using suicide bombers to induce the withdrawal of a superpower and its allies from a Middle Eastern country undoubtedly encouraged the future use of terrorism in the Middle East, casting a malevolent shadow all the way to the present.

The worst political crisis of Reagan's presidency originated in an astounding lapse from Reagan's tough posture towards America's enemies. While Reagan had publicly vowed never to deal with terrorists, in 1985 he became very emotional regarding the fate of several Americans held hostage by the Lebanese terrorist group Hezbollah, which was backed by Iran. Through a series of steps undertaken with Israeli mediation by his White House national security staff, Reagan secretly violated the American embargo against Iran by selling arms to Khomeini's regime in return for the release of hostages by Hezbollah. The deal with the terrorists and their Iranian sponsors was predictably rotten: Hezbollah kept capturing more Americans than it released. Once Reagan's aides descended to the level of secret haggling with unsavory Middle Eastern terrorist groups, they were not much better than those guileless Western tourists that are hopelessly outmatched in any Middle Eastern bazaar.

The American people were outraged in the fall of 1986 when a Lebanese newspaper revealed the ill-conceived bargain with the terrorists. But the situation became much worse for Reagan when Congress and the press began to inquire into what had happened to the proceeds of the secret arms sales to Iran. Since these proceeds were unrecorded in the federal budget, White House staffers decided to divert them to the Contras in Nicaragua, in direct violation of the law that prohibited the use of federal funds in their support. For a few months the ensuing Iran-Contra scandal threatened to reach Watergate proportions, and Reagan was forced to fire several senior White House aides. In the event, Reagan survived the scandal largely because, having been painted by his political opponents as an aging ignoramus not up to the details of his job, he could plausibly claim not to have known or remember the relevant decisions. But his popularity plummeted at the height of the scandal, and never fully recovered for the remainder of his presidency.

Reagan's second term coincided with a powerful worldwide current in favor of liberalism. Revolutionary socialism waned because of its increasingly evident failure in the Soviet Union. Deng Xiaoping's China began in the mid-1980s to implement liberalizing economic reforms, through which it escaped the fate of the decaying Soviet economy and emulated the stunning achievements of the East Asian 'tigers' like Taiwan, Singapore and South Korea. Elsewhere, authoritarian regimes were swept away by a wave of democratization. The Reagan administration had not anticipated these changes, but it embraced and promoted them once they became evident. American policy helped end the Marcos dictatorship in the Philippines in 1986 and the Pinochet dictatorship in Chile in 1988, regimes the United States had long supported. The democratization wave also defused the Reagan administration's confrontation with the Sandinista regime soon after the end of Reagan's presidency. Free elections in Nicaragua in 1990 resulted in the Sandinistas' defeat, transforming them from a revolutionary movement into a democratic opposition party, much to the benefit of stability in Central America. There were large parts of the Third World that were unaffected by the international liberal wave of the later 1980s, especially the Middle East, which remained under the sway of illiberal regimes and anti-Western movements. But the international surge of liberalism climaxed when it reached beyond the Third World and swept over the 'second world' of the Soviet empire.

The end of the Cold War

The Cold War began to wind down with the rise of Mikhail Gorbachev to the Soviet leadership in 1985. Reagan's pressures on the Soviet Union were a major reason for the decision of the Soviet oligarchy to choose a relatively young reformer like Gorbachev as its new leader, after a series of 'geriatric' hard-liners (Brezhnev, Andropov, Chernenko) let the Soviet economy decline steeply in the first half of the 1980s. Experienced Soviet policy-makers like Foreign Minister Gromyko, who had held major policy posts since 1943, supported Gorbachev because they saw clearly the grave dangers for the Soviet Union if there was no change in course.

Gorbachev was a believer in the Soviet system; he wanted to reform it, not end it. But he was aware that reforms could not be implemented unless the pressures of the arms race were lifted. Consequently, he needed to improve relations with the West in order to reach new arms control agreements that would facilitate reduced Soviet defense spending. As a result, Gorbachev went further than any previous Soviet leader towards reducing world tensions and normalizing Soviet relations with the West. Reagan responded positively to Gorbachev's overtures, sensing that he had attained his objective of inducing deep changes within the Soviet Union. Reagan's response was fortunate; had the United States maintained a hawkish policy during Gorbachev's rule, Soviet hard-liners might have resisted his reforms and the decline of the Soviet Union might have been an altogether more dangerous and violent affair.

The Intermediate Nuclear Forces agreement of 1987 was the first major step in de-escalating the arms race. During his trip to the Soviet Union in 1988 Reagan declared that the Soviet Union had changed and was no longer an 'evil empire'. Yet he continued to nudge the Soviet leadership towards demonstrating its intention truly to end the Cold War. In a speech in 1987 in front of the Brandenburg Gate on the Berlin dividing line, Reagan issued his celebrated appeal: 'Mr Gorbachev, open this gate! Mr Gorbachev, tear down this wall!'

Superpower relations continued to improve during the presidency of George H. W. Bush. In mid-1989 Bush and Gorbachev arranged to have a summit meeting at the end of the year in order to sign ambitious new arms control agreements. Yet by the time the summit took place, arms control was overshadowed by much more historic developments that shook the world in the second half of that momentous year.

In retrospect it is clear that Gorbachev's reform policy was ill-conceived from the outset. The main cause of Soviet decline was the centrally planned command economy, which is admirably suited for mobilizing national resources to cope with an urgent short-term emergency such as war, but is incapable of sustaining long-term growth. In the Soviet Union it worked extremely well during World War II, and tolerably well, though at enormous human cost, in the early phases of Soviet industrialization. But by the 1970s it had become so dysfunctional that it no longer produced real growth. By the 1980s the Soviet economy was actually shrinking. The social cost was devastating. Indicatively, in the late 1980s, 35 percent of Soviet hospital beds were in facilities without warm water, 30 percent of hospitals had no internal toilets and one in six hospital beds was in a facility with no running water at all; this in a country that saw fit to maintain many thousand nuclear warheads.

Gorbachev never seriously attempted to reform the Soviet economic system. His *perestroika* amounted to reforms within the centrally planned command economy. His *glasnost* meant more openness and freer debate within the Soviet Union, which in the event gave the peoples of the Soviet Union the freedom to complain, rebel and eventually secede from a failed system. Unlike Deng Xiaoping, who during the same period introduced ambitious free market reforms that in time salvaged the Chinese economy from the pits of Maoism, Gorbachev presided over continuing economic decline. By loosening the controls of a totalitarian regime without addressing the failures of the economic system, he unleashed revolutionary forces that soon swept him and the whole Soviet Union away.

By 1989 internal upheavals were already rocking the Soviet Union. The first proof that Gorbachev had truly changed Soviet policy came in June 1989, when free elections were held in Poland that resulted in the defeat of the ruling Communist Party and the rise to power of the anti-regime Solidarity movement. At the same time, China's communist regime crushed its own dissident movement in the Tiananmen Square massacre, repudiating a Chinese version of *glasnost*. Hard-line communist regimes within the Warsaw Pact called for the crushing of the new government of Poland by military means in the manner of the Soviet invasions of Hungary in 1956 and Czechoslovakia in 1968. But Gorbachev firmly rejected such a course, which would have derailed his policy of normalizing relations with the West and reforming the Soviet Union. As a result, every communist regime in the satellite countries of the Warsaw Pact collapsed before the end of 1989.

The most significant and symbolic event of this momentous period was the fall of the Berlin Wall in November, which produced euphoria in the West. Bush refused to rise to the occasion, reacting publicly with muted language. In fact he shrewdly avoided any display of triumphalism, even at the cost of leaving his domestic gallery unsatisfied, in order not to strengthen Gorbachev's domestic hard-line opponents who viewed the collapse of the Soviet empire as an unmitigated disaster.

The fall of the Berlin Wall brought the German question to the center of international politics. Developments in East Germany made German reunification inevitable once the four occupying powers of 1945 agreed to it. Gorbachev, the French President Francois Mitterrand and especially the British Prime Minister Margaret Thatcher were at first opposed to German reunification. Bush in contrast supported German reunification on one condition, that the reunited Germany remain within NATO. With the support of the United States, the Germans overcame French doubts and British resistance. Gorbachev's opposition was stronger. But, in the end, he was too preoccupied with – and weakened by – the slowly unfolding disintegration of the Soviet Union to be able to resist German reunification; on the day of the Gorbachev-Kohl agreement on German reunification within NATO, Ukraine declared its 'sovereignty'. Thus Germany was reunited in October 1990, and a major reshaping of the European distribution of power was attained bloodlessly.

Bush's Gulf War

At the beginning of August 1990 the focus of the Bush administration shifted to the Persian Gulf, where Saddam Hussein invaded and swiftly conquered Kuwait. In a clear sign that the old superpower antagonisms had ended, Bush's Secretary of State James Baker promptly secured Soviet cooperation against this annexation of a small state by a former Soviet client. By the end of 1990 the Bush administration had assembled an impressive coalition, including most members of NATO, Arab states such as Egypt, Saudi Arabia, Syria, Morocco and the smaller Gulf states, as well as other Muslim states such as Pakistan, Bangladesh, Nigeria and Senegal, all of which contributed military forces for the liberation of Kuwait. The United States deployed in the Gulf region almost half a million troops, 1500 airplanes and fleets with eight aircraft carriers, in what amounted to the largest American military operation since Vietnam.

The coalition liberated Kuwait in early 1991 after a swift campaign in which coalition forces inflicted heavy losses on the Iraqi army while suffering few casualties themselves. Bush then made the subsequently much criticized decision not to push to Baghdad and overthrow Saddam Hussein, though he urged the people of Iraq to rebel against their regime. The Bush administration was not willing to undertake the risks of governing Iraq, which might have led to a prolonged entanglement. Moreover, Bush feared a potential breakup of Iraq if the Kurds in the north and the Shiites in the south seceded. In effect, he wanted an Iraq too weak to resume its expansionism yet strong enough to balance Iran and Syria. This *Realpolitik* avoided a polarizing military occupation, but it cynically left the Shiites to their own fate by allowing Saddam Hussein to crush their rebellion in southern Iraq brutally, in spite of the UN's no-fly zone that prevented him from using air power. The no-fly zone in the north of Iraq was more effective in allowing the Kurds to secure their *de facto* autonomy; unlike the Shiite south, the terrain in Iraq's Kurdish north is rugged and mountainous, favoring local defiance. For the United States the most worrying aspect of the Gulf War's aftermath was Saddam Hussein's continuing fixation on weapons of mass destruction, whereby he violated the cease-fire agreement and paid the penalty of a UN economic embargo.

In the meantime, the Soviet Union's slow disintegration was continuing. Bush was so comfortable in his relations with Gorbachev and so apprehensive about large-scale instability if the Soviet Union broke up violently – as was happening with Yugoslavia's disintegration beginning in June 1991 – that he sought to dissuade the Soviet peoples from seceding. In the event, American policy was unable to prevent the dissolution of the Soviet Union, once Russia herself decided to secede. Fortunately Russia, unlike Serbia in the Yugoslav case, never sought any changes in the borders of the Soviet republics, even though millions of Russians ended up as minorities outside Russia. As a result, the breakup of the Soviet Union was not violent, in stark contrast to the Yugoslav crises of the 1990s.

The dissolution of the Soviet Union was hastened by the failed hard-line coup in mid-August 1991, which undermined Gorbachev's authority and enhanced the standing of Russia's President Boris Yeltsin, who defied the coup and barricaded himself in the Russian parliament. A few months later Yeltsin and the leaders of Ukraine and Byelorussia, who represented the Slavic core of the Soviet domain, decided to dissolve the Soviet Union at year's end. The Soviet Union ceased to exist at midnight on December 31, 1991, completing the dramatic transformation of the map of Europe in the momentous years 1989–91. It is to the credit of the Bush administration that this transformation was almost bloodless, whereas in earlier periods of history similarly massive changes in the international distribution of power took place only through major wars.

American politics during the Clinton presidency

In the spring of 1991 when Bush won the Gulf War, his popularity reached 90 percent. The fall of the Soviet Union and the end of the Cold War followed. Yet in the elections of November 1992 Bush received only 38 percent of the vote, the lowest percentage for a president seeking reelection since Taft's third-place defeat in 1912. Bush's repudiation was decisive, though the winner of the elections Bill Clinton received only 43 percent, less than Dukakis in 1988. The third-party candidate, businessman Ross Perot, got 19 percent, the highest third-party percentage since 1912.

The main reason for Bush's defeat in 1992 was the recession of 1991 that ended the long boom of the 1980s. Technically, the American economy had begun to grow again in 1992, but unemployment did not fall at the start of the recovery. The Republicans are particularly vulnerable in times of economic insecurity, since their policies tend to favor the wealthy. So long as there was growth that benefited most Americans, the majority tolerated the accumulation of fabulous wealth at the top. In 1991–2, by contrast, opinion polls showed that large majorities favored special taxes for the rich and a more progressive income tax. Bush was particularly vulnerable in this climate of opinion, since, unlike Nixon and Reagan, he came from a wealthy family that belonged to the old patrician Republican establishment of the Northeast. Furthermore, Bush had disillusioned his conservative base by violating his 1988 pledge: 'Read my lips, no new taxes!'

Bush's losses were greatest among blue-collar whites that had traditionally supported the New Deal but had voted for Nixon and Reagan. Paradoxically, the Reagan-Bush success in ending the Cold War made national security much less salient and thus removed one factor that since 1968 had led many white blue-collar workers to vote Republican. Ross Perot seems to have attracted large numbers of these blue-collar voters defecting from the Republicans, who apparently were still too alienated by the Democratic Party's identification with minorities and cultural liberalism to vote for Clinton.

The Democratic candidate, Governor Bill Clinton of Arkansas, came from the ranks of the so-called New Democrats who wished to move the party towards the center and to distance themselves from the legacy of the Great Society on the economy and welfare. In these matters, Clinton largely embraced the legacy of the Reagan Revolution. In 1992 he proposed welfare reform that would limit government handouts to two years in order to discourage welfare dependency. In 1996 he declared that 'the era of Big Government is over'.

If Clinton's movement toward the economic legacy of the Reagan Revolution narrowed the gap between the two parties, their differences increased in regard to religion and traditional morality. In a desperate bid to displace the recession from the center of electoral politics, the Republicans in 1992 emphasized family values, which secured them the continuing allegiance of evangelical and fundamentalist Protestants. The Democrats were firmly pro-choice on abortion and in favor of gay rights. The religious cleavage in American politics deepened during the 1990s, with ever-increasing numbers of evangelical and fundamentalist Protestants, as well as the more orthodox Catholics and Jews, voting Republican, while secular and religious groups that embraced cultural diversity tended increasingly to vote Democratic.

During his presidency, Clinton sought both to expand his appeal in the center and to satisfy his core liberal supporters. Consequently, his policies lacked ideological consistency. Clinton's first act as president was supportive of gays serving in the military, pleasing the liberals and enraging cultural conservatives. But he also supported tough policies against crime, which brought him closer to conservative positions. By supporting and passing the North American Free Trade Agreement (NAFTA), Clinton clashed with economic protectionists such as Perot and the labor unions who feared the relocation of industrial plants from the United States to low-wage Mexico.

Clinton's main strategic mistake in his first two years was to push first for a national health system, a major liberal reform, and leave the more conservative welfare reform for later. National health insurance defied the conservative trends on welfare-state issues that the Reagan Revolution bequeathed. Clinton compounded the mistake by placing his wife Hillary in charge of the health reform team, making his personal fortune hostage to the reform's progress. But the unions did not actively support Clinton on health reform – this was payback for NAFTA – while conservatives and the insurance industry lobby alarmed the public by charging that Clinton intended to nationalize 14 percent of the American economy. In 1994 the health bill was voted down in both chambers of Congress, in spite of their Democratic majorities.

Republicans gain control of Congress

Clinton's political situation worsened sharply with the midterm elections of November 1994, in which the Republicans gained control of both chambers of Congress for the first time since 1953–4. For a second time in recent history – the first was in 1980 – the conservatives felt they had stormed the Washington citadel of the federal government. As in 1980, the storming was incomplete, then because of continued Democratic control of the House, now because a Democrat occupied the White House. But the Republicans thought that Clinton had been weakened irreparably, that the Republican Congress would have the political initiative and that Clinton would be defeated in 1996, ending this lamentable parenthesis in Republican presidential rule. In the euphoria of their historic victory, the Republicans underestimated their opponent.

In 1995 the Republican Congress and the Democratic president clashed fiercely over the budget. Led by the Speaker of the House Newt Gingrich, the architect of the Republican victory in 1994, the Republicans sought major cuts in domestic spending in order to reduce the federal deficit. Clinton preferred to reduce the deficit by raising taxes. A deadlock ensued when Clinton vetoed the Republican budget proposals. The Republican leadership was able to deny Clinton the bipartisan majorities he needed to pass his budget proposal; yet the Republicans were far short of the two-thirds majority needed to override Clinton's veto and pass their own budget plan. The budget confrontation lasted well beyond the 30 September deadline (the end of the fiscal year). For months thereafter, federal spending on essential services continued on the basis of temporary legislation, while nonessential parts of the federal government shut down. In the end Congress backed down, because Clinton was able to portray the opposition as dominated by unreasonable extremists, moving public opinion against it. Unlike Reagan, who was politically astute and rarely pushed for unpopular domestic spending cuts, Gingrich proved to be more ideologically rigid and saw his popularity decline.

Clinton's victory in the 1995 budget confrontation paved the way for his reelection in 1996. In order to insulate himself from Republican charges that he was too liberal, Clinton in 1996 made major moves in a rightward direction. First, Congress passed his welfare reform that limited welfare payments to two years. This major reform changed the structure of welfare in the United States. By 2003 less than half of welfare spending went to cash assistance, and more than half went to childcare, education, training and other services intended to help the poor get jobs and stay off welfare. Second, on the basis of his 1994 anticrime act Clinton spent large sums to help state and local governments hire more policemen and build new prisons. He also demonstrated fiscal frugality by downsizing the federal bureaucracy and getting rid of excess personnel. By thus staking ground in the center, or even to the right of center, Clinton broadened his electoral appeal and was able to define his opponent Bob Dole, the Senate Majority Leader during the 1995 budget confrontation, as too right-wing for the mainstream.

In the 1996 election Clinton got 49.2 percent of the vote, just short of the absolute majority that he sought. Dole got 40.1 percent, not much better than Bush in 1992, while Ross Perot got only 8.4 percent, which showed that his influence was waning. Yet the Republicans retained control over both chambers of Congress. The structure of national politics was thus similar to the Eisenhower years, with the role of the two parties reversed. In the 1950s Eisenhower had sought with his 'Modern Republicanism' to move to the center in order to deal with the dominant New Deal coalition that ruled Congress. In the 1990s Clinton sought, as a 'New Democrat', to move to the center, adjusting to the prevailing conservative trends in American society that resulted in Republican rule in Congress. But one important difference was that Eisenhower had been elected twice with solid majorities, whereas Clinton's vote stayed below 50 percent both times.

This fact contributed to the intensity of the Republican attacks against Clinton during the Lewinsky scandal, which broke out in early 1998. When his affair with White House intern Monica Lewinsky was revealed in early 1998, during his trial for sexual harassment allegedly committed while he was governor of Arkansas, Clinton took the highly risky step of denying under oath that they ever had sexual relations. For six months Clinton stuck to his version. Then, in a humiliating reversal in August 1998 he was forced to admit his affair with Lewinsky, after DNA from his semen was found on a dress belonging to her.

A majority of the American people thought that Clinton's public humiliation was enough punishment for his personal misconduct. Nonetheless, the Republicans set in motion – for only the third time in American history – the process of impeaching a president (the previous two were against Andrew Johnson in 1865 and Nixon in 1974). Clinton had indeed committed perjury, but it was in relation to a matter that in the judgment of most Americans had no bearing on his presidential performance and did not justify impeachment.

The Republicans persisted with impeachment against the prevalent attitudes in the opinion polls. Clinton's sexual misconduct especially enraged the Christian Right, which constituted an increasingly important part of the Republican base. Clinton's moves to the right had been on welfare and crime, not on the moral issues that agitated the Christian fundamentalists, who were thus particularly anti-Clinton. Moreover, it was difficult for the Republican leaders to mask the fact that while the Christian Right was a powerful component of the Reagan coalition, it had received little more than rhetoric in return; none of the Supreme Court's 1960s and 1970s decisions on abortion, pornography and school prayers had been reversed. Attacking Clinton was a way for the Republicans to give the Christian Right something concrete in return for their loyal support since 1980. Additionally, the Republicans calculated that they would benefit in the midterm elections of 1998, even though most Americans opposed impeachment, since they expected a disproportionate turnout among religious Americans outraged by Clinton's misconduct. Since the turnout in midterm elections was well below 50 percent, Republicans reasoned that only the more motivated citizens were likely to vote.

Nevertheless, the impeachment project failed because it was opposed by most Americans. The House voted for Clinton's impeachment in the fall of 1998. Then the people voted in the midterm elections of November, and marginally reduced the Republican majority in the House. This was only the second time in American history that the party controlling the White House had made congressional gains in a midterm election. Since the Republicans had expected to make significant gains, they were so shocked that Speaker Gingrich resigned; instead of Clinton, it was his chief opponent who had fallen. Subsequently the Senate acquitted Clinton, who saw his popularity rise during the remainder of his presidency.

Clinton's survival and increasing popularity was related to the fact that several positive trends benefited American society in the second half of the 1990s. The economy enjoyed its longest postwar boom and reached annual growth rates of four percent, while unemployment fell below four percent and inflation remained around a safe two percent. In stark contrast to the period 1966–82, the American economy was outperforming its main rivals, enhancing American economic predominance worldwide. The boom in combination with tax increases passed by Bush and Clinton transformed the large federal deficits that went back to the Reagan era into surpluses at the end of the 1990s.

Another favorable trend was a sharp decline in crime, which was caused by large increases in police forces and the number of people incarcerated; in 1990 America's prisons held 1.1 million inmates, whereas by 1997 they held 1.7 million. The economist Stephen Levitt managed to enrage conservatives and liberals alike with his controversial argument that crime also declined as a result of the 1973 *Roe versus Wade* decision, since the legalization of abortion had presumably reduced the births of unwanted children, who were more likely to become criminals. Levitt also credited the waning of the crack epidemic for much of the decline in crime. Others credited New York's innovative zero-tolerance approach to petty crime under Mayor Rudy Giuliani. The results of this combination of factors can be seen in Table 4.

The decline in crime was beneficial to the African-American community, even though an alarming number – more than one in ten – of young black men were in prison. Decaying inner cities are more likely to revive under lower crime conditions, as soon became evident in parts of New York. There was more hope now that the ghettos would benefit from a virtuous cycle of more investments and job opportunities, less welfare dependency, higher incomes and changing patterns of behavior involving less drug and alcohol abuse and fewer births out of wedlock. The decline in crime was also likely to reduce racial tensions in America's cities,

Table 4 Annual homicide totals

	1992	1997	Percentage decline
New York	2,154	770	64.3
Los Angeles	1,094	574	47.5
Miami	128	103	19.3
Washington, DC	443	300	32.3
Detroit	595	469	21.2
San Francisco	117	59	49.6

which were largely fueled by white prejudice that was inflamed by the crime wave of the period 1965–92.

American foreign policy in the 1990s

With the end of the Cold War, American foreign policy found itself without a clear mission analogous to the containment of the Soviet threat. Two bids by academics to define the new challenges of American foreign policy, in the manner of Kennan's 'X' article of 1947, particularly influenced the American discourse on world affairs in the 1990s. The first was historian Francis Fukuyama's argument about the end of history through the worldwide ascendancy of liberalism as the only socioeconomic model of the future. The appeal of this argument showed that many Americans saw the end of the Cold War as a unique opportunity to complete Woodrow Wilson's program of creating a liberal world order. The second was political scientist Samuel Huntington's argument about the clash of civilizations, according to which the old ideological dividing lines of the Cold War have been replaced by civilizational cleavages. Huntington's argument had an appeal because it explained the ethnic-religious conflicts that broke out in the 1990s in Yugoslavia, the Middle East, the southern periphery of the former Soviet Union, South Asia and other parts of the world.

The appeal of these two arguments shows the two sides of international developments in the 1990s. On the one hand, the advanced world, including parts of the former communist bloc and parts of the developing world, have known peace, stability, democracy and growing prosperity in the context of an intensification of international transactions. On the other hand, major regions of the world witnessed instability and warfare. Secessionist movements led to the breakup of the old Yugoslavia and rocked many other states. Afghanistan, Tajikistan and Algeria witnessed very bloody civil strife between supporters and opponents of Islamic fundamentalism. Worst of all, sub-Saharan Africa suffered civil and international wars that engulfed 20 states and killed some 10 million people.

The United States in the 1990s had an unusually dominant role in managing global affairs on account of its commanding position in the international distribution of power, which became even more dominant in terms of its military and economic superiority by the end of the decade; among major economies only China had higher economic growth rates than America. Inevitably, America was drawn into the problems of the unstable parts of the globe. Three major perspectives regarding American foreign policy can be discerned in the 1990s:

- *Wilsonian Liberalism.* According to this perspective the United States should use its hegemonic position in the international distribution of power in order to promote a liberal world order based on the spread of democracy, free markets and international cooperation. Most Wilsonians are liberal in domestic politics, favor humanitarian interventions and support multilateral institutions in world affairs. But there are also conservative ideologues, sometimes described as neoconservatives, who seek to spread American ideals worldwide, though they are less interested in multilateral institutions and are apt to support unilateral interventions for ideological causes. The neoconservatives are in these respects close to the nationalists, constituting a militant and some-times unilateralist brand of Wilsonian Liberalism.

■ *Nationalism.* This perspective is at the other end of the spectrum from Wilsonian Liberalism and is to some extent the heir of the old isolationist tradition, though actual isolationists such as Pat Buchanan are few in number. The nationalists are wary of multilateral entanglements and seek to confine American interventions to cases where important American national interests are at stake. They are not interested in saving the world except passively by America's example; they do not like humanitarian interventions, strongly dis-trust the UN, but favor the use of decisive force, with coalitions of the willing or alone if necessary, when it comes to defending national interests. This per-spective is strongest in America's heartland, and in the 1990s found expres-sion in the Republican Congress. The congressional Republicans in the later 1990s opposed new multilateral agreements such as the environmentalist Kyoto Protocol and the International Criminal Court; they also resisted plac-ing American troops under non-American UN commands and balked at pay-ing American dues to the UN and the IMF.

■ *Realism.* This pragmatic perspective focuses on power relations and national interests. The Realists support American management of the world economy on the grounds that it benefits the United States, and are in this respect close to the Wilsonian views on the desirability of international economic interde-pendence. They also support American engagement in multilateral institu-tions on pragmatic grounds because it helps legitimize American hegemony. But they are closer to the nationalists in opposing humanitarian interventions and focusing on the defense of the national interest.

American foreign policy in the 1990s vacillated between Bush's Realism, Clinton's Wilsonian Liberalism and the Republican Congress's nationalism. Bush's Realism was evident in the Yugoslav crisis that broke out in 1991. The Bush administration refused to deal with the crisis in 1991 and early 1992, pass-ing the buck to the European Community. European mediation efforts failed and major warfare broke out first in Croatia in June 1991 and then in Bosnia in April 1992. Atrocities committed mostly, though not exclusively, by the Serbs outraged American public opinion, forcing the Bush administration in mid-1992 to take the lead in international diplomatic efforts in search of a solution. Yet Bush resolutely refused to resort to military intervention, being unwilling to entangle the United States in a Balkan guerrilla war in which no significant American national interests were at stake. Paradoxically, his fiercest American critics were liberals who had opposed the Vietnam War 20 years earlier, some of whom described him as a new Neville Chamberlain who was appeasing the Serbian leader Slobodan Milosevic.

Clinton's foreign policy

Clinton was a Wilsonian Liberal who felt that the 'unipolar moment' of American hegemony would sooner or later pass and that the United States should utilize its unique opportunity to promote the transformation of the world in a Wilsonian direction while its supremacy lasted. Unlike Bush, Clinton was therefore prepared to use armed force to end humanitarian disasters. In Europe his greatest success was the proactive policy of enlarging NATO in Central and Eastern Europe, which together with the European Union's parallel enlargement created strong incentives for the states of the region to enhance their democratization, respect human rights, liberalize their economies and avoid ethnic conflict, in order not to be left out.

Clinton's first humanitarian intervention was in Somalia, when he transformed the neutral peace-keeping mission that he inherited from Bush into a peacemaking mission that brought American forces in conflict with some of the parties of Somalia's civil strife. But Clinton withdrew his forces in 1993, after fighting resulted in 18 American deaths. Osama bin Laden, who was involved in Somalia on the anti-American side, declared later: 'When tens of your soldiers were killed in minor battles and one American pilot was dragged in the streets of Mogadishu, you left the area in disappointment, humiliation and defeat.' As with Reagan's retreat from Lebanon after the suicide bombing of the Marine barracks in 1983, Clinton's retreat from Somalia after a small number of casualties encouraged anti-American forces across the world to believe that it was possible for them to stand up to America, in spite of a highly skewed distribution of power in her favor, because of her extreme aversion to casualties.

Clinton's next major humanitarian intervention was far more ambitious and complex, since it aimed at putting an end to the Bosnian War, the bloodiest conflict in Europe since 1945 with terrible atrocities and massive ethnic cleansing. The triangular Bosnian conflict pitted the Bosnian Serbs and the Bosnian Croats against the Muslim Bosniacs. Clinton vacillated during the first two years of his presidency, torn between an intervention demanded by American public opinion and the danger stressed by military experts of getting bogged down in a prolonged conflict with substantial American casualties. Clinton's policy aimed at changing the situation on the ground so that an intervention would be either unnecessary or low-risk. In 1994 American diplomacy forged an alliance between Croats and Muslims, which ended the conflict between them and strengthened them *vis-à-vis* the Serbs. In the summer of 1995, the Croats and Muslims began major offensives against the Bosnian Serbs, while NATO launched an air campaign against Serbian positions in Bosnia. This resulted in a retreat by the Bosnian Serbs until they controlled only 49 percent of Bosnia's territory, as was envisaged by international peace plans. The easy success of NATO's intervention paved the way for the Dayton/Paris agreement of 1995, which pacified Bosnia on the basis of a complex federal system backed by an international peace-keeping force.

Clinton's largest humanitarian intervention was designed to prevent a repetition of Bosnia's humanitarian disaster in Kosovo. Instead of waiting for the Kosovo crisis to escalate into massive ethnic cleansing, the Clinton administration was determined to act early. The Kosovo War broke out in February 1998 when Albanian Kosovars launched a guerilla war with the objective of seceding from Serbia. The guerrilla movement was suppressed by the Serbian counteroffensive in the summer of 1998, but an internationally monitored cease-fire was imposed by the Clinton administration in October. The Serbian leader Milosevic was determined ultimately to expel most Albanian Kosovars from Kosovo in order to retain the province, which by the 1990s was over 90 percent Albanian, yet he did not dare to proceed with ethnic cleansing so long as he risked NATO's intervention.

The Clinton administration moved towards a military confrontation with Milosevic at the beginning of 1999, after the massacre in January of 45 Albanian Kosovars, which indicated that Milosevic would never renounce violence in the pursuit of his objectives. The American demands during the talks in France in February and March 1999 were so harsh on Serbia as to virtually guarantee Serbian rejection. In Kissinger's opinion, these demands 'amounted to insistence on war by a group of nations [i.e. NATO] that had always justified their union as purely defensive'.[4] Congressional Republicans opposed Clinton's policy; the leading House Republican Tom DeLay published an article in the *Wall Street Journal* shortly before NATO's intervention in Kosovo with the title 'Don't Intervene in Kosovo'.

The Clinton administration apparently believed that Milosevic would back down after a brief show of force by NATO. Instead, once he became certain that NATO's intervention was inevitable, Milosevic prepared a massive ethnic cleansing operation. As a result, about half the Albanian population of Kosovo was swiftly expelled within the first few weeks of NATO's air campaign against Serbia in late March and April 1999. NATO meanwhile ran out of military targets, since Milosevic had dispersed and hidden his forces. Clinton wanted no American casualties and thus ruled out a land operation. Having put NATO's credibility at stake but being unprepared to incur American casualties, Clinton had no choice but to bomb general nonmilitary infrastructure targets in Serbia.

After 78 days of bombardments that destroyed significant parts of Serbia's public infrastructure, Milosevic acquiesced in a cease-fire and the deployment of UN peace-keeping forces in Kosovo that guaranteed the return of the expelled Albanian Kosovars. Clinton's Balkan policy was considered a major success with the fall of Milosevic in 2000, since henceforth every Balkan government wishes to join the EU and NATO. Balkan peace and stability depends on the indefinite operation of the international protectorates in Bosnia and Kosovo. But perhaps this is an acceptable price to pay, not only in Wilsonian but also in *Realpolitik* terms, in order to secure the integration of formerly communist Southeast European countries in the West.

From a military point of view, the Kosovo intervention demonstrated the advances in American military capabilities that took place in the 1990s. For the first time ever, a substantial war was won with no casualties on the victorious side. The new integrated weapons systems allowed the American air forces to hit targets from high altitudes with accurate guided missiles and smart bombs, presenting a leap in American war fighting capabilities even from the Gulf War of 1991, let alone Vietnam. The message was clear: the United States is able to bomb any particular point on the planet with an accuracy measured in meters. But when a power enjoys absolute superiority in conventional means, it might induce its enemies to resort to unconventional means, especially if they are

themselves unconventional entities that have thrived in the rubbles of failed
states like Somalia, Sudan and Afghanistan. The military historian Martin van
Creveld issued this warning in 1989: 'Let him who has ears to listen, listen: the
call *Lucifer ante Portas* already reverberates, and new forms of warfare are threatening to put an end to our delicate civilization.'[5] The meaning of his warning
became clearer on September 11, 2001.

NOTES

1. Geoffrey Layman, *The Great Divide: Religious and Cultural Conflict in American Party Politics*, New York: Columbia University Press, 2001, p. 9–10.
2. Bruce J. Schulman, *The Seventies: The Great Shift in American Culture, Society, and Politics*, New York: Free Press, 2001, p. 252.
3. Peter Schweizer, *Reagan's War*, New York: Doubleday, 2002, pp. 141–3.
4. Henry Kissinger, *Does America Need a Foreign Policy?* New York: Simon and Schuster, 2001, p. 428.
5. Martin van Creveld, *Technology and War*, New York: Free Press, 1989, p. 296.

RECOMMENDED READING

Michael Barone, *Our Country: The Shaping of America from Roosevelt to Reagan*, New York: Free Press, 1990.
Michael Beschloss and Strobe Talbott, *At the Highest Levels: The Inside Story of the End of the Cold War*, New York: Little, Brown, 1993.
Geoffrey Layman, *The Great Divide: Religious and Cultural Conflict in American Party Politics*, New York: Columbia University Press, 2001.
James T. Patterson, *Restless Giant: The United States from Watergate to Bush v. Gore*, Oxford: Oxford University Press, 2005.
Peter Schweizer, *Reagan's War*, New York: Doubleday, 2002.
Gil Troy, *Morning in America: How Ronald Reagan Invented the 1980s*, Princeton, NJ: Princeton University Press, 2005.
Sean Wilentz, *The Age of Reagan: A History, 1974–2008*, New York: HarperCollins, 2008.

CHAPTER 10

From the Global Village to Bowling Alone

The neoconservative counterrevolution that began with George Wallace reached its zenith in the 1980s during the presidency of Ronald Reagan. Though he was the oldest president ever to be elected, Reagan projected youthful optimism when he proclaimed, 'It's morning again in America.' In *Reagan's America: Innocents at Home* (1987), Garry Wills summed up the late president's popular appeal. 'Reagan runs continuously in everyone's home movies of the mind. He wrests from us something warmer than mere popularity, a kind of complicity,' Wills explained. 'He is the great American synecdoche, not only part of our past but a large part of our multiple pasts.' Besides his influence on politics, Reagan had a significant impact on mainstream culture as a symbol of renewed American optimism after the disasters of Vietnam, Watergate and the Iranian hostage crisis. No wonder that Sean Wilentz called his history of the years between Richard Nixon's resignation and Barack Obama's election *The Age of Reagan* (2008). Wilentz argues that only a few American presidents have defined their era, including Jefferson, Jackson, Lincoln, Roosevelt – and Reagan.

Yet the Reagan legacy was less impressive than his supporters claimed, though Reagan himself was less of a bumpkin than his opponents charged. He was a skilled politician and a superb communicator with little intellectual curiosity and a short attention span. Though Reagan bristled at being called 'just an actor' by his detractors, he told an interviewer at the end of his presidency that he couldn't understand how anyone could do the job who hadn't been an actor. Perhaps the journalist Frances FitzGerald best summed up Reagan's complex legacy in *Way Out There in the Blue* (2000): 'In fact, it could be argued that what Americans really wanted in the 1980s was an actor for President. Many, after all, were able to persuade themselves that America was "back" and "standing tall" when American troops managed to occupy the island of Grenada.' In this sense, Reagan embodied the spirit of the decade. 'Even at the time, the 1980s was not thought of as a period of national dedication and sacrifice, but rather as a time of false prosperity, indulgence, and speculation, when even the most solid middle-class citizens dreamed of getting something for nothing.'

Reagan did not 'win' the Cold War single-handedly, as some claimed. There were other forces at work undermining the imploding Soviet system. In 1988, another symbol of American power appeared in Eastern Europe when the first McDonald's Restaurant opened in Budapest, Hungary. It was a significant event: an American fast-food restaurant, emblem of global capitalism, in the heart of the communist empire. The restaurant was located near *Vaci utca*, Budapest's fashionable pedestrian mall. Across the street was the Adidas outlet, where Hungarians could buy the overstock of the famous running shoes made for Western export. On Saturdays, long lines in front of Adidas and McDonald's confirmed the triumph of consumer culture over socialist realism. Was this an omen of the collapse of communism in the following year?

'The End of History'?

In 1989, just after the fall of the Berlin Wall, a young Japanese-American social scientist named Francis Fukuyama published a celebrated essay entitled 'The End of History?' Three years later, an expanded version was published as a book, *The End of History and the Last Man* (1992). Fukuyama argued that with the collapse of communism, the age of ideology had come to an end. 'At the end of history, there are no serious ideological competitors left to liberal democracy,' he wrote:

> In our grandparents' time, many reasonable people could foresee a radiant socialist future in which private property and capitalism had been abolished, and in which politics itself was somehow overcome. Today, by contrast, we have trouble imagining a world that is radically better than our own, or a future that is not essentially democratic and capitalist.

But the end of history poses a paradox. According to Fukuyama, the primary human drive is not for self-preservation but for *thymos,* or self-recognition. History begins with slavery and the thymotic desire for individual recognition and ends with democracy and the thymotic desire for equality. It was this belief in *thymos* – the idea that each person must be accorded the right of recognition – that shaped modern history, from the eighteenth-century revolutions in America and France to the recent revolts in Eastern Europe. But with the collapse of the Cold War, the demand for recognition yields to the pursuit of economic self-interest. The end of history may signal the end of violent conflict but it can also lead to a loss of humanity if we exchange the vision of the good life for the animal contentment of the consumer society. 'A dog is content to sleep in the sun all day provided he is fed, because he is not dissatisfied with what he is,' Fukuyama says.

> He does not worry that other dogs are doing better than him, or that his career as a dog has stagnated, or that dogs are being oppressed in a distant part of the world. If man reaches a society in which he has succeeded in abolishing injustice, his life will come to resemble that of the dog.

Accordingly, 'Human life, then, involves a curious paradox: it seems to require injustice, for the struggle against injustice is what calls for that which is highest in man.'

Fukuyama's prophesy of 'the end of history' after the Cold War did not materialize. But the fear that the desire for *thymos* would give way to the pursuit of economic self-interest was borne out. Even the religious Moral Majority embraced the union of God and Mammon; its leader, Jerry Falwell, proclaimed, 'The free enterprise system is clearly outlined in the Book of Proverbs.'

In the 1990s and the first decade of the new millennium, expansive global capitalism enriched many developing countries but created greater inequalities between rich and poor nations and between rich and poor within nations. When he was chief economist of the World Bank, Joseph E. Stiglitz 'saw firsthand the devastating effect that globalization can have on developing countries, and especially the poor in those countries'.[1] He says, 'A growing divide between the haves and the have-nots has left increasing numbers in the Third World in dire poverty, living on less than a dollar a day.'[2] In Europe, too, market-driven economies threatened the existence of even prosperous Scandinavian social welfare systems. In the United States, 'the business of America' once again became 'business' as a buoyant stock market of the 1990s created a million new millionaires and destroyed several million old jobs in an orgy of downsizing. At the beginning of the new millennium, global capitalism metastasized into giant corporate scandals, from Enron in the United States to Parmalat in Italy, culminating in the financial meltdown in 2008. Already in 2003, the historian Russell Duncan predicted, 'The 2001 event which could have the biggest long-term impact on the United States may well not be the war on terrorism, but the Enron scandal.'[3] Duncan turned out to be prophetic. In 2002 the economist Paul Krugman asked 'a scary question': 'How many more Enrons are out there?' It turned out there were too many to count. By the end of 2007 it was revealed that prominent Wall Street firms, major banks, and giant insurance companies were all involved in questionable speculative practices that threatened the global economic system. 'A confluence of three factors in the late 1990s opened the door for financial scams on a scale unseen for generations,' Krugman wrote in *The Great Unraveling* (2004). 'First was the rise of the "new economy" [of informational technology]... Second was the stock market bubble. ... And finally, there was (and is) a permissive legal environment.' Krugman's analysis was also prescient.

Blind faith by the Clinton and Bush administrations in 'the magic of the market' to regulate the economy led to cynical manipulations that undermined the global system. The audacious multibillion dollar fraud perpetrated by a 'respected' investment broker, Bernard Madoff, became the new symbol of Wall Street greed. In 2003 the esteemed economist, John Kenneth Galbraith, noted that public faith in business ethics and leadership had vanished; 'nothing in my lifetime, or yours has happened more completely than the loss of confidence in corporate leadership.' Looking back over 60 years of public life, he concluded. 'I entered the world of politics at a time when there were Fifth Amendment communists, and I've reached the age of ninety-four when there are Fifth Amendment capitalists.'[4]

'Greed is good!'

In *Sleepwalking Through History* (1991), Haynes Johnson showed how we arrived at Enron; he chronicled the astonishing series of major financial scandals that prefigured it in the 1980s. 'The multiple scandals on Wall Street, in Washington, the Chicago futures markets, the savings and loan associations across the country, the evangelical empires, and the amateur and professional athletic franchises all differed in degree and manner. But they contained common threads.' The Reagan administration's faith in deregulation and reduced supervision by federal regulatory agencies like the SEC, offered new opportunities for circumventing the law. Innovative stock brokers like Ivan Boesky and Michael Milken found new methods of creating enormous wealth without producing anything. Soon a new vocabulary of hostile takeovers, leveraged buyouts, insider trading and 'junk bonds' came to dominate American business culture. Clearly, Wall Street ethics had changed. In 1986 Boesky captured the national mood when he told an enthusiastic college audience, 'Greed is all right.'

Thus Gordon Gekko, the charismatic villain of Oliver Stone's film *Wall Street* (1987), was only repeating Boesky when he announced, 'Greed, for want of a better word, is good!' (Stone reprised the current financial crisis in a sequel, *Wall Street 2: Money Never Sleeps*, (2010) where 'greed is now legal'.) Both were echoing President Reagan's remark, 'What I want to see above all is that this country remains a country where someone can always get rich. That's the one thing we have and that must be preserved.' During the Reagan years, middle-class Americans turned from political commitment to the frenzied accumulation of money. According to Johnson, 'Not in decades, perhaps not in the century, had acquisition and flaunting of wealth been celebrated so publicly by so many.' The new culture heroes were 'the rich and famous', like televangelist Jim Bakker who owned six homes and an air-conditioned doghouse, or real estate entrepreneur Donald Trump who owned six helicopters, a $29-million yacht and a 47-room 'week-end cottage' in Greenwich, Connecticut. By the beginning of the 1990s, Boesky, Bakker and Milken were all in prison.

In *American Sucker* (2004), the film critic David Denby recounts his own personal pursuit of the chimera of financial success. In the late 1990s, at the height of the Bull market, he sees friends and colleagues making killings on the stock market and decides to follow suit by plunging into the NASDAQ wonderland of new technology stocks. Soon he is headed for disaster. 'What is this thing called greed?' he asks himself. 'I knew that I had my legitimate need, my serious reason to make money. But I also knew that my hunger had grown larger than mere rational need; my hunger never stopped, it had taken over my mind.' Denby discovers he is not alone; Arthur Levitt, former head of the SEC, tells him, 'We live in a culture of instant wealth, a more materialistic culture than anything I've read about in the history of the United States.' No wonder, then, that the epoch is defined by the Enron scandal. 'The age had found its name, its face, its metaphor,' Denby says, 'and the rage over the scandal burned its way into one's senses like a magnifying glass concentrating light onto a page.'

The buoyant economy of the 1990s created not simply two classes in the United States but two nations, a tendency that accelerated in the new millennium during the presidency of George W. Bush. In *The Revolt of the Elites* (1995), Christopher Lasch cited the moment when the first President Bush expressed astonishment on seeing, evidently for the first time, an electronic scanning device in a supermarket. Clearly, here was a man who had lived his adult life totally insulated from everyday experience. Lasch noted,

> To an alarming extent the privileged classes – by an expansive definition, the top 20 per cent – have made themselves independent not only of crumbling industrial cities but of public services in general. They send their children to private schools, insure themselves against medical emergencies by enrolling in company-supported plans, and hire private security guards to protect themselves from the common life.

This retreat from civic responsibility led Lasch in the last years of his life to question 'whether democracy has a future'.

On the international scene, too, the collapse of the Cold War did not lead to a new democratic world order. Instead, there was something approaching global disorder, culminating in the terrorist attacks of September 11, 2001 and March 11, 2004. In the United States, the political consensus deteriorated into bitter party bickering and increasing public apathy. In 1992, Bill Clinton was elected president with only 43 percent of the vote. During Clinton's presidency, Americans experienced the most divisive political era since the 1960s, culminating in the failed attempt to impeach the president and the controversial election of George W. Bush in 2000. Things only got worse in the next eight years.

'Bowling alone'

Many social scientists noted a marked increase in American political apathy. There were increasing signs that voters were turned off by the electoral process and politics had become a spectator sport. The decline in voting was well known, but over the past three decades voter identification with the two major parties had also dropped precipitously. At the same time that citizen involvement in party activities was falling, campaign spending was rising. Between 1964 and 1996 campaign expenditures increased fivefold as lavish corporate donations to political campaigns made it possible for candidates to raise enormous sums of money. (One major corporate contributor was Enron, whose financial collapse in 2001 created a political and economic scandal.) Cynics used to say that American politicians were the best that money could buy; now it seemed that the politicians were attempting to 'buy' the electorate with the help of the electronic media.

Even more disturbing was the growing distrust of government among voters. The political scientist Robert D. Putnam cited one startling example of increasing alienation:

> In April 1966, with the Vietnam War raging and race riots in Cleveland, Chicago, and Atlanta, 66 percent of Americans *rejected* the view that 'the people running the country don't really care what happens to you.' In December 1997, in the midst of the longest period of peace and prosperity in more than two generations, 57 percent of Americans *endorsed* that same view.

In *Bowling Alone* (2000), he traces the decline in American political participation over the past 30 years in the larger context of collapsing community values and a shrinking civil society.

Putnam measures the decline of American civil society in terms of what social scientists call 'social capital': the social networks, norms of reciprocity and trust that can be compared to notions of physical capital (tools) and human capital (training) in enhancing individual and collective productivity. 'Just as a screwdriver (physical capital) or a college education (human capital) can increase productivity (both individual and collective), so too social contacts affect the productivity of individuals and groups.' The United States has always been envied for its vital civil society and productive use of social capital. Though Americans are known as rugged individualists, throughout their history they have also been great joiners: of churches, political parties, philanthropic organizations, alumni associations and neighborhood groups. These voluntary groups range from the Boy Scouts to Alcoholics Anonymous, from the Jewish B'nai Brith to the Catholic Knights of Columbus, from the National Rifle Association to the National Association for the Advancement of Colored People.

When Alexis de Tocqueville visited the United States in 1831, he observed how Americans habitually organized themselves into informal groups to solve problems that weak local and national governments could not resolve quickly. In *Democracy in America* (1838), he wrote, 'Americans of all ages, all conditions, all minds constantly unite. Not only do they have commercial and industrial associations in which all take part, but they also have a thousand other kinds: religious, moral, grave, futile, very general and very particular, immense and very small.' For him the connection between the vitality of civil society and the practice of democracy was clear. Americans were freer than Europeans not only because they were more egalitarian, but because they created a more inclusive civil society. During the nineteenth century, American civic participation grew rapidly. In the twentieth century, citizens' groups continued to flourish, except during the Depression, until the end of the 1950s. And then something strange happened, says Putnam: 'For the first two-thirds of the twentieth century a powerful tide bore Americans into ever deeper engagement in the life of their communities, but a few decades ago – silently, without warning – that tide reversed and we were overtaken by a treacherous rip current.' Over the past 30 years, 'Americans have been dropping out in droves, not merely from political life, but from organized community life more generally.'

The signs are everywhere, from the fall in churchgoing through the decline in volunteering to the loss of membership in bowling leagues. More Americans than ever are bowling – 91 million in 1996 – but more are 'bowling alone'. Significantly, the dropout rate in civic participation is lower among older Americans born before World War II than among so-called 'Baby Boomers' born between 1946 and 1964. But the dropout rate is highest among 'Generation X' members born after 1965. Moreover, the decline in civic participation is matched by a similar decline in mental health. 'The younger you are, the worse things have gotten over the last decades of the twentieth century in terms of headaches, indigestion, sleeplessness, as well as general satisfaction with life and even likelihood of taking your own life.'

Many reasons have been suggested for this radical social transformation. Liberals point to intensive time and economic pressures. Conservatives note the increasing movement of women into the workforce and the declining significance of the nuclear family. Others point out America's famous geographical mobility and the increase of suburbanization and sprawl. Then there is rising consumerism and the changing scale and structure of a global economy. But Putnam finds that the most likely culprit is the power of television, which keeps most Americans indoors. 'The American house has been TV-centered for three generations. It is the focus of family life, and the life of the house correspondingly turns inward, away from whatever occurs beyond its four walls,' says media critic James Howard Kunstler.

> At the same time, the television is the family's chief connection with the outside world. The physical envelope of the house itself no longer connects their lives to the outside in any active way; rather, it seals them off from it. The outside world has become an abstraction filtered through television, just as the weather is an abstraction filtered through air conditioning.

Media unlimited

Bowling Alone was not the first jeremiad against the abuses of television. Critics have been warning of the growing power of the media for decades. In *The Image* (1962), Daniel Boorstin described how the media transgressed the critical line between reporting news and making news, creating the 'pseudo-event', something that had only been staged in order to be reported. The symbiotic relationship between journalists and public figures contributed to the manufacture of news where there was none. In the process, the 'hero' who was famous for his actions is transformed into the 'celebrity' who is famous for being known. 'The hero was distinguished by his achievement; the celebrity by his image or trademark,' Boorstin said. 'The hero created himself; the celebrity is created by the media.' Instead of Michelangelo, we have Andy Warhol.

In *Amusing Ourselves to Death* (1985), Neil Postman described life in the Age of Celebrity. According to him, 'the most significant American cultural fact of the second half of the twentieth century' is 'the decline of the Age of Typography and the ascendancy of the Age of Television'. As image culture replaces print culture, public discourse is flattened by the electronic media: instead of news we get 'infotainment', hard news presented as soft entertainment. 'Our politics, religion, news, athletics, education and commerce have been transformed into congenial adjuncts of show business,' Postman claimed. 'The result is that we are a people on the verge of amusing ourselves to death.'

Similarly, Neal Gabler finds a troubling confusion between 'art' and 'life' in contemporary society. In *Life: The Movie* (1998) he argues, 'where we had once measured the movies by life, we now measured life by how well it satisfied the narrative expectations created by the movies.' The *fin-de-siècle* poet Villiers de L'Isle-Adam wrote that living should be left to the servants; today Americans apparently believe that living should be left to the media. Instead of Villiers' drama *Axel*, we have television reality programs and Peter Weir's film *The Truman Show* (1998).

This broad assault on media culture continued in the new millennium in Chris Hedges' *Empire of Illusions* (2009). Hedges compares American television viewers to the imprisoned human beings described in Plato's *Republic* who mistake the shadows on their walls for substance. 'We are chained to the flickering shadows of celebrity culture, the spectacle of the arena and the airwaves, the lies of advertising, the endless personal dramas, many of them completely fictional, that have become the staple of new, celebrity gossip, New Age mysticism, and pop psychology.'

In movies like *Network* (1976), *Broadcast News* (1987) and *The Truman Show*, Hollywood eagerly exposed the cultural banality of its arch-rival, television. But, faced with falling attendance in the 1970s, the major film studios cut production by 25 percent and aimed at producing blockbuster hits like Steven Spielberg's *Jaws* (1975) and George Lucas's *Star Wars* (1977). 'Genre, special effects, nostalgia: in the aftermath of the box-office triumph of *Star Wars*, these elements fuelled the movie industry's new marketing machine,' notes Robert Sklar in *Movie-Made America*. This trend continues today in the numbing sequels to earlier hits, from *Lethal Weapon 4* (2006) to *Die Hard 4* (2007). As we entered the new millennium more people than ever were 'amusing themselves to death' in cineplexes, theme parks and shopping malls all over the world.

In the 1980s Hollywood went through yet another transformation as film studios were sold to multinational conglomerates. Beginning in 1985, foreign media giants began buying up American film studios: the Australian-owned News Corporation acquired 20th Century Fox, Sony bought Tri-Star and Columbia Pictures while Matsushita purchased MCA-Universal. Meanwhile Warner Brothers merged with Time Incorporated and Viacom took over Paramount. Now film companies were under even more pressure to produce what the *Wall Street Journal* called 'high profile mass appeal movies with big commercial potential'.

In a strange way, the movie business has come full circle in recent years. In *Seeing Through Movies* (1990), Mark Crispin Miller describes how the new media conglomerates regained the monopolistic power of the old studios. In 1985 the Reagan administration reversed the 1948 ruling that compelled the old studios to break up Hollywood's vertical monopoly. The new ruling allowed the new media giants to revive the old structure in a new context. This, says Miller, constituted 'an enormous structural change in the movie business': the transformation of the old 'vertical' movie monopoly into a new 'horizontal' media monopoly.

> In other words, whereas the old movie companies, controlling every phase of filmmaking from production to exhibition, made only movies, that industry (much changed) is now a major cog, or chip, within a mammoth image-generating system that includes TV production companies and syndication firms, cable distribution networks, record companies, theme parks, and numerous merchandising operations – as well as publishing companies, major magazines, and many newspapers.

Synergy

In the language of the new media conglomerates, the key word is *synergy* – the way the parts relate to and enhance the whole, thus creating a new constellation. Significantly, a similar convergence can be seen in the news media as well. One example is *Time* magazine, which is part of Time Warner. Another is America's oldest continuous newspaper, the *New York Post*, which is owned by Rupert Murdoch's World Corporation, a global television network. A third example is the television network CBS, which is now part of Viacom, a conglomerate involved in making movies, marketing books and broadcasting cable television.

In *Backstory* (2003), Ken Auletta explains how *synergy* is defined by the media conglomerates. 'In the spring of 2003, a news executive at CBS dispatched a proposal to the family of Pfc. Jessica Lynch, who had been captured and wounded in Iraq, offering her exposure on various news programs,' he says.[5]

> But the news executive didn't stop there. She noted that Viacom, the corporate parent, owned Paramount, which could make a movie of Lynch's heroics, and Simon & Schuster, which could offer a book, and MTV, a popular cable network, which might make her a cohost of a video show, and Infinity Broadcasting, the second largest radio network.

We have entered the brave new synergistic world of media conglomerates.

The results of global synergy are visible everywhere. In *Media Unlimited* (2002), Todd Gitlin shows how our lives have become submerged in a flood of media images: movies, television and the Internet have become the vehicles by which we organize our social reality and structure our emotional life. 'To an unprecedented degree, the torrent of images, songs, and stories streaming has become our familiar, our felt world,' he says.

> We are seeing on a world scale the familiar infectious rhythm of modernity. The money economy extends its reach, bringing with it a calculating mentality. Even in the poor countries it stirs the same hunger for private feeling, the same taste for disposable labels and sensations on demand, the same attention to fashion, the new and the now, that cropped up earlier in the West.

In the 1960s, Marshall McLuhan had grandly predicted that the new electronic media would create a utopian 'global village'. But Gitlin notes that McLuhan was only partly right: 'If there is a village, it speaks American. It wears jeans, drinks coke, eats at the golden arches, walks on swooshed shoes, plays electric guitars, recognizes Mickey Mouse, James Dean, E.T., Bart Simpson, R2 D2, and Pamela Anderson.' The predominance of American popular culture approximates a 'global lingua franca'; but this predominance is a two-edged sword. 'American popular culture is the nemesis that hundreds of millions – perhaps billions – of people love, and love to hate. The antagonism and the dependency are inseparable, for the media flood – essentially American in its origin, but virtually unlimited in its reach – represents, like it or not, a common imagination.'

Globalization

The rise of multinational media conglomerates is part of a larger process of globalization. In *The Paradox of American Power* (2002), Joseph Nye notes,

'Globalization – the growth of worldwide networks of interdependence – is virtually as old as human history. What's new is that the networks are thicker and more complex, involving people from more regions and social classes.' In the postmodern era, there is no doubt that globalization has an American accent. Nye cites the French Foreign Minister Hubert Vedrine: 'The United States is a very big fish that swims easily and rules supreme in the waters of globalization.' Americans benefit from this for many reasons, Vedrine explains: because of their size, their language, their promotion of market economies and rugged individualism.

Americanism and Americanization

No wonder that many identify globalization with Americanization. We all recognize the impact of American cultural imperialism: what Austrian scholar Reinhold Wagnleitner calls signs of 'Coca-Colonization'.[6] The former French Minister of Culture, Jack Lang, charged that American cultural imperialists interfered 'in the interior affairs of other countries, and more seriously, in the consciousness of the citizens of those countries'. Like the pods in the cult horror film, *Invasion of the Body Snatchers,* Americans were taking over the 'trains of thought' and 'ways of life' of Frenchmen and Danes alike.[7] Perhaps some readers feel that Americans are tampering with *their* subconscious, but before we can explore that subject we must understand what is meant by American cultural imperialism.

In *If You've Seen One You've Seen the Mall* (1996), Dutch historian Rob Kroes argues that in any discussion of cultural imperialism it is important to distinguish between *Americanism* and *Americanization*. According to Kroes, Americanism has two distinct meanings. In its positive sense, the term is identified with freedom, equality and the American Dream. In its negative sense, it is identified with consumption, mass culture and the American Way of Life. He says, 'In its negative sense the term symbolizes America as the antithesis to Europeanism, to everything that European intellectuals conceive of as their common cultural heritage.'

The word Americanization has an older pedigree. According to Richard Pells, the term originated in Britain in the 1830s and spread to the continent in the 1850s. But only in the twentieth century did it take on an ominous significance. In 1901, the British journalist William Stead published *The Americanization of the World*. At first, Americanization referred to technological prowess, but with America's rise to international prominence after World War I, Europeans began to pay increasing attention to growing American cultural and economic influence as well.

Kroes shows how the values associated with Americanism have been absorbed into the process of Americanization. He identifies the two essential aspects of Americanism as freedom and affluence. 'In these contours the post-war world came to conceive of America in its imaginary guise of a dreamland, a realm of freedom and abundance,' he notes. 'Even today, these are still the two aspects that centrally define the appeal of America as a cultural symbol.' In this way, drinking a Coke and wearing blue jeans are associated with living the American Dream. But Americanization has not simply been imposed from outside by nasty capitalists and cultural imperialists. The ideas have been introjected as well. In the process, American icons have become global, as Italian jeans manufacturers and German cigarette makers advertise their wares against a background image of the American West. In other words, there is no mystery why American capitalists sell their products as extensions of the American Dream. The mystery is why Europeans consume the same dream as well.

But the mystery is not limited to Europe. Recent experience in China suggests that something similar is going on there. In *Many Globalizations* (2002), Yunxiang Yan, an anthropologist at UCLA, reports on the ambiguous behavior of Chinese youths after the NATO bombing of the Chinese Embassy in Belgrade in May 1999. Surprisingly, many young protesters appeared at the US Embassy in Beijing chanting 'Down with American Imperialism' while at the same time drinking Coca-Cola. Meanwhile, others posted anti-McDonald's slogans on the streets and then went to eat at a local Kentucky Fried Chicken (KFC) outlet. Similarly, when the China Central Television Station (CCTV) cancelled its scheduled broadcast of the National Basketball Association (NBA) games to protest the Belgrade bombing, many viewers called to complain. Professor Yan even interviewed a student who had demonstrated in front of the American Embassy *and* protested the cancellation of the NBA broadcast. When asked to account for his seemingly contradictory behavior, the student replied: 'No, there were no contradictions. Yes, I hate American hegemony, and I love the NBA games. But they are two different things. NBA games belong to the world, and everyone has the right to enjoy them.' In an epiphany, Yan 'suddenly realized that, at least for youths like him, there might actually be a truly global culture that can be enjoyed and appropriated by people from different cultural backgrounds, while they are politically nationalistic at the same time.'

McDonaldization

One name given to this phenomenon is *McDonaldization*. But here we are talking about something more than simply hamburgers. In a special issue of *American Studies* (Summer/Fall 2000), George Ritzer and Elizabeth L. Malone argue, 'This is the process by which the principles of the highly successful and revolutionary fast-food restaurant are coming to dominate more and more sectors of American society and an increasing number of societies throughout the world.' They describe the principles involved as: *'efficiency, calculability, predictability, and control, which are often achieved through the substitution of nonhuman, for human technology.'*

McDonaldization refers to Americanization as a revolutionary new process of production and distribution. But it is also intimately connected with new means of consumption. The proliferation of consumer outlets is not new; many of them can be traced back to commercial innovations in American life during the 1950s. Think of business franchises like McDonald's (started in 1955); superstores like Toys R Us (opened in 1957); theme parks like Disneyland (opened in 1955); and indoor shopping malls (first established in 1956). Today, these American commercial innovations have been globalized.

The impact of McDonaldization on the rest of the world is a subject of great controversy. Critics claim it is a form of cultural imperialism that threatens to destroy local cultures and homogenize the world. This is not a new charge, especially in France where they take their food culture seriously. In 1948, when Coca-Cola applied for a license to establish a local bottling plant, the French Communist Party opposed it on the grounds that the company also worked as an American spy network. More recently, in 1999, members of a so-called 'peasants' confederation' called Attac trashed a new McDonald's in the town of Millau because it represented American cultural imperialism and threatened French agriculture and the local cuisine.

But there is another side to the debate. Others argue that McDonaldization strengthens local institutions, including cuisine. Some point to the proliferation of local imitators of homogeneous fast-food chains. In Russia the most successful chain is called Russkoye Bistro; it serves blinis not hamburgers. Russkoye Bistro has over 100 outlets and serves 40,000 customers a day. 'If McDonald's had not come to our country, then we probably wouldn't be here,' says the company's deputy director; 'we need to create fast food here that fits our lifestyle and traditions...We see McDonald's like an older brother...We have a lot to learn from them.' In a similar fashion, Chinese entrepreneurs copied the popular KFC franchise by opening Ronghua Chicken and Xiangfei Roast Chicken chains.

This local appropriation of fast-food culture suggests that we are describing a phenomenon that more closely approximates *globalization* than *Americanization*. Either way, we are describing a process of homogenization through the spread of indigenous clones. But the globalizing process may transcend Americanization in other ways as well. During the Cold War French Communists accused Coca-Cola salesmen of being secret agents of the American government but today the reverse may be true. In *The Lexus and the Olive Tree* (1999), Thomas Friedman recounts an anecdote about the time the then American Ambassador to Israel, Martin Indyk, dressed in a baseball cap with the McDonald's logo, officiated at the opening of the first McDonald's restaurant in Jerusalem. Suddenly a teenager also wearing a McDonald's hat approached him and asked, 'Are you the ambassador? Can I have your autograph?' The Ambassador was flattered and replied, 'Sure, I've never been asked for my autograph before.'

As Ambassador Indyk took the hat and prepared to sign his name on the bill, the teenager said to him, Wow, what's it like to be the ambassador from McDonald's, going around the world opening McDonald's restaurants everywhere?'

Somewhat stunned, Ambassador Indyk looked at the Israeli youth and said, 'No, no. I'm the *American* ambassador – not the ambassador from McDonald's!'

The Israeli youth looked totally crestfallen. Ambassador Indyk described what happened next: 'I said to him, "Does this mean you don't want my autograph?" And the kid said, "No, I don't want your autograph," and he took his hat back and walked away.'

McWorld

The development of efficient techniques of cultural distribution has created mass culture and spread American values over the world. In the process, the term

Americanization has given way to the term globalization. In *Jihad vs. McWorld* (1995), Benjamin R. Barber calls this global colony 'McWorld'. By *McWorld*, he means not only American cultural imperialism but Western economic power that colonizes the entire world: the 'onrushing economic, technological, and ecological forces that demand integration and uniformity and that mesmerize peoples everywhere with fast music, fast computers, and fast-food – MTV, Macintosh, and McDonald's – pressing nations into one homogeneous global theme park, one McWorld tied together by communications, information, entertainment, and commerce.' McWorld responds to the demands of multinational corporations, not to the needs of sovereign nations. Their customers are defined not by nationality or ethnicity but as interchangeable consumers in a global land of desire. The chairman of one multinational corporation claimed: 'I do not find foreign countries foreign.' Welcome to McWorld, says Barber.

By *Jihad*, Barber means not simply the moral armed struggle of believers against faithlessness identified with militant Islam but a parochial anti-modernism which celebrates difference, demonizes 'the Other' and privileges tribe over nation, collectivism over individualism, religious values over secular, and local institutions over global. It is a movement that, in various guises, encircles the globe, from the Ayotallahs of Iran to the ethnic cleansers of the former Yugoslavia; from the new political right in Germany and France to the new Religious Right in the United States. 'Caught between Babel and Disneyland, the planet is falling precipitously apart and coming reluctantly together at the very same moment.'

Jihad and McWorld struggle against each other; but they need each other as well. They are adversarial *and* symbiotic. The contradictions are often comical. The French government sets quotas on Hollywood films but subsidizes Euro Disneyland; the Japanese government limits beef imports but welcomes a thousand McDonald's restaurants. At times the contradictions are schizophrenic. In Iran, the faithful heed the mullahs in mosques and then watch Western soap operas on Star Television via satellite dishes. In Russia, the Orthodox Church renews its faith and then enters a joint venture with California businessmen to market natural waters as the Saint Springs Water Company. In Germany, neo-Nazis use rock music to attract recruits to their war against decadent culture; in the United States, religious fundamentalists fight secular modernity on the Internet.

Clearly, McWorld can disrupt fragile Third World societies, but is this true in Europe? Richard Pells thinks not. In *Not Like Us* (1997), he argues that the Americanization of Europe is a myth: 'A powerful and enduring myth, often cherished by the Europeans themselves because they can use it to explain how their societies have changed in ways they don't like, but a myth nonetheless.' Despite the overwhelming American presence in the European marketplace, Europeans have not become closet Americans. Instead they have adapted American culture to their own tastes and traditions. To prove his point, Pells tells the story of the creation of Euro Disneyland. He reminds us that the original Disneyland's model was European, Copenhagen's Tivoli, which opened in the nineteenth century. He says, 'Disney wanted to reproduce Tivoli's Danish sense of decorum and safety, its cleanliness and meticulously planned use of space,' in a modern version.

The first Disneyland opened in Anaheim, California, in 1955. A second theme park, Disney World, opened in Florida in 1971. Their success encouraged the Disney Corporation to export the idea first to Tokyo in 1983 and then to Paris in 1992. From the beginning, Euro Disney ran into problems, first with French intellectuals who termed it a 'cultural Chernobyl', and then with customers who found it too restrictive and too expensive. In exporting its culture, the Disney board of directors forgot that Paris is not Anaheim. The weather is different and so are the local customs. Disney CEO Michael Eisner complained, 'Everybody arrives at 9:30, leaves at 5:30, and they want lunch at 12:30.' During its first three years of operation, Euro Disney lost 1.5 billion dollars. There followed a financial restructuring and a cultural accommodation. Prices were lowered; wine was served with meals. By the end of 1995, Euro Disney was showing a modest profit. But after September 11, 2001, that profit disappeared.

According to Pells, the Euro Disney story is an instructive example of how American mass culture has had to accommodate to local conditions. 'European lifestyles and attitudes were only partially altered by the presence of America's mass culture and merchandise,' he says. 'To a considerable extent, Europeans resisted the standardization and homogeneity allegedly inflicted on them by their American masters.' Thus the Americanization of Europe is primarily a symbolic event, made manifest by the high visibility of American brand names and trademarks:

> Drinking a Coke, eating a Big Mac, buying a pair of Nikes, watching a Steven Spielberg movie, or going to Euro Disney did not mean that one had become 'Americanized.' Sometimes a movie is just a movie and a cheeseburger is just a cheeseburger. Americans never supposed that driving a Toyota or a Volvo implied a surrender to Japanese or Swedish values. Neither did the purchase of American-made sneakers by a Danish adolescent or the decision of a Belgian family to have dinner at the nearby Pizza Hut signify an embrace of the American way of life.

But there is another point as well. European and Asian companies are increasingly active in the global culture industry as American newspapers and publishing houses, television stations and movie studios are acquired by multinational giants like Australia's Rupert Murdoch, Japan's Sony Corporation and the German Bertelsmann media concern. Those who worry about Americanization might take solace in the fact that many American icons are now foreign owned. William H. Marling points out, 'Burger King is owned by an English firm, Diageo/ 7-Eleven is owned by a Japanese company, Ito-Yakado Corporation. Even Mister Donut is Japanese.'

Pells concurs. 'In fact, the postwar relationship between the United States and Europe was never as unequal as European writers and political leaders claimed,' he says. 'It was marked more by a process of cross-fertilization, a reciprocal exchange of ideas about filmmaking and fashion, architecture and literary criticism, furnishings and food. In this sense, too, American culture was partly "Europeanized." In the end, there was no such thing as a completely Americanized society – not in Europe and not even, as it turned out, in the United States.'

Chronicles of the Cold War

As we neared the end of the Cold War, a deepened sense of skepticism surfaced in American writing. E. L. Doctorow viewed history as a process of recomposition 'in an endless process of dissatisfaction'. Thomas Pynchon's fiction was organized around the principle of entropy. Similarly, other American writers concerned themselves with the end of history as the century began to draw to a close. In the 1980s, American writing already sounded an apocalyptic note, echoing the urgency of Jonathan Schell's controversial bestseller, *The Fate of the Earth* (1982). Whether dealing with the fall of empire (Mailer's *Ancient Evenings*, 1983), the collapse of political systems (Bellow's *The Dean's December*, 1982) or the end of the world (Malamud's *God's Grace*, 1982), American writers projected the imagination of disaster.

John Updike

No writer captured this sense of decline better than the late John Updike in his remarkable tetralogy about Harry Angstrom, nicknamed 'Rabbit'. Angstrom is 'a man as ordinary as any American is ordinary' and thus he is an apt witness to the transformation of American life in the late twentieth century. He first appeared in *Rabbit, Run* (1959) as a fugitive from the Eisenhower years who tries unsuccessfully to escape from a dull marriage by pursuing a life of the senses. Rabbit fails to avoid the consequences of his actions but at the end of the novel he is still struggling, still running. Thereafter, Updike decided to return to his hero at the end of each subsequent decade as a means of synthesizing the times. Though his fiction is not political in the conventional sense, Updike's characters are immersed in the political life of their times. 'My fiction about the daily doings of ordinary people has more history in it than history books,' he observed, 'just as there is more breathing history in archeology than in a list of declared wars and changes of government.'

At the end of the turbulent 1960s, Updike resurrected Rabbit as an uneasy witness to 'Vietnam distress, race riots, marches, agitation of all sorts'. In *Rabbit Redux* (1971), Harry is abandoned by his wife and takes in a homeless teenage girl and a mysterious black activist, a gesture that ends in catastrophe. 'America and Harry suffered, marveled, listened, and endured. Not without cost, of course.' At the end of the novel, Rabbit returns to his wife and begins the long march to affluence as America moves from the crisis-rammed 1960s to the more 'amorphous' 1970s. *Rabbit is Rich* (1981) takes place a decade later at the time of the oil crisis and Harry, now a successful Toyota car dealer, watches with dismay as America is 'running out of gas'. He has made it into the middle class at the precise moment when inflation and depletion began to erode American self-confidence. Thus the title is ironic. 'The general sense of exhaustion, inflation, President Jimmy Carter fainting during one of his trots – all that seemed to add up to a national picture,' Updike noted. Ten years later, in *Rabbit at Rest* (1990), Harry, now semi-retired in Florida, experiences the simultaneous collapse of his health and the family business. The novel opens in late 1988, just after the presidential election and the crash of Pan American flight 103 in Lockerbie, Scotland. 'Everything falling apart, airplanes, bridges, eight years under Reagan of nobody minding the store, making money out of nothing, running up debt, trusting in God.'

The movement in the Rabbit tetralogy is apocalyptic. 'History,' Harry thinks in *Rabbit is Rich*. 'The more of it you have the more you have to live it. After a while there gets to be too much of it to memorize and maybe that's when empires start to decline.' By the end of the 1980s, an aura of closure was in the air, from Paul Kennedy's *The Rise and Fall of Great Powers* (1988) to Francis Fukuyama's 'The End of History?' Earlier, in *The Sense of an Ending* (1967), Frank Kermode noted that the apocalyptic imagination was 'endemic in what we call modernism'. But he suggested sensibly that apocalyptic thinking has been shared by all ages, that 'crisis is a way of thinking about one's moment, and not inherent in the moment itself.' Updike admitted that *Rabbit at Rest* ends with Hurricane Hugo, a symbol of natural disaster, and not the most important human event of 1989: the collapse of communism in Eastern Europe. Yet he was prescient enough to see that we had reached a historical turning point. Watching the imminent collapse of the communist regimes, Rabbit asks slyly: 'If there's no Cold War, what's the point of being an American?'

Philip Roth

Updike was not the only writer of his generation to confront the cultural contradictions of the Cold War. Whereas he crafted his 'Rabbit' tetralogy over three decades, his contemporary, Philip Roth, published his own retrospective Cold War trilogy in just over four years: *American Pastoral* (1997), *I Married a Communist* (1998) and *The Human Stain* (2000). Previously, Roth had created a fictive *alter ego* named Nathan Zuckerman who appeared in several books collected into one volume entitled *Zuckerman Bound* (1985). A decade later, in the Cold War trilogy, Nathan is transformed from protagonist to witness. 'I think of [them] as a thematic trilogy, dealing with the historical moments in postwar American life that have had the greatest impact on my generation,' Roth explains.

> Which moments? The first was the McCarthy era…Even more potent was the impact of the Vietnam War. That was the most shattering national event of my adulthood…The third moment was 1998, the year of the presidential impeachment. In 1998 you had the illusion that you were suddenly able to know this huge, unknowable country, to catch a glimpse of its moral core.[8]

The hero of *American Pastoral* is named Seymour 'Swede' Levov. The grandchild of Jewish immigrants, Seymour is called 'Swede' not only because he has blonde hair, but because he acts like a 'real' American. He marries Dawn Dwyer, a beauty contest winner who is Irish Catholic. Both Swede and Dawn believe in the American Dream and they begin to live it, joining the exodus from the city to the suburbs. They move to an idyllic village called Old Rimrock that has existed since the time of the American Revolution. Old Rimrock represents the 'real' America they seek. Swede works hard and become a successful businessman. Dawn becomes a farmer and raises prize cattle. Like Adam and Eve in the

Garden of Eden, they are living the American pastoral ideal. But as in the Bible there is a snake in the Garden.

The snake in the Garden is History and it comes in the form of their daughter, Meredith, who grows up in the turbulent 1960s and rejects the bourgeois world her parents have made. She begins as a rebellious child, grows into an adolescent revolutionary and ends up a teenage terrorist, deliberately blowing up the local post office and accidentally killing a local doctor. The year is 1968 when the Vietnam War has poisoned the mainstream of national life. In rejecting her parents' version of the American Dream, Meredith transports them 'out of the longed-for American pastoral and into everything that is its antithesis and its enemy, into the fury, the violence, and the desperation of the counterpastoral – into the indigenous American beserk'.

Roth's next novel, *I Married a Communist,* shares some themes with *American Pastoral.* Both tell stories of American upward mobility and Jewish assimilation in the postwar years – and their betrayal. His protagonist is Ira Ringold, a man of political passions and private appetites, a Jewish working-class stiff who accidentally becomes a radio star on the basis of his physical resemblance to Abraham Lincoln. He marries refined Eve Frame, a former actress in silent films who is now a star of stage and radio. The marriage is the fulfillment of Ira's dream of personal happiness but both partners have secrets: they are in flight from their past histories. To protect her career, Eve writes a memoir entitled *I Married a Communist,* which reveals her husband's left-wing politics. Just as *American Pastoral* portrayed the deceptions of the 1960s, so *I Married a Communist* depicts the self-deceptions of the 1950s.

Deception is everywhere – in the communist betrayal of American idealists and in the anticommunist betrayal of American institutions. 'To me it seems likely that more acts of personal betrayal were tellingly perpetrated in America in the decade after the war – say, between '46 and '56 – than in any other period in our history,' Ira's brother Murray explains. 'It was everywhere during those years, the accessible transgression, the *permissible* transgression that any American could commit. Not only does the pleasure of betrayal replace the prohibition, but you transgress without giving up your moral authority.' Thus the significance of Senator McCarthy was less political than cultural. Murray says. 'I think of the McCarthy era as inaugurating the postwar triumph of gossip as the unifying credo of the world's oldest democratic republic.' In this manner, McCarthyism transformed the national motto from 'In God We Trust' to 'In Gossip We Trust'.

Nathan ponders the relationship between private and public betrayals. Eve's betrayal of Ira is a private action that has unintended public consequences. In the novel, Eve is finally destroyed by the forces she sets in motion by writing her book. In the real world, McCarthy was censured by the Senate in 1954 and died the death of a pitiful drunk in 1957. His right-hand man, Roy Cohn, ruthless hunter of communists and homosexuals, died of AIDS. But there is not much solace to be derived from such reversals of fortune. 'It's all error,' Nathan tells Murray. '*There's* the heart of the world. Nobody finds his life. That *is* life.' Murray apparently agrees. 'Every action produces loss,' he says. 'It's the entropy of the system.' 'What system?' Nathan asks. Murray replies: 'The moral system.'

The last volume in Roth's trilogy, *The Human Stain,* begins in 1998 during the revelations of Bill Clinton's affair with Monica Lewinsky. 'It was the summer in America when the nausea returned, when the joking didn't stop, when the speculation and theorizing and the hyperbole didn't stop,' he writes. 'It was the summer when – for the billionth time – the jumble, the mayhem, the mess proved itself more subtle than this one's ideology and than one's morality. It was the summer when a president's penis was on everybody's mind, and life, in all its shameless impurity, once again confounded America.'

But *The Human Stain* is only peripherally about Bill Clinton's penis. Rather it depicts the genteel life and violent death of Coleman Silk, a retired professor of classics at a conservative New England college, who, at the age of 71, enters into an intense affair with an uneducated working-class woman half his age named Faunia Farley. Silk scandalizes the genteel college community with his affair just as he had done, a few years earlier, when he was accused of making a racial slur against two black students who had failed to attend his classes. We are in a period of cultural madness when the political correctness of the left and the moral correctness of the right demand no deviation from behavioral conformity.

But Coleman has a more scandalous secret than either his purported racism or his evident randiness. He was born into a genteel middle-class black family that believes in social responsibility, self-improvement and racial pride. But he wishes to live his life on his own terms; with light skin and green eyes, he decides to pass for white. To make his disguise even more impenetrable, he chooses to pass himself off as a Jew. 'As a heretofore unknown amalgam of the most unalike of America's historic undesirables, he now made sense.' Coleman's reinvention of himself is, of course, in the tradition of American heroes like Jay Gatsby. He is not a revolutionary who wants to overturn society but a rebel who refuses to accept his assigned place in the American social order. But is he merely another American dreamer or a figure in a Greek tragedy who learns 'how accidentally a fate is made … or how accidental it may all seem when it is inescapable'?

The question points to the title. For Nathan, the human stain is the fact of our mortality, symbolized by the diapers he must wear after a successful operation for prostate cancer. For Coleman, the human stain is the stigma of race that he tries to eradicate by simply declaring himself white. But for Faunia, the human stain is a sign of our human imperfection. She says, 'we leave a stain, we leave a trail, we leave our imprint. Impurity, cruelty, abuse, error, excrement, semen – there's no other way to be here. Nothing to do with disobedience. Nothing to do with grace or salvation or redemption. It's in everyone. Indwelling. Inherent. Defining.'

Roth's trilogy is a major imaginative achievement. All three novels deal with hysterical episodes in modern American history: the McCarthyism of the 1950s, the counterculture of the 1960s and the neopuritanism of the late 1990s. They all have protagonists whose faith in the American Dream is their final undoing. And, finally, they reveal Roth's rejection of utopian thinking. Like Faunia, he seems reconciled to 'the inevitably stained creatures that we are'. Roth's enemies are utopian perfectionists in the disguise of rabid anticommunists, frenzied cultural radicals, self-righteous feminists, puritanical politicians and guardians of political correctness.

The following year, Roth added a coda to his trilogy in the form of a novella, *The Dying Animal* (2001). Like *American Pastoral*, it describes the impact of the rambunctious 1960s on the nation's psyche. Like *I Married a Communist*, it treats the strain of rabid anticommunism, in this case within the Cuban-American community. Like *The Human Stain*, it depicts an affair between a young woman and a much older man. Moreover, the specter of 1998 hangs over the novella: the young woman, Consuela, with her 'pornographic underwear', is a Cuban echo of that Jewish siren, Monica Lewinsky. The novel ends with a climactic meeting on the eve of the new millennium between the dying girl and the aging narrator. In the coda to his chronicle of postwar American life, Roth sets the reality of 'the human stain' and 'the dying animal' against the eternal promise of 'the American Dream'.

In the new millennium, Roth continues to pursue his revisioning of the American past in a series of recent novels, including *The Plot Against America* (2005), *Exit Ghost* (2007) and *Indignation* (2008), demonstrating that, in his seventies, he can still brilliantly expand his fictional horizons.

Waiting for the millennium

The collapse of the Cold War brought us not to the end but to a new situation full of uncertainty. This new age of anxiety was reflected in books as different as Don DeLillo's *Mao II*, Norman Mailer's *Harlot's Ghost* and Jane Smiley's *A Thousand Acres*, all published in 1991. In DeLillo's prize-winning novel, the protagonist, Bill Gray, is a reclusive writer who attempts to escape from his writer's block by becoming involved in a Lebanese hostage drama that will place him on the stage of history. 'There's a curious knot that binds novelists and terrorists,' Bill explains.

> In the West we become famous effigies as our books lose the power to shape and influence ... Years ago I used to think it was possible for a novelist to alter the inner life of the culture. Now bomb-makers and gunmen have taken that territory. They make raids on human consciousness. What writers used to do before we were all incorporated.

Richard Powers

At the end of the century, several novelists attempted to sum up contemporary American experience from a consciously 'millennial' perspective. Among the most talented is Richard Powers, who has already published ten highly praised novels. Powers is fascinated by our ambivalent relationship with science and technology. His second novel, *Prisoner's Dilemma* (1988), dealt with game theory, his third, *The Gold Bug Variations* (1991), with molecular biology, and his fifth, *Galatea 2.2* (1995), with artificial intelligence. His most accessible novel, *Gain* (1998), deals with chemistry. Like the earlier *Operation Wandering Soul* (1993), it is also concerned with matters of health and sickness, life and death. *Gain* tells two stories: one describes the evolution of a soap manufacturing company and the other focuses on the progress of one woman's cancer. Two unlikely subjects of fiction, soap and cancer, are interwoven into a fascinating narrative about the relationship between individuals and corporate institutions, the pleasures and perils of progress, and the complexities of contemporary life.

In *Gain*, Powers invents a multinational corporation that has a long history. Clare Soap began 170 years ago when three brothers in Boston joined a recent Irish immigrant in manufacturing a domestic soap. By dint of hard work and ingenuity, they prospered and Clare Soap grew from cottage industry to local family business to nationwide company to, eventually, a global corporation selling everything from detergents to fast foods. The story of Clare Soap is, of course, the story of America and its economic rise from colonial status to world power. It is also the narrative of American capitalism from its beginnings in man-ufacturing necessities to its present state of marketing desires. The three Clare brothers represent different aspects of the American character: Samuel believes in *religion*, Resolve believes in *business*, and Benjamin believes in *science*. Soap is the perfect product for their obsession with Perfectibility and the American faith in Progress. 'Soap appealed to Samuel because it put the purchaser next to godli-ness. Resolve liked it because the purchaser used it up.' The marriage of God and Mammon described by Powers resembles the union that Max Weber identified between 'the Protestant ethic and the spirit of Capitalism'.

Think not only of Weber but also of Marx. In its first 100 years of existence, Clare Soap survives a dozen economic crises. 'Panics and depressions grew so frequent that bad times now outnumbered good. Advancement seemed a mat-ter of eternal contraction and collapse. Industry began to resemble those cities situated in an earthquake zone, constantly rebuilding from their own rubble.' Capitalism is a whirlwind and the society it creates is constantly reformed, in Joseph Schumpeter's famous phrase, by 'the gales of creative destruction'. Resolve Clare understands that capitalism is like a natural force: 'His genius lay in seeing that progress demanded the destruction of much that had once been considered wealth. Manufacturing, like the very project of civilization that it advanced, was a snaking, torrential Shenandoah [River] beyond anyone's abil-ity to dam.' Scientists like Benjamin Clare believe they can tame this force of nature. 'In his ultimate heaven – nothing so mundane as God's – all growth lived off some other's compost, like a gentleman farmer's estate, or a balanced aquarium.' But growth in business, as in nature, resists control. The dream of order is a chimera, especially in expansive market economies 'where money parted from value'. Powers cites the nineteenth-century social critic John Jay Chapman: 'Business has destroyed the very knowledge in us of all other natural forces except business.'

Here the two narratives of *Gain* coalesce. A young woman, Laura Bodey, lives in the Middle-American city of Lacewood, home of the agricultural division of the Clare Corporation. (Indeed, without Clare there would be no Lacewood.) Her family, with its two wisecracking children, is familiar from American tele-vision sitcoms. But this family is dysfunctional: Laura is divorced, her kids are disturbed, her errant ex-husband is depressed. Then she mysteriously contracts uterine cancer. As Clare Soap Company expands into a global corporation, so Laura's cancer metastasizes into a life-threatening disease. Suddenly it seems that just about *everyone* in Lacewood has contracted some form of cancer. Is the

Clare Corporation responsible? Many citizens think so and they start a class action suit against the corporation, much like recent suits against the American tobacco companies for inflicting cancer on smokers. But Laura is reluctant to join in because she recognizes how much of her life has been shaped by corporations like Clare. She thinks, 'It makes no difference whether this business gave her cancer. They have given her everything else. Taken her life and molded it in every way imaginable, plus six degrees beyond imagining. Changed her life so greatly that not even cancer can change it more than halfway back.' Laura has chosen a lifestyle that gave her everything: consumer choices, modern conveniences, managed health care – and perhaps even cancer. She confesses that if she were given the choice she would do it all over again.

Jonathan Franzen

At the end of the nineteenth century, William Dean Howells spoke of the romance of money as 'the poetry of the age'. Now, at the end of the millennium, Powers confronts the triumph of global capitalism and describes our romance with private consumption, perfect health, economic growth, world markets and technological solutions. Another young writer with similar concerns is Jonathan Franzen. While working on his third novel in 1996, he published a celebrated essay on the problem of writing fiction at the end of the millennium entitled 'Perchance to Dream'. He wrote, 'After the collapse of the Soviet Union, the American political economy had set about consolidating its gains, enlarging its markets, securing its profits, and demoralizing its few remaining critics.'

In *The Corrections* (2001), Franzen recreates middle-class family life in the American Moment. The Lamberts are a typical Middle-American family consisting of the father Alfred, his wife Enid, and their three grown-up children: the successful businessman Gary, the failed academic Chip and the talented cook Denise. But typical is perhaps the wrong word to describe them. Tyrannical Alfred, a retired railroad engineer, is a stern father, an undemonstrative husband and an old-fashioned moralist who reads Schopenhauer. Passive-aggressive Enid is a more devious demagogue who tyrannizes her family with love. All three children are in various stages of rebellion. Each wishes to 'correct' the mistakes of the parents and find an alternative to their dysfunctional family life. The crisis comes to a head when Alfred is diagnosed with Parkinson's disease and the onset of dementia. The narrative moves inexorably towards a climax at the final family Christmas gathering just before the end of the last millennium.

In Franzen's novel, 'corrections' come in many forms: old-fashioned discipline, newfangled psychotherapy, alternative lifestyles, biochemical solutions. But none of them seems to work. Gary tries to improve on the family model by becoming more successful than his father. But he ends up depressed and alcoholic. Chip rebels against traditional puritanism by joining the counterculture and writing an essay called 'Creative Adultery'. But he fails at all three endeavors and is forced to flee to, of all places, Lithuania. Denise becomes a master chef to escape her claustrophobic family, creating in the kitchen an alternative crew that prizes both '*privacy* and *autonomy*'. But she destroys her privacy and autonomy when she sleeps not only with her boss, but with her boss's wife.

The best scenes in *The Corrections* are the clinical descriptions of family turbulence. Here the dysfunctional family mirrors the larger dysfunctional society. America in the 1990s is a cultural wasteland dominated by dollars. But so is the rest of the world. When Chip goes to Vilnius to make his fortune in the post-communist world, he finds a nation of gangsters, whores and apparatchiks whose sole ambition is to become a second-rate Western country. 'Chip was struck by the broad similarities between black-market Lithuania and free-market America.'

The only difference he can find is that while the American elite offers bread and circuses, the new Lithuanian oligarchy uses guns and intimidation. Franzen's jaundiced view of the wages of globalization was inadvertently prophetic: *The Corrections* was published in 2001, the week before the destruction of the World Trade Center.

Don DeLillo

In its old-fashioned manner of storytelling, *The Corrections* defies postmodern literary prescription and satirizes posthumanist social theory. In its attempt to bridge the gap 'between private experience and public context' it is reminiscent of Don DeLillo's epic novel, *Underworld* (1992). In *Underworld,* someone tells the following story about the Cold War: 'They did a bomb test in the nineteen-fifties in which a hundred pigs were dressed in custom-made GI field jackets and positioned at well-spaced intervals from the blast site … Then they exploded the device. Then they examined the uniforms on the barbecued pigs to evaluate the thermal qualities of the material. Because that was the point of the test.' 'Picture it,' he says. 'A breed of large fat hog with drooping ears. Wearing khaki uniforms with zippers, seams, everything, and with drawstrings drawn because that's how the regulation reads. And a voice on the loudspeaker's going, Ten, nine, eight, seven.' Then he asks: 'Is this when history turned to fiction?'

In *Underworld,* history is a form of fiction where the Cold War is not only a geopolitical event but a state of mind as well. Another character says of the Cold War, 'It was stable, it was focused, it was a tangible thing. It was greatness, danger, terror, all those things. And it held us together, the Soviets and us. Maybe it held the world together.' But with the collapse of the Soviet empire we are lost in a defamiliarized world. 'Many things that were anchored to the balance of power and the balance of terror seem to be undone, unstuck. Things have no limits now.' *Underworld* is an imaginative history of our free fall through four decades of the Cold War into the current epoch of drift.

In *Underworld,* DeLillo writes the secret history of the Cold War. After the prologue, the novel moves backwards in time, from 1992 to 1951. The epilogue returns us to the present. He works on a grand scale, covering four decades and several continents. Public figures like FBI director J. Edgar Hoover and standup comedian Lenny Bruce combine with a large cast of fictional characters including Nick Shay, a young juvenile delinquent who becomes an expert in 'waste management' and his brother Matt, a child chess prodigy who becomes a scientist working on nuclear weapons. DeLillo shows us how world events impinge upon private lives. He begins with a memorable baseball game in New York that occurs on the same day in 1951 that the Soviets explode a nuclear device in Kazakhstan. We watch children going through atomic air-raid drills in the 1950s and New Yorkers coping with power blackouts and garbage strikes later on. We see the 1962 Cuban missile crisis refracted through the brilliant comic monologues of Lenny Bruce. We witness the domestic turmoil over Vietnam as demonstrators invade Truman Capote's famous celebrity party at the Plaza Hotel in 1967.

The memorable epilogue 'Das Kapital' takes place in present-day Kazakhstan where Nick watches Russian scientists trying to cleanse the contaminated countryside with the aid of nuclear weapons. Weapons and waste: two sides of the same coin. He records this conversation:

> I tell Viktor there is a curious connection between weapons and waste. I don't know exactly what... He says maybe one is the mystical twin of the other. He likes the idea. He says waste is the devil twin. Because waste is the secret history, the underhistory, the way archeologists dig out the history of early cultures, every sort of bone heap and broken tool, literally from under the ground.

All those decades, he says, when we thought about weapons all the time and never thought about the dark multiplying byproduct.

'And in this case,' I say. 'In our case, in our age. What we excrete comes back to consume us.'

DeLillo is an archeologist digging up the buried nightmares of the Cold War, recycling the waste of 40 years of futile conflict. Here every event, every character has its devil twin and the title *Underworld* takes on multiple meanings: dream world, criminal world, counterculture, garbage dump, hell. In this underworld nothing is ever lost, the repressed returns to take its revenge. 'All the banned words, the secrets kept in white-washed vaults, the half-forgotten plots -they're all out here now, seeping invisibly into the land and air, into the marrowed folds of the bone.' There are no winners, only losers in this Cold War. The epilogue ends where the prologue began: in New York and Kazakhstan. Both are much poorer now: Russia symbolized by a hospital full of sick children, pathetic mutants deformed by nuclear radiation; America symbolized by an urban slum of the homeless, orphaned and dispossessed, where children are casually raped and murdered. The lesson of the Cold War, he tells us in the last pages, is: 'Everything is connected in the end.'

NOTES

1. Studs Terkel, *Hope Dies Last*, New York: New Press, 2003, p. 90.
2. Joseph E. Stiglitz, *Globalization and its Discontents*, New York: Norton, 2002, p. ix.
3. Ibid., p. 5.
4. Russell Duncan and Joseph Goddard, *Contemporary America*, Basingstoke and New York: Palgrave Macmillan, 2003, p. 223.

5. For another insightful view of the Jessica Lynch story, see Susan Faludi, *The Terror Dream*, New York: Metropolitan Books, 2007, pp. 165–95.
6. Reinhold Wagnleitner, *Coca-Colonization and the Cold War,* Chapel Hill, NC: University of North Carolina Press, 1994.
7. Quoted in Richard Pells, *Not Like Us,* New York: Basic, 1997, p. 274.
8. Charles McGrath, 'Zuckerman's Alter Brain', *New York Times* (May 7, 2000), p. 8.

RECOMMENDED READING

Benjamin R. Barber, *Jihad vs. McWorld,* New York: Random House, 1995.

Thomas L. Friedman, *The Lexus and the Olive Tree*, New York: Farrar, Straus & Giroux, 1999.

Francis Fukuyama, *The End of History and the Last Man,* New York: Free Press, 1992.

Neal Gabler, *Life: The Movie,* New York: Vintage, 2000.

Chris Hedges, *Empire of Illusion.* New York: Nation Books, 2009.

Samuel P. Huntington, *The Clash of Civilizations and the Remaking of World Order*, New York: Simon & Schuster, 1996.

Haynes Johnson, *The Best of Times*, New York: Harcourt, 2001.

Rob Kroes, *If You've Seen One You've Seen the Mall,* Urbana, IL: University of Illinois Press, 1996.

Paul Krugman, *The Great Unraveling*, New York: Norton, 2004.

William Marling, *How 'American' Is Globalization?* Baltimore: Johns Hopkins University Press, 2006.

Richard Pells, *Not Like Us,* New York: Basic, 1997.

Robert Putnam, *Bowling Alone,* New York: Simon & Schuster, 2000.

Sean Wilentz, *The Age of Reagan*, New York: HarperCollins, 2008.

PART VI
America after
September 11, 2001

9/11

Year	Politics	Culture
2000	• Al Qaeda attacks USS *Cole* • Governor Bush defeats Vice-President Gore in presidential election	• Michael Chabon, *The Amazing Adventures of Kavalier and Clay* • E. L. Doctorow, *City of God* • Philip Roth, *The Human Stain*
2001	• Congress passes Bush's tax cuts and education reform • 9/11 • US invasion of Afghanistan overthrows Taliban regime	• Jonathan Franzen, *The Corrections* • Richard Russo, *Empire Falls* • Amy Tan, *The Bonesetter's Daughter* • Mel Brooks, *The Producers* (play)
2002	• Bush seeks UN support to overthrow Iraq's Saddam Hussein regime • Republicans marginally increase their majorities in Congress	• Stephen A. Carter, *The Emperor of Ocean Park* • Ha Jin, *The Crazed* • Jeffrey Eugenides, *Middlesex* • Suzan Lori-Parks, *Topdog/Underdog*
2003	• Security Council rejects new US resolution on Iraq • Invasion of Iraq, overthrow of Saddam Hussein • Occupation faces guerrilla resistance in Iraq	• T. C. Boyle, *Drop City* • Don DeLillo, *Cosmopolis* • Richard Powers, *The Time of Our Singing* • Jonathan Lethem, *The Fortress of Solitude* • Robert Lowell, *Collected Poems* • David Marannis, *They Marched into Sunlight*
2004	• Kerry wins Democratic nomination for presidency • Guerilla resistance in Iraq intensifies • Bush is reelected by a clear margin • Republicans increase their majorities in Congress	• Michael Moore, *Fahrenheit 9/11* • Toni Morrison, *Love* • Anne Tyler, *The Amateur Marriage: A Novel* • James Mann, *Rise of the Vulcans*
2005	• Elections and referendum on constitution in Iraq amidst the continuing Sunni insurgency • Hurricane Katrina results in the flooding of New Orleans	• E. I. Doctorow, *The March* • Cormac McCarthy, *No Country for Old Men* • Philip Roth, *The Plot Against America* • Joan Didion, *The Year of Magical Thinking* • August Wilson, *Radio Golf* • Ang Lee, *Brokeback Mountain*
2006	• Major escalation of sectarian violence in Iraq • Democrats gain control of both chambers of Congress • Bush replaces Secretary of Defense Donald Rumsfeld with Robert Gates	• Cormac McCarthy, *The Road* • Richard Powers, *The Echo Maker* • Thomas Pynchon, *Against the Day* • Thomas E. Ricks, *Fiasco* • Al Gore, *In Inconvenient Truth* • Barack Obama, *The Audacity of Hope*
2007	• Bush adopts new counterinsurgency strategy and troop surge in Iraq • Financial crisis begins	• Michael Chabon, *The Yiddish Policeman's Union* • Don DeLillo, *Falling Man* • Junot Diaz, *The Brief Wondrous World of Oscar Wao* • Robert Hass, *Time and Materials: Poems 1997–2005* • Coen Brothers, *No Country for Old Men* (film)
2008	• Violence de-escalates drastically in Iraq • Barack Obama defeats Hillary Clinton in Democratic primaries and caucuses • John McCain wins Republican nomination and chooses Sarah Palin as running mate • Financial crisis reaches panic levels and threatens global economic collapse • Massive cash injection by the Bush administration and the Federal Reserve to save the banking system • Obama defeats McCain in presidential race	• Peter Matthiassen, *Shadow Country* • Sean Wilentz, *The Age of Reagan* • Danny Boyle, *Slumdog Millionaire*, is the first Bollywood film to win the Oscar
2009	• Inauguration of Obama, first African American president • Major economic stimulus package passes Congress • Grassroots anti-big government Tea Party movement emerges • Health care reform is stalled in Congress	• Barbara Kingslover, *The Lawna* • Joshua Ferris, *The Unnamed* • Kathryn Bigelow, *The Hurt Locker*, wins Oscars for Best film, Best Director • James Cameron, *Avatar*, biggest movie money-earner of all time
2010	• Republican Scott Brown wins Ted Kennedy's Senate seat in liberal Massachusetts • Obama passes health care reform in Congress • Giant oil spill in Gulf of Mexico	• Don DeLillo, *Point Omega* • Ralph Ellison, *Three Days Before the Shooting* • Jonathan Franzen, *Freedom*

CHAPTER 11

American Politics in the Twenty-First Century

George W. Bush rose to the presidency with the most controversial presidential election in American history. In spite of the slimness of his victory, Bush pursued an ambitious agenda in continuation of the Reagan Revolution. Then a new and incalculable factor impinged on American politics. The 9/11 attacks displaced all else at the top of the American political agenda and abruptly ushered in a new era of insecurity. Bush responded by swiftly overthrowing the Taliban in Afghanistan, with almost universal support from the international community. But then he squandered international goodwill towards the United States by invading Iraq on weak grounds. The prolonged insurgency in Iraq after the overthrow of Saddam Hussein and the revival of Taliban power in much of rural Afghanistan entangled the United States in two guerrilla wars for the rest of the decade, stretching the US military thin and sapping American self-confidence. The American people punished the Republicans for Bush's increasingly unpopular Iraq war by electing Democratic majorities in both chambers of Congress in the midterm elections of 2006, opening the way for Obama's historic victory in 2008. The election of an African American to the presidency suggested that the American people were ready for change in politics and government. The rise of Obama was at first thought likely, even by respectable conservative commentators, to lead to a realignment of the American party system and result in a prolonged Democratic primacy. Obama inherited ongoing wars in Iraq and Afghanistan and the worst financial crisis since the Great Depression, which broke out at the end of Bush's presidency. Additionally Obama promoted his own reform agenda on health care and climate change. Even though he performed creditably well on most of these fronts, by the end of his first year the high expectations that greeted his accession to the presidency had been somewhat lowered.

The rise of George W. Bush

If the Clinton presidency showed structural similarities to the Eisenhower presidency, in the sense that a popular 'anti-regime' president was forced to adjust to the ruling coalition of the opposite party in Congress, the elections of 2000 resembled those of 1960. In both cases the vice-president was nominated by his party in the hope that he would win the election as the successor of a popular president against the forces of the ruling coalition. The result of the presidential election was in both cases extremely narrow but in the end both vice-presidents,

Richard Nixon and Al Gore, lost to the candidate of the ruling coalition, John F. Kennedy and George W. Bush.

Bush's rise to the presidency resulted from the failures of Newt Gingrich's congressional revolution in 1995–8. The budget crisis and the shutting down of much of the federal government in 1995 portrayed the Republicans as heartless enemies of the welfare state. The bid to impeach Clinton in 1998 depicted them as fanatical Puritans who sought to purge the president for his personal failings, not his policies. To counter that legacy, Bush presented himself as a different kind of Republican who stood for 'compassionate conservatism'. His objective was to raise the standard of tax-cutting Reaganism, yet to avoid the image of social heartlessness and Puritanical fanaticism that marked the Gingrich period. Nonetheless, he relied heavily on the Christian Right to defeat Senator John McCain in the primaries. On the Democratic side, the nomination went to Vice-President Al Gore, who had two major advantages over Bush in the general election. First, he could reap the political benefits of the Clinton boom of the 1990s, the longest in American history, as well as the decline in crime. Second, he had the chance to occupy the middle ground, given Bush's identification with the Christian Right. But Gore chose to move to the left, abandoning the centrist orientation of the 'New Democrats' that Clinton had followed. Gore's leftward movement gave Bush the opportunity to move into the middle ground by emphasizing that he would use the large federal budget surplus that the boom produced to pursue Reaganite tax cuts. In this manner, Bush largely neutralized the advantages that the 1990s boom conferred on Gore.

The 2000 election results were among the most even in American history. The Republicans maintained a very narrow lead in the House and kept control over the Senate only by Vice-President Cheney's tie-breaking vote. (The Senate was evenly divided; had Gore won the presidential election, his running mate, Senator Joe Lieberman, would have left the Senate and the Republicans would have had a 51 to 49 seat majority.) In the presidential election Gore got about half a million more votes than Bush, yet narrowly lost in the Electoral College. But the final outcome remained uncertain for over one month after the vote because Gore asked for recounts of the Florida vote, in which on the first mechanical count Bush had a tiny lead of some 500 votes. The two candidates were so evenly matched in the Electoral College that Florida would determine the overall outcome.

For 36 days the American people witnessed the spectacle of administrative and legal maneuvers by the Gore and Bush camps over whether new Florida vote counts should take place or not. When a second mechanical vote count in Florida confirmed Bush as the winner, Gore pushed for recounts by hand in certain counties where the mechanical count was alleged to be flawed. In the subsequent maneuvers, several institutions made decisions that appeared to be partisan. Florida's Secretary of State Katherine Harris (an aide of Florida's Republican Governor Jeb Bush, George W.'s brother) interpreted Florida's contradictory legislation in a manner that favored Bush in rejecting recounts by hand. Florida's Supreme Court, where six out of the seven justices were appointed by Democratic governors, interpreted the same contradictory legislation in a manner that favored Gore in ordering recounts by hand. The US Supreme Court, a majority of whose members were appointed by Republican presidents, interpreted federal legislation and the Constitution in a way that favored Bush and determined the election in his favor. Though these decisions were harshly criticized, their legitimacy was not questioned; evidently, the American people would tolerate what appeared to be partisan decisions by nonpartisan institutions so long as they demonstrated due deference to the American tradition of the rule of law.

The geography of the 2000 elections showed a clear cleavage between the two parties. Bush won every state in the South – Florida marginally, of course – and the entire Western hinterland except New Mexico. Gore won the entire Northeast except New Hampshire, and the three West Coast states. The two candidates split the Midwest. This geographical division demonstrated the significance of the cultural cleavage in contemporary American politics: Bush was strong mainly in the parts of America in which the evangelical and fundamentalist Protestants are strong demographically.

The beginning of Bush's presidency coincided with the end of the 1990s boom. As the American economy slid into a recession, in the spring of 2001 Bush was able to pass in Congress massive tax cuts totaling $1.3 trillion over the ten-year period 2001–11. Bush thus picked up Reagan's mantle and continued his politics, unlike his father who had raised taxes and alienated his conservative base. The combination of tax cuts and recession-induced revenue declines turned the large federal surpluses of the later 1990s into large deficits by 2002. Deficit spending is appropriate in a recession in terms of short-term Keynesian demand stimulus. But Bush also believed in the long-term supply-side effects of lower taxes in terms of fueling higher growth trends. Much like Reagan, he seemed prepared to live with large federal deficits as the price for lower taxes, partly in order to constrict liberal pressures for federal spending increases.

Immediately after their tax cut victory, the Republicans suffered a major setback when one of their senators defected and gave control of the Senate to the Democrats – by a 51–49 margin – for the first time since 1993–4. This unexpected debacle demonstrated the fragility of the ruling Republican hold on power in the federal government. In spite of the rightward shift in American politics since 1968 and especially 1980, the Republicans before 2003 held the White House, the House and the Senate simultaneously for no more than a few months in early 2001. Only with the midterm elections of 2002 did their hold on all three elective bases of federal power become firmer.

9/11

The political 1990s can be said to have lasted from the dissolution of the Soviet Union on December 31, 1991 until September 11, 2001. It was a period in which the advanced world enjoyed unparalleled prosperity under conditions of high security. Foreign policy was of low priority for most Americans; it occupied only half a debate from the three Bush-Gore debates of the 2000 elections. Then the prevalent sense of security was abruptly shattered and a new era of insecurity began. On the morning of September 11, 2001, 19 terrorists boarded and hijacked four airplanes that took off from East Coast airports. At 8.46 am the first plane hit one of the World Trade Center's Twin Towers in New York.

The second tower was hit at 9.03 am and the Pentagon at 9.37 am. The fourth plane was brought down by its passengers, who were alerted by relatives via cell phones about the intentions of the hijackers.

With the suicide attacks of 9/11, a nonstate actor crashed into the world of sovereign states and became the most serious actual threat to the security of the advanced world. This new threat has been likened to piracy or even to the barbarian tribes that invaded civilized states and empires in premodern times. These comparisons point to an important aspect of the new challenge, namely that it constitutes a failure of the Westphalian system of sovereign states, which are supposed to monopolize the use of force and to subjugate all nonstate actors that possess means of violence.

The spread of the European system of sovereign states across the globe in the past two centuries constitutes a central development in the modern political organization of mankind. The sovereign state is the main guarantor of stability and security in contemporary human societies. Internal sovereignty refers to the ability of the state to secure its citizens from internal nonstate threats, while the evolution of the international society of sovereign states has fostered a host of institutions and practices that support the international sovereignty of states against external threats. The system has not provided absolute security, since there are still wars between and within states as well as lesser security threats, for example from organized crime. Moreover, in some parts of the world sovereign states have collapsed, producing conditions of anarchy that became breeding grounds for nonstate threats. Nonetheless, the system appeared to have secured the advanced world and much of the developing world from major security threats.

The 9/11 attacks were a shock because a nonstate actor succeeded in striking at the center of the most powerful nation in the world. This was the worst external attack inflicted on the United States since the British occupied Washington and burned the Capitol and the White House in the War of 1812. One would have to go back several centuries to find a similar example of a great power being struck at its center by an external nonstate actor.

Several factors magnified the threat-perceptions in the advanced world emanating from 9/11. Terrorists prepared to commit suicide attacks cannot be deterred by ordinary means. From the American point of view, it proved easier to deter the mighty Soviet Union than Al Qaeda. Fears about weapons of mass destruction (WMD) falling into the hands of ruthless terrorists magnified the threat-perceptions powerfully. It should be stressed that such fears preceded 9/11.

The origins of this new terrorist threat are to be found in the Islamic resistance to the Soviet invasion of Afghanistan in the 1980s, in which more than 35,000 non-Afghani volunteers took part. In the minds of these Islamist warriors, the collapse of the Soviet Union was caused by their *jihad*. This skewed perception gave Osama bin Laden and his comrades the confidence of men who believed that they had overthrown a superpower. In one of his last interviews to a Western journalist in the later 1990s, bin Laden boasted that his new *jihad* would bring about the disintegration of the United States into smaller successor states. This statement only makes sense in the light of his belief that he had already defeated and dismembered the other superpower of the Cold War.

After Afghanistan, an 'Islamist international' organized by Al Qaeda became involved in a vast and heterogeneous field of operations. According to the Middle East scholar Bernard Lewis, radical Islamists consider it unnatural and blasphemous for Muslims to be ruled by non-Muslims. Consequently they supported unrest among Muslim minorities in Eritrea, Bosnia, Chechnya, Kashmir, the Philippines, Central Asia and China. Thus they have picked fights with the United States, Russia, China and India simultaneously.

Another tenet of Al Qaeda's ideology is that foreigners must be driven out of the house of Islam. In his first post-9/11 message, Osama bin Laden referred to the humiliations of the past 80 years, since the dissolution of the Ottoman Empire and the colonization of most of the Middle East. The European colonizers have long gone, but their rule has been replaced by American domination of the region. What particularly offended the radical Islamists was the American military presence in Saudi Arabia, the holy land of Mecca and Medina. Furthermore, Israel is seen as a foreign body in the house of Islam that must be expelled from the region like the Crusader states in the Middle Ages.

Ultimately, the main target of Al Qaeda's operations is not non-Muslims, but the states in the Muslim world that have abandoned traditional Muslim values and seek to modernize, or westernize, their societies. For the Islamic fundamentalists, all the ills of the Muslim world have been caused by abandonment of 'authentic' Islam. Their aim is to mobilize and radicalize the Muslim peoples, in order to overthrow their governments and install theocracies. The rule of the Taliban, in which women were barred from work and school and were stoned to death for uncovering as little as an elbow in public, provides an idea of their vision of the future of Islam. In their struggle against various 'infidel' governments, they have clashed with the regimes of Algeria, Egypt, Saudi Arabia and the smaller Persian Gulf states, Sudan, Nigeria, Indonesia and Morocco, among others.

The international response: The consensus phase

International Islamist terrorism is a form of unconventional warfare, an 'asymmetric' campaign that avoids confronting enemies by conventional means in which they enjoy overwhelming superiority. One factor that made asymmetric attacks before 9/11 successful was an asymmetry in the interests at stake. The mighty United States was induced to withdraw from Lebanon in early 1984 after a suicide attack on the Marine barracks in October 1983 killed 241 Marines. It withdrew from Somalia in 1993 after an engagement that caused the death of 18 American troops in Mogadishu. These were effective asymmetric attacks because the American interests in Lebanon and Somalia were not important enough to merit even such relatively limited casualties. Al Qaeda even got away with its attacks against the American Embassies in Kenya and Tanzania, as well as against the *USS Cole,* with only limited American retaliation. In spite of these attacks, the United States continued in effect to tolerate *de facto* the Taliban regime, which openly harbored Al Qaeda. If the Islamist terrorists had continued to strike at minor American targets in order to attain limited objectives of marginal interest to the United States, they might have induced limited American retreats in the manner of Lebanon and Somalia. The key to the success of such an asymmetric strategy is that it aims to bring about a Mogadishu, not a Pearl Harbor, in the words of the strategic analyst Kenneth McKenzie.

But the objectives of Al Qaeda were hardly limited. Its 9/11 attacks indicated a willingness to strike at the most vital American interests in the heart of the United States. This was indeed a Pearl Harbor, not a Mogadishu. Consequently, it radically altered the American cost-benefit calculations in the struggle against international Islamist terrorism. Costs that were previously unthinkable for all practical purposes, such as the launching of American invasions in Central Asia and the Middle East, came now to be seen as a reasonable price for securing the United States from renewed attacks on the scale of 9/11 or worse.

Even though the new threat came from a nonstate actor, the system of sovereign states was central to the American counterterrorist strategy. The world is divided into sovereign states, which by definition means that Al Qaeda's network operates within state boundaries. If states were able and willing to exercise their internal sovereignty, they should be able to destroy any group that defied their sovereign monopoly on the use of force. When President Bush declared, shortly after 9/11, that 'you are either with us or against us', he was in effect issuing a stern warning to the sovereign states that they should do their best to hunt down the terrorists in their domains. States that actively supported, harbored, tolerated, or merely failed actively to pursue, terrorist elements in their domains would henceforth be held accountable by the United States and forced to mend their ways.

American policy focused first on Afghanistan, Osama bin Laden's base since the mid-1990s, when he helped the Taliban rise to power. The Taliban regime was internationally isolated, having diplomatic relations with only three states: Pakistan, Saudi Arabia and the United Arab Emirates. Moreover, it did not exercise full internal sovereignty since it was challenged in parts of the country by the Northern Alliance, which was supported by Russia and Iran. The Taliban openly aligned themselves with Al Qaeda, even after 9/11, presumably being unable to fathom the international consequences of their stance.

The swiftness and decisiveness of the American military intervention in Afghanistan in the fall of 2001 resulted from Russia's crucial support, which secured for the American armed forces the use of former Soviet bases in Central Asia as well as access to the Northern Alliance. It also depended on the collaboration of Pakistan, which previously had been the Taliban's most significant external supporter, but which turned against them after 9/11. NATO provided moral and political support by activating for the first time ever its Article 5 common defense clause, under which all its members are bound to assist any member that has been attacked.

The swift overthrow of the Taliban resulted from a combination of strategically decisive factors. Prior to the military campaign, the CIA weakened the Taliban's hold over Afghanistan's provinces by injecting large amounts of cash that detached Afghani tribes from the Taliban regime. American Special Forces infiltrated Afghanistan with Russian assistance, in order to collaborate with the Northern Alliance. As a result, the American air campaign was able to provide close tactical support for the Northern Alliance's ground offensives. This collaboration was militarily decisive because the Northern Alliance offensives forced the Taliban army to concentrate its troops at the fronts, thereby providing easy targets for the American air forces. In addition, the air campaign devastated regime targets throughout Afghanistan. It took just a few weeks of this kind of combined military pressure on the ground and from the air to destroy the Taliban regime, forcing the remnants of its leadership and its Al Qaeda associates to flee to the mountains at Afghanistan's borders with Pakistan.

The fall of the Taliban deprived Al Qaeda of a safe base for the operation of its training camps. Osama bin Laden and his leadership group disappeared into the mountainous regions that straddle the Afghanistan-Pakistan borders, unable to maintain tight operational control over Al Qaeda's worldwide affiliates. Across the globe, states hunted down Al Qaeda operatives and financial supporters dealing the terrorist organization major blows. In the next few years Al Qaeda was transformed into a loose confederation, with its central leadership providing political inspiration and general guidance, while the local affiliates in various parts of the world acquired operational autonomy.

Though much weakened, Al Qaeda and its affiliates have remained a major terrorist threat. Major terrorist strikes took place after 9/11 in Bali, Riyadh, Casablanca, Moscow, Istanbul, Madrid, London and various Indian targets. Many more terrorist plots were neutralized at the planning stage by the authorities in the United States and Europe. Some terrorist plots failed by sheer luck, as with the airplane bombing attempt in the United States on Christmas Day, 2009. Hunting down the remnants of the international Islamist terrorist networks before they strike major targets again, and above all before they get their hands on weapons of mass destruction, is one of the top security priorities of most states worldwide.

Bush's home front

9/11 inevitably had an enormous impact on American domestic politics. Bush was transformed from a tax-cutter to a national security president (though he continued to cut taxes). For some 30 weeks after 9/11 ordinary politics were in suspension, with the president towering above all other politicians as the national leader around whom an insecure nation rallied. But Bush squandered his authority as a leader above partisan politics by using his popularity to campaign actively in the 2002 midterm elections, in which the Republicans regained control of the Senate and marginally increased their small majority in the House. This partisanship helped revive the intense polarization in American politics that marked the 1990s.

One consequence of 9/11 was that the pendulum between security and civil liberties swung violently towards the security end, much as it had with the 1920 Palmer raids and the internal security mechanisms during the Red Scare in the later 1940s. Shortly after 9/11, Congress passed Bush's draconian Patriot Act, which allowed the government to collect all kinds of private information about citizens, including records from libraries, universities, telephone operators and medical facilities, without needing to demonstrate a connection with terrorism. Thousands of immigrants were detained, often for lengthy periods, and most of them were charged with nothing more than visa violations. The Bush administration maintained that such violations of civil liberties were justified in the war against terrorism; the government could not run the risk of allowing deadly terrorists to plot their next attack unmolested by the authorities because of the overly generous rights granted to suspects under American law. But as 9/11 receded into memory, the pendulum gradually began to swing again in the direction of affirming and protecting civil liberties. Indeed, as early as 2003 and 2004 the courts began to strike down parts of the Bush administration's draconian security measures.

One novelty with international ramifications was the creation of an extra-legal zone in the American base at Guantanamo, Cuba, where hundreds of prisoners from dozens of countries were held without either the POW rights accorded by international law or civil rights guaranteed by American domestic law. When the British courts confronted the matter of British citizens held in Guantanamo, the Master of the Rolls Lord Phillips declared: 'We find surprising the proposition that the writ of the United States courts does not run in respect of individuals held by the US government on territory that the United States holds...under a long-term treaty.' But the Bush administration was not prepared to release Guantanamo prisoners and run the risk of unleashing future terrorists against the United States. Thus an unsatisfactory arrangement that deprived these prisoners of legal rights remained in place well into Obama's presidency.

After 9/11 Bush drastically increased defense spending, to the point where the United States accounted for almost half of all military expenditures on the planet. On the other hand, defense spending remained less than four percent of GDP, which was much lower than in the 1980s. The creation of the Homeland Security Department and related domestic security spending also resulted in new burdens on the federal budget. Yet Bush did not issue a 'blood and tears' call for sacrifices from American taxpayers. On the contrary, he continued to cut taxes after 9/11. He also supported major new domestic spending programs especially on education and Medicare. As a Reaganite, Bush believed in the supply-side pro-growth consequences of lower taxes over the longer term, but he seemed not to share Reagan's distrust of big government.

Consensus fractured: The Iraq war

In 2002 the Bush administration adopted the controversial doctrine of preemptive strikes in the war against terrorism. The new doctrine was a proactive policy that sought to neutralize terrorist threats before they became imminent, since another terrorist attack on the scale of September 11 might remain undetected by American intelligence, if allowed to mature. In the context of the new doctrine, the Bush administration moved toward the American nationalist tradition of disdaining multilateral constrictions and being willing to use force unilaterally if necessary for defending vital national interests. The most urgent aspect of the preemptive strikes doctrine was the objective of keeping weapons of mass destruction out of the hands of Islamist terrorists. The first application of the doctrine was the overthrow of Saddam Hussein in Iraq. The Bush administration launched this audacious and controversial attack, which became the defining feature of the Bush presidency, for a number of reasons.

First, the Bush administration seems genuinely to have believed that Saddam Hussein had weapons of mass destruction and that he might pass them on to Islamist terrorists, even though he did not have ideological links to Al Qaeda. Moreover, by overthrowing Saddam, Bush sought to deter other anti-American regimes from developing WMD, which might then fall into terrorist hands. By early 2003 the Bush administration became impatient with the slow pace of the UN monitoring of Iraq's alleged WMD. In February, Secretary of State Colin Powell made the case for military intervention in the UN Security Council when he detailed extensive intelligence on Iraq's possession of WMD. Unfortunately, US intelligence turned out to be flawed; no WMD surfaced after Iraq was occupied. Thus Bush's formal grounds for invasion were revealed as false.

Second, by invading and occupying a major Arab state in the heart of the Middle East, the Bush administration sought to force changes in the policies of other states in the region. Under the shock of the American attack in Iraq, Saudi Arabia was to be induced to eliminate Al Qaeda's Saudi funding sources and to move against radical Saudi imams and religious foundations espousing a particularly virulent antimodern and xenophobic Wahhabi version of Islam. Iran was to be induced to end its nuclear program and to stop supporting terrorism. Syria was to be induced to desist supporting Palestinian groups that launched suicide bombers against Israel. The Palestinians were to be induced to move towards peace with Israel. This tough reasoning in favor of the invasion drew from the American nationalist tradition.

Third, according to an ideological reasoning put forth not only by the neo-conservatives in the Bush administration but also by some liberal commentators like Thomas Friedman and Christopher Hitchens, the overthrow of Saddam Hussein's Ba'athist totalitarian dictatorship and its replacement by a democracy would open the way for the spread of democratic ideas across the Middle East. The war in Iraq was designed as the first step in a long-term effort to push the Middle East towards modernization.

Fourth, Iraq possesses massive oil resources relatively near the surface, that is, extractable at low cost. It is the only country that could rival Saudi Arabia's leading position in the oil market. Given the role of Saudi factors in manning and financing Al Qaeda, the Bush administration had reason to back another horse to secure oil supplies over the long run.

The implementation of Bush's Iraq policy met with difficulties from the start. The United States could not persuade the UN Security Council to endorse an attack on Saddam Hussein, with France and Germany leading the diplomatic resistance. Europe's governments were deeply divided and almost half the members of NATO refused to follow America when Bush launched his attack without a Security Council endorsement. The conventional operations in March and April 2003 overthrew Saddam Hussein's regime in three weeks. This was the war that the Bush administration had been prepared for. But it had done inadequate planning for the post-Saddam occupation. It had reduced the ground forces for the operation from 500,000 in the original plan to 145,000, which was adequate to overthrow Saddam Hussein but inadequate for the subsequent occupation.

For several weeks after Saddam's fall, every kind of public facility in Iraq was looted in an orgy of disorder. The American troops stood passively at the sidelines. It took weeks before the American commanders discovered that under international law the military force that overthrows a regime is legally responsible for maintaining law and order. By the time the American forces moved against the lootings, they were no longer seen as the invincible force that had shocked and awed Iraqis with its swift victory over Saddam Hussein.

Once the Bush administration began to focus on the task of governing Iraq, it had to confront the animosities between Iraq's main population groups. Since the 1920s the Sunni 18 percent of the population had ruled over the Shiite 60 percent and the Kurdish 20 percent The Kurds had established their autonomy in northern Iraq since 1991, but the Shiites had been brutally repressed in the wake of the 1991 war. The stability of Iraq required compromises between the three groups. The Sunnis needed to learn to share power with the other two groups. The Kurds and the Shiites had to be convinced not to abuse their majority power in order to inflict revenge on the Sunnis.

Paul Bremer, the head of the occupation in Iraq, committed key blunders in May 2003, which turned the Sunnis against the Americans. First, he disbanded the Iraqi army, sending hundreds of thousands of armed men into unemployment. Second, he ordered the firing of all civil servants who held the top four ranks in the Ba'athi party. These overwhelmingly Sunni officials often were only nominally Ba'athist; in a totalitarian regime people go through the motions of party membership for narrow careerist purposes. Third, Bremer announced that the handing over of power to an Iraqi government would take a long time, thereby convincing many Iraqis that the Americans came not as liberators but as dominators.

The Sunni insurgence that broke out in the summer of 2003 spread across the Sunni regions of central Iraq. The American military were not prepared for a counterinsurgency campaign. American tactics, including night raids into homes with helicopters hovering menacingly over neighborhoods, may well have turned more Iraqis into insurgents than those they neutralized. It took years before the American military adopted a successful counterinsurgency strategy and tactics.

The Iraqi nationalist resistance organized mainly by former Ba'athists was soon added by an insurgency by Islamists affiliated to Al Qaeda. Under the Jordanian Zarqawi, Al Qaeda in Iraq conducted a devastating campaign of terrorism. Unlike the Iraqi nationalists who hit occupation and official Iraqi targets, Al Qaeda in Iraq aimed at civilian targets, particularly Shiites. Its first major attack against Shiite mosques in March 2004, which caused 270 deaths, was a grim foretaste of what was to come in the following years.

The key to the success of American policy in Iraq was the Shiites. The Kurds were uniformly in favor of the American enterprise and the Sunnis increasingly against. The Shiites, who with 60 percent of the population could make or break the project, were at first overwhelmingly favorable. Their most revered religious leader, the Grand Ayatollah Ali Sistani, prompted Shiite politicians to work with the Americans and demanded elections as early as possible, making Bush wonder how a Shiite ayatollah could outflank the Americans on the democracy issue. But the young firebrand Shiite cleric Moqtadr al-Sadr, son of a revered grand ayatollah killed by Saddam Hussein's regime, aroused the Shiite underclass against the occupation with nationalistic rallying cries. Sadr thus defied the Shiite establishment, which looked down on him as an inexperienced upstart, and organized a militia to promote his cause.

In spring 2004 the situation in Iraq worsened. The Sunni insurgency pushed the American forces out of Fallujah, a major town in the Sunni triangle north of Baghdad. The legitimacy of the American occupation was dealt a dreadful blow with the publication of photos showing humiliating torture of Iraqi prisoners by American guards at the Abu Graib prison. Most ominously, Moqtadr al-Sadr launched guerrilla attacks against occupation forces in the hitherto relatively peaceful Shiite parts of Baghdad and southern Iraq. The Sadrist insurrection ended quickly, since the Shiite establishment turned against it, but Sadr and his militia survived as a force in Iraq's fragile politics. From spring 2004 onwards a majority of Americans declared in opinion polls that the war had been a mistake.

The second Bush term

In the aftermath of the Republican gains in the midterm elections of 2002, Bush's leading strategist, Karl Rove, and other leading Republicans saw the 2004 elections as an opportunity to bring about a lasting period of Republican hegemony. But Bush's reelection prospects weakened with the growing instability in Iraq, which produced a serious drop in his popularity. Bush's effort to expand his appeal to parts of the electorate that voted for Gore in 2000 was hampered by the fact that he was a highly polarizing president, much beloved by his supporters but also much despised by his detractors. This was largely a consequence of the cultural polarization that has increasingly characterized American politics since the 1990s and that produced the clear geographical divide in the 2000 presidential vote. It was also the result of Bush's war in Iraq, which, like Vietnam, deeply divided America and undermined Bush's post-September 11 image as a unifying national leader above the fray of partisan politics.

The great polarization in American politics resulted in 2004 in the hardest fought election campaign in decades. The forces arrayed behind Bush and his Democratic opponent, Senator John F. Kerry, were exceptionally mobilized. The unions, environmentalists and pro-choice groups, on the one hand, and evangelical pastors, Catholic prelates and the National Rifle Association, on the other, joined the fight as if they were adjuncts of the Kerry and Bush campaigns respectively. Each side spent a phenomenal $125 million in drives to register voters and get them to the voting booths on election day; in 2000 the Republicans had spent only one-third as much. The opposing forces seemed so evenly matched that another protracted process with recounts in marginal states, as in 2000, was widely feared.

In the event, Bush won a clear victory. It was not a landslide. He got 51 percent of the popular vote against Kerry's 48 percent. In the Electoral College he got 286 electoral votes against Kerry's 252, which meant that if closely fought Ohio with its 20 electoral votes had gone the other way, Kerry would have won. Still, unlike in 2000, it was an unambiguous victory. The Congressional elections were also favorable for the Republicans, who increased their Senate majority from 51–49 to 55–45. They increased their majority in the House of

Representatives as well, thus controlling all elective parts of the federal govern-ment by comfortable margins for the first time since the 1920s. Geographically the 2004 election enhanced the clear regional divide that had been evident in 2000. Bush won the entire South and the Western hinterland, including New Mexico, which in 2000 had gone for Gore. Kerry won the three West Coast states and the entire Northeast, including New Hampshire, which in 2000 had gone for Bush. The Midwest remained split, though it became slightly more favorable to Bush. The divisions in American society seemed to harden into two geographically distinct blocs.

Bush's reelection was a personal triumph. His presidency went downhill thereafter. In the early months of 2005 he toured the country to raise support for social security reform, only to see the reform's popularity decline; the more Americans heard about it, the less they liked it. In late August 2005 Hurricane Katrina resulted in the flooding of much of New Orleans. The Federal Emergency Management Agency's response was widely perceived as inadequate, forcing Bush to dismiss its chief. In conjunction with the continuing instability in Iraq, Katrina enhanced the image of the Bush administration as incompetent. In the fall of 2005 Bush did succeed in having John Roberts confirmed by the Senate as the new chief justice of the US Supreme Court. But then he nominated White House counsel Harriet Miers to a second opening in the Supreme Court. Miers was per-ceived even among leading conservatives as so inadequate, that Bush embarrass-ingly had to withdraw her nomination. The subsequent confirmation of Samuel Alito to the Supreme Court did not undo the damage to Bush's standing.

To Bush's personal decline was added an outbreak of scandals engulfing other Republicans. US Representative Tom DeLay, one of the most powerful Republican leaders in Congress, was forced to resign after being charged with violations of campaign finance law. In early 2006 Republican lobbyist Jack Abramoff, who had worked closely with DeLay, was convicted for bribes, fraud and tax evasion. The scandals hit the White House when Lewis Libby, Vice-President Cheney's chief of staff, was indicted and later convicted for perjury and obstruction of justice in the investigation of the leak of Valerie Plame's secret identity as a CIA agent. The leak, which actually came not from the White House but the State Department, had taken place in 2003 after Plame's husband, former ambassador James Wilson, had failed to corroborate Bush administration claims related to Saddam Hussein's supposed weapons of mass destruction programs.

The decline in Bush's standing and Republican disarray was evident in 2006, when the president's own party rose against his proposed immigration reform, which would have legalized the 12 million illegal immigrants in the United States. In this matter the Democratic minority in Congress was more favorable to Bush's proposals than the Republican majority, which thereby alienated much of the growing Latino voting population. But the decline in the Republican Party's fortunes in 2006 derived above all from the worsening situation in Iraq.

The agony of Iraq

While the Sunni insurgency was raging, the Bush administration made sig-nificant steps towards setting up a viable Iraqi government. In June 2004 Iraqi sovereignty was restored under a government led by a secular Shiite. In January 2005 there were parliamentary elections. The results showed the prevalence of sectarian loyalties. The one secular party that fielded candidates from all three main sects received only 15 percent of the vote. The Kurds and most Shiites voted for sectarian parties, while the Sunnis mostly abstained from the vote and were thus under-represented in parliament. In the new government the president was Kurdish and the prime minister Shiite.

In October the Iraqi people voted in a referendum on the new constitution, which preserved the autonomy of Kurdistan but otherwise deferred to the future the final federal structure of Iraq. In the Kurdish and Shiite provinces the new constitution was approved by over 90 percent of the votes. Nonetheless, it would not have passed, if three provinces had voted against it by more than two-thirds of the votes. It was rejected in three Sunni provinces, but in one of these the no vote was only 55 percent, less than two thirds, securing passage of the constitution. In December 2005 there were new parliamentary elections, which confirmed the primacy of sectarian loyalties. This time the Sunnis participated in large numbers, in order to secure a greater say in subsequent political developments.

In spite of this political progress, in 2006 violence escalated disastrously. Some Sunni insurgents, and especially Al Qaeda in Iraq, hit Shiite civilian targets with devastating results. In February 2006 the Shiites were outraged, when one of their holiest mosques was blown up in Samara. Shiite militias retaliated by raiding Sunni neighborhoods and killing indiscriminately. The Iraqi police had been infiltrated by Shiite militiamen and thus offered little protection to the Sunnis. Much of Iraq, and especially Baghdad with its mixed population, sank into ever worsening violence, while millions of mostly Sunni Iraqis fled to neighboring countries. Leading Sunnis now demanded that the American forces remain in Iraq, since only they could be relied upon to protect the embattled Sunni communities, even while they continued to be attacked by Sunni insurgents.

The relentless news flow of ever worsening atrocities in Iraq demoralized the American people. Bush's popularity sank to 30 percent or lower, never to recover. The Republican Party was decisively punished in the midterm elections of November 2006 for entangling America in the Iraqi nightmare. In the House of Representatives the Democrats gained 31 seats and acquired a 233–202 majority. In the Senate, where only one-third of the seats was up for reelection, the Republicans lost six seats. The two parties were equal with 49 senators each, but the two Independents voted with the Democrats on the chamber's organization, that is, the senate leadership and all the committee chairs went to the Democrats.

The day after the elections a chastened Bush fired Defense Secretary Rumsfeld, who had become identified with the failed strategy in Iraq. Rumsfeld had resisted calls for a troop increase in Iraq on the grounds that the Iraqis should be pushed to take responsibility for their own internal security by building up competent security forces. Defiantly, given widespread American disenchantment with the war, Bush decided in January 2007 on a surge of American troops in Iraq from roughly 130,000 to 160,000. He also appointed as the new commander in Iraq General David Petraeus, who had just overseen the rewriting of the army's manual on counterinsurgency and was thus well suited for a drastic change in the strategy on the ground.

With the surge in troops, Petraeus was able to station American troops permanently within even the toughest neighborhoods of Baghdad, to provide round-the-clock support for the still inexperienced Iraqi army units and gain the trust of the local population. This resulted at first in a rise in American casualties. Iraqi civilian casualties also kept rising in early spring 2007. It was only in late summer 2007 that the new strategy brought results, when Sunni nationalist insurgents started to cooperate with the Americans against Al Qaeda in Iraq, the brutal methods and Islamist extremism of which had repulsed them. In parallel Petraeus pressured the Iraqi government, led by the Shiite prime minister Maliki, to move against the Shiite militias. Maliki made his move in March 2008, destroying the hold of Muqtada al Sadr's militia over significant Shiite parts of Iraq.

From September 2007 onwards American and Iraqi casualties began to decline steeply. One year later the situation had improved sufficiently for Obama to declare that 'the surge succeeded beyond our wildest dreams.' Obama, who had opposed the surge, was being politically shrewd; being inexperienced on national security, he stood to gain by a decline in the salience of national security issues in the 2008 elections. But his statement did reflect the new reality on the ground.

In the end Bush managed to salvage his audacious Iraq project, though not his presidency or the fortunes of his party. When he went into Iraq, he failed in what Clausewitz deemed as 'the first, the most majestic, the most decisive act of judgment,' that the leader recognizes correctly the nature of the war into which he is entering and 'does not mistake it for or try to make it into something, which in the nature of circumstances it cannot be.'[1] Bush thought he was entering into a conventional war to overthrow Saddam Hussein and was not prepared for a counterinsurgency struggle. It took years of agony, and the loss of much blood and treasure, to correct that disastrous mistake.

The rise of Obama

Barack Obama's rise to the top of American politics was the fastest in modern times. From 1997 to 2004 Obama served in the Illinois state senate, hardly a post pointing to the US presidency. His rapid ascent began in March 2004, when he won the Democratic Illinois primary for the US Senate by an unexpected landslide. On account of this victory, he gave the keynote speech at the 2004 Democratic National Convention and thus became nationally known. In November 2004 he was elected to the Senate. By October 2006, with less than two years as Senator, Obama was generating enough excitement with his new book *The Audacity of Hope* for the *Economist* to publish an article with the title 'Obamamania'.[2]

Nonetheless, when Obama announced his candidacy for the presidency in February 2007, his prospects seemed remote. The front-runner in the Democratic field was Hillary Clinton, who with her husband Bill Clinton had connections with Democratic heavyweights across the country. But Obama soon showed that he had the charisma and organizational skills to challenge the formidable Clinton machine. During 2007 his fundraising operations rivaled Clinton's; by the end of the year opinion polls placed Obama second after Clinton in a field of eight Democratic candidates.

During January 2008 the Democratic race narrowed down to an Obama-Clinton duel, already ensuring that this would be a historic election; never before had either a woman or an African American attained a major party's presidential nomination. Obama established an early lead in the delegate count by winning Iowa in early January. Then Clinton narrowed Obama's delegate lead by winning New Hampshire. This pattern was to repeat itself all the way until June, with Obama repeatedly surging ahead but then Clinton fighting back ferociously and narrowing his lead. On Super Tuesday in early February, when 22 states voted, Obama's lead dwindled to a few delegates. Then Obama won the next 11 ballots in a row and seemed unstoppable. But in early March Clinton revived her campaign by winning the popular vote in Ohio and Texas.

During this duel Clinton's attacks against Obama evolved significantly. At first she tried to define Obama as unelectable in the November general election, by pointing out his inexperience and hinting that the time was not yet ripe for an African American president. But as Obama swept even states with few blacks and above-average income levels, she switched to painting him as too distant from working-class Americans. It was indeed the case that Obama was strongest among blacks, the young and affluent wine-drinking liberals, whereas Clinton did better among beer-drinking working-class whites.

Obama countered by presenting himself as the candidate of hope and change, while defining Clinton as a return to a divisive past. When he declared that neither Nixon nor Bill Clinton had changed the direction of American politics, whereas Reagan had, Obama was implicitly comparing himself to past presidents who had brought about major realignments in American politics and lasting primacy for their parties. At the same time he was implicitly comparing the Clintons to Nixon in the sense of them being highly divisive and polarizing figures, carrying debilitating negative baggage from the 1990s.

One dangerous moment for Obama came in February, when an old video clip surfaced on YouTube showing his former Chicago pastor, the Reverend Jeremiah Wright, ranting 'God damn America' from the pulpit. Obama neutralized this threat with a widely admired speech on race and religion, in which he skillfully distanced himself from recent black grievance politics and presented himself as a bridge across the racial divide. This fit well with his broader unifying appeal. Being the first post-1960s presidential candidate whose adulthood began after the intense divisions of the 1960s had subsided, Obama promised to overcome recent cultural divisions. While his pro-choice position on abortion was unquestionable, for example, he found respectful ways of talking about the pro-life position that appeased religious Americans.

While the Democratic duel continued into late spring, on the Republican side Senator John McCain clinched the nomination by early March. Six months earlier he had been written off, his popularity low and his campaign bankrupt. But McCain had for years advocated large increases in the troop levels in Iraq. The success of the surge strategy turned his fortunes around. Nonetheless, large parts of the Republican base were unexcited, especially social and fiscal conservatives who had rooted for former governors Mike Huckabee of Arkansas and Mitt Romney of Massachusetts respectively. Moreover, turnout in the Republican primaries had been much lower than on the Democratic side. Bush's unpopularity and the recession that began in late 2007 made 2008 very unpromising for the Republicans.

By the time Obama secured the nomination in June, he had prevailed in a grueling political marathon having made very few missteps. His impressive self-discipline under fire and his superb campaign organization demonstrated his leadership qualities, neutralizing the factor of his relative inexperience. The rock-star adulation that he evoked from his supporters demonstrated his charisma. His fundraising operation broke all records, relying largely on an unusually broad pool of small donors contributing through the Internet; such often young supporters could at critical junctures be induced to contribute small sums again and again, while remaining below individual campaign finance law contribution limits. His fundraising was so successful, that Obama made the unprecedented decision to forego public funding in the general election campaign in order not to be constrained by the concomitant overall campaign spending limit.

In the summer of 2008 the two candidates chose their running mates. Obama played safe by choosing Joe Biden, US Senator since 1973 when Obama was still in sixth grade. Being a white Roman Catholic with a working-class background and enormous experience in foreign affairs, Biden nicely balanced the ticket. McCain, who is 25 years older than Obama, chose the young social conservative Governor Sarah Palin of Alaska, hoping to fire up the Republican base while himself trying to revive his old appeal among independents. For a short time it seemed to work; McCain's postconvention bounce was the only moment in 2008 when his popularity rose above Obama's. But his choice soon backfired, when Palin revealed her embarrassing ignorance of national issues on televised interviews. Compared with Obama and his cerebral, highly methodical and deliberative decision-making approach, McCain now seemed impulsive, bordering on reckless.

While the campaign was moving towards the fall debates phase, in mid-September the worst financial crisis since the Great Depression temporarily overshadowed all else. With the global capitalist system seemingly on the brink of collapse under Bush's watch, the fortunes of the Republican Party sank to their lowest levels in decades. National security, the only issue where McCain did better than Obama in opinion polls, was displaced by the economy as the voters' dominant concern. With Obama's popularity surging well above McCain's, the latter's last hope of turning the campaign around was in the debates. McCain was particularly combative in the last and liveliest of the three presidential debates, hoping to bait Obama into some gaffe but instead he appeared as condescending. Obama kept his cool, remained courteous towards his older Senate colleague and demonstrated his mastery of the issues.

In the November elections Obama got 53 percent of the popular vote, the highest percentage by a Democrat since Lyndon Johnson's 1964 landslide. He did particularly well among African Americans, the young and Latinos. Women and low-income voters also gave him large majorities, as did the top income earners with annual incomes above $200,000. McCain did well only among seniors and working-class whites. Geographically, Obama won every state that had voted for Kerry in 2004 and broke into Bush's red-states bloc, winning Nevada, Colorado and New Mexico in the Western hinterland; Florida, Virginia and North Carolina in the South; and almost the entire Midwest. Obama thus diminished the previous division of the United States into two geographically distinct political blocs.

The Democrats also made major gains in Congress. In the House of Representatives they gained 21 seats and acquired a 257–178 majority. In the Senate they gained eight seats and, together with the two Independents who leaned towards the Democrats, held a 59–41 majority, just one short of the filibuster-proof 60–40 majority.

The 2008 election constituted a decisive repudiation of Bush. Obama's message of hope and change clearly resonated in American society. Obama now sought to turn his historic victory into a lasting realignment of the American party system. He had campaigned in favor of health care reform and controlling climate change. But his first priority was the financial crisis and the deepening recession.

The financial crisis of 2008

In the fall of 2008 the global economy came to the brink of an economic disaster similar to the Great Depression. In the event, massive government intervention limited the damage; the recession was deep but relatively short. Nonetheless, it is not yet clear how soon the United States will overcome the effects of the financial crisis of 2008 and whether the American economy will return to the relatively high average growth rates of the 1983–2006 period.

The financial crisis originated in an accumulation of excess liquidity in the American financial system in the years up to 2006. One reason for this was the large surplus in China's bilateral trade with the United States, which meant that China was accumulating dollar reserves so vast that they could only be invested in a financial system as large and deep as that of America. Another reason was the Federal Reserve's cheap money policy to counter the effects of the bursting of the dotcom bubble in 2000; the Fed's interest rate declined from 6.5 percent in 2000 to one percent in 2003. With the financial system awash with cheap cash, investors turned to ever riskier forms of investments that promised higher returns.

The result was a housing bubble that peaked in 2006. Encouraged by policies from the 1990s favoring loans to less affluent Americans, mortgage lenders extended loans to ever riskier clients; these sub-prime mortgages rose from ten percent of all mortgage loans in 2004 to 20 percent in 2006. Investment bankers then packaged such high-risk and high-return mortgages in investment products, assuming that the risks would be cancelled out by the packaging. Banks and other institutional investors bought these investment products all over the advanced world, enjoying high returns so long as the bubble grew. Particularly exposed to these risky assets were the American investment banks, which unlike the commercial banks were less regulated by the authorities and thus less constrained in their risk-taking behavior.

The housing bubble burst in 2007. With steep declines in housing prices, more and more borrowers could not refinance their mortgages and defaulted. Over one hundred smaller mortgage lenders went bankrupt. Now the packaged high-risk mortgages became toxic assets, exposing their owners to enormous losses.

What ensued in 2008 was a banking crisis. Unlike earlier runs on the banks in the nineteenth and early twentieth centuries, when retail clients panicked and withdrew their savings, in 2008 it was wholesale institutional investors such as hedge funds that led the run. The first investment bank to go under was Bear Stearns in March; it was acquired very cheaply at the expense of its shareholders by JP Morgan Chase with assistance from the Federal Reserve. Uncertainty turned into panic in mid-September, when Lehman Brothers went broke. Unlike Bear Stearns, Lehman was one of Wall Street's top investment banks. Banks now needed all the liquidity they could get to stave off runs. Therefore they stopped giving emergency loans to one another, which meant that the next victim of a run would get no lifeline from the financial sector. A collapse of the banking system similar to the early 1930s seemed possible.

With banks keeping liquid assets to survive a possible run, credit dried out in the American economy. Major corporations including General Motors and Chrysler could not get emergency loans to cover their cash flow needs. With the banking system on the verge of collapse, corporations secured liquidity by slashing production below sales, thereby cutting costs and selling off their inventory. Unemployment shot up sharply and GDP declined steeply in late 2008 and early 2009. But this was going to be a V-shaped recession; once inventory was exhausted, corporations increased production sharply in later 2009.

In the meantime, the federal government intervened massively to save the banking system. With a speed reminiscent of the early days of the New Deal, the Bush administration proposed and the Democratic Congress approved the $700 billion Troubled Asset Relief Program (TARP) a mere fortnight after Lehman's fall. TARP funds bailed out tottering banks, though only after a major consolidation of the financial sector that effectively eliminated investment banking as it was known in the previous decades. The insurance giant AIG was bailed out to save banks it had insured not only in the United States but also in Europe. TARP funds were also used to bail out General Motors and Chrysler. In the process the federal government became a major shareholder of leading banks and corporations, radically changing American political economy at least temporarily. This massive government intervention in the economy began under Bush. More was to follow under Obama.

Obama's presidency

At the start of Obama's presidency the United States was still engaged in wars in Iraq and Afghanistan, while having to cope with the worst postwar financial crisis and the ensuing deep recession. To deal with these major problems, Obama assembled unusually strong teams in the fields of economics and international affairs. The mobilization of Democratic talent in his administration included his former rival Hillary Clinton as Secretary of State. Obama reached across the aisle by keeping Bush's Secretary of Defense Robert Gates, who had turned the war around in Iraq and would be charged with the task of repeating the feat in Afghanistan. Obama described his administration as 'a team of rivals', citing the title of a book about Lincoln's cabinet.

Obama's inauguration thrilled most Americans and the rest of the world. When he was born in 1961, the South still had segregation and the ascension of an African American to the presidency seemed unimaginable. Obama's rise fulfilled Martin Luther King's dream four decades after the great civil rights leader's death. Moreover, most people in the United States and abroad had high expectations about Obama after the failures and international tensions of the Bush years. But high expectations are difficult to meet, especially when held by people with diverse and even contradictory viewpoints. Using the initial good-will towards his presidency to forge a new dominant Democratic coalition at home and to overcome lasting problems abroad would prove a difficult challenge for Obama.

Obama's first priority was to pass a massive $787 billion stimulus package to help pull the economy out of the recession. He sought a bipartisan approach, even meeting Republican senators on Capitol Hill in the first days of his presidency. But he delegated the management of the legislative process to congressional Democratic leaders, who were less willing to conciliate the minority party. The result was a package that leaned towards public spending favored by liberals rather than tax cuts and incentives for small businesses favored by conservatives and even centrist Democrats. Some of the new spending furthered other parts of Obama's agenda, such as research on energy efficiency and renewable energy sources. The stimulus received no Republican votes in the House and only three in the Senate, thus keeping alive the intense partisan polarization in Congress.

In spring 2009 the Obama administration completed the bailout of General Motors and Chrysler. It also arranged for a public-private scheme for removing toxic assets from financial institutions. Private investors and the government jointly bought toxic assets at low prices and would share ensuing profits; but the government alone would assume all losses if these purchases proved unprofitable. Effectively subsidizing Wall Street investors may have been wise in terms of dealing with the financial mess, but it proved unpopular both among liberals on the left and conservative populists on the right. Nonetheless, disaffection with Obama's policies remained contained at this stage. In April the Democrats scored a major victory when the Republican Senator Arlen Specter switched parties and secured for them, together with the two Independents, a filibuster-proof 60–40 majority. The Senate thus confirmed Obama's nomination of Sonia Sotomayor to the Supreme Court without difficulties.

In the summer of 2009 Obama moved his domestic agenda beyond dealing with the economic crisis and pushed for an ambitious health care reform, which had eluded Truman, Nixon and Clinton. Obama hoped to pass health care reform by August, before Congress's summer recess, in order to attain an early momentum in his overall domestic reform agenda. It was not to be.

The Democratic Party's triumph in 2008 and the Republican Party's steep decline in opinion polls masked the fact that the ideological orientation of Americans had remained unchanged. Opinion polls in the first half of 2009 showed that only 21 to 24 percent of Americans identified themselves as liberals, whereas 35 to 40 percent identified themselves as conservatives, unchanged from previous years. The moderates, who had leaned towards Obama in 2008, moved rightwards during 2009.

The reason evidently was that most Americans were uncomfortable with the massive intrusion of the federal government in the economy. Bank and corporation bailouts that made government a major shareholder in leading units of the economy, the massive stimulus spending, a federal budget deficit projected for 2009 to reach 12 percent of GDP and the ensuing drastic increase in the national debt were highly unsettling developments for most Americans. Now Obama proposed to add major government intervention in the health care sector. A grassroots backlash developed with the emergence of the inchoate tea party movement, which opposed big government. By December 2009 in one poll only 28 percent were positive on the Republicans and 35 percent on the Democrats, but an astonishing 41 percent were positive on the unorganized tea party movement.

Congressional Democrats elected in 2006 and 2008 in previously Republican and thus rather conservative states and districts became worried about their reelection prospects and hence delayed and diluted health care reform in Congress. Even though the Republican Party remained low in the polls, Republicans benefited from the backlash. In early November 2009 Republicans won gubernatorial elections in New Jersey and Virginia, states that Obama had won with 57 percent and 53 percent respectively in 2008. Nonetheless, different versions of health care reform passed the House and the Senate by the end of 2009. But before the two versions were reconciled, in January 2010 liberal Massachusetts elected Republican Scott Brown to Ted Kennedy's old Senate seat. This was a stunning setback for the Democratic leadership; Massachusetts had not elected a Republican to the Senate since 1972 and had given Obama 62 percent in 2008.

For a while panic prevailed amongst congressional Democrats. Health care reform seemed dead. But Obama kept his cool, regrouped his party and turned the situation around. Since the Democrats had lost their filibuster-proof majority in the Senate, the House had to pass the Senate bill without amendments. With the help of the able Speaker Nancy Pelosi, Obama was able to pass the Senate health care bill through the House in March, thereby achieving a historic reform that had eluded several of his predecessors. This great legislative victory revived the morale of the Democratic Party and Obama's presidential fortunes. Even though the reform seems likely to result in Democratic losses in the November 2010 midterm elections, it also seems likely to benefit Obama in the longer term.

It would be premature to make judgments about Obama's prospects in 2012, though after Massachusetts it seemed less likely that he would succeed in bringing about the lasting realignment in American party politics that he hoped for. But Reagan's popularity had plummeted during the steep 1981–2 recession and then recovered splendidly in 1983, when unemployment declined. Obama's popularity may well recover similarly, once the economic recovery leads to a fall in unemployment. The prospects for his presidency seem less bright in 2010 than they were at his inauguration, but his health care reform demonstrated. his resilience in the face of adversity. The man who made history by the mere fact of being elected president is likely to make history as a major reformer as well.

America and the world in 2010

By the end of Bush's presidency, American global influence was in retreat. The United States was mired in the Iraq and Afghanistan wars that sapped its morale. The American capitalist model became less appealing internationally with the financial crisis. Bush's Wilsonian vision of spreading democracy in the Greater Middle East did not inspire most Americans, who according to opinion polls were in an isolationist mood. Russia, China, Venezuela and other states openly defied the will of the United States in ways that seemed unthinkable at the start of the twenty-first century. Even America's European allies were sometimes defiant, as when some of them blocked in mid-2008 the accession to NATO of Ukraine, Georgia and the Former Yugoslav Republic of Macedonia that Bush supported.

Nonetheless, the position of the United States in the international distribution of power remained dominant. The American economy accounted for more than a quarter of the global economy and American defense spending was nearly half of global defense spending. The United States remained the only power with a global reach. Moreover, it remained allied with the wealthiest nations in the world. The United States, the EU, Japan, Australia, Canada and New Zealand as a bloc accounted for some two-thirds of global GDP. The United States and its allies faced no significant conventional threats from other states; terrorism and other nonstate threats remained the dominant security concerns of the advanced world. The challenges for America's leaders were those of a hegemonic power; they related to managing international politics, dealing with peripheral crises across the globe and providing some semblance of global governance.

In the first year of his presidency, Obama strove to improve America's position in the world by emphasizing international cooperation and multilateralism. He certainly improved America's international image and generated much goodwill across the world. But there were no major breakthroughs in the problems that he inherited. He continued the process of winding down the American military presence in Iraq. In late 2009 he decided on a surge of American troops in Afghanistan, hoping that this, together with improvements in the counterinsurgency strategy, would turn the war around in the manner of Iraq. But the political situation in Afghanistan was more difficult than that in Iraq, since the corrupt Afghani government exercised only a tenuous and geographically limited control over Afghanistan's fractured and tribal society, making the outcome of the venture uncertain. Obama's push to revive the Middle East peace process was unsuccessful. Iran continued its nuclear program, defying Obama's December 31, 2009 deadline and refusing to cooperate with the international community. The global climate change conference in Copenhagen in December 2009 did not produce a breakthrough on a front that Obama had emphasized in his election campaign. At the end of his first year Obama had thus not yet left a deep mark on world affairs.

Nonetheless, Obama was successful in managing the global economic system at a time of strong protectionist pressures. One of the greatest achievements of postwar American policy was the operation of the open international economic system, which provided unparalleled prosperity to North America, Western Europe and parts of East Asia. After the end of the Cold War, this system expanded to include the economies of the former Warsaw Pact countries as well as China.

Undoubtedly the open international economic system is the most powerful engine of economic growth in history. All states that participated in it have in the long run witnessed unprecedented overall prosperity. Yet the very dynamism of the international market system has redistributive effects that may undermine it: First, markets redistribute resources and wealth within a nation at the expense of internationally uncompetitive sectors and firms. The employers, unions and regions of the declining sectors often press for protection from international competition. In a recession such protectionist pressures increase.

Second, international markets redistribute wealth between nations. Differential growth rates over the long run change the international distribution of power, with profound political consequences. Ever since Thucydides, major changes in the distribution of power have been recognized as among the most important causes of wars, since the rising powers challenge the international *status quo* that favors established but declining powers. But this is not a likely danger in the foreseeable future, since it will take at least several decades for a rising power such as China to become so strong as to be able to challenge the present international arrangements of the dominant West. In the foreseeable future it is more likely that changes in the distribution of power will increase economic rather than military competition between nations and regional blocks, especially if the declining economic powers follow protectionist policies to maintain their position.

Changes in the distribution of power may threaten the global economy in another way. In the past the global economy functioned best when the distribution of economic power was hegemonic and one dominant economy was able to bear the burden of managing the open international economic system. The first golden era of the global economy in the nineteenth century was based on British economic hegemony: in 1850 Britain produced half the industrial product of the world. The post-World War II international economic system was based on American economic hegemony: in 1950 it was the United States that produced half the industrial product of the world.

Between these two golden eras of the global economy, in the interwar years, there was no economic hegemon. Britain had fallen behind the United States and Germany, neither of which was able or willing to take over the responsibility of managing the global economy. America's international economic policy after World War I, in particular, was myopically selfish with its insistence on repayment of her war loans by her allies (how different from the Marshall Plan after WWII!), who in turn insisted on reparations from Germany to repay the American loans, thereby weakening the foundations of the European economic system. When the shock of 1929 shook the global economy neither the United States nor Germany sought to bear the burden of managing the system. Britain tried, but was no longer able to do so. As the leading economies resorted to protectionism – Britain was last to do so in September 1931 – international trade collapsed and the world economy experienced its worst depression in the industrial age.

Was a repetition of the collapse of the 1930s possible in 2008–9? Policy makers have, of course, learned the lessons of that catastrophe and were hence unlikely to repeat the same mistakes. But the relative decline of American economic hegemony since the 1950s and the emergence of powerful regionalisms have complicated the problem of managing the global economic system. The European Union (EU), NAFTA and, in a less formalized way, East Asia have emerged as rival economic blocs. Under conditions of an 'oligopolistic' distribution of economic power, it is more conceivable that an economic shock may spiral out of control if none of the three main blocs is willing to bear the burden of international economic management and each seeks to 'pass the buck' to the others. It is to Obama's credit that this did not happen in 2009 and that the leading economic powers cooperated well in order to prevent a collapse of the open international economic system.

NOTES

1. Carl von Clausewitz, *Vom Kriege*, Frankfurt a. M.: Ullstein Materialien, 1980, p. 36, my translation from German.
2. *Economist*, October 28, 2006.

RECOMMENDED READING

Robert Draper, *Dead Certain: The Presidency of George W. Bush,* New York: Free Press, 2008.

Robert Gilpin, *Global Political Economy: Understanding the International Economic Order,* Princeton, NJ: Princeton University Press, 2001.

James Mann, *Rise of the Vulcans: The History of Bush's War Cabinet,* New York: Viking Books, 2004.

Barack Obama, *The Audacity of Hope: Thoughts on Reclaiming the American Dream,* New York: Vintage Books, 2006.

Thomas E. Ricks, *Fiasco: The American Military Adventure in Iraq,* London: Allen Lane, 2006.

Linda Robinson, *Tell Me How This Ends: General David Petraeus and the Search for a Way Out of Iraq,* New York, Public Affairs, 2008.

The 9/11 Commission Report Final Report of the National Commission on Terrorist Attacks Upon the United States, New York: Norton, 2004.

CHAPTER 12

Hard Facts and Millennial Fictions

September 11, 2001

In the United States the new millennium began not on January 1, 2000, but on September 11, 2001. On that clear autumn morning, 19 Muslim terrorists hijacked four commercial airliners and crashed three of them into two major symbols of American power: the World Trade Center in New York City and the Pentagon just outside of Washington, DC. In a matter of minutes, the American sense of reality was abruptly changed. As Richard Bernstein writes in the reconstruction of these events compiled by the staff of *The New York Times*:

> Out of a clear blue sky using our own engines against us, armed with nothing but knives, terrorists had struck simultaneously at the chief symbols of American commercial and military might. The inconceivable had happened, and it had happened even though we were supposedly protected by the world's biggest defense budget, by the greatest military power in world history, and by an at least creditable intelligence establishment that was supposed to find out about things like terrorist attacks before they happened. The phrases that were heard over and over again were 'Everything has changed' and 'Nothing will be the same again.'

In *Out of the Blue* (2003) Bernstein catalogues the complete destruction of the vast World Trade Center which housed some of the nation's leading banks, stock brokerages, law offices, investment houses, real estate agencies, telecommunications companies as well as New York State government tax and finance departments. In all, 2823 people were killed, 400,000 tons of structural steel was destroyed along with 208 passenger elevators, 300 computer mainframes, 23,000 fluorescent lightbulbs, 49,000 tons of air-conditioning equipment, 12,000 miles of electrical cable and 220 acres' worth of reinforced concrete flooring. 'A few ten- to twelve-story segments of wall remained after the collapses, like relics of an ancient city sacked by barbarians,' he writes. 'All the rest, all the persons and paraphernalia of American capitalism compacted into the sixteen-acre site of the trade center in an astounding three-dimensional Jackson Pollock-like dystopia of ash-covered wreckage that smoldered and burned literally for months.'

How can we understand this first decisive event of the new millennium? First, the lethal terrorist attack on the United States did not come 'out of the blue'. Bernstein traces it back to 1979, a fateful year for militant Islamism.

In February, Ayotallah Khomeini established an Islamic republic in Iran and identified the United States as 'the Great Satan' for its support of the deposed Shah. In November, Islamic radicals seized the Holy Mosque in Mecca and held it until they were driven out by Saudi Arabian government forces. In December, the Soviet Union invaded Afghanistan, unleashing a backlash in the form of a national resistance movement, including Muslim volunteers from the Middle East and Pakistan.

In that same year a charismatic Palestinian religious scholar named Abdullah Azzam moved from Egypt to Peshawar, Pakistan, to help recruit young Arabs for the Afghan resistance. Azzam was a fundamentalist who believed in creating a pure Islamic state in Afghanistan. His Office of Services soon became the hub of a successful global network for training Muslim *mujaheedeen* to enact *jihad* against the Soviet Union. Among his earliest disciples was Osama bin Laden. Bernstein says, 'In some ways Osama bin Laden is a prototype of a common kind of modern-day political figure, the child of wealth and privilege who devotes himself to overturning the establishment that gave him his privileges in the first place.' But the first generation of Third World revolutionaries had been Marxists; bin Laden is part of another generation who are Islamic fundamentalists. At first, Azzam and bin Laden were close allies; but then they split over whether *jihad* should be limited to Afghanistan or expanded to include other 'corrupt' Muslim societies like Egypt and Saudi Arabia. Azzam was assassinated in 1989 under mysterious circumstances and bin Laden took over the task of globalizing the war against the infidels. In this manner Al Qaeda was born and grew.

We can trace the murderous progress of Al Qaeda from the killing of American soldiers in Somalia and the car-bombing of the World Trade Center in 1993 to the attacks on American embassies in Kenya and Tanzania in 1998 and on the battleship *USS Cole* in 2000. In retrospect it seems that its expansion was preordained by the failures of America's intelligence agencies and the inability of the American government to find an effective response. 'Indeed, before September 11, no administration – and this includes the Bush administration in its first nine months – was willing to undertake major military and diplomatic moves that would have been necessary to destroy Al Qaeda.'

Terror and liberalism

The causes of the new global terrorism are disputed. While economic inequality is certainly one cause of terrorism, the destruction of the World Trade Center was not the result of the class struggle. Instead, the terrorists were acting under a different imperative. As Thomas Friedman points out in *Longitudes & Attitudes* (2002), 'If we've learned one thing since 9/11, it's that terrorism is not produced by the poverty of money. It's produced by the poverty of dignity.' Muhammad Atta, the ringleader of the September 11 attack, came from a middle-class Egyptian family and studied architecture in Hamburg. He was most likely converted to Islamic fundamentalism during a pilgrimage to Mecca. Osama bin Laden, son of a Saudi business tycoon, was outraged by the presence of American infidels on Saudi holy ground during the Gulf War. Their reasons were religious, not economic. Although many Western intellectuals have rejected

Samuel Huntington's controversial thesis that future conflicts will be fought along cultural and not economic lines, bin Laden and his followers seem to have adopted the idea. Huntington wrote, 'In the post-Cold War world, for the first time in history, global politics has become multipolar *and* multicivilizational.' The current *jihad* against Western infidels seems closer to his 'clash of civilizations' than to Marx's class war.

In modern times, the connection between grievance and violence is an old story. 'To know the reality of politics,' Norman O. Brown wrote in *Love's Body* (1966), 'we have to believe the myth, to believe what we were told as children.' In *Moses and Monotheism* (1939), Freud recounted the ancient myth of the sons' rebellion against the father and the subsequent quarrel over the paternal inheritance. The sons kill the father in order to become brothers; but then they quarrel over who shall take the place of the father. Brown sees history as the performance of myth: the 'pursuit of liberty' turns out to be 'the old, old story' of the reenactment of the primal crime and the subsequent dispute over the father's property, his power. Thus all revolutions follow the same pattern: they begin with 'liberty, equality, fraternity' and end up with tyranny. 'Liberty, equality,' Brown wrote, 'it is all a dispute over the inheritance of the paternal estate.' He concluded, 'All fraternity is fratricidal.'

In *Terror and Liberalism* (2003), Paul Berman brilliantly updates Brown's argument by invoking Albert Camus, who identified the intimate connection between totalitarianism and terror. According to Berman, Camus 'had noticed a modern impulse to rebel, which had come out of the French Revolution and the nineteenth century and had very quickly, in the name of an ideal, mutated into a cult of death.' It was inspired by the 'Ur-myth' of the corruption of the city of Babylon and its ultimate purification in the apocalyptic battle between the forces of light and darkness at Armageddon. In the twentieth century, this impulse became ideological. 'It was the war between liberalism and the apocalyptic and phantasmagorical movements that have risen up against liberal civilization ever since the calamities of the First World War.'

In the ensuing years, Lenin, Stalin, Mussolini, Franco and Hitler all followed the same script. They began with the Bolshevik Class Struggle, the Fascist Crusade, or the Nazi Race War; and they all ended up with the massacre of innocent civilians. Today, for the Islamic fundamentalists it is *jihad* and suicide bombers. In each case, revolution is based on restoration: the Fascist resurrection of the Roman Empire; the Nazi creation of the Third Reich; or the Islamic revival of the seventh-century Caliphate of the Arab Empire. Berman sees Saddam's Ba'athism and Osama's Islamism as 'two branches of a single impulse, which was Muslim totalitarianism – the Muslim variation on the European idea.' Thus Huntington's 'clash of civilizations' must be amended to account for this common impulse.

In 2001 Middle East violence made its way to American shores. Geography had historically insulated the United States from foreign threats; even during the Cold War, the threat of domestic attack remained remote. But an unintended consequence of globalization has been to increase American vulnerability. 'That's a major lesson of September 11,' says the historian John Lewis Gaddis in *Surprise, Security, and the American Experience* (2004): 'the very instruments of the new world order – airplanes, liberal policies on immigration and money transfers, multiculturalism itself in the sense that there seemed to be nothing odd about the hijackers when they were taking their flight training – can be turned horribly against it.' Moreover, bin Laden and his associates have turned the organizing principles of globalization against itself. An explosive blend of apocalyptic theology and business practice permits Al Qaeda to address the grievances of Muslims that globalization generates without providing a viable alternative except suicidal violence.

What should be America's role in this new world disorder? Friedman argues that while Americans can fight the war on terrorists, the war against the fundamentalists must be fought inside the Muslim world. The role of the West is to help 'educate' authoritarian regimes to become more open, democratic and progressive. Left out of the process of modernization, he says, Arab citizens know how to blow up planes but not how to build them. This process will not be easy because the demographic patterns are against us. Gaddis disagrees. He calls for a pragmatic policy that serves American national interests: 'We'll have to define our allies more in terms of shared interests, and less in terms of shared values.' But whether an open-ended war on terror is pragmatic is still an open question. Paul Hirst concludes, 'The problem with a "war" on terrorism is that it has to be fought but cannot be won. Equally, the terrorists face the problem that they can disturb the peace but they do not have the ideas to change it.'[1] This is the awful paradox of the new millennium.

World Trade Center

'In New York, history is divided between the period before September 11, 2001, and the period after it,' notes Paul Goldberger in *Up from Zero* (2004). The destruction of the World Trade Center (WTC) was a terrible blow for the city. The story of its construction is just as complex as the story of its destruction. The WTC was conceived in the 1950s and completed in the 1970s but its origins lie further back in time. It was the offspring of an independent public agency called the Port Authority of New York and New Jersey (PA), which was founded in 1921. 'To understand the World Trade Center,' Angus Gillespie explains in *Twin Towers* (1999), 'we first have to understand the Port Authority, the organization which built it. It is a complex story of money and politics, law and engineering, public service and personal pride.' The story begins more than 100 years ago.

In the nineteenth century, as the United States expanded rapidly in the years before the Civil War, New York became the nation's commercial hub, economic marketplace and immigrant gateway. Thanks to its deep natural harbor, the city was also the nation's leading port. By 1860, two-thirds of America's imports and one-third of its exports traveled through the Port of New York. But the development was lopsided. Access to the harbor was through the Hudson River which separates New York and New Jersey. Most of the wharves and piers were built on the New York side, but most of the railroads terminated on the New Jersey side. This was also a source of commercial friction; thus the PA was established in 1921 to settle disputes between the two states and facilitate the transportation of goods and people across the Hudson River. Originally, it was supposed to build infrastructure like bridges and tunnels; later its mandate was interpreted more broadly to include building a world trade center. After World War II, it became clear that America's economic future lay in international commerce. Soon the function of the PA was expanded from building bridges to developing trade. From there it was but a short step to entering the real estate market and building a skyscraper to end all skyscrapers.

The two key figures in creating the WTC were Austin Tobin and David Rockefeller. Tobin joined the PA in 1927 and was appointed its executive director in 1942. He was a skillful and autocratic administrator who was responsible for the successful development of the three large New York-area airports over the next two decades. Rockefeller, the youngest of five brothers in one of America's richest families, headed the powerful Chase Manhattan Bank. In the early 1950s, he decided to build the new 60-story Chase Manhattan Bank Tower near Wall Street. It was a brave decision because at that time lower Manhattan was a run-down area of older commercial buildings housing small businesses and factories. To protect his investment, Rockefeller established a new business organization, the Downtown-Lower Manhattan Association (DLMA), to promote new real estate construction – and raise real estate values – in the shabby neighborhood. In 1958 the DLMA sponsored a study to plan the revival of lower Manhattan. When the plan was unveiled in 1960, it included a proposal for the World Trade Center. Soon Rockefeller persuaded Tobin that the proposed WTC would be good for the city and good for the PA.

But it was a controversial decision for many reasons. First of all, it put the publicly funded PA in the real estate business competing with powerful private developers. Second, it was part of a larger plan to renovate older neighborhoods that were visually shabby but socially viable and economically successful. In *Divided We Stand* (2000), Eric Darton notes, 'For more than two decades, well into the 1970s, large sections of American cities where properties were deemed "undervalued" had become fair game for federally subsidized clearance and redevelopment plans. In many cases, these areas included viable – even vibrant – residential, industrial, and business districts.' In the late nineteenth century, the future site of the WTC had included a large settlement of Arab immigrants called the 'Syrian Quarter,' which was a vital center of small-scale commercial activity. In the 1930s, it became the hub of the city's electronics trade, known as 'Radio Row'. Lower Manhattan was not derelict; it was simply 'underdeveloped' by David Rockefeller's standards.

In fact, Rockefeller and the DLMA had a grand vision of the future city. It involved an ambitious plan to transform New York from an industrial to a postindustrial city. In the 1950s, New York still had a varied economy involving commerce, manufacturing, shipping and services. In 1959 there were nearly one million manufacturing jobs in the city employing mainly blue-collar workers. But Rockefeller's urban vision did not include a large manufacturing sector, an active port or blue-collar workers. Instead he envisaged a postindustrial urban economy based on a dynamic financial, service and commercial sector with an expanded white-collar office work force. Pundits called this new economy FIRE, which stood for Finance, Insurance, and Real Estate.

Whatever else one might think, Rockefeller's plan worked. By the 1970s, the number of manufacturing jobs in the city was reduced to 553,000. Today there are fewer than 300,000. What impact the elimination of so many manufacturing jobs will have on the future economy of New York is still to be determined. But the city's total economy was gravely wounded by September 11. The removal of 260,000 tons of debris at Ground Zero alone cost five billion dollars. Unemployment rose to eight percent in 2002 and is even higher in the current recession. Critics charge that New York's FIRE-based economy is under siege and that the city is undergoing its worst economic crisis since the 1970s when it faced bankruptcy.

As plans for the projected WTC moved forward in 1962, Tobin and the PA began the arduous task of finding clients for the giant new complex. This was not easy in a city that already had unused office space. At this point, New York Governor Nelson Rockefeller came to the aid of his younger brother, David. Nelson announced that the State of New York would concentrate many of its offices there, thus saving the project from the embarrassing spectre of too many vacancies. Small wonder then that when the project was completed, critics saw it as a Rockefeller family venture to enhance the Chase Manhattan Bank Tower and thus they dubbed the twin towers 'David' and 'Nelson'.

Building the WTC

Now the task fell to Tobin to find a suitable architect and here he made a surprising choice. Minoru Yamasaki was a Japanese-American architect based in the Midwest. 'In the end, Tobin delivered the World Trade Center into the hands of a kindred spirit: an ambitious climber with the soul of an engineer,' says Darton uncharitably. Strangely enough, Yamasaki had designed only one giant project before, the massive Pruitt-Igoe public housing project in St. Louis. Like similar projects built in the postwar period, it turned out to be a disaster. On July 15, 1972, while the WTC was under construction, municipal demolition experts imploded Pruitt-Igoe as thousands of former residents cheered. The WTC was not the first Yamasaki project to be blown up.

But to be fair to Yamasaki, the idea of building the world's tallest building was not his. The planners knew there was a limited market for commercial space in the WTC so they thought that the tallest building in the world would attract tenants. The result was a monstrous complex covering 40 hectares and comprising one million square meters of office space – or almost twice as much floor space as in the Pentagon. 'With the World Trade Center, the skyscraper mutated into a creature of a fundamentally different species,' says Darton. 'The trade center's scale and form had exploded the structure beyond any relationship to its surroundings. Its proportions simply gave people nothing in which they could recognize a human referent.'

Criticism rained down on the project from all sides. First, there were charges of simple graft. Second, there were skyrocketing costs. From an original estimate of $350 million in January 1964, the final cost was, as some critics had predicted, $1 billion. Environmentalists pointed out that there were no light switches in the towers so tenants were compelled to waste electricity. But the primary criticism was aesthetic. Michael Tomasky observed: 'to say that the towers were a symbol that New Yorkers were particularly proud of would be to stretch the point. As is well known, the World Trade Center was unloved by architecture critics and by New Yorkers in general.'[2]

Now that this 'unloved' landmark is gone, what of the future? The prize-winning design for the defunct site was the work of Daniel Libeskind, the brilliant Polish-Jewish-American architect who emigrated to the United States in 1959. But, nearly a decade after its destruction, the entire project is still mired in legal disputes and even Libeskind's celebrated Freedom Tower won't be completed before 2013. When it is finally constructed, the Manhattan skyline will be transformed once again, thus both closing a tragic page in the city's history and opening up a new and hopefully brighter chapter in its future. But whatever its final form, the new project will always live in the shadow of the old skyscrapers. As Darton observed prophetically in 2000, in some sense, those critics who praised the WTC twin towers as 'the first buildings of the twenty-first century' were correct. 'The problem was that they couldn't know what the twenty-first century was going to be about.'

Heavenly and unheavenly cities

The reelection of George W. Bush in 2004 demonstrated that Americans were still as divided as they were in 2000. Some attributed this division to the traumatic September 11 attack; but Americans were already deeply split over other key issues involving race and immigration; economic inequality and social values; indeed, the very meaning of the American Dream. This division is not new in American life; it can be traced back to the seventeenth century and the homogeneous group of English settlers who founded the early colonies. They created a society of like-minded individuals who maintained social cohesion by excluding anyone who didn't agree with them. John Winthrop's vision of 'a city on a hill' became the touchstone of this orthodoxy. 'Never has the ideal of community been more forcefully stated in America,' notes the urban historian Thomas Bender. 'The Puritans envisioned a single moral community, one that acknowledged no distinction between private and public values.'

In *The Unfinished City* (2002), Bender argues that America's national myths stem from such provincial sources. 'The most influential myths of America, those that have been incorporated into the culture, are very much identified with the regions of their origins: Puritan New England and Jeffersonian Virginia.' They succeeded in placing the small town and the agrarian community at the heart of the nation's vision of itself. Cosmopolitan cities like New York are the antithesis of what the Puritans had in mind. 'The New York experience and the outlook associated with that experience posit a political and cultural life based upon difference, while the myth of rural and small-town America excludes difference from politics and culture.' For some, New York City remains an un-American place.

This mistrust is neither new nor localized. 'Cities have always been viewed as instruments of luxurious corruption – parasites on the virtuous and fruitful occupations of country folk,' Joseph Rykwert noted in *The Seduction of Place*

(2000). While American fundamentalists consider the city a foreign country, Islamic terrorists identified it as the center of the American empire. Rykwert observed, 'From wherever it is seen – Europe or Asia, Latin America or the Pacific Rim – New York now seems to be the capital (financial, administrative – even cultural) of all the world.' But with the destruction of the World Trade Center, the image of the city was transformed; suddenly New York became the symbol of a more vulnerable America in the new age of global terrorism. Shortly after the terrorist attack, Don DeLillo described this transformation in an essay entitled 'In the Ruins of the Future'. 'Technology is our fate, our truth. It is what we mean when we call ourselves the only superpower on the planet,' he wrote. 'Now a small group of men have literally altered our skyline. We have fallen back in time and space.'

In the new millennium, New York became the site of a remarkable variety of interpretations. For instance, Doctorow's *City of God* (2000) and DeLillo's *Cosmopolis* (2003) are quite short but both novels have large ambitions in depicting the millennial moment in the global capital of the postmodern world. Both describe New York as shaped by money, multiplicity, ethnic diversity and the spectacle of constant change. Though neither is about the September 11 tragedy, both describe the cosmopolitan conditions that make New York the obvious target of *jihad*.

City of God takes place in end-of-the-millennium New York. It begins with the mysterious theft of a gigantic cross from a derelict Protestant church in lower Manhattan but this unsolved mystery forms only one strand of the novel. Instead it moves from the street to an interior space. Doctorow's discontinuous narrative purports to be the work of a writer named Everett who keeps a diary of his chaotic life in New York City. But Everett does not tell a single story; instead we look over his shoulder as he creates a synchronic account of postmodern life. We soon realize that we are reading his notes for a novel in which he records ideas for stories, conversations with friends, meditations on urban life, popular culture, sex, religion and cosmology. Doctorow explains, 'He's a kind of Everyman of what we know and think today. As a writer he is a carrier of our prevailing ideas of this time in history, a repository of our cultural detritus, and he has grown up haunted by the great disasters of his century. All of this finds expression in his compulsive need to record the life of his mind.'

Everett lives in an imperfect world far from Augustine's City of God. Life in Manhattan may not be heavenly, but the city is the site of an extraordinary democratic experiment. Everett thinks, 'And so each of the passersby on this corner, every scruffy, oversize, undersize, weird, fat, or bony or limping or muttering or foreign-looking, or greenhaired punk-strutting, threatening, crazy, angry, inconsolable person I see ... is a New Yorker, which is to say as native to this diaspora as I am, and part of our great sputtering experiment in a universalist society proposing a world without nations where anyone can be anything and the ID is planetary.'

Cosmopolis takes place on a single day in April 2000. The protagonist is Eric Packer, a fabulously wealthy currency trader who, at the age of 28, is the *wunderkind* of the postindustrial world. Packer has everything – and nothing. He has a new rich and beautiful wife whom he barely knows and rarely sees; a luxurious

48-room apartment in the world's tallest apartment building where he spends sleepless nights; and a burning desire to own everything, which he cannot fulfill. In the course of the novel he will lose his fortune, his illusions and his life.

But Eric is already partially dead. His real world is virtual: the data stream reproduced on the bank of computers and television screens which fill his cork-lined stretch limousine. From there he runs his global empire of ones and zeros, trading in the world's currencies and watching the world's violence on CNN – the murder of the managing director of the IMF in North Korea and the assassination of a powerful Russian mogul in Moscow. Packer is insulated from the outside world by his limousine, advisers and bodyguards. Even money has lost its reality for Eric; he recalls a line from a poem by Zbigniew Herbert which stands as the epigraph to the novel: 'a rat became the unit of currency.'

But on this April day all Eric Packer wants is a haircut. This simple task develops into a Homeric journey that takes him across New York City. The trip becomes an odyssey that will strip him of his defenses, liberate him from his *ennui* and lead him to a final confrontation with his nemesis and alter-ego, a derelict former employee who is a casualty of the globalizing process that Packer has helped create. Thus the real protagonist of *Cosmopolis* is the city itself. The entire novel takes place on a single New York street that runs crosstown from east to west, embracing the different worlds of the United Nations, the Diamond Mart, Times Square and Hell's Kitchen. DeLillo has chosen an actual street – 47th Street – because it reveals the cosmopolitan character of the 'unfinished city'. It is a metonym of Manhattan.

Both DeLillo's cosmopolis and Doctorow's metropolis are distinguished by their inclusive pluralism. Packer's employees are the city's new immigrants: advisers from chaotic Eastern Europe, bodyguards from the war-torn Balkans, his Muslim driver 'a victim of rooted violence driven by the spirits of his enemies forebears.' Similarly, Doctorow's global city is populated by new immigrants. 'The migrant wretched of the world, they think if they can just get here, they can get a foothold. Run a newsstand, a bodega, drive a cab, peddle. Janitor, security guard, run numbers, deal, whatever it takes. You want to tell them this is no place for poor people. The racial fault line going through the heartland goes through our heart.'

Yet despite racial antagonisms and ethnic suspicions, they are all part of a shared experience in a democratic experiment. So Doctorow writes, 'For all the wariness or indifference with which we negotiate our public spaces, we rely on the masses around us to delineate ourselves. The city may begin from a marketplace, a trading post, the confluence of waters, but it secretly depends on the human need to walk among strangers.'

DeLillo's next novel, *Falling Man* (2007), depicts New York after the destruction of the Twin Towers. It describes the survivors who live in what DeLillo earlier called 'the ruins of the future', symbolized by the recurring image of an anonymous figure falling from the burning North Tower. Twenty years earlier, in *Libra*, DeLillo had described the assassination of President Kennedy as 'the seven seconds that broke the back of the American century.' Now in *Falling Man* he depicts the destruction of the Twin Towers as the end of American innocence. As a survivor watches a videotape of the destruction of the Twin

Towers, he comments: 'It looks like an accident, the first one. Even from this distance, way outside the thing, how many days later, I'm standing here thinking it's an accident.' Then he adds, 'The second plane, by the time the second plane appears...we're all a little older and wiser.'

Other writers have tried to recapture the nightmare experience of fear and disorientation that Susan Faludi aptly calls *The Terror Dream* (2007). In Ken Kalfus' *A Disorder Peculiar to the Country* (2006), a WTC survivor is told by a sympathetic doctor, 'Well, that was something terrible, Mr. Harriman. Now you know what it's like to live in history.' In Jess Walter's *The Zero* (2006), an elderly woman asks anxiously, 'When do you think it will get back to normal?' Even foreign writers have joined in. In 2009 Joseph O'Neill, an Irish lawyer living in New York, became a celebrity when his novel, *Netherland* (2007), was praised by President Obama. *Netherland* is a contemporary revisioning of *The Great Gatsby*; O'Neill's West Indian hero is a postmodern version of Fitzgerald's dreamer living on the margins of the post-9/11 city. O'Neill acknowledges his debt to Fitzgerald but he sees *Netherland* as 'a post-American novel'. He says, 'I increasingly think that the integrity of the United States, the idea of the US as this special, sealed-off zone of opportunity and freedom, is anachronistic. Has this idea actually ever been true? Globalization has undermined the exclusiveness of the American experience.' Thus *Netherland* is both a vision of the post-holocaust city populated by new immigrants and a meditation on the American Moment.

Immigration: The promised city

The planes that smashed into the World Trade Center killed people from 62 countries and every religious faith. Over 400 victims came from India and Pakistan alone. Though some were tourists, most were New Yorkers and many were recent immigrants who worked in the buildings. In New York City, generations of new immigrants have helped to create a dynamic cosmopolitan society; without them, crucial sectors like transportation, information technology and public health could not function. 'The immigrant communities of the past have left an indelible imprint on the city,' says the anthropologist Nancy Foner. 'New York is constantly invigorated as new groups plant their roots here, and the newcomers themselves are – and will be – irrevocably changed by their own journeys through New York.'

In the twentieth century the United States – and New York – experienced two great waves of immigration and inner migration that transformed the nation and the city. The first wave occurred between 1880 and 1914 and consisted mainly of Italian Catholics and Russian Jews. The second wave, beginning in the 1960s and persisting today, contains many ethnic groups from the Caribbean, Mexico, Latin America, Asia, Africa and Eastern Europe. 'Today, a new wave of immigrants is again changing the face of the city,' Foner notes; 'immigrants already constitute over a third of the city's population. More than two and a half million have arrived since 1965, and they are now streaming in at a rate of over one hundred thousand a year.' In other words, the percentage of foreign-born in New York City today is the same as it was 150 years ago.

In *From Ellis Island to JFK* (2000), Foner measures the impact of recent immigration on the city's social and economic structure. She notes that in 1998, 37 percent of the city's population was foreign-born – 'an astounding 2.8 million immigrants'. Even more surprising are the social and cultural differences between the two waves of immigration. 'A hundred years ago, immigrants arrived at Ellis Island dirty and bedraggled, after a long ocean journey in steerage; now they emerge from the cabin of a jet plane at John F. Kennedy International Airport, often dressed in designer jeans or fashionable attire.' New York's new immigrants are not only ethnically diverse; they are differentiated by education, social background and class as well. Whereas earlier immigrants were often poor and uneducated, today's newcomers are a more varied group, including many middle-class professionals. 'Diversity, the buzz word of the 1990s, is an apt description of the newest New Yorkers. In almost every way – economically, educationally, and culturally – they are more diverse than their predecessors a hundred years ago, and this has enormous implications for understanding what happens when they settle in New York.'

What Foner describes in New York is also true of the rest of the country. In *The Lexus and the Olive Tree* (1999) Thomas Friedman noted that about one-third of the scientists and engineers in California's Silicon Valley are foreign-born. He cited a study by the Public Policy Institute of California which found that in 1996, there were 1786 Silicon Valley technology companies run by Indian and Chinese immigrant executives. These firms employed 46,000 people and sold $12.6 billion worth of goods and services. One biotech company had a staff that consisted of three Vietnamese, two Canadians, a German, a Peruvian, a Malaysian, an Iranian, an Indian, a Chinese, and eight native-born Americans. The CEO said, 'I cannot think of another country in the world where you could so easily put such a team together.'

Who are the new immigrants?

The new immigrants comprise a significant portion of the population. According to the 2000 Census, there are more than 30 million living in the United States; one-third of them arrived in the 1990s. Added together with their children, they number 60 million people – or an astonishing 20 percent of the population. They also reflect changing attitudes towards gender, race, ethnicity, and transnationality. Consider the issue of gender. One hundred years ago, 80 percent of the Italian immigrants were men. Today more than half of new immigrants are women. They are not only more numerous but more independent and, in many cases, better educated than their Italian and Jewish counterparts who arrived before even American women had the vote. According to Foner, 'Contemporary immigrant women benefit from, among other changes, the expansion of educational and employment opportunities for women, from liberalized legislation concerning divorce and gender discrimination, and from social welfare programs that have made it easier for them to manage on their own.' Many women experience more personal and economic freedom than in their homelands though, she notes, they still encounter 'the persistence of male privilege' in their adopted country.

There has also been a great change in the realm of race. We know that racial categories are social constructions rather than scientific facts. In the late nineteenth century, Italians and Jews were considered inferior races. American-born workers called themselves 'white men' to differentiate themselves from these new immigrants. Prejudice against Jews and Italians declined when immigration from southern and eastern Europe stopped in the 1920s. At the same time, the massive migration of blacks from the South after World War I and the post-World War II migration of Hispanics from Puerto Rico created a new racial dynamic in New York City. When immigration laws were reformed in the 1960s, a new wave of immigrants poured in, primarily from the Caribbean, Latin America, Africa and Asia. Thus the modern multicultural society was created.

However, contemporary talk about race and ethnicity can be misleading. Though many people still think in terms of a simple racial paradigm of white, black, Hispanic, and Asian, the reality is much more complex. For instance, blacks in New York are divided into two main groups, African Americans and West Indians. These two groups do not necessarily live in the same neighborhoods, compete for the same jobs or identify with each other. West Indians often distinguish themselves from African Americans by emphasizing their cultural, linguistic and behavioral differences. Foner says, 'In other words, race unites West Indians and African Americans; ethnicity divides them.'

The situation is even more complex among Hispanics who display a remarkable racial and ethnic diversity, including black Dominicans, white Argentinians and red Mexican Indians. Moreover, ethnic diversity is complicated by class differences. 'Most Brazilian New Yorkers are from the middle strata of Brazilian society and are well educated; they consider it an insult to be confused with the rest of the city's Latino population, who typically come from poorer backgrounds and have less education.' Thus Latin American immigrants often identify themselves by nationality to distinguish them from black Americans and Puerto Ricans, the city's poorest and most stigmatized minorities.

Indeed, the term, 'Hispanic'. is a good example of how racial categories are constructed. The term was created only a few decades ago by government census takers as a convenient way of covering the various Spanish-speaking groups. Though Spanish-speaking immigrants tend to identify themselves by nationality, they are increasingly characterized as a racial group in public discourse. According to Foner, 'There has been a gradual racialization of Hispanics – a belief that physical characteristics, particularly skin color, are involved. Indeed, by treating Hispanics as a group equivalent to blacks in antidiscrimination and affirmative-action policies, the federal government has contributed to raising Hispanic to the status of a racial category.'

While blacks and Hispanics continue to be racially stigmatized, the growing Asian community is often named as the city's most successful 'minority', comparable in achievement to the Jews of 100 years ago. There is a certain bitter irony in this. For much of American history, Asian immigrants were barred from becoming citizens. Though African Americans became US citizens after the Civil War, legal measures like the 1882 Chinese Exclusion Act denied citizenship to Asians. It was not until 1943 that Chinese immigrants were granted the right to citizenship and not until 1952 that other Asians were granted the same rights.

All that has changed now that many Asians have become successful, assimilated Americans. Though part of their success stems from a culture-bound work ethic, Foner suggests that another reason is class-bound. According to the 1990 census one-third of adult Asian immigrants in New York City were college graduates. But only about 10 percent of the West Indian and Latin American adult immigrants had finished college. She describes a new racial hierarchy that is evolving in New York, which places Asians above Hispanics and blacks. 'This enormous change in perceptions of Asians has led to speculation that, with more intermarriage and intermingling, the category "white" may eventually be expanded to include Asians as well as lighter-skinned Hispanics, although a more pessimistic view holds that persistent discrimination will prevent Asians from ever being accepted as belonging to white America.'

Finally, there is the issue of transnationality: the feeling of belonging to two different cultures. Old and new immigrants have tried to maintain strong familial, economic and cultural ties with both their homeland and their host country. But present-day transnational communities are more complex because of new technologies and the global economy. Jet planes, mobile telephones and the Internet simplify and multiply communication between continents. The global economy encourages international business operations. Thus Indian immigrants repatriate money earned in New York as venture capital for new businesses in Andhra Pradesh; Chinese 'astronauts' shuttle back and forth between Taiwan or Hong Kong and New York; and Hispanic businessmen divide their time between the Dominican Republic and the United States. The new transnationalism, which appears to be both far-reaching and long-lasting, raises interesting questions about the durability of traditional concepts of national identity and even citizenship in the brave new world of mass migration and global economy.

Remaking the American mainstream

The United States has always been a nation of immigrants; but it has often been a nation that feared new immigrants as well. In the 1850s a new anti-immigrant political party called the American or 'Know-Nothing' Party flourished on a fear of Irish Catholics and German socialists. In the 1920s, another backlash against new immigrants from eastern and southern Europe culminated in restrictive immigration laws. In a similar spirit, there is a growing movement to restrict immigration today. In a controversial book entitled *Alien Nation* (1995), Peter Brimelow argued that American society will break down if non-European immigration continues to grow and the white European population continues to decline. Brimelow sounds like a homegrown American chauvinist but, in fact, he is himself an immigrant – from Great Britain! Recent efforts to make English the national language and to restrict the rights of illegal immigrants suggest that America is experiencing another wave of anti-immigrant feeling. The continuing War on Terror has not improved the climate.

Some of Brimelow's arguments were echoed in Samuel Huntington's *Who Are We?* (2004). Huntington made a distinction between Settlers and Immigrants.

The original English settlers were immigrants who created the social, cultural and political foundations of the new nation; the immigrants who came after settled in a country whose framework was already established. 'Anglo-Protestant culture has been central to American identity for three centuries,' he argued. Its seminal contributions have been the English language, Christian religion, Protestant work ethic and the English concept of the rule of law. 'Historically, millions of immigrants were attracted to America because of this culture and the economic opportunities it helped to make possible.' Instead of the melting pot of cultural fusion or the salad bowl of multiculturalism, he proposed a third culinary metaphor: tomato soup, or Anglo-Protestant conformity. 'The culinary metaphor is an Anglo-Protestant tomato soup to which immigration adds celery, croutons, spices, parsley and other ingredients that enrich and diversify the taste, but which are absorbed into what remains fundamentally tomato soup.'

But now Huntington saw a fly in his soup. He feared that the core Anglo-Protestant values were being undermined by massive Mexican immigration, with its demand for bilingual education, binational citizenship and a separate Hispanic culture. Instead of one English-speaking nation, he presented the alarming prospect of two nations where one speaks only Spanish. He warned, 'Mexican immigration is leading toward the demographic *reconquista* of areas Americans took from Mexico by force in the 1830s and 1840s.' Some of his conclusions are contradicted in Richard Alba and Victor Nee's *Remaking the American Mainstream* (2003). According to them, Hispanics – including Mexicans – are assimilating to American norms in education, employment and citizenship though at a slower rate than other groups.

Like Huntington, the two authors believe assimilation is desirable. They argue, 'Assimilation has reshaped the American mainstream in the past, and it will do so again, culturally, institutionally, and demographically.' Unlike Huntington, they view assimilation as a dynamic process in which both the new immigrant and the national mainstream are changed. Instead of imposing an ideal national identity from the top down, they propose a dialogic approach. 'Coercive assimilation, which can be seen in the state- and elite-led policies of the early twentieth century, which disparaged immigrant cultures and attempted "pressure-cooker" acculturation, is not usually very effective because it stimulates active resistance in its subjects.' On the contrary, assimilation is most effective when it is the result of individual choices. In a felicitous phrase borrowed from the Beatles, they describe assimilation as 'something that frequently enough happens to people while they are making other plans.'

Alba and Nee's argument is bolstered by recent research which shows a surprising change in migratory patterns. Between 1965 and 1990 the majority of immigrants settled in five states: California, New York, Texas, Florida, and Illinois. Since then, there has been a remarkable diffusion, as Douglas S. Massey demonstrates in *New Faces in New Places* (2008). 'During the 1990s,' says Massey, 'something dramatic happened – there was a marked shift of immigrants away from global cities and the states and regions where they are located toward new places of destination throughout the United States.' Now immigrants, including Mexicans, are moving to new locations in Arkansas, Georgia, Iowa, Nevada and North Carolina. Once again the face of America is being transformed.

Huntington insisted that Americans have always resisted expanded immigration; the current vitriolic debate on immigration reform suggests he may be correct. But a recent comprehensive study of national attitudes suggests Americans still believe that the United States should remain an immigrant society despite the presence of many illegal immigrants. In *One Nation, After All* (1998), Alan Wolfe showed that a majority of middle-class Americans dismiss Brimelow's proposals in *Alien Nation*. One respondent spoke for the majority when he said, 'I think that anybody who denies immigrants ultimately denies America.' Surprisingly, attitudes towards immigration and immigrants defy traditional political analysis; Americans do not divide into right and left on this issue as one might have expected. Though many Americans support some restrictions, disagreements about immigration in the middle class are less ideological than methodological. There is broad agreement on a vision of a future America, says Wolfe: 'a society that respects law, a society that takes care of people, a society that is open to opportunity.' That society, it seems, will always have room for new immigrants.

Race: Nashville and beyond

The success of the United States as an immigrant society must be set beside its failure to achieve racial equality. The legacy of racial prejudice continues to haunt American efforts to create a society worthy of its essential document, 'The Declaration of Independence'. The terrible consequences of failing to confront America's institutionalized racism were revealed once again in December 2003 with the sensational disclosure that the recently deceased senator from Mississippi, Strom Thurmond, Dixiecrat candidate for president in 1948 and an outspoken opponent of racial integration for most of the twentieth century, was the father of a black daughter whom he had secretly supported and publicly abandoned for seven decades.

In *The Image* (1961), Daniel Boorstin wrote, 'From the beginning, the great promise of America was to open doors, so that men could try to work out their problems for themselves – not necessarily alone, but in communities of their choosing, and toward often-uncertain ends which appealed to them.' As we have seen, perhaps nothing reflected the promise of America better than the Civil Rights movement. David Halberstam, the late journalist who covered the movement 40 years ago, concluded: 'I can think of no occasion in recent postwar American history when there has been so shining an example of democracy at work because of the courage and nobility of ordinary people – people hardly favored at the time of birth by their circumstances – than what happened in those days in the South. By that I mean the five years which began in February 1960 with the sit-ins and ended with the Voting Rights Act in 1965 after the Selma protests.'

The beloved community

In 1998 Halberstam published a narrative of four decades of African-American experience in microcosm. *The Children* is a moving account of the lives of several important black activists who first met in Nashville, Tennessee in 1958. It began when James Lawson, Jr. came to study theology at the newly integrated

Vanderbilt Divinity School. He had spent three years in India studying Gandhi's method of nonviolent civil disobedience to see what lessons might be learned for the civil rights struggle in his own country. Then in 1955 he read in the Indian newspapers about the Montgomery Bus Boycott. Lawson knew it was time to go home.

He established a workshop in nonviolence, which attracted a small but dedicated core of black students. They included Diane Nash, a runner-up in the Miss Illinois beauty contest; James Bevel, one of 17 children from a small town in Mississippi; Gloria Johnson, a medical student who had graduated from a prestigious New England women's college; and John Lewis, a slow-speaking country boy from Alabama who studied at American Baptist College. They participated in the Nashville sit-ins and later became leaders in two major civil rights organizations, SNCC and SCLC, the Southern Christian Leadership Conference.

They were all part of a close-knit group that Lawson called 'the beloved community'. In the 1960s they achieved some remarkable victories; but at the moment of their greatest triumph, things began to fall apart. A second generation of activists, more alienated and less religious than the first, took over SNCC and demanded the exclusion of white members. Soon Martin Luther King's 'loving disobedience' was being replaced by 'black rage'. The rise of black nationalism subverted the original goal of integration; the belief in nonviolent civil *disobedience* gave way to the rhetoric of violent *disallegiance*. With King's murder in 1968, an era in the struggle for civil rights was over.

As the civil rights movement deteriorated, the members of 'the beloved community' dispersed. Thirty years later their lives were irrevocably changed. Lawson moved to a large, middle-class black church in Los Angeles. Johnson became the first black professor of psychiatry at Harvard Medical School. Lewis was elected to the U.S Congress. But not everyone succeeded. Diane Nash married and divorced James Bevel. She raised their two children as a single parent while he continued to drift through the fringes of American politics. Another early activist, Marion Barry, was twice elected mayor of Washington, DC, became involved in corruption scandals, was imprisoned on a narcotics charge, and was reelected Mayor in 1994 after his release from prison.

The black community after the 1960s

The story of the demise of Nashville's 'beloved community' is a parable of what has happened to the larger African-American community after the heyday of the civil rights movement. When the communal spirit dissolved, black society itself fragmented. One observer said: 'As [some] Negro families succeed, they tend to move out of these economically and socially depressed areas to better neighborhoods where they and their children have a better opportunity to lead a better life. They leave behind the least educated and the most deprived – unwed mothers, deserted wives, the physically and mentally handicapped, and the aged. As a result there is a concentration of misery in the very hearts of our largest cities.'[3]

During the 1970s and 1980s black communities split apart and black America was increasingly divided into a two-class society. On the one hand, increased opportunities enabled 35 to 45 percent of black families to enter the middle class. On the other hand, another 30 percent of the black population declined into deeper poverty. 'Significantly, black families living on the margins of the nation's urban ghettos made substantial gains,' William Chafe wrote in *The Unfinished Journey* (1986); 'but in the heart of the ghetto, every indicator of poverty showed deterioration. In the past, blacks from all classes had been united by neighborhood bonds, common institutions, and a shared commitment to self-help and progress. Now, the middle-class leadership of those communities moved into desegregated suburbs, leaving the least well off to endure crime, massive unemployment, malnutrition, and urban chaos. In the past, the majority of poor families had lived in rural areas of America. Now, more than 70 per cent lived in inner cities.'

By the beginning of the 1990s the successes of the civil rights movement were tangible. There were black mayors in large Northern cities, black sheriffs in small Southern towns, a Black Caucus in Congress, and a significant showing of black talent in both the Clinton and Bush administrations. Affirmative-action policies had encouraged more black men and women to become doctors, lawyers, businessmen and stockbrokers. But the civil rights movement failed to regenerate itself, was unable to produce a second generation of leaders who could command the allegiance of the whole black community. Moreover, it failed to sustain its earlier vision of a racially integrated society.

At the beginning of the new century, black and white Americans were still debating the condition of America's multiracial society. There was no doubt that many African Americans had moved upward; but it was just as certain that nearly as many had moved downward. In *Blurring the Color Line* (2009) Richard Alba reports that in 2000 more black men were in prison than in college; in 1980 the situation was reversed by a wide margin. 'For the black community, imprisonment has become an affliction far greater than it ever was in the pre-civil rights era. The United States has become the world's leader in putting its own citizen's behind bars, and this incarceration has had a disproportionate impact on ethnoracial minorities, who make up 60 per cent of prisoners.'

The debate over racial progress often amounted to an argument over whether the glass is half-full or half-empty. The pessimistic view is presented by Andrew Hacker in *Two Nations: Black and White, Separate, Hostile, Unequal* (1992). 'A huge racial chasm remains,' says Hacker, 'and there are few signs that the coming century will see it closed.' A more optimistic view is offered by Stephan and Abigail Thernstrom in *America in Black and White* (1997). They point to evidence of dramatic racial progress in areas like education, employment, median income and life expectancy at birth. In fact, the Thernstroms conceived their book as an answer to Hacker: 'One nation (we argue), no longer separate, much less unequal than it once was, and by many measures, less hostile.'

Facing up to the American dream

But the problem of racial divisions goes beyond the parameters of inequality and threatens the very fabric of American ideology. As President Clinton defined it in 1993, 'The American dream that we were all raised on is a simple but powerful one – if you work hard and play by the rules you should be given a chance to go as far as your God-given ability will take you.' But as economic inequalities increase and equal opportunities for the poorly educated decrease in the era of globalization and economic recession, many blacks and whites may be sentenced to a life term in the permanent new underclass. They may begin to reject the universal appeal of the American dream and seek other creeds that promote social anomie, racial prejudice or class antagonisms.

In *Facing Up to the American Dream* (1995), Jennifer L. Hochschild noted that while blacks and whites define the American dream of equal opportunity similarly, they interpret it in different ways. Whites believe that African Americans are now included in the dream; they point to the rapid expansion of a black middle class and their increased visibility in business, politics and culture. Blacks, on the other hand, still feel that the terms of the dream exclude them; even successful blacks are made to feel that they have 'made it' less on their own merit than because of special programs of affirmative action. Thus African Americans are caught in a racial Catch-22: if they succeed it is not through their own efforts; if they fail it is because of their own efforts. 'If a substantial number of Americans lose faith in any foundational precept or the whole gestalt,' she concluded, 'the American dream can collapse in upon itself as thoroughly as any savings and loan bank.' This could mean the end of the American Moment; it is the real challenge of the twenty-first century.

Multiracialism: 'The new face of America'

Meanwhile there were other significant cultural changes taking place in American society. In *Racechanges* (1997), Susan Gubar cites examples of a new interracial consciousness reflected in popular culture: 'In 1993, two phenomena…dramatically underscored the importance of cross-racial patterns of imagery.' First, a *Time* magazine article on 'The New Face of America' featured a computer-created cover of a 'new Eve' composed of white, black, yellow, brown and red racial and ethnic features. In the same year, the late pop star Michael Jackson issued a new music video entitled 'Black and White', which used the same Morph 2.0 computer program to blend images of black, white, male, female, Native American and Asian faces. At the same time, a new generation of popular culture icons – movie actors, pop stars and sports celebrities – entered the scene. Significantly, many were interracial: golf champion Tiger Woods, baseball star Derek Jeter, actress Halle Berry, singer Mariah Carey, actor Joaquin Pheonix, musician Alicia Keys, playwright August Wilson, and television personality Paula Abdul. Finally, in 2000, the census added a new multiracial category to the list of traditional racial identities. More than six million Americans identified themselves as 'multiracial' though many more clearly were.

Richard Alba and Victor Nee argue that the American mainstream is in the process of being redefined in ways that undermine the foundation of identity politics. 'Given demographic trends, the mainstream is likely to evolve in the direction of including members of ethnic and racial groups that were formerly excluded,' they predict; 'in the next quarter century, we expect some blurring of the main ethnic and racial boundaries of American life.' Just as excluded ethnic groups like Italians and Jews were 'whitened' in the early twentieth century so, one hundred years later, Cubans and Chinese are also entering the American mainstream. 'For portions of nonwhite and Hispanic groups, the social and cultural distance from the mainstream will shrink: these individuals will live and work in ethnically and racially mixed milieus, much of the time without a sense that their social interactions are greatly affected by their origins.' While this will not mean an end to racial inequality, still 'it will alter the racial compartmentalization of American society to an important extent.'

In *Remaking the American Mainstream*, Alba and Nee also suggest that intermarriage will be the primary vehicle for redefining American identity. 'Indeed, this process is already visibly underway, but it will expand in the future.' In fact, the exogamous rate among many ethnic groups, especially in Asian-American communities, is climbing at an astonishing rate. In *Blurring the Color Line* (2009), Richard Alba reports, 'Intermarriage rates, mainly with white American partners, have soared to the point that about one of every two young US-born Asian Americans marries a non-Asian.' While this status change has not erased all racial stereotypes, says Alba, 'the changes have been profound, nevertheless.'

In the 1980s a new phenomenon appeared on the multiethnic Berkeley campus: the rapidly-growing population of students of mixed racial origin founded an organization called MISC (Multiracial Intercultural Student Coalition). They confounded supporters of orthodox identity politics because they refused to identify with a single racial or ethnic group. As their children grow up they will create a new social dynamic. By 2009, the Associated Press reported, 'Multiracial Americans have become the fastest-growing demographic group, wielding an impact on minority growth that challenges traditional notions of race.'[4] So multiracial Americans may become the new face of the nation.

If MISC is a harbinger of the future then America may become a pluralistic society of a different kind. Instead of multiculturalism within the society we will have multiculturalism within the individual. Over 150 years ago, in 'Song of Myself' Walt Whitman sang of the American as a cosmos containing multitudes. Today, the critic Leon Wieseltier argues in *The New Republic*, 'The American achievement is not the multicultural society, it is the multicultural individual.' He says, 'Identity is a promise of singleness, but this is a false promise. Many things are possible in America, but the singleness of identity is not one of them.'

Dreams from My Father

The cultural changes of the past 20 years set the stage for the fundamental political changes to come. Just as a new cultural paradigm predated Kennedy's presidency in 1960, so a new multiracial paradigm anticipated Obama's election in 2008. Among the first to notice was the journalist Andrew Sullivan. Writing in *The Atlantic* (December 2007), he advanced three reasons for Barack Obama's emerging popularity: his independence, his youth and his face. 'Barack Hussein Obama is the new face of America,' wrote Sullivan. 'A brown-skinned man whose father was an African, who grew up in Indonesia and Hawaii, who attended a majority-Muslim school as a boy.'

But Obama was not always the ideal multiracial candidate. In 1995, before he became a politician, Obama published a revealing autobiography, *Dreams from My Father*. In this beautifully written book, he traces his remarkable life from his birth to a white mother from Kansas and a black father from Kenya. Obama's father abandoned the family when his son was two, moved to Harvard to study and returned to Kenya soon after. In fact, Obama only met his father once again when he was ten years old. His book is about the search for the missing father.

Despite being raised in a white family environment, Obama was aware of racial prejudice at an early age. He notes, 'In 1960, the year my parents were married, *miscegenation* still described a felony in over half the states in the Union.' As he grew up he embarked on a search for his black roots. 'Away from my mother, away from my grandparents, I was engaged in a fitful interior struggle. I was trying to raise myself to be a black man in America, and beyond the given of my appearance, no one around me seemed to know exactly what that meant.' When he reached adolescence, he began to act out his black rebellion. As he recalls, 'I was living out a caricature of black male adolescence, itself a caricature of swaggering American manhood.'

Obama's embrace of his racial identity was a sign of the times. When a friend from a mixed marriage insisted she was not 'black' but '*multiracial*', Obama disagreed. 'That was the problem with people like Joyce,' he recalls. 'They talked about the richness of their multicultural heritage and it sounded real good, until you noticed that they avoided black people.' But when his search for the absent father later takes him to Africa, he discovers the confusion is global. In Kenya, his aunt describes a similar multicultural muddle where her daughter speaks bits of English, Luo, Swahili and German. 'Sometimes I get fed up with this,' she says. 'But I'm beginning to resign myself – there's nothing really to do. They lived in a mixed-up world. It's just as well, I suppose. In the end, I'm less interested in a daughter who's authentically African than one who is authentically herself.'

Obama's search for his roots takes him to Kenya, Harvard and Chicago. Soon it becomes clear that his search for the absent father is also a search for his place in the larger community. He learns, 'Communities had to be created, fought for, tended like gardens.'

They expanded or contracted with the dreams of men – and in the civil rights movement those dreams had been large…Through organizing, through shared sacrifice, membership had been earned. And because membership was earned – because this community I imagined was still in the making, built on the promise that the larger American community, black, white, and brown, could somehow redefine itself – I believed that it might, over time, admit the uniqueness of my own life.

Dreams from My Father is a moving racial odyssey that reflects its times. But the man who was elected president in 2008 was not quite the same man who wrote the book 13 years before. In the new edition, published in 2004 after the death of his mother, Obama wonders why he focused on his missing black father when he was raised by his white mother. 'I think sometimes that had I known she would not survive her illness, I might have written a different book – less a meditation on the absent parent, more a celebration of the one who was the single constant in my life...I know she was the kindest, most generous spirit I have ever known, and that what is best in me I owe to her.'

In his second, less personal book, *The Audacity of Hope* (2006), Obama returns to his complex relations with his parents. 'My fierce ambitions might have been fueled by my father – by my knowledge of his achievements and failures, by my unspoken desire to somehow earn his love, and by my resentments and anger toward him.' But it was his mother's 'fundamental faith' in the value of human life that shaped those ambitions to study political philosophy, become a community organizer and enter political life.

A deliberative democracy

In *The Audacity of Hope*, Obama acknowledges that he is the prisoner of his own biography. He writes, 'I can't help but view the American experience through the lens of a black man of mixed heritage, forever mindful of how generations of people who looked like me were subjugated and stigmatized, and the subtle and not so subtle ways that race and class continue to shape our lives.' But he is also heir to an American democratic tradition based on the Constitution and the rule of law.

James Madison, father of the Constitution, said famously, 'if men were angels they wouldn't need governments.' But the obverse was also true: if men were devils they couldn't form governments. Madison and his colleagues enshrined in the Constitution their vision of limited government based on the separation of powers and the Bill of Rights. Obama also sees 'our democracy not as a house to be built, but as a conversation to be had.' Accordingly, 'the genius of Madison's design' is in its flexibility. 'It provides us with a framework and with rules, but fidelity to these rules will not guarantee a just society or assure agreement on what's right.' This framework helps us to 'organize the way by which we argue about our future.' It is 'designed to force us into a conversation, a "deliberative democracy" in which all citizens are required to engage in a process of testing their ideas against an external reality, persuading others of their point of view, and building shifting alliances of consent.'

Obama identifies one impulse shared by all the Founding Fathers: 'a rejection of all forms of absolute authority, whether the king, the theocrat, the general, the oligarch, the dictator, the majority, or anyone else who claims to make choices for us.' A deliberative democracy is a site of conversation, not a monologue. Beyond that, says Obama, 'was a rejection of absolute truth, the infallibility of any idea or ideology or theology or "ism", any tyrannical consistency that might lock future generations into a single, unalterable course, or drive both majorities and minorities into the cruelties of the Inquisition, the pogrom, the gulag, or the jihad.'

From the public sphere to cyberspace

President Obama's 'conversation' takes place in what sociologists call the 'public sphere': the open space uncontrolled by governments where ideas are debated and public opinion is formed. In *The Structural Transformation of the Public Sphere* (1962, translated 1989) Jurgen Habermas described how in the eighteenth century the public sphere thrived in English coffee houses. (By 1710 there were 3000 coffee houses in London.) But today public opinion is formed in the mass media which we receive in the privacy of our homes. Now the advent of new digital media has transformed the way public opinion is transmitted.

After Watergate, the press was ascendant but then the reputation of newspapers suffered as their existence was threatened by journalistic scandals, declining readership, falling profits, staffing cuts, corporate takeovers, growing bankruptcies and the increasing dominance of Internet competition. 'Americans have never been truly fond of their press,' noted James Fallows in *Breaking the News* (1996). 'Americans believe that the news media have become too arrogant, cynical, scandal-minded, and destructive. Public hostility shows up in opinion polls, through comments on talk shows, in waning support for news organizations in their showdowns with government officials, and in many other ways. The most important sign of public unhappiness may be a quiet consumer's boycott of the press. Year by year, a smaller proportion of Americans goes to the trouble of reading newspapers or watching news broadcasts on TV.'

The decline of traditional news outlets continues in the new millennium. In 2009 Todd Gitlin described the 'many crises' faced by the news media and concluded that traditional information sources were being radically transformed. He noted that the average American newspaper reader is 55 years old while the median age of evening news television viewers is 61. As the young turn to other information outlets offered by computers and cell phones there is a paradigm shift in how Americans view the world. 'We may well be living amidst a sea change in how we encounter the world, how we take in its traces and make sense of them, a change comparable to the shift from oral to written culture among the Greeks and the shift to printing with movable types in 15th and 16th century Europe.'[5]

World Wide Web

The advent of the World Wide Web, developed by Tim Berners-Lee in 1991, ushered in a new age of global digital communication with its promise of universal demographic and democratic access. The new e-technology giants like Microsoft, Yahoo and Google announced 'the democratization of information' and began paving the broad 'Information Superhighway'. A Microsoft engineer compared cyberspace to what Frederick Jackson Turner called the frontier in nineteenth-century America: 'the engine driving an economic democracy'. He argued the information highway would break '*the tyranny of geography* – the stranglehold of location, access and transportation that has governed human societies from their inception.' A Yahoo executive reiterated the ethos when he stated: 'We believe the Internet can positively transform lives, societies and economies. We believe the Internet is built on openness.' The motto of Google is: 'Don't be evil.'

There is no doubt that the Internet can be a democratizing force. It makes available to a global audience information that was once limited to a privileged few. It has also had a profound impact on global politics. In 1997 Jody Williams was awarded the Nobel Peace Prize after she used the Internet to organize the International Campaign to Ban Landmines from her home in rural New England. In the new millennium, as social networks like YouTube and Facebook proliferate, their role in organizing presidential campaigns and political protests increases. In *The Argument* (2007), Matt Bai showed how the Internet recently transformed the Democratic Party, culminating in Barack Obama's innovative campaign for the presidency. In *Bad Elements* (2001), Ian Buruma described how Chinese dissidents used cyberspace to counteract the Chinese regime's crackdown on opposition after the Tiananmen Square massacre in 1989. More recently, Iranian demonstrators used social networking to organize massive street protests against the fraudulent presidential election in 2009.

But after two decades the 'openness' of the Internet is still contested. First, there is the question of global access. Uneven development has prevented the creation of 'a level playing field'. In the United States there are 600 phones per 1000 inhabitants while in Chad there is one phone per 1000 inhabitants. Technological backwardness is a primary reason for Africa's faltering economic and social development. Second, 'the democratization of information' is challenged in three crucial areas: control by government; control by private corporation; and control by nobody, anarchy.

Don't be evil

The Internet can be a two-edged sword. Instead of democratizing information, authoritarian regimes try to monopolize it. In Russia, President Putin silenced his critics by closing down independent television stations on dubious technical grounds. In China, the regime protects its citizens from unhappy news by employing a gigantic censorship apparatus called The Great Firewall which filters out references to taboo subjects like Tiananmen, Tibet and Taiwan independence. Even more troubling was the revelation that major American internet providers and software companies are coconspirators in this process of censorship. Eager for access to China's huge potential market, giants like Microsoft, Yahoo and Google signed agreements allowing them to operate in China but at the cost of free expression. Yahoo even admitted giving confidential data to Chinese officials that helped send a Chinese journalist to prison for ten years.

The saga of authoritarian government control took a new turn in 2010 when Google discovered that its sensitive Chinese accounts were being intercepted by mysterious hackers who were traced to two Chinese educational institutions with close ties to the military establishment. Google responded by taking its motto seriously. It refused to comply with Chinese censorship rules, closed its Internet operation on the mainland and moved it to Hong Kong. The mainland regime replied by blocking the giant American operator. In July the Chinese government renewed Google's permit to operate on the mainland but it continues to block access to the website sporadically.

In little more than a year, international icons like Google, Facebook, Twitter and YouTube have disappeared from Chinese cyberspace; evidently, the regime's goal is to create a tightly controlled alternative social networking reality for its citizens. In the new millennium China is moving away from Habermas' Public Sphere and toward Huxley's Brave New World.

When Tim Berners-Lee first introduced the World Wide Web he had no interest in profit. But others immediately saw the commercial possibilities. 'Five years later it was a mainstream commercial technology, the religion of corporate apparatchiks everywhere, who now walked around spewing the new clichés about the importance of "knowledge sharing," "being webified," and "thinking outside the box,"' says Michael Lewis in *Next: The Future Just Happened* (2001).

The Google motto is 'Don't be evil' but not all privately funded media activity is benign. In their desire to square 'media openness' with the bottom line, Internet corporations have been caught in a murky ethical area dancing with dictators and pursuing monopolistic control. Critics note that cyberspace is already controlled by a handful of giant corporations, placing more power in fewer corporate hands. But the question remains: how is the consolidation of media power in private hands qualitatively different from the consolidation of media power in the hands of an authoritarian government?

A third threat to democratization is the misuse of the media in a playing field without rules or regulation. The Internet can be misused by child pornographers and racist demagogues; the public sphere can be subverted by dictators and terrorists; cyberspace can be manipulated by unscrupulous bankers and businessmen. But this subversion took a bizarre new turn in September 2005 when the conservative Danish newspaper *Jyllands-Posten* published a series of cartoons depicting the prophet Muhammad in a variety of poses. 'We have a tradition of satire in Denmark,' the cultural editor Flemming Rose wrote in the *Washington Post*. 'We do the same with the royal family, politicians, anyone. In a modern secular society, nobody can impose their religious taboos in the public domain.'

However, local Islamic clerics were shocked by the cartoons and began an unsuccessful campaign to force the Danish government to apologize for the sacrilege. By January 2006 news of the Danish sacrilege was spreading over the Internet to Muslim countries from Lebanon to Indonesia. Fueled by wild rumors that the Koran was about to be burned in Denmark, riots broke out in Syria, Lebanon and Afghanistan. Danish embassies were torched in Beirut and Damascus. The Saudis started a boycott of Danish products. Angry mobs elsewhere burned the Danish flag and respected Islamic clerics demanded that the Danish editor be put to death.

The controversy, stoked by the Internet, produced more heat than illumination. But the ironies were abundant. Danish businessmen, stung by an Islamic boycott of their products, quickly abandoned western ideas of freedom of speech and hastened to apologize to the Muslim public. Muslims were particularly offended by one cartoon's association of Islam with violence; now violent Muslim mobs were confirming the connection by burning down embassies and thirsting for blood. In *The New Republic*, Leon Wieseltier observed, 'Scores of people died in the cartoon riots. It was not the cartoons that killed them; it was their conviction that violence is a variety of cultural criticism.'[6] Now, after two decades, the Internet is still in its adolescence, flawed in construction but indispensable in usage. As Richard Powers observes in *Generosity* (2009): 'Information may travel at light speed. But meaning travels at the speed of dark.'

Book business

In the age of electronic media, do books have a future? Jason Epstein, the legendary Random House editor, believes they do but in a new form. In *Book Business* (2001), he notes that book publishing is not a rational business. Whereas cars, refrigerators and soap powder can be standardized, centrally planned, and mass produced, books are individual items up to the time of their printing. In other words, books belong to an older mode of small-scale production: what we call 'a cottage industry'.

But in the late twentieth century, commercial publishing was radically transformed by economics and demography. The rise of giant media conglomerates led to the commercial consolidation of the book business while the suburbanization of America led to the decline of independent booksellers and the homogenization of literary culture. This consolidation was mirrored in the consolidation of the list of bestsellers. Epstein notes that between 1986 and 1996, nearly two-thirds of the 100 bestselling titles in America were written by only six writers: Tom Clancy, John Grisham, Stephen King, Dean Koontz, Michael Crichton, and Danielle Steel.

Today book publishing faces a new crisis as we enter the era of advanced information technology. Will book publishers and booksellers alike be replaced by the Internet and the electronic book? Epstein imagines a time in the near future when we will order a book at our local kiosk and have it printed electronically while we wait. Ironically, the future book business will be less like today's media conglomerate than yesterday's cottage industry: 'decentralized, improvisational, personal'. This will radically change the function of the publishing house but will it eliminate the bookstore? Epstein thinks not. He says, 'a civilization without retail booksellers is unimaginable. Like shrines and other sacred meeting places, bookstores are essential artifacts of human nature. The feel of a book taken from a shelf and held in the hand is a magical experience, linking writer to reader.' But the bookstore of the future will have to be markedly different from today's mass-market emporiums. 'Tomorrow's stores will have to be what the Web cannot be: tangible, intimate, and local; communal shrines, perhaps with coffee bars offering pleasure and wisdom in the company of others who share one's interests, where the book one wants can always be found and surprises and temptations spring from every shelf.'

So we end where we began, reading our 'sacred' cultural texts as part of the national 'conversation' cited by Obama. 'The books we read read us,' notes Josephine Hendin, pointing to the necessity of art in a critical time. 'In the American moral crisis,' Saul Bellow writes, 'the first requirement was to experience what was happening and to see what must be seen.' For Bellow, writing is an act of recovering reality and a process of discovering its meaning. The artist's job is 'to recover the world that is buried under the debris of false description or nonexperience.' For John Barth, the act of storytelling does not recover reality but creates it: 'the truth of fiction is that Fact is fantasy; the made-up story is a model of the world.' For Doctorow, the act of writing becomes a metaphor for the act of living: 'The insufficiency of fiction and the need to reform it, I take as a metaphor for our need to transform our lives and remake ourselves.'[7] While politicians and presidents speak sententiously of a New World Order, our artists continue to remind us that we have neither reached the End of History nor fulfilled the American Dream. As Joyce Carol Oates remarks: 'America is a tale still being told – in many voices – and nowhere near its conclusion.'

NOTES

1. Paul Hirst, 'Future War', www.openDemocracy.net (October 18, 2001).
2. Michael Tomasky, 'The Story Behind the Towers', *New York Review of Books*, (March 14, 2002), p. 8.
3. Quoted in William H. Chafe, *The Unfinished Journey*, New York: Oxford University Press, 1986, p. 442.
4. Hope Yen, 'Multiracial people become fastest-growing US group', Associated Press (May 28, 2009).
5. Todd Gitlin, 'Journalism's Many Crises', www.openDemocracy.net (May 20, 2009).
6. Leon Wieseltier, 'Jollies', *New Republic* (March 20, 2006).
7. E. L. Doctorow, 'Living in the House of Fiction', *The Nation* (April 22, 1978), p. 461.

RECOMMENDED READING

Richard Alba, *Blurring the Color Line*, Cambridge, MA: Harvard University Press, 2009.
Richard Alba and Victor Nee, *Remaking the American Mainstream,* Cambridge, MA: Harvard University Press, 2003.
Richard Bernstein, *Out of the Blue,* New York: Times Books, 2002.
Eric Darton, *Divided We Fall,* New York: Perseus Books, 2000.
Susan Faludi, *The Terror Dream,* New York: Metropolitan Books, 2007.
Paul Goldberger, *Up from Zero,* New York: Random House, 2004.
Andrew Hacker, *Two Nations: Black and White, Separate, Hostile, Unequal,* New York: Ballantine Books, 1995.
David Halberstam, *The Children,* New York: Random House, 1998.
Jennifer L. Hochschild, *Facing Up to the American Dream,* Princeton, NJ: Princeton University Press, 1995.
Samuel Huntington, *Who Are We?* New York: Simon & Schuster, 2004.
Douglas S. Massey, ed., *New Faces in New Places,* New York: Russell Sage, 2008.
Barack Obama, *Dreams from my Father* (revised), New York, Crown, 2004.
Stephen and Abigail Thernstrom, *America in Black and White: One Nation, Indivisible,* New York: Simon & Schuster, 1997.
Mary C. Waters and Reed Ueda, eds., *The New Americans,* Cambridge, MA: Harvard University Press, 2007.
Alan Wolfe, *One Nation, After All,* New York: Viking, 1998.

Postscript

And what of Henry Luce's prophesy of 'the American Century'? During the 70 years since his famous *Life Magazine* editorial, the United States rose to dominate global politics, economics and culture. But in the new millennium its sustaining power has been challenged. The neoconservative strategists surrounding President George W. Bush had hoped to extend the American Century into the distant future; but their disastrous policies undermined the American economy at home and subverted American prestige abroad. Even a sympathetic critic, Francis Fukuyama, acknowledged its failures in *America at the Crossroads* (2007): 'One of the striking things about the performance of the Bush administration is how poorly it has followed through in accomplishing the ambitious objectives it has set for itself.' Perhaps the most revealing epitaph of the Bush years came inadvertently from the grammatically challenged president himself, when he said, 'Our enemies are innovative and resourceful, and so are we. They never stop thinking about new ways to harm our country and our people, and neither do we.'

The breathtaking election of Barack Obama and his message of hope created a new wave of optimism in America. His dazzling rise to the American presidency reached its apogee in the premature awarding of the Nobel Peace Prize in 2009, only months after he had assumed office and weeks after he had made the controversial decision to increase American troop levels in Afghanistan. Now Obama must deliver more than soaring rhetoric if he is to achieve the Herculean tasks of resuscitating the economy, regulating Wall Street, reforming the health care system, rescuing the environment and raising America's standing in the world.

Though many analysts pronounce this mission impossible and predict the decline of the United States in the twenty-first century, perhaps Zaheed Zakaria provides the shrewdest assessment of the future in *The Post-American World* (2008). He predicts not the fall of the United States but 'the rise of the rest,' especially emerging Asian powers like China and India. Meanwhile the American public grapples with global problems of social, economic and technological change. 'The irony is that the rise of the rest is a consequence of American ideas and actions,' says Zakaria. 'Generations from now, when historians write about these times, they might note that, in the early decades of the twenty-first century, the United States succeeded in its great and historic mission – it globalized the world. But along the way, they might write, it forgot to globalize itself.'

It may be that the dream of the American Century is coming to a close. But we still live in the American Moment.

Index